TWILIGHT OF THE RENAISSANCE

The Life of Juan de Valdés

Diplomat, courtier, and heretic, Juan de Valdés (c.1500–1541) was one of the most famous humanist writers in Renaissance Spain. In this biography, Daniel A. Crews paints a lively portrait of a complex and fascinating figure, focusing on Valdés's service as an imperial courtier and on how his employments in Italy – after brushes with the Spanish Inquisition – influenced both Spanish diplomacy and his own religious thought. *Twilight of the Renaissance* documents Valdés's political activities in Charles V's Italian alliance system and negotiations with the papacy, while vividly portraying an intriguing and complex Renaissance figure.

Crews examines how Valdés, who was praised by two popes and the emperor, was also branded a heretic almost immediately after his death. By considering Valdés's spirituality, as well as his egotism, this incisive work reveals how the libertine atmosphere of the late Renaissance challenges the saintly Socratic image Valdés fashioned for himself in his writings.

An exciting glimpse into late-Renaissance politics and culture, *Twilight of the Renaissance* brings new insights into Valdés's life and political career, while also studying the relationship between the Spanish language and imperial propaganda efforts.

DANIEL A. CREWS is a professor in the Department of History at the University of Central Missouri.

DANIEL A. CREWS

Twilight of the Renaissance:

The Life of Juan de Valdés

UNIVERSITY OF TORONTO PRESS
Toronto Buffalo London

© University of Toronto Press 2008
Toronto Buffalo London
utorontopress.com

Reprinted in paperback 2020

ISBN 978-0-8020-9867-2 (cloth)   ISBN 978-1-4875-2609-2 (paper)

Library and Archives Canada Cataloguing in Publication

Title: Twilight of the Renaissance : the life of Juan de Valdés / Daniel A. Crews.

Names: Crews, Daniel A., 1956– author.

Identifiers: Canadiana 20200289063 | ISBN 9781487526092 (softcover)

Subjects: LCSH: Valdés, Juan de, –1541. | LCSH: Holy Roman Empire – Politics and government – 16th century. | LCSH: Papal States – Politics and government – 16th century. | LCSH: Holy Roman Empire – History – Charles V, 1519-1556. | LCSH: Papal States – History – 1417–1605. | LCSH: Naples (Kingdom) – History – Spanish rule, 1442–1707. | LCSH: Italy – Church history – 16th century. | LCSH: Holy Roman Empire – Court and courtiers – Biography. | LCSH: Papal States – Court and courtiers – Biography. | LCSH: Naples (Kingdom) – Court and courtiers – Biography. | LCSH: Authors, Spanish – Classical period, 1500–1700 – Biography. | LCSH: Renaissance – Italy. | LCGFT: Biographies.

Classification: LCC BR350.V35 C74 2020 | DDC 270.6092–dc23

University of Toronto Press acknowledges the financial assistance to its publishing program of the Canada Council for the Arts and the Ontario Arts Council, an agency of the Government of Ontario.

In Memory of Gordon Kinder 1927–1997

Contents

Preface ix
Maps xi

Introduction   3
1   Rebellion's Child   8
2   Reform School   27
3   Italian Design   47
4   Cardinal Relations   73
5   The Valdesian Sodality   91
6   Offices and Audits   113
7   Regensburg Justification   135
Conclusion   160

Appendices   169
Abbreviations   191
Notes   193
Bibliography   253
Index   273

Preface

A biography of the sixteenth-century Spanish humanist Juan de Valdés is long overdue. His association with heretical doctrines has fuelled a historiography strong on theological analysis, but weak on the details of his life and political career. The only biography to give equal weight to Valdés's non-religious activities was published in 1875, and is obviously dated. The image of Valdés the courtier is more complex than either the saintly figure Valdés's disciples fashioned after his death, or the secret Protestant portrayed in more recent studies.

It is impossible to remember, much less credit, all to whom I am deeply indebted for a project that has taken so long to bring to completion. I would like to thank Walter Brown, Hines Hall III, Donna Bohanon, and my fatherly major professor, Richard G. Eaves, for mentoring me through the travails of graduate study and for moulding my historical methodology. Good history requires the pursuit of relevant archival material. In this endeavour my work was ably supported by Miguel Jiménez Monteserín, Cuenca's Municipal Archivist, and most heroically by doña Isabel Aguirre Landa, Head of the Reading Room at the General Archive of Simancas, the greatest archive in the world. In the course of my professional development, I received kind encouragement for my work on Valdés from Helen Nader, José Nieto, Jack Owens, Christoph Strosetzki, and Nigel and Clive Griffin. I thank Keshav Bhattarai for producing my maps, and Ruth Doyle and Al Iantorno for some Italian translation. The following friends and colleagues deserve special recognition for helping to hammer the research into some intelligible form. Richard Clement aided the collection of material, sometimes on short notice, as Head of the Department of Special Collections of the Kenneth Spencer Research Library at the University of Kansas. A glutton for punishment, he also suggested stylistic improvements on two versions of the manuscript. Missouri colleagues William Maltby, William Foley, and the late Raymond Leonard also read various drafts and provided good direction for emendations as well. Professor Sara T. Nalle has been a guiding saint almost from the moment I began the project. She directed my earliest research in Cuenca, selflessly provided hours of paleographic labour transcribing numerous difficult documents, and critically commented on a near-final draft. For many years the late Gordon Kinder provided inspiration for my research. He tirelessly worked on a considerable number of transcriptions, but most importantly his periodic visits to my home included a bit of good-natured goading, compelling me to work harder to complete a seemingly endless task. Without his mentoring, I would not have begun the book project, much less finished it. Whatever the reader may find useful in this study is due to the combined contributions of these professors, friends, and colleagues; I take full responsibility only for any flaws or errors. Finally, I express my deepest gratitude to my wife Rhonda and son Dylan for putting up with a time traveller who too often finds wandering among the dead more pleasurable than 'living in the now.'

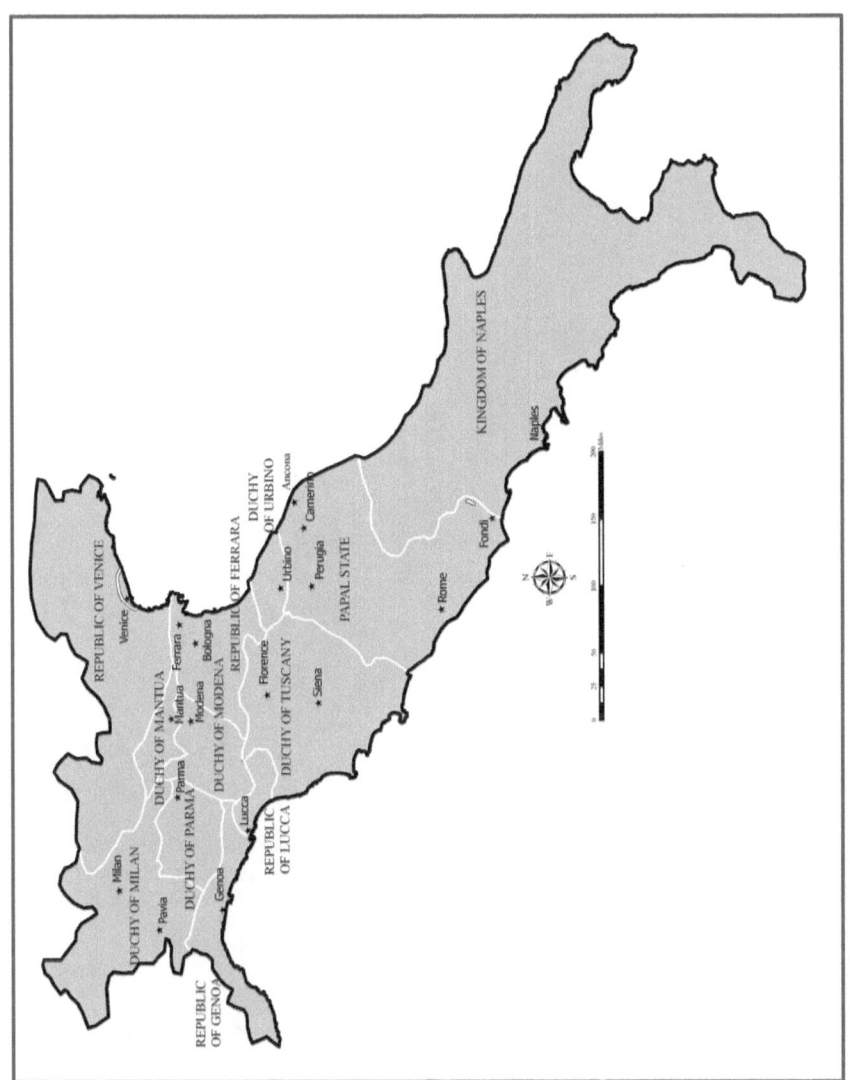

Map 1: The Italian States, 1559

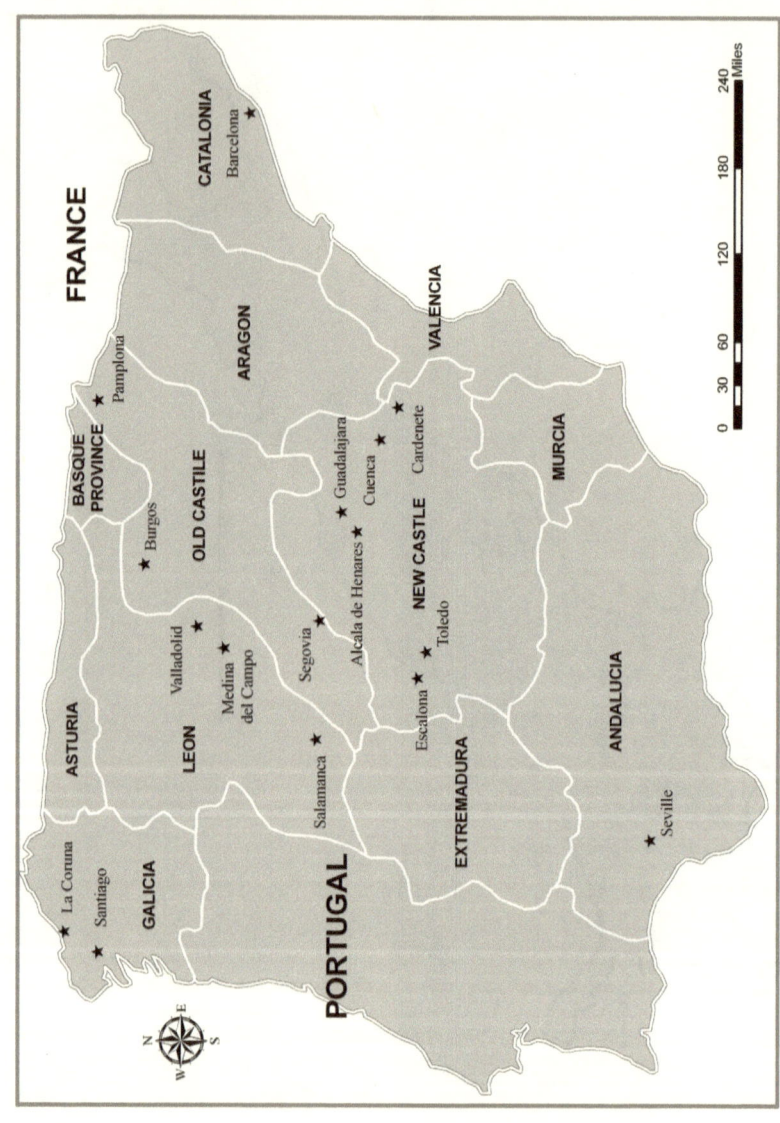

Spain 1469-1714

TWILIGHT OF THE RENAISSANCE

Introduction

After spending a day with Giulia Gonzaga, Juan de Valdés gushed: 'It is the greatest sin that she is not lord over the whole world. God would thus have provided that we poor beggars benefit from her divine conversation, gentility, and, not an inferior point, her beauty.'[1] That ethereal encounter in 1535 would ensure Valdés's status as one of the most renowned courtiers in Italy. Within a month he would become Giulia's solicitor, and within six months she became the focus of his humanist circle in Naples. Henceforth Giulia's fame and Valdés's influence were inextricable. She was, according to contemporary poets, the most beautiful woman in Italy, hailing from one of the greatest Italian families of the Renaissance. At age thirteen she married Vespasiano Colonna, some twenty-eight years her senior, who left her a young widow two years later. With her husband's demise, a complicated and interminable legal feud ensued between members of the powerful Gonzaga and Colonna clans which precluded the possibility of her remarriage and led her to seek Valdés's courtly influence.

Valdés first met Giulia when she was the mistress of the pope's nephew, Cardinal Ippolito de' Medici, and the centre of his literary circle. In August 1535 Medici died in her arms under mysterious circumstances. Valdés had made a career of gathering intelligence from cardinals more or less inclined to Emperor Charles V's policies, including Ippolito and Giulia's cousin, Cardinal Ercole Gonzaga. She trusted Valdés and soon moved to Naples to be near her legal adviser and soon-to-be spiritual guide.

Valdés came from far different social circumstances than Giulia. The Valdés were *hidalgos* (knights) descended from converted Jews (*conversos*) in La Mancha. His grandfather, father, uncle, and older brother had served the crown with arms. Juan's father, Fernando de Valdés, amassed sufficient wealth and influence to become a city councillor in Cuenca and to place two older sons in Emperor Charles V's court. Juan too eventually joined the imperial court after a difficult career path. In 1529 he published a book that the Spanish Inquisition withdrew from circulation because of its criticism of the Church. The Holy Office had previously penanced his father, and oldest brother, and had burned a maternal uncle at the stake for Judaizing. Inquisitorial investigation encouraged Juan to depart Spain for Italy; he never attempted to publish another book.

Aided by his brother Alfonso, an influential imperial secretary, Juan clawed his way into Charles's personal service, first serving at the court of Pope Clement VII, and then inheriting Alfonso's post as imperial secretary in 1532. Despite valued service at the Second Treaty of Bologna (1533), factional machinations and Juan's refusal to return to Spain caused the secretarial appointment to lapse temporarily. The new Viceroy of Naples, Pedro de Toledo, returned Juan to Rome in 1534 as his personal intelligence agent. Utilizing his contacts at the papal court, Juan played a behind-the-scenes role in averting war between Charles and Pope Paul III during the famous Tunisian expedition in 1535. During these negotiations Charles appointed Juan as a secretary in his personal service and afterwards Juan reaped rewards and offices in Naples as well as a nice prebend from the pope. He had apparently cleansed himself of any stains of heresy from Spain.

When Juan agreed to become Giulia's legal adviser, he was just finishing work as solicitor for the Cardinal of Ravenna. In that case he had impressed the papal court by mitigating papal punishment of a notoriously corrupt cardinal. Juan was not above passing bribes and exerting political pressure, but he knew Giulia's case would be even more difficult because the viceroy favoured the Colonnas. Juan's job was less to bring Giulia victory than to prevent conflict between the two powerful imperial allies. So the litigation dragged on, with Juan unable to offer anything more to Giulia than spiritual advice, which she insisted he write down in the form it became known as, *The Christian Alphabet*. Meanwhile Juan met with Charles and his courtiers in Naples, advised the viceroy on Italian affairs, and collected offices in the Neapolitan administration. Despite a comfortable income, he was not satisfied until he finally gained appointment as an adviser to Francisco de los Cobos, Charles's most powerful secretary, who had ultimate responsibility for all Italian and Spanish affairs of state.

The last three years of Juan's life were spent defending Viceroy Toledo from an unfair administrative review, pressing Giulia's case to an acceptable conclusion, and writing an enormous body of religious tracts and scriptural commentary. In letters to Cobos, Valdés protected Toledo's reputation in general, but complained about him in regard to Giulia's case. The viceroy had supported all of Juan's promotions and everyone at court considered them very close. By the standards of the day, Valdés was a disloyal client, but he may have been motivated by a growing personal relationship with Giulia. That relationship was the foundation of the famous Valdesian circle in Naples.

Originally Valdés's group merged an imperialist desire to spread the Spanish language with the Italian vernacular movement and its celebration of beauty and linguistic style. By 1538 Valdés's circle had evolved into a *spirituali* centre, one of numerous evangelical reform groups in Italy. The change of course resulted from a combination of factors: Giulia's spiritual needs, given her interminable legal problems, Pope Paul III's creation of a Reform Commission in 1537, and Charles V's religious colloquies in Germany aimed at a religious settlement between his Lutheran and Catholic vassals. Despite his earlier brush with the Spanish Inquisition, Juan re-entered the dangerous waters of religious reform. Through his circle Valdés influenced Cardinal Contarini, the papal legate at the fateful Diet of Regensburg, 1541. The Regensburg agreements did not create a permanent religious peace, but they were a step in that direction. Shortly after this, Valdés died, bemoaned by his followers as a departed saint who had worked himself to death in spiritual labour.

> Where are we to go now that Señor Valdés is dead? Certainly this has been a great loss for us and for the world, because Señor Valdés was one of the rare men of Europe. ... He controlled his frail, thin body with a small part of his soul, while with the major part and with pure understanding, almost as if he had no body, he was always elevated in the contemplation of truth and divine things. ... When such fortunes, letters, and virtues are united in a soul, it seems to me that they make war on the body, and they seek to leave with the spirit for the mansion from which it came.[2]

Two popes, the emperor, and the most beautiful woman in Italy had praised Valdés's virtues and service. Soon after Valdés's death, Francisco de los Cobos compared his political career with that of his more renowned brother Alfonso and concluded: 'I consider this one [i.e., Juan] the greater, very honoured.'[3]

Despite such acclaim, Juan de Valdés's name became synonymous with heresy after his death, a reputation he tried to avoid in life. Valdés's doctrine of justification was identified with the Regensburg doctrine of double justification, a thorn in the side of the papacy as it suggested a degree of compromise with the Lutheran doctrine of justification by faith alone. Giulia Gonzaga saved many of Valdés's religious writings and permitted their publication in Rome and Venice during the first two sessions of the Council of Trent to bolster the position of reformers in the council.[4] Despite strong support from several representatives, the doctrine of double justification was condemned in 1547. Valdés's followers were forced to renounce his doctrines, flee to Protestant lands for safety, or await execution following the final ratification of the decrees of Trent in 1563. With the 1550 publication of the *One Hundred and Ten Divine Considerations* in Protestant Basel, and the persecution of Valdesians in Italy, several Protestant leaders determined that Valdés was one of their own. In succeeding years Juan's and his family's encounters with the Spanish Inquisition, and the treatment of his followers by the Papal Inquisition, naturally led scholars to ignore his career as a courtier in Italy and to focus their attention on his heterodox religious doctrines.

Not until the early twentieth century did historians begin to link Juan de Valdés to the diplomacy of Charles V and muted allegations of overt heresy. When Marcel Bataillon discovered and published Juan's *Dialogue on Christian Doctrine* in 1925, he interpreted it as an Erasmian work that complemented the reforms and policies advocated by Juan's brother Alfonso and Grand Chancellor Mercurino Gattinara.[5] In 1931 José Montesinos reinforced the Bataillon thesis by publishing the Spanish courtier's correspondence with Cardinal Ercole Gonzaga, and a few years later Benedetto Croce uncovered some diplomatic letters Valdés wrote to Cobos late in his career.[6] Bataillon produced a synthesis of Valdés's intellectual and political life in his 1938 masterpiece, *Erasmus and Spain*, which cast Juan de Valdés as a leading actor in Charles V's so-called 'Erasmian' policy.[7] Though numerous studies of Spanish intellectual and political history subsequently endorsed Bataillon's Erasmian interpretation, since the 1930s researchers have failed to search for additional archival material related to Valdés's political career.[8]

More recent theological studies have questioned the extent of Erasmus's influence on Valdés. In 1970 José Nieto set forth the thesis that Valdés was the product of Spanish pre-Lutheran reformation doctrines identified with the teachings of the lay preacher Pedro Ruiz de Alcaraz. Further, he argued that Valdés's apparent Erasmianism in the 1529 *Dialogue on Christian Doctrine* was merely a rhetorical mask that he removed in his later writings.[9] Carlos Gilly and Gordon Kinder have driven Valdés further into the Protestant camp by finding evidence of early Lutheran influence in Spain and in the *Dialogue on Christian Doctrine*.[10] Though deserving considerable credit for placing Spain in the general stream of Reformation thought, these studies have added little to an understanding of Valdés's political career and its relation to his religious writings.

The uncovering of a considerable amount of fresh archival material elevates Juan's role as a courtier in the cultural context of the late Italian Renaissance. Juan excelled at gathering information in a world fixated upon beauty and love. In Valdés's Italy, the intellectual liberty associated with literary and artistic genius eventually gave way to a rather free discussion of religious doctrines; but in 1545 the convocation of the Council of Trent and the first Schmalkaldic War ushered in an era of doctrinal rigidity and enforced conformity. Though cliché, he was a man shaped by a distinct though brief period in history.

Viewed as an Erasmian or as a Protestant, Valdés was a failure. Regensburg did not establish a permanent religious peace, nor did Valdés's doctrines create a viable religious sect. However, viewed as a courtier, he had a more immediate goal, maintaining Charles's Italian alliance system in the face of the Franco-Turkish threat and papal obstruction, and making himself wealthy and famous in the process. In that regard he was more successful. He catered to cardinals useful to Charles's policies even if they lacked impeccable reputations. He worked to prevent a complete break between pope and emperor at the 1533 Treaty of Bologna and during the Tunisian campaign of 1535. Most importantly, he gave indispensable support to the 'Great Viceroy,' Pedro de Toledo, helping to make him the fulcrum of Charles's Italian diplomacy.

The life of Juan de Valdés presents the enigma of a suspected heretic from La Mancha ascending to fame and a degree of influence in both the papal and imperial courts. The answer to the puzzle lay in Valdés's amazing character and personality. A difficult upbringing in a volatile social environment gave him a strong sense of liberty and hardened him for service with a variety of patrons in an Italy resentful of Spanish dominion. His successful clientage eventually gave him the security to return to religious writing useful to the policy of his supreme patron, Emperor Charles V. Considering all his obstacles, Juan de Valdés was a consummate courtier during the twilight of the Renaissance.

1 Rebellion's Child

La Mancha, a land of windmills and arid plains, provides the colourful if impoverished setting for the misadventures of Don Quixote. But La Mancha was more than the realistic reference point for Miguel Cervantes Saavedra's fictional masterpiece; it bordered the spiritual heart of Castile. Toledo, capital of the ancient Visigothic kingdom and primal see of the Spanish Church, proudly looked down upon the Tajo River and across the plain of La Mancha. In the early sixteenth century, a *manchego* could easily envision himself/herself at the epicentre of a great political and spiritual transformation. Toledo was the heart of Castile, and Castile was the heart of an emergent global, Christian empire.

The La Manchan perspective that all roads led to Toledo increasingly came under assault as Spain transitioned to the rule of the foreign Habsburg dynasty. Dramatic expansion of the Burgundian wool trade in Burgos,[1] and the growing American trade in Seville, advanced an export economy that undermined the old textile and market cities of central Castile. The export orientation meant higher prices for raw wool and food on the one hand, and greater competition from foreign goods on the other.[2] The political centre also gravitated away from La Mancha as Castile experienced a 'legal revolution'[3] that made Valladolid, home of the Royal Chancellery, the unofficial capital prior to the rise of Madrid later in the century. After the death of the beloved Isabel in 1504, both King Ferdinand and the young Charles focused their attention on dynastic concerns rather than Castilian reform. Thus the turbulent era following Isabel's death culminated in a revolutionary bloodletting, the Comunero Revolt, that began and ended in Toledo.

The succession crises following Isabel's death spawned two political factions that would endure decades into the reign of Charles V, and would have a significant impact on the career of Juan de Valdés. The rightful heir of Castile, Isabel's daughter Juana, was deemed incapable of governing, leaving Juana's father, Ferdinand of Aragon, and her husband, the Burgundian Philip of Habsburg, to compete for the rule of Castile. The Ferdinand party was more inclined to the status quo, while the party of Philip, and later the double regent and Archbishop of Toledo, Jiménez de Cisneros, favoured political and religious reform.[4] Juan's father, Fernando de Valdés, became a leader of the Burgundian faction in Cuenca in part to protect his and the city's grain lands from the Duke of Infantado, a leader of the Ferdinand faction. Since the Ferdinand faction dominated during most of the period, Juan's childhood was anything but secure.

Family, Friends, and Foes

Juan's nuclear family was large and close knit. Mutual support contributed to the 1540 establishment of a Valdés *mayorazgo*, an entailed estate.[5] This vaunted privilege crowned the Valdés family's long and difficult climb up the social ladder. According to Miguel Jiménez Monteserín's genealogy of the Valdés, Juan's paternal ancestors descended from *hidalgos* who resided in the village of Villanueva in Asturias in the fourteenth century. His grandfather, Andrés de Villanueva, appears to have moved to Cuenca to serve the resident bishop. Andrés married a *converso*, who bore Juan's father sometime between 1450 and 1453. Fernando and his brother Alonso de Valdés entered the service of Pedro Carillo de Albornoz as captains in the Cuenca militia: Alonso as *Alcaide* (governor) of the fortress of Beteta, and Fernando as *Alcaide* of fortresses in Pareja and Casasana. In 1481 Fernando married María de Barrera, who had three *converso* grandparents.

The *Ejecutoría* that created the Valdés *mayorazgo* registers eleven children for Fernando and María, seven males and four females, and lists their birth order by gender. Andrés, the oldest son, was followed by Diego, a canon of Cartagena; Gregorio de Alarcón, 'who died unmarried in his father's house'; Cristóbal, a Franciscan friar; Francisco, a *criado* (servant) of the Marquis of Moya who died in 1523; Alfonso, the imperial secretary; and Juan, the youngest male. The female Valdés were Teresa Gómez de Valdés, 'who died soon after marrying'; María de Valdés, who married Luis de Salazar in Cuenca; Catalina, who died as a child; Margarita, who became a Conceptionist nun; and Isabel, who married Luis de Orduña in 1523.[6] The only firm date of birth is 1484 for Andrés.[7]

The birth date of Juan de Valdés remains a debatable subject. In 1970 José Nieto rejected the traditional estimation, 1498–1500, in favour of 1509–10, based on a questionable interpretation of an Inquisition document.[8] Historian Dorothy Donald and the former archivist of Cuenca, Elena Lázaro, favour the year 1490 as Juan's birth date, based on a 1506 letter from Fernando de Valdés to Cuenca's city council. In it Fernando says his son Juan, who must have returned to Cuenca, could vouch for Fernando's description of events at the Cortes of Valladolid held that year.[9]

Both revisionist chronologies have problems. In 1512 an Inquisition witness claimed that four years earlier he saw Fernando de Valdés praying in Hebrew with 'his sons, Valdés el *mozo* [unmarried young man], and three other *mochachos*.'[10] Thus in 1508 two or three of Juan's older siblings appeared to be *mochachos*, i.e., under fourteen years of age. Archbishop Bartolomé de Carranza testified before the Papal Inquisition that he first met Valdés in 1526 or 1527 when Juan was a youth (*juvenis*) studying Latin at the University of Alcalá.[11] The 1534 Inquisition testimony of Juan de Vergara is more damaging to the Donald-Lazaro chronology. Vergara claimed that he supported the publication of Juan's first book in 1529 because he knew Valdés to be a 'virtuous young man [*mancebo virtuoso*].'[12] *Mancebo* could refer to a broad age range, but the context here would make it relative to the age of the speaker: Vergara was born in 1492.[13] It is logical to assume that Vergara viewed Juan de Valdés as considerably younger than himself.[14]

Some confusion about Juan's lineage results from the fact that his father apparently had an illegitimate son named Fernando who also had a son named Juan de Valdés.[15] This Fernando was a Captain of the Royal Guards (*continos*) who died in battle against the French in Navarre in 1512. In 1517, and again in 1535, the captain's son petitioned the crown for a grant based on his father's admirable service.[16] Interestingly, our Juan also tried to benefit from the captain's heroic demise. In 1521 the governors of Castile asked that Charles employ Juan de Valdés in his service, and identified him as the nephew of Alonso de Valdés, the 'Captain of the common infantry who died in Pamplona. ... And another *uncle* of his was Hernando de Valdés who was Captain of the Guard of the Catholic king, Your Majesty's grandfather, who was killed at Valdeconcal in battle with the French.'[17] The Valdés *Ejecutoría* identifies Juan's uncle Alonso de Valdés as the commander of the Cuencan militia at Navarre in 1521,[18] while Fernando the bastard is not mentioned. Perhaps the Valdés family wanted to hide the captain's illegitimacy by labelling him Juan's uncle in the request, and by omitting him from the 1540 *Ejecutoría*.

Weighing all the evidence, the traditional view of Juan's possible dates of birth, 1498–1500, seems a plausible compromise between the revisionist alternatives. Without doubt the Carranza and Vergara references are to the famous humanist; he appeared to be a *juvenis* and *mancebo* in the late 1520s. Yet Valdés was old enough to be nominated for imperial service in 1521 and, according to the Cuencan archivist, Miguel Jiménez Monteserín, he had to be at least twenty-five in 1529 when he received a prebend (Church office), the *mayoralia* of San Lázaro in the diocese of Cuenca.[19] The account of Juan's reporting to the city council in 1506 suggests that he was quite a precocious youth and highly esteemed by his father.

Whatever his age, the family favoured Juan over older siblings. Diego and Alfonso generously remembered Juan in their testaments, but failed to mention Cristóbal, who left Cuenca in 1537, and had no further contact with the family. In terms of office and prebends, Juan also bested Cristóbal. In 1529 Fernando transferred his prebend of the *mayoralia* of San Lázaro to Juan, and in 1532 Juan began serving as a Papal Chamberlain in Rome with Alfonso's support.[20] In April 1520 Fernando transferred his hereditary office of *regidor*, city councilman, to Andrés.[21]

Andrés, Diego, Alfonso, and Juan all served the emperor at some point as *continos*, royal guards, or knights, originally created in the fifteenth century to protect the monarch from disloyal aristocrats. By the sixteenth century they were also employed as functionaries for the court. Though the term *contino* was also used as a generic term for someone in imperial service, from this study, it appears the office was transferable within a family and that it provided a slot at court for one member of the Valdés family. In 1516 Andrés held the office that he may have inherited from his illegitimate brother Fernando, the Captain of the Royal Guards. Following King Ferdinand's death in January 1516, Andrés made out his last will and testament and then left to join Charles's court in Flanders along with many other supporters of the Burgundian faction. With Andrés's assumption of the *regimiento* of Cuenca in 1520, Alfonso took his older brother's slot at Charles's court and received the transfer of the 'power' of Andrés's office of *contino* in 1520. However, Andrés did not permanently transfer the position and salary to Alfonso until 1523.[22]

Diego entered Charles's service as a *contino* in 1519, if not before,[23] and documents continued to refer to him as such as late as 1528. Andrés transferred his 'power' as *contino* to Alfonso because Diego had to serve in Madrid while Alfonso attended the court in Flanders; hence Alfonso became the Valdés *contino* at court even though Andrés pocketed the pay.[24] At some point Diego entered the clergy, and may have briefly served as a royal chaplain in 1529.[25] He became a cathedral canon in Cartagena, and in 1530 acquired prebends in Zaragoza, Cuenca, Salamanca, and Segovia. In 1534, Pope Clement VII would recommend that Juan inherit Diego's prebends.[26] For Diego, Alfonso, and later Juan, the *contino* post gave them a position in Charles's personal service, opening an avenue for other influential and lucrative positions. With the exception of Cristóbal and Isabel, the youngest daughter, the surviving Valdés siblings cooperated to secure the family's social status and honour. Diego named his sister María, who had married Luis Salazar, as his universal heir.[27]

Alfonso made Juan his universal heir on condition that he provide care for their sister Margarita, the Conceptionist nun. Both Diego and Alfonso left their ancestral lands to Andrés with Diego making an additional contribution of 270 ducats for the family chapel. Juan bequeathed half his ancestral inheritance in Cuenca and considerable liquid assets in Naples to Andrés's oldest son and first holder of the Valdés *mayorazgo*, Juan Alfonso de Valdés,[28] who married the daughter of María Valdés and Luis Salazar.

Fernando's *converso* connections facilitated the family's social ascent. During much of the fifteenth century, *converso* influence within the Cuenca city council increased and then peaked in the 1480s when seventeen of twenty regidores were *conversos*.[29] Fernando allied himself with Luis Carillo, the most aristocratic member of the city council and commander of the city militia. Fernando was also a *criado* of the *converso* Andrés de Cabrera, who became the Marquis of Moya in 1482. The new marquis then sponsored Fernando's appointment as hereditary *regidor* in Cuenca the same year.[30] Three times Fernando served as one of the city's two *procuradores* sent to represent Cuenca at the Castilian *Cortes* (Parliament). In 1493 the city council sent him on a special mission to negotiate with the king and queen, and he was later put in charge of organizing the city's mourning for the beloved Queen Isabel.[31]

Fernando advanced financially as well as politically. He owned a large home near the Plaza de San Salvador in Cuenca, a country home and estate in Verdelpíno six kilometres north of Cuenca, a two-trough fulling mill, and grain lands in Olmedilla.[32] He successfully petitioned the crown in 1486 about an attempted reduction of the city's jurisdiction over neighbouring lands, and in 1492 convinced the city council to pass financial incentives to encourage settlement of Olmedilla.[33] Fernando's defence of Cuenca's jurisdiction over Olmedilla initiated a feud with Diego Hurtado de Mendoza, the Duke of Infantado and *guardia mayor* of the region.

During the aristocratic anarchy in the middle of the fifteenth century, the Mendozas frequently clashed with the house of Pacheco, led by the Marquis of Villena, for dominance of the region surrounding Cuenca.[34] Renewal of the Mendoza-Pacheco rivalry ensured that the transition to Habsburg rule in Spain would be contentious, particularly in Cuenca. Cuenca's liberty depended upon keeping the cathedral fortress overlooking the city from falling into hostile hands. The Catholic monarchs neutralized the cathedral by allowing the city to retain control of it provided it would not be fortified. The city, which supported Ferdinand and Isabel in the War of Succession, rose in revolt against Ferdinand when he tried to seize the cathedral with royal troops at the end of that war.[35] Between 1493 and 1518 the see was vacant because of a conflict between the Catholic Monarchs and the papacy over patronage. Finally in 1518 the crown and the papacy agreed on the election of Diego Ramírez Villaescusa as bishop, but he could not take up residence in Cuenca until 1523 because he presided over the Chancellery of Valladolid.[36] The long vacancy enabled the Mendoza faction in Cuenca to establish its dominance over the cathedral chapter.

Infantado methodically sought to gain mastery over the city with the aid of relatives. Canon Diego Manrique, a Mendoza kinsman, led the cathedral chapter with the aid of other relatives, Juan del Pozo Manrique and Gómez Cerilla. Outside the chapter the Mendozas could count on the armed muscle of Rodrigo Manrique, the brother of Diego Manrique, who was *Comendador* of Salamanca and a constable (*alguacil*) of Cuenca.[37] A 1501 suit before the Royal Council records that the Cuenca city council prevented Diego Hurtado from entering the city.[38]

The situation changed after Queen Isabel's death, as Ferdinand needed Mendoza support. In 1505 the Cuenca city council petitioned the crown to stop the illegal fortification of its cathedral by Diego Hurtado and his minions on the cathedral chapter.[39] After Charles's succession to the throne, the *regidores* of Cuenca petitioned the emperor to force Bishop Ramírez de Villaescusa to come to the city and control the chapter.[40] Between 1504 and 1523 the city submitted seven cases to the Royal Council involving either the cathedral chapter or the city's territorial jurisdiction.[41] The new bishop, a leader of the Burgundian faction, probably feared Mendoza's influence.[42]

Isabel left the crown of Castile to her daughter Juana, but should she prove incapable of governing, Isabel stipulated that Ferdinand would rule Castile as governor in Juana's name.[43] However, Ferdinand alienated Castilians by insulting the memory of their beloved queen with his quick marriage to a French princess.[44] Juana's husband, Philip of Habsburg, quickly proclaimed himself king, making the choice between Ferdinand and Philip as the *de facto* ruler of Castile a divisive question for the aristocracy. The Marquis of Villena took the lead in organizing most grandees in support of Philip, forcing Ferdinand to relinquish his powers in Castile and to return to Aragon.[45] Philip convoked a meeting of the Cortes in Valladolid where Fernando de Valdés, aided by his son Juan, served as one of Cuenca's two representatives.

Because of the Mendoza threat, Fernando took the momentous step of aligning Cuenca with the Marquis of Villena and the Burgundian faction to recognize Philip as king of Castile. Fernando praised Philip effusively in letters to the city council.[46] While Villena stood by Philip's side instructing him on proper procedure in the Cortes, Fernando led the cities in swearing their allegiance to the Habsburg dynasty. He boasted to the Cuenca city council that he had won the city fame and honour by being the first to grant obedience to Philip and Juana. 'We were the cause of others [cities], other caballeros and the council doing the same, and my son Juan de Valdés ... is able to say so in public.'[47]

Unfortunately for Fernando, Philip died a few months later and Diego Hurtado de Mendoza asserted authority in Cuenca even though Ferdinand's position as governor of Castile was not official until 1510.[48] Fernando later alleged that the Duke's faction killed three minor officials, seriously wounded a *regidor* and another prominent citizen, and prevented the royal investigator from entering the city.[49] These were difficult days for Fernando de Valdés. In December 1506 the city council had reappointed him as a representative to the next Cortes, but revoked his authority after the Mendoza coup.[50] The Mendoza faction succeeded in removing Fernando from the council for three years (1509–12), supposedly for financial misconduct, but Valdés won exoneration on appeal to the Royal Council.[51] During the period of Fernando's absence from the city council the Mendoza faction encouraged an anti-*converso* offensive by the Inquisition in Cuenca, which initiated *procesos* against seven *regidores* of *converso* descent in 1510 and 1511.[52]

Fernando's fortune eventually changed for the better after Ferdinand's death in 1516. In November 1517 he was selected as a representative to join the new Habsburg monarch in his first Cortes in Valladolid in early 1518. It was a propitious moment and location for the Valdés clan. The biographers of Alfonso de Valdés agree that he studied Latin and law under the tutelage of Pedro de Angleria, the Italian humanist brought to the royal court by Ferdinand and Isabel to provide such instruction.[53] Alfonso's letters to Angleria from the imperial court in Flanders, Angleria's favourable comments about Alfonso's father, and Alfonso's subsequent offices leave little doubt that he spent years of training under Angleria in Valladolid. With Angleria's assistance, Fernando undoubtedly helped secure Alfonso a future place in Charles's service, joining his older brothers Andrés and Diego. Juan probably attended the court as well, following it south from Valladolid in early April 1518. When Fernando and Juan arrived in Cuenca later that month, Juan participated in the ceremony of the *pleito-homenaje* that Charles granted Fernando. Juan's father placed his clasped hands between the hands of Luis Carillo and swore three times that he would not surrender either of the two fortresses he guarded to anyone but Charles. He then proceeded to transfer his military authority to his oldest sons, Andrés and Diego.[54] The Valdés patriarch used his personal honour to secure the positions of Andrés and Diego firmly with Charles.

Defensive Revolution

A few documents and inferences from some comments in Juan's later writings indicate that he actively participated in the defence of his family's interests from Mendoza attack during and immediately following the Comunero Revolt. Two autobiographical statements in Juan's *Dialogue on Language* give clues about his life before he entered the University of Alcalá in 1526. First, he claimed to have been brought up 'in the kingdom of Toledo and at the court of Spain.'[55] Later he added, 'ten years, the best of my life, I spent in palaces and courts where I did not exercise more virtue than reading these lies [tales of chivalric romance].'[56] Given his father's clientage with the Marquis of Moya, he probably spent considerable time at Moya's bleak palace in the impoverished village of Cardenete near Cuenca.[57] A January 1523 document mentioned Juan and his brother Francisco as *criados* of Moya.[58]

However, Juan was not completely trapped in the grim environs of Cardenete. Given his comment that he had been 'brought up at the court of Spain,' and the fact that Valladolid functioned as the juridical home of the royal court, Juan may have spent some time studying

Latin and law under Angleria, as did his brother Alfonso.[59] More concretely, Juan's acquisition of legal Spanish, that odd mixture of Spanish and Latin, indicates that he may have worked in the chancellery. The University of Alcalá provided no training in civil law, yet Valdés's later service as Giulia Gonzaga's solicitor and his work with the audit of Naples required mastery of this unique language.

In the *Dialogue on Language*, Juan strongly defended the use of legal Spanish from an attack by Pacheco, a Spanish nobleman in the discussion. After Valdés stated his famous linguistic rule that Spanish should be written as it is pronounced, Pacheco interjected that the Chancellery of Valladolid would reject the rule because *letrados* could only raise themselves above the vulgar by buying a little Latin to mix with their Spanish. Valdés responded, 'It is the most uncouth thing in the world to make laws about matters where every plebian and vulgar person thinks that he is able to be master.'[60] The exchange suggests that Juan knew the language and had experience in the courts.

Unlike Alfonso, Juan did not have a position at the imperial court. If he began training in Valladolid, as seems likely, he would have abandoned it because of the Comunero Revolt and the threat it posed to his family. Thus he would have returned to Cuenca and later Moya's miserly court, where he was joined by uncle Alonso, who led the Cuenca militia to Cardenete to suppress Moya's rebellious peasants. However, scandal quickly struck the Valdés family in 1521 when the Marquis sued Juan's uncle for seducing his wife.[61] Juan probably left Moya's court at the time, as a debt for five bushels of wheat places him back in Cuenca in June 1521 only two days after the Valdés lawyer recorded the verdict on his uncle's indiscretion.[62] Some time between the scandal and 1523 Juan moved to Escalona, the famous court of the Marquis of Villena.

While the Valdés family participated in the Comunero Revolt, they remained completely loyal to Charles and the Habsburg dynasty.[63] Wishing to avoid the appearance of disloyalty, Fernando de Valdés resigned as *regidor* in April 1520 in favour of his son Andrés, though he continued meeting with the city council. The city officially joined the comuneros on 10 July, and on 21 July the lieutenant of the *corregidor* handed his staff of justice, the symbol of royal authority, to Andrés de Valdés and Gregorio Chinchilla.[64] If one abandons grand interpretations of the revolt as a modern revolution based on constitutional or class conflict, then the actions of the family become more comprehensible.[65] In Cuenca the Comunero Revolt simply renewed the city's old feud with Mendoza, and in this matter the Valdés family could not be neutral.

After the revolt ended, Fernando de Valdés claimed that as soon as Cuenca joined the rebellion, Infantado's relatives, Rodrigo and Diego Manrique, forcibly removed a *regidor* from office and seized control of the city's finances, sending some funds to the Comunero *Santa Junta*, but keeping most for themselves. The city council, led by Luis Carillo, quickly restored order and exiled the Manrique brothers from the city, but made no attempt to recall Cuenca's representatives from the *Santa Junta*.[66] On 18 October Rodrigo Manrique launched a devastating raid on the city coordinated with the cathedral chapter. The attackers were repelled, but they encamped outside the city to prevent provisions from entering. The city council was forced to request troops from the *Santa Junta* to lift the siege.[67] Thereafter the city moved toward the royalist camp, but continued its feud with the Duke of Infantado.

Perhaps to demonstrate Cuenca's loyalty to the crown, the city council ordered Juan's uncle Alonso to lead Cuencan troops to pacify the lands of the Marquis of Moya. Soon after this, the city council voted to accept a *corregidor*, even though it continued to maintain representation on the Comunero *Santa Junta*.[68] On 1 January 1521 Charles wrote a letter thanking Cuenca's city council for its return to royal service.[69] Unfortunately for Cuenca and the Valdés clan, Mendoza had also joined the royalist camp. Charles's desire to bring as much pressure as possible on Toledo, the last bastion of the comuneros, led him to appoint Infantado as a special envoy in September 1521 to assist the two grandees he selected the previous year to serve as governors with Adrian of Utrecht.[70]

Fearing Mendoza revenge, the council petitioned for a general pardon, which it received on 13 March 1521. Andrés de Valdés emphatically proclaimed that he and his family did 'not want the said pardon, because they had never in any manner acted in disservice to your majesty.'[71] Andrés added that the sending of delegates to the Junta was forced on the *regidores* under the threat of death. On 15 April Andrés de Valdés informed Charles that as *regidor* and *contino* he had helped pacify the city and deserved a reward.[72] In late June Fernando de Valdés wrote the governors again, repeating how the city had saved the Marquis of Moya when all his lands were aflame, and reminded the governors of Charles's previous promises to the city.[73] To prove its loyalty, the city council dispatched much of Cuenca's militia, again commanded by Juan's uncle Alonso, to turn back the French invasion of Navarre. With the Cuenca militia thus engaged, Mendoza proceeded to occupy the city in July and to fortify the cathedral, but failed to pacify the countryside, as remnant comunero troops raided villages of the nobility two years after the revolt ended.[74]

Despite his frail body, Juan apparently participated physically in the violent factional conflicts. In 1523 Juan's father testified as a character witness for one Cristóbal of Alcalá. He declared that he had 'troubled days from a son of his' who engaged Cristóbal's son in a knife fight, but Fernando insisted that he bore no enmity toward the father or the son.[75] Juan's youth, his temper, and his presence in the city at the time of the incident make him the likely aggressor. Further, Juan probably lost the fight, as the winner's family would have little reason to hold a grudge. Thus the governors' recommendation to employ Juan in imperial service in December 1521 may have resulted from Fernando's desire to get his troubled son out of the region.

Mendoza's clients became overconfident and openly made jokes, probably anti-Semitic in nature, about Cuenca's *regimiento*.[76] Fernando and Andrés de Valdés finally ended the Mendoza 'tyranny' by suing the Duke and his kinsmen before the royal court in Valladolid for violating the city's rights and publicly disrespecting the *regimiento*. The dates of depositions and testimony are between April and September 1524, though the suit would have been filed much earlier. The verdict in the case is not archived with the depositions, but a later Inquisition document refers to the sentence against the Mendoza that included stiff fines and the loss of Diego Hurtado's appointment as *guardia mayor*.[77]

With Charles's support, the Valdés family had successfully defended its honour in court against one of the most powerful grandees in Spain. Charles's favour for the Valdés was based on his immediate needs as well as the family's past loyalty. Charles must have been happy to see Fernando de Valdés among the delegates at the contentious 1523 Cortes in Valladolid. Very grudgingly the representatives agreed to a new *servicio*, but only on condition Charles not ask for another. They pointed out that the demand for the last *servicio* led to the revolt, and cancellation of the *servicio*. Further, they argued that damage from the conflict made it difficult to impose more taxes.[78] Charles's plans to marry Isabel of Portugal and his military campaigns in Italy forced him to convene the Cortes two years later to request another *servicio*. Prior to its meeting, Andrés de Valdés replied to Charles's request of him as a 'servant [*criado*] of your Royal House and *regidor*' of Cuenca. Andrés agreed to use his influence on the city council to ensure that the representatives selected for the 1525 Cortes of Toledo would have the power to vote a new *servicio*.[79] Charles's dependence on the Valdés family before, during, and immediately after the Comunero Revolt contributed to the rise of the Valdés brothers in imperial service.

Spiritual Upheaval

The year 1521 witnessed a turning point in the life of Juan de Valdés. The hated Duke of Infantado had taken control of Cuenca, uncle Alonso had scandalized the family, and young Juan had some kind of spiritual experience. In his 1541 *Commentary on Matthew*, Valdés wrote: 'I was compelled to come to Christ ... I am certain that I could not have resisted it if I wished.'[80] Elsewhere in the same work he commented that the revelation of God through Christ should not be called knowledge, 'just as the knowledge, which I had of Christ and of God twenty years ago, comparing that with what I now have, I do not call knowledge.'[81]

Juan's spiritual interest found an outlet in the *alumbrado* movement. These popular preachers were usually *converso*, lay, and often female. The *alumbrados* drew on the spiritual literature published by Cardinal Cisneros, the Inquisitor General as well as the Archbishop of Toledo, who also served as their protector.[82] In the concise words of Spanish literary historian Otis Green, 'Cisneros himself ... could not be separated from the complicated interplay of orthodoxy-heterodoxy in the early years of Spain's uncertain vacillation between innovation and tradition.'[83] Cisneros opened the door for experimental forms of religious piety. In addition, Cisnerian and later Erasmian reformers and their opponents reflected the factional strife of Charles's early court.[84]

Because the region of Toledo was the heart of the *alumbrado* movement, some scholars have suggested a link between the *alumbrados* and the Comunero Revolt.[85] However, the primary evidence linking *alumbrados* to comuneros is a bit vague. A letter written by the Admiral of Castile to Charles just after the Battle of Villalar declared that 'This wicked sect of liberty was very fixed in the hearts of this people.'[86] An inquisitor commented that the *alumbrados* 'pretended to have a zeal for [Christian] perfection just as the comuneros pretended to have a zeal for a republic, but later no one excused their guilt.'[87] In his autobiography, Charles V called the comuneros heretics, and compared them to the Lutherans.[88] He also permitted the Inquisition to expand its authority to investigate the *alumbrados* in 1519 after some discussion early in his reign to limit the Inquisition's authority.[89] The courts of Villena and Infantado were *alumbrado* havens, but these grandees abandoned open support of the Comunero Revolt early. The evidence does not seem sufficient to make *alumbrado* doctrines integral to the origin of the revolt. Perhaps it is more accurate to conclude that, as the early *alumbrado* trials progressed, inquisitors became increasingly concerned with the *alumbrados'* potential political transcendence in the wake of the spread of Lutheranism and the Peasants War in Germany.

Juan's *converso* lineage probably contributed to his attraction to *alumbrado* sermons. The high degree of intermarriage and close-knit social networks of upper-class *conversos* suggest that in Cuenca a gulf separated *conversos* from Old Christians. Though *alumbrado* doctrines were not particularly Jewish, and the Inquisition made surprisingly few accusations of Judaizing, the fact that nearly all *alumbrados* investigated by the Inquisition were *conversos* implies that the movement stemmed from '*converso* religiosity.'[90] Their de-emphasis of rituals appealed to *conversos*, who were appalled by some of the magical and superstitious aspects in the local religious beliefs of Old Christians.[91]

Before the Inquisition condemned their doctrines, the term *alumbrado* was used pejoratively as a synonym for a religiously inspired person who was fraudulent, crazy, lascivious, or some combination of the three. As a group they were quite egotistical and jealous, often eager to accuse their rivals before the Inquisition. Scholars generally agree that many *alumbrados* preached heretical doctrines, but differ over the classification of their heresy: mystic, Protestant, or Epicurean.[92] In addition to the courts of the Marquis of Villena and the Duke of Infantado, the *alumbrados* conglomerated near the universities of Salamanca and Alcalá, where they intermixed with 'Erasmians,' particularly after the Inquisition's edict condemning *alumbrado* doctrines in 1525.

In the 1480s some spiritual Franciscan convents began practising *recogimiento*, exercises directed at a spiritual union with God. For at least two hours a day a *recogido* would seek seclusion to pray orally, especially the Lord's Prayer, meditate on Christ's passion, and engage in mental prayer. In the latter stage, the mind was focused on nothingness, permitting God to take control of the will. According to an *alumbrado* instruction manual, 'This thinking nothing is to think of him entirely.'[93] By emphasizing interior feelings, the *alumbrados* feminized religion by enabling women openly to discuss their love of God independent of the male ecclesiastical hierarchy.[94] Thus many leaders of the movement were *beatas*, women who dedicated themselves to God, usually symbolized by their wearing clothing resembling a religious habit. Isabel de la

Cruz and María Cazalla in Guadalajara, and Francisca Hernández in Salamanca and later Valladolid, communicated with each other, though their specific doctrines varied.[95] Intimate seclusion with disciples for spiritual healing naturally led to allegations of sexual misconduct. Though certainly a minority, some *alumbrados/alumbradas* claimed the conjugal act was a way to achieve union with God.[96] The poor but beautiful Francisca Hernández had the ability to prevent students studying for the clergy from masturbating. Since some fondling seems to have been part of the cure, she and her followers contributed to the image of *alumbrados* as sex-crazed deviants.[97]

Alfonso and Juan may have had contact with Francisca's group. Given the proximity and interconnections of the Chancellery of Valladolid to the famed law school at the University of Salamanca, students and courtiers from both cities intermingled. Until 1522, the intellectual leader of Francisca's devotees was Bernardino Tovar, older half-brother of Juan de Vergara, a former secretary of Cisneros. The Valdés brothers would later work closely with Vergara and his brother Francisco at the University of Alcalá, but this family connection likely began when Tovar was a student at Salamanca, and after he followed Francisca to Valladolid. In the later Inquisition trial of Juan de Vergara, a witness named Juan and Alfonso among a couple of dozen disciples of Tovar,[98] and Tovar became Juan's close friend at Alcalá. Alfonso has been so closely identified with Erasmus that scholars have overlooked the fact that the Inquisition censured his *Dialogue of Mercury and Charon* for *alumbrado* errors with specific quotations and page citations.[99] The most probable direct source of Alfonso's contact with *alumbrado* doctrines was Bernardino Tovar.

The possible connection of Juan to Francisca Hernández's group suggests that he may have initially been attracted to the *alumbrados* for less-than-divine reasons. The typical literature popular among young knights was not entirely puritanical. Juan's expression of a lack of virtue in voraciously reading the tales of chivalric romance hints at his thought process. These romances celebrated the free and impulsive love of the late medieval 'courtly love' tradition. For example, *Amadis of Gaul*, Valdés's favourite, begins with Elisena's blushing amorous eyes and a quick bedding with King Perion, thinly veiled with 'secret matrimony.'[100] Juan's authoritative ranking of Spanish love poems in the *Dialogue on Language* further evidences his interest in the language of love.[101] Thus his initial attraction to *alumbrado* gatherings where young men and women had freer, and in the minds of inquisitors scandalous, association may well have stemmed from physical as well as spiritual inspiration.

Further insight into Juan's sexual experience is suggested in his praise of *La Celestina*. In Valdés's view, Castilian stylistic elegance peaked with its composition: 'In my opinion no book written in Castilian has language more natural, more appropriate or more elegant.'[102] It combined the 'free love' tradition of chivalric romances with healthy doses of similar themes from Petrarch and Boccaccio.[103] Published in 1499, Fernando de Rojas's story of a go-between (pimp), maidenhead sewer, and sinister con woman delves deep into the underworld of rogues who prey on the gullible. Using Petrarch's principle that the good is communicable, Celestina twists it to convince the fair maiden Melibea that it is sinful not to share one's charms.[104] When asked about character development in the work, Valdés claimed that Celestina 'in my view is perfect [*perfetíssima*] in regard to everything that pertains to a go-between.'[105] Perhaps unconsciously, Valdés proclaimed himself an authority on pimps.

When Valdés arrived at Alcalá, he quickly gained fame for his skill at making up bawdy stories. Diego Gracián de Alderete wrote Juan's professor of Greek, 'you have such an abundance of tales you can already tell me; above all having there Juan de Valdés, who has excellent skill in finding them.'[106] Though no letters from Juan to Gracian have yet been discovered, a few from Gracian to Juan have survived. They consist largely of an exchange of off-colour jokes about monks and nuns. In one letter Gracián claimed to have observed some Benedictines lying out, idly working on their tans, when one exclaimed: 'If only we had a young nun at our side in order to amuse ourselves!'[107]

The Franciscan tertiary Isabel de la Cruz countered *alumbrado* sexual excesses by launching a rival doctrine to *recogimiento* called *dejamiento*, giving oneself over to the love of God. Since Isabel's Inquisition trial is lost, the best exposition of her doctrine comes from the trial of her primary disciple, Pedro Ruiz de Alcaraz, whose sermons Juan de Valdés frequented at Escalona. Convinced that their teaching was superior to all other *alumbrados*, Alcaraz and Isabel became fervent missionaries, establishing *dejado* cells in many towns and Franciscan convents in La Mancha.[108] Before his torture, Alcaraz tried to avoid identification with Isabel. The inquisitors wrote that he had learned 'many things from her that seemed good to the accused, but on the other hand she also told him many things that to him seemed to be from the Devil.'[109] Alcaraz's cowardly attempt to distance himself from Isabel failed entirely. Throughout his trial the Inquisition repeatedly lumped Isabel and Alcaraz together as if they were practically one and the same.[110]

According to Alcaraz, *dejamiento* meant constantly glorifying in God's love through mental prayer: 'Knowing the great love of God for man and its manifestation in our fortunes [leads to the] ... experience of man glorying in God.'[111] Glorying in God's love meant constantly thanking God in thought and silent prayer while performing routine daily activities. Concentration on God's love and the benefits it brought led to good works. Anyone who performed works from fear rather than love lost the spiritual benefit of charity: 'They have little experience of the effect of charity.'[112]

> At the end of our lives it is the love of God, and not any other love, that is love of God rather than love of self, that generates all good works and keeps all your goals upright; and if the love of God is principally in you, all your desires and works will be for God; ... the love of God as the law of God obligates us to love him with all our heart and all our soul and all our forces. And from this the love of neighbour is born.[113]

By undercutting human agency in works, Alcaraz's justification by love threatened both the rituals and the income of the Church.

Inquisitors repeatedly called Alcaraz 'an idiot without letters' because he lacked higher education, but Alcaraz rejected the *recogidos*' view that knowledge of letters inhibited spiritual enlightenment.[114] The historian Gordon Kinder concluded from meticulous analysis of Alcaraz's letters of defence that he was far from ignorant. Alcaraz referred to most books of the New Testament, and eleven in the Old Testament. He cited numerous religious authorities repeatedly in his defence: Thomas à Kempis (31), Bernard of Clairvaux (18), St Augustine (18), Angela of Foligno (11), Thomas Aquinas (8), Hughes de Balma (7), Gregory the Great (6), Benedict of Nursia (6), John Climacus (5), St Jerome (3), St Bonaventure (3), Alonso Fernández de Madrigal (2), Peter Lombard (2), and Hugh of St Victor (2). Single references were made to more than a dozen other authors, including Erasmus.[115] Alcaraz denied ever saying that some are invited by love of God and others by the love of the servants of God, a doctrine that seduced, literally, many *alumbrados*.[116] For Alcaraz the 'experience' of the love of God required study rather than sexual promiscuity.

Valdés also read many of these materials. The religious literature he recommended in his 1529 *Dialogue on Christian Doctrine* was almost identical with the devotional books he later praised in the *Dialogue on Language*. These books include Friar Ambrosio Montesino's 1512 Spanish translation of parts of the New Testament (*Epistles and Gospels*), Ludolf of Saxony's *Life of Christ*, the letters of St Jerome and his *Lives of the Fathers*, the letters of St Catherine of Siena, Jean Gerson's *Contempt of the World*, St Gregory's *Morals on the Book of Job*, works by John Climacus, and short works of St Augustine.[117] Thus mystical literature (Climacus, Gerson, and St Catherine) and works about the early church attracted Valdés's attention. His predilections were typical of popular reading material, including his later favour of Erasmus's works.[118] Though his reading preferences were not exceptional, this literature filtered through the mind of a young *converso* keenly aware of the persecution of his family by Old Christians.

In early 1523 the Marquis of Villena lured the popular Alcaraz to his court at Escalona with a high salary. Almost immediately a group of disciples flocked to his sermons. His devotees included many women and young men, *muchachos*, leading to later charges that he discussed religious doctrines with those incapable of understanding them.[119] His salary and the cliquish nature of his group caused friction at Escalona, and soon the court divided into rival *alumbrado* camps: the followers of Alcaraz's *dejamiento* versus the followers of *recogimiento* led by Francisco de Ocaña. Ocaña was a Franciscan friar who had the support of Juan de Olmillos, the guardian of a nearby Franciscan convent.[120] Issues of contention between the two concerned methods of prayer and prophecy.[121]

Soon after his arrival at Escalona, Alcaraz attended one of Francisco Ocaña's sermons and claimed Ocaña created a great disturbance at Villena's court by declaring that 'the Church ought to be reformed and those that now lead it ought to be thrown out like pigs.' Further, Ocaña predicted that in 1524 the king of France would be 'dispossessed of his Kingdom by the emperor and the father guardian [Olmillos] and I will go to Rome and reform the Church. ... the father guardian and I and Francisca Hernández who is in Valladolid will make the light that God has guarded to reform the souls [*espiritus*] and this good old man, the marquis [of Villena], will place the pope on his chair.'[122]

Alcaraz could tolerate the prophecies no more, probably fearing that Villena might favour Ocaña's ingratiating predictions. After questioning Ocaña, Alcaraz went to the Franciscan provincial in Toledo informing him of Ocaña's 'illusion and fraud from the devil.'[123] The investigation backfired, as eventually the Inquisition focused its attention on Alcaraz, who was more vulnerable to charges of heresy because he was neither a member of the clergy nor formally educated. He was arrested on 26 May

1524 and convicted of *alumbrado* heresies five years later.[124] His trial provided most of the material for the edict condemning *alumbrado* doctrines in September 1525.[125]

Though inferring theology from the adversarial nature of an Inquisition trial is dangerous, the reasons for Alcaraz's popularity in the depressed conditions of post-comunero La Mancha are obvious. He was an extremely intelligent and charismatic iconoclast. Repeatedly the Inquisition charged him with making jokes about customary rituals – confession, transubstantiation in the Mass, indulgences, using the name of Jesus and Mary, bowing to a cross, fasting during Lent, etc.[126] Only one allegation of Judaizing surfaced, 'That he ate in the manner of the Jews on Saturday.'[127] The inquisitors condemned him for the audacity of lecturing from the Bible in Spanish and telling his listeners that they 'had the spiritual capability of understanding sacred scripture.'[128] Thus the inquisitors claimed Alcaraz set out to make a 'New Law ... speaking in secret in isolated places with maidens and young, beautiful women which has caused scandal and rumours among those who saw them.'[129]

Juan attended Alcaraz's meetings regularly, as indicated by the three references to him in Alcaraz's trial.[130] The first is the December 1525 testimony of Francisco de Azevedo merely listing Valdés with several others who frequented Alcaraz's meetings, where Alcaraz read from the Bible in Latin and discussed the letters of St Paul.[131] The second reference came in November 1526 from a defender of Alcaraz who claimed he heard the Marquis of Villena say licenciado Santander did not like Alcaraz and 'he told the same to Juan de Valdés, *criado* of the said marquis. He also heard the said licenciado Santander say he would damage Alcaraz by putting the Inquisition on him.'[132] This testimony places Valdés among Alcaraz's defenders, and in the margin 'Alcalá' is written, indicating that Valdés had already entered the university. [133] The next month Alcaraz's wife pleaded with inquisitors to call Juan to testify on her husband's behalf. She claimed that he would be able to declare 'the intention of what my husband said; I ask Your Honours that if he is not in the *proceso*, Your Honours would order him to declare what he knows about it.'[134] Valdés was never called for testimony, and Alcaraz was scourged in Toledo, Guadalajara, Escalona, and Pastrana and sentenced to life imprisonment, and lost his property. He was released in 1539.[135]

Valdés must have been close to Alcaraz, but he had reason to fear being dragged into Alcaraz's investigation. *Conversos* were the primary target of the Spanish Inquisition. Juan's maternal uncle Fernando, a priest in the Valdés parish, was burned at the stake for Judaizing in 1491. Though Juan's father was only one-quarter *converso*, he had several *converso* friends who were executed for Judaizing as well. Fernando's name appears either as a witness or suspect in several Inquisition trials between 1510 and 1530. Three witnesses claimed to have seen him frequent the secret 'synagogue' of Pedro Suarez de Toledo, who was also burned at the stake. There are references to the lost trial of Fernando de Valdés in which he confessed and was reconciled for words and deeds against the Inquisition, a crime for which Andrés de Valdés was forced to do penance as well.[136] The Alcaraz investigation would not be the last brush Valdés had with the Spanish Inquisition.

2 Reform School

Trouble stalked Juan de Valdés. He had survived the turbulent waters of comunero-era La Mancha only to be thrown into the perilous sea of Charles V's reformation diplomacy. Though Charles had condemned Martin Luther's doctrines at the Diet of Worms in 1521, he could not enforce the diet's edict because of the Franco-Turkish threat to his territories. Francis I, fearful of Charles's encirclement of France, tried to take advantage of the Comunero Revolt by attacking Spain and the Spanish vice-royalty of Naples. Francis's imprisonment following his capture at the Battle of Pavia (1525) was only a temporary setback. After his release he joined Pope Clement VII to form the League of Cognac (May 1526), an impressive alliance which included Milan, Florence, and Venice with the support of Henry VIII.[1] As Charles committed his forces to Italy, the Ottoman Turks led by their greatest sultan, Suleiman the Magnificent, conquered Hungary in 1526 and by 1529 arrived at the gates of Vienna in the Habsburg heartland. Charles had to maintain religious peace in Germany, and needed Lutheran aid to defend his realms in Italy as well.

Under the direction of Grand Chancellor Gattinara, Alfonso de Valdés used Erasmus's doctrines in support of Charles's diplomacy. Gattinara and Alfonso capitalized upon the University of Alcalá's humanist pedigree and temporarily transformed the university into an imperial propaganda machine. According to John Headley, the symbiotic relationship between the university and its press and the imperial court was the first systematic use of the printing press by a government to shape European public opinion.[2] With quasi-official sanction, Alcalá scholars felt free to blend together doctrines of the *alumbrados*, Erasmus, and even early Protestant reformers into a stimulating brew misleadingly labelled Spanish

Erasmianism by modern historians.³ No work better expressed this intellectual hybrid than Juan de Valdés's *Dialogue on Christian Doctrine*.⁴

Juan's stature at the university during the propaganda campaign suggests that he did more than merely ride the Spanish Erasmian bandwagon. Américo Castro defined Spanish Erasmianism as 'an imperialist movement that aspired to depict a national outline in the face of Rome and Luther, rivals and opponents of Charles V.'⁵ Whether one considers it an imperial ideology or propaganda,⁶ diplomatic necessity drove the movement more than consistency with the writings of the Dutch humanist.⁷ But after Charles and Clement VII made peace in 1529 and entered into an alliance, the university, and Juan de Valdés, were left vulnerable to a political backlash and inquisitorial investigation.

Curricular and Extra-Curricular Activities

Cardinal Cisneros founded the University of Alcalá in 1508 to unite the linguistic and rhetorical tools pioneered by Italian humanists with theological studies to improve the quality of Spanish clergy. It quickly gained fame for its chairs of Greek and Hebrew established to advance prospective clergy in biblical philology. Of course the study of Greek furnished an aspiring humanist an intimate association with classical literature as well as with biblical criticism. Cisneros employed the linguistic expertise of university scholars in the task of collecting biblical manuscripts and publishing the Old and New Testaments in the ancient languages of Hebrew, Aramaic, and Greek to supplement the Latin *Vulgate*. The *Polyglot Bible* was printed between 1514 and 1517, but would not be distributed until 1522. *Conversos* edited the Old Testament, and the famous Spanish humanist Antonio de Nebrija worked on the New Testament.⁸

Nebrija had studied law, medicine, history, and literature at the University of Bologna before returning to Spain to teach grammar at the University of Salamanca from 1505 to 1513. He held the principal chair of grammar (i.e., rhetoric) at Alcalá from 1513 until his death in 1521 or 1522.⁹ Nebrija's work represents the maturity of linguistic study at Alcalá before the mantra of Erasmus echoed through its halls. Indeed, when Erasmus's New Testament appeared in 1516, Nebrija published a criticism of his translation.¹⁰ Like the Roman ciceronians, he believed linguistic precision aided cultural expansion. He wrote, 'Language was always the companion of empire, and in such a way that together they began, grew and flourished.'¹¹ He then turned the ciceronian position around to encourage the spread of the Spanish vernacular rather than the Latin of Cicero and Virgil. He urged Charles to unify the 'barbaric peoples and nations of foreign languages' by spreading Spanish laws and speech to reflect Spain's political domination.[12] To further this end Nebrija wrote the first textbook on Spanish grammar, a work Juan de Valdés later used to teach Spanish at the court of the Viceroy of Naples.[13] No Spanish humanist would work harder to make Nebrija's dream of a Spanish imperial language a reality than Juan de Valdés.

Nebrija paved the way for the university's commitment to Charles's imperial policies. Prior to the Battle of Pavia, Erasmus's influence at Alcalá was limited to the use of his *Adages* to teach Latin grammar.[14] But after the battle, Grand Chancellor Gattinara commissioned Alcalá's printer and friend of Juan de Valdés, Miguel Eguía, to publish the major works of Erasmus as part of his propaganda campaign, and even asked Erasmus to join the effort by editing Dante's *Monarchia*.[15] According to Bataillon, the Spanish translation of Erasmus's *Enchiridion* enabled the Erasmian movement to absorb the *alumbrados*, giving them 'a European language, at the same time familiar to the humanists and accessible to all spiritualists.'[16] Though Bataillon has rightly been criticized for an over-identification of Erasmianism with the *alumbrados*, many *alumbrado* followers became staunch supporters of Erasmus in the late 1520s, as the latter, given Charles's favour, appeared to be a safer avenue for religious reform.[17] The synthesis of native aspirations with Erasmus's works created an intellectual movement that was often more Spanish than Erasmian. For example, Juan de Valdés did not mind pricking the Dutch humanist's ego by proclaiming the Spanish translation of the *Enchiridion* equal to the original in style.[18]

Erasmianism quickly dominated the intellectual environment at Alcalá to the extent that the 1527–8 *visita* of the university revealed that the regency of the chair of St Thomas was vacant and, when lecturers were found, they 'read propositions from Erasmus more than from St Thomas.'[19] In their report the reviewers threatened the university's rector and Board of Overseers with excommunication and a stiff fine if they did not force their theology faculty to use the books listed in their constitutions.[20]

Alfonso de Valdés was the undisputed leader of the Spanish Erasmian movement and Juan's primary mentor. With Alcaraz's investigation, Juan likely sought the protection of his brother Alfonso at the imperial court. In 1525 the court resided four months at nearby Toledo, meeting with the Castilian Cortes and celebrating Charles's great victory over France at the Battle of Pavia. Alfonso seems to have directed Juan to the

University of Alcalá so he could aid the imperial propaganda campaign. Given his numerous responsibilities, Alfonso needed his brother's help.

During his first sojourn with the imperial court, Alfonso attended the Diet of Worms in 1521, reported to Angleria on the events of the diet, and met Erasmus, who had been employed as a councillor to Charles since 1516. Angleria was a close friend of fellow Italian Grand Chancellor Mercurino Gattinara. After the court returned to Spain, Gattinara took Alfonso into his service and swiftly promoted him.[21] As a result of Charles's administrative reorganization (1523–6), the Council of State, which coordinated diplomatic reports, served directly under the Grand Chancellor. Thus Gattinara held a double grip on Italian affairs because he also served as Chancellor of the Council of Aragon that oversaw the administration of Spanish dominions in Italy.[22] From imperial scribe in 1522, Alfonso climbed to Latin Registrar for Italian affairs and Contrarelator for recording taxes. In 1525 Gattinara appointed Alfonso Chancellor of Naples, thereby transferring all his authority in the viceroyalty to him. If that was not enough work, Alfonso became Charles's Latin Secretary in January 1526 with responsibility for Charles's foreign correspondence in Latin.[23]

These appointments were in addition to Alfonso's previously unrecognized service as Charles's chronicler. There is an undated request in the Simancas Archive for payment to Alfonso because 'he has written the chronicle of Your Majesty for five years to this point,' and funding 'would enable him to continue with better spirit.'[24] Since he is identified as Chancellor Gattinara's secretary, the request had to have been made prior to Gattinara's death in 1530. Angleria, who served as chronicler, must have transferred the position to Alfonso some time before or during the year 1525. The appointment highlights the official nature of Alfonso's compositions. Alfonso's separate propaganda tracts may have been 'the chronicle' referenced in the request, as the cover sheet of the document identifies it as a 'crusade matter,' and all Alfonso's known tracts emphasized the need for Christians to unite behind Charles to battle the Turks.

Alfonso's first propaganda tract was commissioned to glorify the imperial victory at Pavia. In it he employed an Erasmian plea for peace to forge a Christian alliance to wage war on the Turks. The miracle of Pavia was a sign from God that Christian states should end their 'civil wars' and join Charles's battle against the Turks.[25] But a new war followed Pavia rather than peace. The War of the League of Cognac culminated in the 1527 sack of Rome by Charles's army, which included

German Lutherans. In view of the events, Alfonso needed even more masterful rhetoric,[26] and displayed it in the introduction of his *Dialogue on Events in Rome*. He was 'writing not to ignorant people but to Spaniards whose minds can easily comprehend anything, no matter how arduous.'[27] According to Alfonso, the sack was divine retribution for corruption of the Church. Since the pope ignored both Erasmus and Luther, God sent the imperial army as a final warning.[28] It was now left to Charles to bring about the necessary reform, which would achieve for him 'more fame and glory in this world than any other prince before him. To the end of time, people will say that Jesus Christ founded the Church, and that Emperor Charles V restored it.'[29] In his second book, *Dialogue of Mercury and Charon*, Alfonso continued to portray Charles in messianic and crusader terms. 'Take up arms against the infidel not only because they have tormented and enslaved Christians and denied the holy catholic faith of Christ, more because they will destroy Christendom and profane the temples of Christ, and his holy name they will banish from the face of the earth.'[30]

The memoirs of a Spanish noble who knew both Juan and Alfonso well mentioned 'the good doctrine he [Juan] learned from his brother [Alfonso].'[31] The reference implies that Alfonso directed Juan's education. While no correspondence between the Valdés brothers has been discovered,[32] there are numerous references to it in the letters of their associates. A mutual friend of the brothers wrote to Juan in January 1527 about his pleasure in seeing a letter from him 'in the house of your brother the secretary.'[33] In June of the same year Doctor Luis Núñez Coronel concluded a letter to Alfonso: 'greetings to your brother and to you and both of you write me in return.'[34] In a letter to a diplomatic agent in Germany Alfonso stated: 'I know that you are well informed because of the letter from my brother.'[35] Bartolomé de Carranza testified that Juan met with Alfonso at the imperial court in Valladolid in 1528.[36] A letter from Alfonso to the Polish ambassador at the imperial court in February 1529 indicates that the two brothers reunited in Toledo a month after Juan's *Dialogue of Christian Doctrine* left the Alcalá press.[37]

The structure of Alcalá's curriculum indicates the type of education Juan de Valdés would have acquired at Alcalá beyond Erasmian immersion. Alcalá's constitutions provided for instruction in Arts, Theology, Medicine, Canon Law, Rhetoric, Grammar, and Languages (i.e., Greek and Hebrew). Rhetoric was merged with grammar, making the chair of Rhetoric the principal professor of Grammar, who instructed students in advanced Latin.[38] The typical curriculum began with three years of grammar in the minor colleges of San Eugenio and San Isidoro. Students honed their Latin with heavy doses of Nebrija, some of Erasmus's *Adages*, as well as Cato, Juvenal, Quintilian, and Virgil among other classical authors. Mastery of Latin was essential because all instruction and all daily conversation had to be in Latin. The grammar colleges also offered two additional years of Greek if a student did not want to advance immediately to an arts college.[39] Grammar was the core curriculum, but Cisneros did not provide for the granting of degrees in it. Rather it prepared the student for the study of the Arts culminating in a Bachelor of Arts degree.[40] But advanced study in Latin, Greek, and Hebrew was often integrated into graduate work, especially in Theology.

In 1528 the creation of the College of San Jerónimo, i.e., the Trilingual College, further enhanced the teaching of classical and biblical philology. The study of Greek was transferred to it from the grammar colleges. Now a student could study languages for nine years before having to move to another college: three in advanced Latin, i.e., rhetoric, three in Greek, and three in Hebrew. Founded by the university's rector and friend of Juan de Valdés, Mateo Pascual, the college quickly established the university's fame with its rigorous linguistic training. In addition to the regular course work, each year the student had to present a comedy or tragedy in his chosen language in the university's theatre.[41]

Juan de Valdés did not progress along a normal degree route. Students with the proper political connections would concentrate their studies in grammar and rhetoric, and aspire to 'cape and sword' offices that included positions in high councils, the diplomatic corps, the military, or local government. The granting of these positions depended more on family influence than on a specific degree.[42] In his *Dialogue on Language* Valdés defined the word *bachillería* as a popular term for anyone pretending to be a know-it-all, demonstrating his condescension toward those who pursued degrees rather than knowledge.[43]

The citation of Juan de Valdés in the trial of Alcaraz places him at the university in 1526; he probably had already left the university shortly before Erasmus invited him to join him in January 1530.[44] As mentioned previously, Bartolomé de Carranza testified that he first met Juan in 1526 or 1527 when Valdés was a student of Latin at Alcalá.[45] Juan must have been studying advanced Latin, i.e., rhetoric, when he met Carranza. Not only does evidence point to his earlier study of Latin in Valladolid, he later claimed to have been an avid reader of Latin books before entering Alcalá.[46] The Alcaraz trial also contained testimony that Valdés had listened to Alcaraz read scripture in Latin.[47]

In January 1529 Valdés published his *Dialogue on Christian Doctrine*, which evidenced his mastery of Greek by including a translation of the Sermon on the Mount from Greek into Spanish. Most likely Valdés entered the Trilingual College in 1528 and afterwards focused on the study of Greek. It was an appealing residence for him because he had familiarity with Hebrew from his *converso* background.[48] In his later career Valdés translated the Psalms from Hebrew into Spanish and frequently translated Hebrew terms in his commentaries on the New Testament. The Trilingual College would have enabled Valdés to polish his Latin and Hebrew while focusing on Greek.

Juan's stature at the university further indicates that his studies were quite advanced. He was a good friend with many of the university's luminaries, including its rector, its printer, the primary chair of Greek, Francisco de Vergara, and his brother Juan de Vergara, who had helped to edit the *Polyglot Bible*. Most prominently he corresponded directly with Erasmus, who in 1528 commended his study of the 'liberal disciplines ... where you gain such honour.'[49] In 1532 the newly appointed primary chair of St Thomas, Hernán Vázquez, openly admired the work of Juan de Valdés.[50]

Juan became a true Hellenophile through his studies with Francisco de Vergara. The 1527–8 *visita* rated Francisco as one of the outstanding lecturers in the university.[51] Francisco's students began their Greek translations with Aesop, Lucan, and precepts of Isocrates and Scripture. The next stage consisted of more Isocrates and early Greek fathers, such as Crysostrom and Basil, followed by Aristotle's *Politics* and *Ethics* and Plutarch. Final training included translation of Thucydides, Plato, Demosthenes, Pausanius, and Hellenic poets and playwrights.[52] Juan later praised the classical authors for 'the natural propriety and purity of the language.'[53]

Juan's association with Francisco's elder brother, Juan de Vergara, a secretary to the Archbishop of Toledo, deepened his foundation in classical literature and biblical philology. Juan de Vergara worked on the Latin translation of the Greek Septuagint in the *Polyglot* and was later commissioned by Cisneros to edit and translate the complete works of Aristotle from Greek to Latin.[54] Vergara had been a personal friend and staunch defender of Erasmus since the early 1520s. His vast library included books by Protestant reformers, the ownership of which had been forbidden by the Inquisition. Vergara claimed that he was not aware of the prohibition until 1530, and prior to that he believed, 'A man of my position ought to be able to own and to read such books.'[55] Vergara even admitted initially favouring Luther:

When Luther only touched on the necessity of reforming the Church in articles concerning moral corruption, the whole world approved. ... The same thing occurred in Spain during the Comunero Revolt. In the beginning when it seemed that it only sought reform of some things, everyone favoured it; later when the people began to disagree and to profane the movement, the wise separated themselves from it and persecuted it.[56]

In the various trials of Erasmians in the early and late 1530s, the same accusations recur. They did not attend mass, confess, or take communion regularly. They criticized monks and conservative theologians for their ritualism and lack of scriptural knowledge. They associated with known *alumbrados* and approved certain doctrines of Luther. They used Scripture to justify their doctrine and praised works by Erasmus, whose orthodoxy some inquisitors questioned.[57] These charges neatly summarize the intellectual environment during Juan de Valdés's tenure at Alcalá.

Spanish opponents of Erasmus had denounced him as a semi-Lutheran as early as 1522.[58] The conflict escalated with the translations of the *Enchiridion* and *Colloquies* into Spanish, and other publications at Alcalá. Many of Spain's leading theologians met in a special council to review the works of Erasmus and decide whether they should be expurgated, or banned. The council opened in June 1527, but an outbreak of plague in mid-August forced its adjournment after twenty-one contentious sessions.[59] While the council was meeting, Alfonso de Valdés and Inquisitor General Alonso Manrique asked the pope, who was still a prisoner of the emperor in Rome, for a papal brief to prohibit clerical abuse of Erasmus. Clement VII, wily as ever, only prohibited attacks on those of Erasmus's works that were written to refute Luther.[60] Nevertheless, the Erasmians proclaimed victory after Manrique suspended the council. Charles personally assured Erasmus in December of the same year that he should no longer fear persecution in Spain.[61]

Following the council, Juan de Valdés penned a victory joke to Erasmus involving a fictional friar's sermon of condemnation on Erasmus's *Enchiridion*.

> 'What do they think now, those who never put down the *Cherrion* or *Chicharron* that they continually read in assemblies and public streets, since the other day the ground opened up and swallowed the Archdeacon of Alcor, who translated the *Enchiridion* of Erasmus?' Everyone there

believed the story true. An indulgence seller happened to be passing through and responded to the sermon: 'It is truly true that the ground suddenly opened up and swallowed the Archdeacon of Alcor, but it was to separate him from the evil company of friars, who are the most vile thing in the world. But it vomited him up in Palencia, where I saw him yesterday safe and sound.'[62]

Juan would not have the last laugh. The 1527 council was a Pyrrhic victory because it authoritatively demonstrated the apparent similarity of some Erasmian and Lutheran positions.

Clement VII now seized the initiative and launched his own attack against the Erasmians at the imperial court. He sent the famous humanist and diplomat Baldesar Castiglione to Spain to press the Inquisition to seize Alfonso de Valdés as a Lutheran heretic because of his *Dialogue on Events in Rome*. After failing in that attempt, Castiglione heaped his vituperation on Alfonso, calling him 'the greatest enemy and most perfidious heretic who has ever stood up against the Church of Christ. I do not see how you could more clearly demonstrate that you are a Lutheran yourself, for you practically say that he should be canonized.'[63] Castiglione decided to try and undermine his enemy at court by enlisting the support of Jean Lallemand, the Secretary of State (i.e., Secretary of the Council of State), to spread rumours to encourage prominent men to denounce Valdés.[64] Sensing a plot, Alfonso personally went to Charles, who sanctioned Lallemand's imprisonment as a traitor to the emperor in December 1528, and a few days later Castiglione died. Alfonso coldly celebrated 'God's judgment' on his enemies.[65]

The Shipwreck

At the moment of apparent Erasmian triumph, Juan's *Dialogue on Christian Doctrine* issued from the University of Alcalá's press in January 1529. Since Juan had already applied for imperial service, the work was intended to complement Alfonso's more obvious propaganda tracts and to help Juan gain a position on the emperor's payroll. The book presents the Archbishop of Granada as a model Erasmian reformer, closely paralleling Latancio's comment in Alfonso's *Dialogue on Events in Rome*. 'You do not believe that there are many wise bishops of good conscience who could serve as examples to others? To tell the truth, it seems to me that now this is the best remedy until there may be a general reformation of the Church.'[66] Barely more than a hundred pages, Juan's controversial little book was probably written in 1528 and hastily sent to press as Protestants and Catholics awaited Charles's decision on his papal prisoner. It was an ideal time to encourage Spanish bishops to initiate reforms autonomously.

Some hundred and thirty Spanish authors used the dialogue form in the sixteenth century, but arguably none more effectively than Juan de Valdés.[67] Juan placed his discussion in a realistic, contemporary setting, the Jeronymite monastery of Santa María de la Granada.[68] Eusebio, the fictional author, observed a well-intentioned but poorly trained priest instructing children, and invited the priest to accompany him on a visit to the saintly Archbishop of Granada, Fray Pedro de Alba. Since Alba died in June 1528, Valdés opportunistically employed his name as the Socratic voice for his doctrines. Most of the work is a rather mild catechism for Christian education in the following topical order: the Apostles Creed, Ten Commandments, Sermon on the Mount, Seven Mortal Sins, the Cardinal and Theological virtues, the gifts of the Holy Spirit, the Commandments of the Church, the Lord's Prayer, a very short summary of the Bible, and recommendations for further study.

The atmosphere of the dialogue and the name of Eusebio were borrowed from Erasmus's famous colloquy 'The Godly Feast.'[69] After a good meal the discussants enter a pleasant garden where the Erasmianized archbishop stresses scriptural study and proper mental attitudes over the mechanical rituals of the Church. The archbishop praises Erasmus highly as a theologian, despite opposition to him among the 'ignorant,' and recommends his *Colloquies* and *Enchiridion* to the priest for study.[70] But the *Dialogue* is not overly bound to Erasmus's doctrines beyond its surface. The archbishop rejects Erasmus's translation of the Lord's Prayer, where the Dutch scholar substituted 'deliver us from the evil one' for the traditional 'deliver us from evil.'[71] Further, though Valdés had a good grounding in the classics and would later praise them, in this work they receive no mention even though Erasmus considered them essential for moral edification and Christian growth. Rather than canonizing Socrates,[72] the archbishop cites traditional theologians to support his advice to the priest.[73]

Alcaraz's influence most prominently permeates the dialogue's discussions of prayer and contemplation.[74] On this topic the archbishop frequently refused to expand his answers, indicating that Valdés feared taking the issue too far, or that these sections were censored by the pre-publication review of the work.[75] Still, his opposition to the predominantly mechanical nature of prayer is obvious. The archbishop insists that rote, oral prayer did not necessarily make one a good Christian. He complained that he saw Christians ignoring the reading of the epistles and gospels in Church to recite prayers, only to leave the building gossiping about their neighbours. Eusebio satirically adds: 'This is because their tongues moved so fast going through the Psalms that they could not stop them.'[76]

Citing the Psalms and Paul's Epistles as examples, the archbishop defines proper contemplation as constantly praising God for his law that required fulfilment with love.[77] This contemplation enables the soul to receive 'knowledge of the supreme good, greatness and mercy of God, and awareness of our own smallness and weakness. With it one learns his obligations to God, his neighbours, and himself. In sum, there is no good that cannot be obtained by this continual contemplation.'[78]

In the discussions of the Ten Commandments and Lord's Prayer, Valdés copies some long excerpts from Lutheran works.[79] Most of these passages refer to original sin and the role of the law in making people conscious of their sinful nature as the first step toward justification, and would not be considered heretical. In fact María Cazalla actually praised these particular passages from the book before inquisitors who made no objection to them.[80] One should not over-emphasize the extent of Lutheran influence in the *Dialogue*. Valdés steers clear of the primary Lutheran doctrine of justification by faith alone in his discussion of faith as one of the three theological virtues. These virtues of faith, hope, and charity were so intertwined that anybody who perfectly possessed one had them all. In this manner faith and works were united: 'The living faith is the root of the works of charity ... [but] if one did not practise charity he would not have true faith.'[81]

Valdés illustrated his conception of faith with the story of a man with a wax head caught in a forest-fire. A guide came to the man and said that if the man would hold his hand and never leave his side, he would be taken to safety. Though it seemed impossible, and the man stumbled and fell a few times, his confidence in his guide grew and he was saved. Similarly the Christian's initial faith led to an experience of faith that increased his love of God and therefore his desire to practise charity. Valdés concluded his story by emphasizing that 'charity is none other than the love of God and neighbour.'[82] The centrality of the love of God in Valdés's conception of faith, and the identification of hope with experience, suggests that Valdés drew upon Alcaraz's doctrines in an attempt to find an acceptable compromise between Catholic and Lutheran views on the relation of faith and works.

The most confrontational section of the work dealt with the commandments of the Church in regard to confession, fasting, and tithes. Like Erasmus, Valdés believed only mortal sins needed to be confessed.[83] It would be best not to have to confess more than the Church's requirement of once a year, and ideally not to have to confess at all. Unfortunately Christians confessed routinely out of superstition. Confessing minor things over and over 'does more harm than good.'[84] Confessors too often had the habit of teaching sin as they inquired about matters that should have been left unmentioned. The archbishop admitted that he had 'learned many ways of sinning from stupid confessors.'[85] According to the archbishop, fasting simply meant abstaining from delicacies and eating moderately from the food the land provided. Avoiding overeating 'subjugates sensuality to reason, and the flesh to the spirit.'[86] Those who paid twice as much for fish as meat to bring it to their plate and then ate to the bursting point pursued vice rather than virtue.

Throughout, the *Dialogue* asserts that outside the archbishop's diocese the Church had neglected its job of providing proper Christian doctrine. If the Church did not provide this education, it did not deserve its income from the laity.

> As long as they do not receive this doctrine from us, believe me that we do not deserve the rents they give us. Not only are we obligated to give doctrine for their rents, but to spend them on those things that the Church wishes them to be spent on. Truly, I do not know how clergy are not sickened at spending their rents given to aid the poor on profane and worldly things.[87]

The *Dialogue on Christian Doctrine* has been cited as one of the first attempts in the Spanish language to promote lay spiritual education.[88] But that was not its primary threat. At a moment when the papacy was temporarily paralysed, Valdés used the model Archbishop of Granada to call on other bishops and archbishops to immediately begin reforming their dioceses. The archbishop lamented that the situation of the Church 'requires a general remedy, but I feel there is little concern about enacting this remedy.'[89] Valdés never mentioned papal authority in his book. Inquisition records indicate that the work was bulk-ordered by clergy as soon as it was printed. As with his later writings, the real danger of Valdés's doctrines was less their appeal among lay masses than their appeal within the ecclesiastical hierarchy.

The publication of Juan de Valdés's *Dialogue on Christian Doctrine* provided new ammunition for the anti-Erasmians. In Valdés's haste to publish, he ignored, or barely heeded, suggestions for revisions. According to the later testimony of María Cazalla, 'Tovar reprehended the said Valdés because he had published the said book so quickly without correcting and amending it more.'[90] A panel of Alcalá theologians reviewed the book before publication. All that is known of their assessment comes from two members of the panel who testified in February and March 1532 in the trial of Juan de Vergara, and from Vergara's responses to their charges.

Vergara and Tovar ran afoul of the Inquisition because of Tovar's relationship with the *alumbrada* Francisca Hernández.[91] Tovar was among her well-to-do followers essential to her comfortable life style. After Vergara ordered an end to the relationship, she proclaimed Tovar and Vergara Lutherans, and to ensure her mild punishment, she turned state's evidence, naming others at Alcalá Lutheran, but not Juan de Valdés. Vergara's intervention in Tovar's case led to his trial[92] and subsequent testimony about his involvement in the publication of the *Dialogue on Christian Doctrine*. According to Doctor Alonso Sánchez, a canon of the Church of San Yuste in Alcalá who served on the panel, its other members included the abbot of San Yuste, Pedro de Lerma, fellow San Yuste canons Doctor Hernán Vázquez and Doctor Juan de Medina, Doctor Hernando de Balvas, Doctor Francisco de la Fuente, Doctor Diego de la Puente, Doctor Bernardino Alonso, Doctor Francisco de Vargas, and occasionally Doctor Cristóbal de Loaysa. They met in the office of the rector of the university, Mateo Pascual, who joined some of the sessions. In reporting his views to the panel, Doctor Vázquez apparently served as the primary investigator. Vázquez criticized several parts of the book, had some sections removed, but 'worked to gloss over, defend and excuse as much of the said book as possible.'[93] Sánchez claimed Vergara urged moderation in the examination 'because Valdés was his friend.'[94] The panel sent its report to Inquisitor General Manrique, a fervent Erasmian.

The second witness, Juan de Medina, questioned Valdés about troublesome passages. Valdés 'urgently begged this witness to take no note of such propositions nor bring them to light, Valdés swearing he had never meant them in such a sense.'[95] The initial report must have been negative because Inquisitor General Manrique sent Sancho Carranza de Miranda, a canon of Seville and former Alcalá professor, as his messenger to the panel. He instructed them 'not to classify the propositions in the said book of Christian doctrine but to craft corrections for the book and return it for printing.'[96] Medina elaborated more than Sánchez on

Vergara's intervention. He claimed that Vergara told him 'to take it as an order that he was to give direction as to how the said book of Christian doctrine may be amended and returned to the printer. ... [But] if there were some erroneous or heretical things in it, he should declare it and not hide it.'[97] As secretary of the Archbishop of Toledo, Vergara exercised considerable clout, and Medina believed Vergara would 'weigh any affront to Valdés.'[98]

On 4 November 1533 the inquisitors confronted Vergara with these testimonies and added that Vergara kept the book a secret from the Archbishop of Toledo, Alonso de Fonseca.[99] Vergara responded to Sánchez's charge by merely saying the majority of the Alcalá assembly disagreed with Sánchez about the particulars of emendation. He claimed that he did know Valdés resided in Alcalá at the time, and that he had not talked with him about the book, nor had he read it. He knew Canon Carranza liked the book and ordered several copies for his clergy, but some of them found a few minor things in need of revision. Doctor Coronel joined Carranza on a Council of the Inquisition supporting a second emendation because they thought the book valuable.[100] For his part, Vergara thought Valdés should not have been 'going into matters he had not studied,' and recalled hearing his brother Tovar mentioning the work.[101]

Initially Vergara seemed determined to distance himself from Valdés. On 22 February 1533 Vergara's secretary, Cristóbal Gumiel, testified that Vergara wrote a letter to Valdés in Murcia or Cartagena just prior to his departure for Italy. Gumiel claimed the letter was very vague for fear of being intercepted, so it did not advise Valdés to stay in Spain or to leave.[102] Four months later the inquisitors asked if Vergara had asked anyone who had left Spain to return. He replied that he wrote Valdés and Mateo Pascual to return because their absence hurt Tovar's case. He thought their testimony would show that Tovar was only guilty of 'some words that were common opinions passed among *letrados* [at Alcalá] but scandalous to idiots.'[103] Pascual returned, but Valdés gave unspecified reasons why he could not. In a much later testimony, 25 February 1535, Gaspar Lucena claimed Pascual and Valdés left Spain together and that Vergara wrote to both, warning them that Rome was not safe, and advised them to leave the city.[104] He did not indicate that Vergara advised a return to Spain.

When Vergara made his final response to the charges against him on 6 March 1534, he no longer attempted to distance himself from Valdés. This time when asked about his intervention for Valdés, Vergara admitted favouring publication of the book because he knew Valdés to be 'a virtuous young man'[105] and side-stepped his comments in the initial Alcalá review by focusing on the post-publication inspection by the Inquisition. He again claimed that he had not read the work, but favoured it because Doctors Carranza and Coronel held it in such high esteem. Vergara turned the Inquisition to his defence by saying an Inquisition Council 'examined it either to make a damnable condemnation, or to make benevolent and modest emendations.'[106] They chose to recall the book for emendation.

In the mid-1970s Martínez Millán discovered an order from Inquisitor General Manrique dated 22 August 1529 to confiscate all copies of the *Dialogue on Christian Doctrine*. The order stated, 'There are many erroneous and ill sounding things in it and thus it is declared by many doctors of theology who have seen and examined it and agree. ... The said book is not to be sold nor distributed by any manner or person because later it will be more difficult to correct.'[107] The Inquisition did not condemn the book, but rather ordered its correction, thereby implying that they considered the book to have merit.

The trial of the feisty María Cazalla reveals further evidence about the Inquisition's view of the *Dialogue on Christian Doctrine*. The Cazalla home was known as an Erasmian-*alumbrado* centre. María and her brother Bishop Pedro de Cazalla were closely connected to the Vergaras and had sponsored the ministry of Isabel de la Cruz from its inception.[108] María knew Valdés's book well and also detailed information about the Inquisition's review of it.

In the initial questioning, inquisitors asked if María had praised Valdés's book. She admitted doing so many times but added that some things 'could have been said better and without scandal such as in what is said about tithes and first fruits, and also confession.'[109] The eleventh of thirty-two charges formulated against her stated that she had criticized St Thomas, Duns Scotus, and scholastic authorities while praising Erasmus, 'and praising highly the book titled *Christian Doctrine* having in it, as it has, errors against our faith.'[110] She responded that she did not recall criticizing 'these doctors,' and admitted she had praised Erasmus. 'Concerning the *Christian Doctrine*, I read it and praised some things in it that seemed good, such as in what manner we become aware of sins and how we transgress God's commandments.'[111] After hearing a Franciscan friar criticize the book, she put it in a chest and told her daughters not to read it 'until Your Majesties determine what to order because I do not consider something good or a good guide without the Catholic Church considering it good.'[112]

In March 1533 María Cazalla added an emphatic statement to her testimony about Valdés's book. 'Since it is not condemned by Your Majesties, it has no error in it.'[113] The problem for María was that she knew the book had been ordered confiscated for correction. A year earlier she wrote a servant of Tovar from prison that inquisitors asked her about the book. She claimed to have responded truthfully 'that it had excessive things in the said book that were the reason that they will emend it in order to have it printed [i.e., reprinted].'[114] Her accusers knew she praised the book after it was prohibited; hence in her sentence she was faulted for having 'praised highly the book called *Christian Doctrine* having in it, as there is, errors against our faith.'[115] After carefully reviewing all the references to the *Dialogue on Christian Doctrine* in María's trial, it is difficult to dispute Milagros Ortega-Costa's conclusion that it was only a minor accusation against her.[116]

The image of the Inquisition hounding Valdés out of Spain after publication of his dialogue needs qualification. Juan temporarily joined Alfonso at the imperial court in Toledo after his book's publication. In February 1529, Alfonso de Valdés wrote the Polish ambassador that he could not send him a copy of his *Dialogue on Events in Rome* because of 'the grave illness of my brother Juan.'[117] John Longhurst and many subsequent Valdesian scholars have interpreted this as a code meaning Juan was already in trouble with the Inquisition.[118] Yet in late October 1528 the *visitadores* at Alcalá noted that the university had been under quarantine for thirty days due to plague.[119] Juan may have actually been too ill to revise his work properly after the Alcalá review, therefore explaining Tovar's complaint that Valdés rushed the publication. Erasmus wrote to Juan in late March that he was grieved to hear Juan was 'moved to and fro by such molestation and dangers. I am glad to know from your letter that you remain afloat in this shipwreck.'[120] Erasmus excused Juan from writing to him, saying that in the future his letters to Alfonso should also be considered to him, and that he would consider letters from Alfonso coming from Juan as well.[121] But Erasmus's concern does not prove that Valdés had to flee Spain immediately. If Juan had felt he needed protection, he would have left with the imperial court in July.

Juan's immediate response to the reaction against the book was to draw closer to the Church. The title page of the *Dialogue* identifies the anonymous author as a *religioso*, indicating that Juan had already taken some sort of vows. On 4 May 1529 his father Fernando gained Charles's permission to transfer his *mayoralía* of San Lázaro to Juan because he had gout and Juan 'has letters.'¹²² Unlike Alcaraz, the Inquisition could not charge that he was unqualified to write about religious matters. In addition, should it become necessary to leave Spain, the prebend would provide Juan an annual income of more than sixty-six ducats.¹²³

Valdés's situation changed drastically following the disgrace of the Erasmian Inquisitor General Alonso Manrique in August. The demise of Manrique resulted from his role in the marriage of the rich, young Countess of Valencia, doña Luisa de Acuña, the most eligible young woman in Spain. Charles and Queen Isabel, fearing rivalry among the grandees could ignite disorders, commanded the countess to the royal court. Nevertheless, after Charles left Spain Manrique engineered her marriage to one of his relatives during a visit by the countess to the convent of Santo Domingo el Real. Queen Isabel banished Manrique to Seville and Charles upheld her decision.¹²⁴

With Manrique's disgrace, *de facto* control of the Holy Office fell to the anti-Erasmian faction at court (i.e., the old Ferdinand faction), headed by Gattinara's great rival Francisco de los Cobos. Cobos had served Ferdinand first in Castilian finance and later in the administration of the Indies. By 1520 Charles had entrusted him with Castilian administration and in his governmental reorganization made him Secretary of the Council of Finance, and Secretary of the Council of the Indies.¹²⁵ After the fall of Lallemand, Charles made Cobos the new Secretary of State, meaning all diplomatic matters came under his purview.

Cobos favoured Lallemand's pro-French policy, and opposed Gattinara's costly central European objectives and questionable compromises with Lutherans. Cobos and Gattinara, Charles's primary advisers, were cut from very different cloth. Gattinara, a man of great culture and intellect, shaped Charles's foreign policy around an Erasmian ideology that employed humanist propagandists like the Valdés brothers.¹²⁶ Cobos lacked formal education and rose to power as an accountant, but he knew the value of every office and where to place loyal servants to maximize his influence and personal income.¹²⁷ He was also more concerned with the financial burdens of Charles's policies on his Spanish subjects.

Cobos's most powerful ally was Juan de Tavera, President of the Council of Castile. In 1534 Tavera became Archbishop of Toledo, and with Manrique's disgrace *de facto* Inquisitor General. As Secretary of the Council of Indies, Cobos could count on the support of Charles's confessor García de Loaysa, who was also president of the Council of the Indies.[128] Immediately after Manrique's disgrace the Inquisition ordered the confiscation of the *Dialogue on Christian Doctrine* for emendation. If not for Manrique's foolish and selfish mistake, Valdés might have revised the book. With Alfonso's court enemies now in control of the Inquisition, Juan prepared to leave for Italy to warn his brother and seek his protection. In September 1529 Juan made arrangements for his brother Andrés to collect his salary from San Lázaro in his absence.[129]

In his letter to Juan dated 13 January 1530, Erasmus clearly throws out a lifeline and seems to be aware of Juan's impending departure. He begins the brief note stating, 'I owe everything to your brother, beloved Valdés, he does not know when to stop loving me, defending me and in deserving well of me. Since he is absent it is just that you are here as his substitute.'[130] Erasmus wrote that Juan could gain more (i.e., confidential) information from his young protégé Francisco Dilfo, who had just arrived in Spain seeking a political appointment.[131] Erasmus expected Juan's immediate departure and offered him a safe refuge. As will be seen in the next chapter, Juan had probably already left Spain. The Inquisition's verdict on Alcaraz and the arrest of Francisca Hernández in 1529 were stepping-stones to a purge of Erasmians at Alcalá. Other arrests soon followed: Tovar in 1530, Miguel Eguía, Alcalá's printer, in the fall of 1531, Alcalá's rector, Mateo Pascual, upon his return to Spain in 1533, and Vergara himself the same year.[132]

John Longhurst's research on the Vergara trial led him to conclude that Juan and Alfonso were both tried and condemned as Lutherans *in absentia*.[133] The early nineteenth-century historian of the Inquisition, Juan Antonio Llorente, also stated that Juan was tried and condemned as a Lutheran, and that Alfonso was suspected of Lutheranism and investigated by the Inquisition. However, Llorente's chronology is worthless, and his list of Valdesian books problematic. He obviously incorrectly transcribed documents from the Carranza trial, and he cites no evidence Juan was condemned before his death.[134] In an exhaustive study of the Inquisition in the early twentieth century, Henry Charles Lea did not find sufficient evidence that the Spanish Inquisition proclaimed either Alfonso or Juan heretical prior to their deaths. Specifically he noted that Juan was not considered heretical when he corresponded with Bartolomé de Carranza in 1539.[135] Longhurst cites four pieces of evidence from Vergara's trial to back his assertion. Two were passing references to the 'processo of Juan de Valdés,' and the other two were separate testimonies from a single witness. In May 1532 Diego Hernández listed Juan first on a list of Tovar's disciples and labelled him 'damaged [*dañado*].'[136]

The only evidence pointing to Juan's condemnation for Lutheranism was a second testimony of Diego Hernández's in 1533. Then he claimed that Juan de Castillo, a professor of Greek at Alcalá, told him the names of seventy Lutherans in Spain, and he listed them all, including Juan and Alfonso, but few on the list were ever condemned for Lutheranism.[137] Diego Hernández's testimony was highly suspect and the inquisitors knew it. He had been María Cazalla's confessor until he seduced a nun, convincing her it was not a sin; he also liked to wear women's clothes. The wayward priest sought revenge for his humiliating dismissal by labelling María and all her associates Lutherans.[138] Merely on the basis of Hernández's testimony, it seems unlikely either Juan or Alfonso was formally condemned *in absentia* because political opponents of Alfonso de Valdés would have seized upon it.

The Spanish Inquisition was not monolithic in its opinions of the various Erasmians, but it reacted to shifting court factionalism quickly. The disgrace of Inquisitor General Manrique, followed by Gattinara's death in 1530, enabled Cobos and Tavera to use the Holy Office to undermine Gattinara's supporters such as Alfonso and Juan de Valdés. Alfonso's book on the sack of Rome had passed a preview by the Inquisition before its publication, and survived Castiglione's scathing attack in 1528. The March 1531 censure of Diego de Valdés for possessing his brothers' books focused almost entirely on Alfonso's *Mercury and Charon*. The Inquisition censured it for jokes about indulgences and friars, and some statements considered similar to *alumbrado* errors, but not for Lutheranism. Diego's possession of Alfonso's first book on the sack of Rome and Juan's *Dialogue on Christian Doctrine* were merely mentioned in passing as if they were not considered as problematic.[139]

Six months later, Inquisitor Pedro Olivar penned a delayed censure of Alfonso's *Dialogue on Events in Rome*. Though he found nothing specifically heretical in the work, he noted that Alfonso did not remove comments on saints and relics as he had asked prior to its publication. The primary reason he gave for belatedly banning the book was its slander of the pope in the vernacular. 'The Lutheran trouble had its beginning in just this sort of thing.'[140] These censures indicate that Alfonso's works were the primary target of investigation, and their timing suggests political and factional motivations.

Though inquisitorial scrutiny of Alfonso and Juan contributed to a brief decline of Alfonso's influence at court, and certainly to Juan's difficulty in obtaining a suitable position in imperial service, it is doubtful either was actually condemned for Lutheranism prior to his death.

Both Alfonso and Juan maintained Charles's personal favour and that probably explains why their investigation by the Inquisition was left open. But at least one inquisitor, Diego Ortiz de Angulo, the fiscal in both the Alcaraz and Vergara cases, maintained that Juan de Valdés was guilty of *alumbrado* errors as late as 10 December 1534.[141] Whether or not the Valdés brothers would have been tried had they returned to Spain, as Francisco de Enzinas speculates in his memoirs, is a different and purely hypothetical question.[142] Considering the fate of those who left Spain and returned, Juan made the correct decision to remain safe in Italy. Unfortunately for Juan's career, Cobos would soon assert his authority in Italy as well.

3 Italian Design

Juan de Valdés needed all the wit and charm he could muster to survive the enmity of the Cobos faction. He endured by gaining the trust of friends and patrons at the papal court useful to the maintenance of Charles's Italian alliance system. Historians reviewing Charles V's diplomacy in the 1530s have focused primarily on conciliar negotiations and Charles's crusade against the Turks, but he did not pursue either of these goals consistently.[1] They were secondary and indeed dependent upon Charles's ability to maintain his dominion in Italy. In 1529 Charles and his Italian allies had defeated Francis I and his Italian allies. If Charles wanted to avoid prompt eviction like the French, he had to make former enemies friends without alienating his supporters.

Winning influential friends among the Romans was no easy task, considering their resentment of Spaniards for the sack of Rome. However, the Medici papacies had made Rome a humanist heaven. More than 40 per cent of papal officials were humanists by training and the city was relatively free of seigniorial servility.[2] Clement VII gave major posts to several leading humanists – Gian Matteo Giberti, Jacobo Sadoleto, Paolo Giovio, Angelo Colocci – as well as lesser positions to many others including Valdés.[3] Churchmen controlled the city and many of them rose to positions of influence based on their mastery of classical philology. Valdés was finally in a position to make his mark in life, and he could ask for no better guide in this brilliant environment than Juan Ginés de Sepúlveda, the most acclaimed Spanish humanist in Rome. Fortunately for Juan, Sepúlveda wanted favour with Erasmus and the imperial court so he provided Juan passage into the world of Roman humanism, a world that extended from the papal court, to the *familia* of cardinals, academic associations, and the sodalities of individual humanists in the curia.[4]

Brotherly Direction

Circumstantial evidence suggests that Juan attended the imperial court prior to his joining Sepúlveda in Rome in the summer of 1531. In December 1529 Alfonso de Valdés asked for and received a plenary indulgence from Pope Clement VII for himself, Juan, and nine other family members and friends.[5] The same month Alfonso's expense account from Bologna lists a Domine Hiouannes (Sir Juan) receiving four hundred escudos worth of supplies.[6] Since this is the only entry that is not to Señor Valdés, it implies that Juan had joined his brother at the imperial court. Juan's arrival and report of inquisitorial investigations in Spain probably led to Alfonso's request for the papal indulgence to protect himself and his family.

Nicholas of Peronet, lord of Granvelle, assisted Alfonso in his negotiations at the 1529 Treaty of Bologna and at the 1530 Diet of Augsburg. Granvelle joined the Council of State in 1528 and upon Gattinara's death in 1530 assumed control over negotiations in northern Europe. In 1535 Juan would serve Granvelle as secretary, suggesting a previous association. The Treaty and League of Bologna signed at the end of December 1529 created the framework for the stabilization of Italy under a loose Spanish dominion. It reaffirmed the previous Peace of Cambrai with France that removed France from Italy, and the 1528 Treaty of Barcelona with the pope that pledged the restoration of papal territories seized by Venice, Urbino, and Ferrara after the sack of Rome.[7]

The 1529 Treaty of Bologna granted Urbino independence from the papacy, but it had to transfer Perugia back to the pope. Satisfied with Urbino as a buffer, Venice returned Ravenna and Cervia to the papacy as well. To appease Clement for the loss of Urbino, Charles restored Medici rule in Florence, using Spanish troops to overthrow the short-lived republic in favour of Clement's nephew, Alessandro de' Medici, who was now betrothed to Charles's illegitimate daughter Margaret. Clement invested Charles as king of Naples and joined Charles's Italian League consisting of Charles, his brother Ferdinand, Venice, Savoy, Milan, Mantua, Monferrato, Urbino, Sienna, and Lucca. By placing all members of the defensive league under imperial protection, Charles effectively precluded any further territorial revisions among its members without his consent.[8] The most difficult issue concerned Ferrara's seizure of Modena from the Papal States. The Duke of Ferrara was not included in the peace, but Charles had previously agreed to the return of Modena to the papacy in the Treaty of Barcelona.[9] With great difficulty Charles persuaded Clement to let him begin a new investigation into the issue and the duke placed Modena under imperial authority until Charles made his decision.[10]

Having agreed to Charles's league and dominion of Italy, Clement expected the emperor to help re-establish papal authority in Germany as stipulated in the Treaty of Barcelona.[11] The rapprochement of pope and emperor stiffened the orthodox party in Germany, while Cardinal Campeggio, who accompanied Charles to Augsburg, recommended extreme measures. The imperial court seemed surprised at the obstinacy of the Protestant minority, despite Gattinara's warning of difficulties. Unfortunately the Grand Chancellor died six weeks before the Diet opened, leaving his assistant, Alfonso de Valdés, in a weak position.[12] Despite meeting with Philip Melanchthon for four days, and translating his *Augsburg Confession* into Spanish for the emperor, Alfonso failed to convince Charles that Lutheran doctrines were not heretical, or that reunion could occur if the papacy would make minor concessions.[13]

The diet ended as a diplomatic disaster. The Protestants demanded communion in both kinds, marriage of clergy, retention of seized church lands, deletion of the canon at mass, and a general council to resolve other problems. The College of Cardinals rejected these demands in July. While Charles agreed to arrange a meeting of a general council, Clement undermined his efforts, fearing his possible deposition.[14] As negotiations turned sour, Alfonso retired to his lodgings, anticipating a long and bloody war among Christians that would likely result in Turkish conquest of Germany and possibly Italy.[15] With good reason he longed for 'the better times [of] the Grand Chancellor.'[16] In September Charles presented the Protestants an ultimatum to give up their practices by 14 April 1531 and wait on the general council.[17] Soon after, Protestant princes formed a defensive alliance, the League of Schmalkald.

Charles decided not to appoint another Grand Chancellor after Gattinara's death. Instead he gave control over foreign relations with Germany, France, Burgundy, and England to Granvelle, and the relations with Spain, Italy, and the Mediterranean to Cobos. Cobos now wielded unrivalled influence at court and wanted authority over the administration as well as the foreign affairs of Italy. But Alfonso de Valdés stood in his way as Gattinara had placed him in charge of the Neapolitan Chancellery.[18] In order to undermine Alfonso, Cobos enlisted the aid of Charles's confessor, García de Loaysa, who arrived in Rome in 1530 as a special envoy. For years Loaysa had been the leading anti-Erasmian at Charles's court.[19] Loaysa asked Charles to replace Alfonso as his Latin secretary because he was incompetent and deceitful: '[In Rome] they laugh at his Latin and say that it is pierced with lies.'[20] In August 1530 Alfonso informed the staunchly imperialist Benedetto Accolti, Cardinal of Ravenna, that he knew Loaysa undermined him in Rome.[21] Alfonso lost his position as Latin secretary later that year.[22] After the diet adjourned, Clement advised Charles to condemn all Lutheran doctrines except clerical marriage and communion in two kinds, which could be enacted by the College of Cardinals.[23]

The lack of consensus within the Spanish diplomatic corps played into Clement's hands. Though dependent on Spanish troops to re-conquer Florence, the pope easily stymied Ambassador Miguel Mai's attempts to negotiate the convocation of a general council. At the Diet of Augsburg, Loaysa urged Charles to forget about a council and to settle the Lutheran matter with force of arms. The pope opposed a council and the other princes would not support it. According to Loaysa, if Charles stopped pressing for a council, the French would loose their influence in the College of Cardinals.[24] Imperialist cardinals quickly discerned the shifting winds. Mai wrote Cobos in July that, with the exception of Cardenal Ravenna, none of the supposedly imperialist cardinals deserved a subsidy because they would not support the council.[25] When the College of Cardinals opposed voting a subsidy for the Turkish war, Clement suggested that Charles seek a subsidy to fight the Lutherans instead.[26]

Cooperation between Clement and Charles proved elusive. Clement's unwillingness to call a general council led Charles to believe he worked in collusion with the French.[27] To firm up his Italian alliance and help block a possible French invasion, Charles decided to invest the Duke of Ferrara with Modena on 3 April 1531. The duke's hatred of the Medicis ensured that Clement's loyalty to Charles's Italian league would remain a matter of doubt.[28] Meanwhile rumours of a massive Turkish invasion force, 300 ships and an army of 250,000, led even Loaysa to support granting the Lutherans official toleration in a national diet pending a general council.[29] Charles expressed his view of the situation in an April 1531 letter to Empress Isabel. Negotiations for a council bore no fruit, and his brother Ferdinand begged him to use all means for an understanding with the Lutherans, 'so more damage will not be done in the future. In order to encourage it more zealously, he asks that I send appropriate persons who on my behalf understand it [i.e., Lutheran negotiations] and I hope to God that it is managed well and in harmony.'[30] Charles needed someone both he and the Lutherans trusted; he needed Alfonso de Valdés.

Charles asked Alfonso to seek a comprehensive agreement on all matters that did not affect 'the essence of the faith.'[31] However, Alfonso had changed his opinion of the Lutherans since the Diet of Augsburg. He confided to Erasmus that the Lutherans were indeed 'heretics, or certainly schismatics. In the meantime, I insist in my sermons, seeing already the Germans cannot be persuaded of their error, that the result [of a compromise] will not be the infection of Spain by the heretical pestilence.'[32] This comment indicates that Alfonso had little hope of the Lutherans returning to the Catholic fold, and that he was willing to accept their independence from Rome in return for military support against the Franco-Turkish alliance.

The Peace of Nürnberg[33] gave the Lutherans the constitutional right to continue their practices as set forth in the Augsburg Confession, and to preach these doctrines in non-Lutheran areas. Further, it forbade the Imperial Chamber to hear suits regarding matters of faith. All concessions were to last until the convocation of a 'general free council' which Charles vowed to do all in his power to convoke within a year. If a council could not be convoked, he would summon an assembly of the German nation to reach a national religious settlement. For this reason Charles would not convene another diet for eight years, fearing that a premature settlement might be forced upon him.[34] Finally the Lutherans had a firm religious peace and naturally feared losing what they had gained in a general council. They contributed generously to Charles's massive multi-national force, 'the finest army that had been seen in Christendom for centuries.'[35] Facing a united Christian army who had the advantage of holding defensive fortifications, Suleiman called off the invasion. Unfortunately Alfonso could not bask in his great triumph for long; he died of the plague a month later, utterly alone.[36]

In the summer of 1531 Juan de Valdés arrived in Rome as an intelligence agent for his brother to help prevent the débâcle at Augsburg from recurring at Nürnburg. Entering elite circles would not be easy, given the city's suspicions of Spaniards. Indeed, during the sack of Rome Italians thought the Lutherans behaved fairly well until they learned the demonic tricks of their Spanish allies such as testicle roasting, pulling out teeth, or forcing their victims to eat their own noses, ears, etc.[37] Despite the insistence of many historians, the sack of Rome did not suddenly end the Italian Renaissance, but it certainly altered the course of Roman humanism.[38] Many humanists perished in the sack, and the cost of rebuilding the city combined with the loss of papal revenue from Protestant lands meant that the papacy had much less patronage to dole out to its humanist clients. Since the golden age the ciceronians had proclaimed imminent was now considered past,

Roman humanists lost their sense of self-importance as the harbingers of a glorious future.[39] After the sack their primary concern centred on the survival of Italian letters.

Appealing to a brotherhood of letters, Pierio Valeriano's *The Ill Fortune of Learned Men* demonstrates the transition. The dialogue is set in 1529 though composed primarily in the 1530s.[40] The Venetian ambassador and future cardinal Gasparo Contarini serves as the Socratic master. At the end of the work, Contarini assures his friends they need no longer fear another 'hideous and dangerous war' because Clement had invited the emperor to Italy 'to discuss openly the value of peace to the Christian polity. ... And I, indeed, who in previous years was the ambassador to the court of this very Caesar on behalf of our Venetian Republic, easily observed in Charles himself a certain great and outstanding benevolence and character quite unlike the deeds his armies committed with licentious daring in Italy. And so Colocci, I would like you to begin to be optimistic about the peace of Italy and thus the tranquility of all good men.'[41] The first Treaty of Bologna is thus presented as beginning a more hopeful future, and Contarini's centrality in the dialogue seems to allude to his leadership of reform-minded cardinals prior to his death in 1542. Despite the sack, Roman humanists were prepared to allow Spanish humanists like Valdés into their circle out of necessity.

Juan Ginés de Sepúlveda had studied at Juan's alma mater of Alcalá before attending the University of Bologna, where he received his doctorate in Theology and Arts in 1523. In 1522 he gained widespread fame by savagely attacking Pietro Alcionio's translation of Aristotle's *De animalibus*. Though Alcionio was a respected ciceronian, Sepúlveda showed Roman humanists that a Spaniard could have a keen mastery of Greek by publishing his own translation of the work highlighting Alcionio's errors.[42] His book won him a stipend from Cardinal Giulio de' Medici, the future Pope Clement VII, and from 1523 until 1526 he served as official translator and commentator on Aristotle at the papal court. One of Sepúlveda's good friends and patrons was Alberto Pio, at whose home Sepúlveda resided for some time. Pio became an open enemy of Erasmus after the sack of Rome and his tracts influenced the anti-Erasmians in Spain.[43]

Erasmus had long tweaked the Roman humanist ego by insulting Italian military weakness, and most cruelly by attacking their beloved ciceronianism a year after the sack.[44] Deciding to respond with a similar low blow, Pio accused Erasmus of starting the Lutheran revolt. In his *Twenty-Three Books* Pio combed Erasmus's works for parallel sentiments with

Luther. Erasmus had Pio in mind when he complained in 1530 that 'the Italians set the imperial court against me.'[45] Though Pio died in 1531 shortly after submitting the book to press, Erasmus proceeded to respond in print with an unmerciful attack on him. Erasmus's indecent critique motivated Sepúlveda to write his *Anti-Apology for Alberto Pio* in defence of his old patron.[46]

Sepúlveda met the imperial court in Genoa in 1529, but, given his anti-Erasmian efforts, relations were not yet close.[47] In 1531 Charles commissioned him to write a propaganda tract (*Democritus*) to encourage support for war against the Turks. Aware of Charles's favour of Erasmus, Sepúlveda asked Alfonso to write Erasmus to soften Erasmus's expected response to the *Anti-Apology*. Meanwhile Alfonso sent Sepúlveda some of Erasmus's books. Sepúlveda admitted he had only a 'casual encounter' with Erasmus's works because his books circulated much more slowly in Italy than in Spain.[48] Sepúlveda was sufficiently influenced by the Valdés brothers, and his own desire for advancement, to revise his book in defence of Pio. The *Anti-Apology* was initially published in Paris in 1531, but a revision was quickly printed in Rome in 1532. Sepúlveda sent Erasmus a copy of the Roman edition hot off the press with a letter of apology. He professed that the first edition was not written 'with a hostile spirit ... [but] in a place or two I had to make concessions to the bad humour of the Italians who said they would be angry with me if I did not do so.'[49] Sepúlveda claimed he wanted to write a longer revision of the work, but 'certain gentlemen of the greatest respectability and good friends of both [of us]' advised him only to cut out certain parts that 'might exasperate your excitability.'[50]

Sepúlveda gave the revised book to Juan de Valdés to review and pass on to Alfonso: 'I have given your brother the manuscript for him to send, and if it does not have flaws I would recommend it efficaciously, as the Poet says, "he believed it ought to be recommended by your own."'[51] Alfonso tactfully replied: 'I read with great avidity your nocturnal works, which I will not extol, because there is no necessity of extolling your merit, and because my praise would more likely stain than favour it. Without reservation I recommend my studious brother to you, a very erudite gentleman.'[52] Alfonso left the 'recommendation' Sepúlveda sought to his younger brother.

Between the lines of this correspondence there appears to be a *quid pro quo*: if Sepúlveda would help Juan in Rome, the Valdés brothers would intercede on his behalf with Erasmus. 'You beseech me in addition that I may receive your brother, if he presents himself to me, as if he were you ... I have offered him with great pleasure all that I value, and I promise to fulfil your offer as long as I live.'[53] Erasmus waited until October to respond to Sepúlveda's letter. He informed Sepúlveda that he had indeed read the Paris edition earlier and that he was 'much more content' with the Roman edition's taste. [54] He ended the letter assuring Sepúlveda that he would not respond with an attack in print. For the rest of his life Erasmus corresponded with Sepúlveda on friendly terms.

With his future appearing bright, Juan asked Sepúlveda about the meaning of recent abnormal celestial phenomena in the skies above Rome. Juan wondered if the heavenly oddities were 'an instant promise that could not be denied'[55] and asked Sepúlveda what ancient authorities thought of such occurrences. First Sepúlveda listed his own observations of the phenomena: a comet on 7 August, three suns five days later, another comet the next day, and a rainbow after sunset on the twenty-ninth. According to Sepúlveda, Pliny and Lucan believed comets foretold civil war, whereas Seneca, in a lone example, noted that a comet 'appeared to greet the earth at the beginning of Caesar Augustus's principate.'[56] Less dramatically, Aristotle asserted comets augured drought and winds. Implicitly Sepúlveda backed the great philosopher. The ancients generally agreed that multiple suns and rainbows both resulted from the sun's rays colliding with dense clouds; thus Aristotle said they foretold imminent rain. While Pliny and other ancients believed a rainbow at night impossible, Aristotle recorded observing the phenomenon, as did Sepúlveda.

One must wonder about Juan's response to the long explanation that said absolutely nothing, but told much about the humanist culture of Rome. Sepúlveda summarized ancient wisdom about these omens as maybe very bad, or maybe very good, but the infallible Aristotle said to expect drought, or heavy rain! Perhaps wary of which way political winds might blow in the future, Sepúlveda dodged Juan's inquiry, but he had displayed proper erudition by quoting several classical works at length. According to Peter Partner, humanism at the papal court was employed primarily as 'an evasive technique.'[57] In Sepúlveda, Juan had an excellent model to follow. Sepúlveda's service to the Valdés brothers probably contributed significantly to Charles's appointment of him as court chronicler in 1535, a position Alfonso had previously held.

Sepúlveda's mentoring undoubtedly toned down Valdés's ideas of religious reform. A humanist advanced in Rome by being skilled in languages, well read in contemporary literature, adaptable and humorous, but not by being an over-zealous reformer. Indeed, the curial mindset of venal Rome considered reform a violation of self-interest.[58] There is no record of correspondence between Juan de Valdés and Erasmus after 1530, and Valdés made only passing references to Erasmus in his later writings after highly praising him in the *Dialogue on Christian Doctrine*.[59] The Papal Secretary Pietro Carnessechi was Clement's primary adviser late in his papacy.[60] He befriended Valdés in Rome and later became one of his leading followers in Naples. In testimony before the Papal Inquisition, he gave the following insightful description of Valdés in Rome.

> Although I had known Juan Valdés in the time of Pope Clement, I cannot say that I knew him as a theologian before the year 1540 in Naples. For in Rome I did not know that he applied himself to the study of sacred literature, but I knew him as a modest and well-bred courtier, and as such I liked him very much, so that the intercourse and familiarity I afterwards had with him at Naples, was a continuation of our friendship made at Rome.[61]

Sepúlveda's anti-Erasmian credentials helped Juan win trust at the papal court. Two of Sepúlveda's patrons, Clement VII and Cardinal Ercole Gonzaga, became important patrons for Valdés as well. Clement gave Juan an important position at court and Cardinal Gonzaga became Juan's best informant inside the College of Cardinals.

The Cardinal of Ravenna, Benedetto Accolti, naturally would have aided Juan as well. During Alfonso's ill-fated negotiations at the Diet of Augsburg, Ambassador Mai considered Ravenna the only cardinal worth an imperial subsidy.[62] The cardinal advised Alfonso about machinations in Rome, and apparently helped secure Juan's appointment as a Secret Chamberlain to Clement VII. In February 1532 Ambassador Mai relayed advice to Charles from Ravenna, Charles's 'good servant.' He switched his writing into cipher and reported that the cardinal recommended that some men from the imperial court could aid negotiations in Rome. He then switched back to normal cursive and wrote, 'I have entrusted Juan to go to the pope and he shows him benevolence.'[63] Given Mai's later recommendation of Valdés for diplomatic service, and the fact that Juan gained his chamberlain post soon after this letter, it appears likely that Ravenna initiated Juan's appointment.

Papal and Imperial Employment

There were approximately sixty chamberlains who served as clerks in the papal antechamber. They were classified as part of the pope's *familia* rather than the curia per se, but they exercised both administrative and household functions. In the hierarchy of the *familia*, chamberlains occupied second place, just below the twenty-odd domestic prelates.[64] Special robes indicated the office's dignity and legal privileges, which included access to the papal palace as well as the curia. Though it was one of the few positions in Renaissance Rome that could not be bought, it was certainly valuable. In 1517 a chamberlain pledged his office against a loan of 5,300 florins.[65] The secret, or private, chamberlains like Valdés participated in the shadowy venal world of Rome, collecting payments for offices, or other off-the-record fees funnelled into the pope's secret accounts.[66] Clement quickly showed favour to Valdés, praising him as a 'beloved son ... whose virtue and doctrine we especially love.'[67] In a later document Clement added his admiration for Juan's 'studious caution.'[68]

When ambassador Mai heard of Alfonso's illness in Nürnburg, he recommended Juan to Cobos, complaining that he was over-burdened with work and could not leave Rome to meet the court. Mai seemed aware of Alfonso's terminal condition, adding, 'If something is from him [Alfonso] would you consent to make use in what you can this brother who is here, a learned and prudent man.'[69] Juan met the imperial court at Mantua in November 1532, where he received the news of Alfonso's death. There Charles appointed Juan as an imperial secretary with a salary of sixty thousand maravedíes a year. The language of the letter implies that he had been given Alfonso's secretarial position at court, though his pay was 40 per cent less.[70]

Charles's quick victory over the Turks in Hungary and sudden appearance in Italy surprised Clement. Fearful of the implications of the Nürnberg Peace and Charles's promise of a free general council, Clement had engaged in negotiations with the French for the marriage of his niece Catherine to Henry, Duke of Orleans. The pontiff liberally bestowed Modena on the newlyweds even though it was still held by the Duke of Ferrara. Francis I intended to join the territory with Milan and Genoa, which he claimed as his own, to form a new Italian state.[71] When Charles inquired about Clement's meetings with the French, the pope claimed it was about the illness of two French bishops.[72]

In tense negotiations between pope and emperor, Juan de Valdés had an odd, dual responsibility at the second Treaty of Bologna (1533). He served Charles as an imperial secretary, and he served Clement as a 'Chamberlain of Honor.'[73] The primary issue was Modena, which Charles had agreed to return to the Papal States in the 1529 Treaty of

Barcelona.⁷⁴ Juan had inherited Alfonso's legal papers concerning imperial, papal, and Ferrara claims to Modena, and he would continue to serve the duke's interests afterwards. ⁷⁵ Combined with his friendship with Carnessechi, Clement's primary adviser, Valdés had good connections for useful information. Charles stuck by his earlier decision and proclaimed Modena imperial territory and officially transferred it to Ferrara. With the addition of Ferrara and Genoa, Charles firmed up his Italian League, which now included all of Italy with the exception of the Venetians, who gave tacit consent to it. The new alliance also specified military obligations in the event of a French invasion.⁷⁶ According to the contemporary historian Paolo Giovio, the loss of Modena encouraged Clement to continue his rapprochement with the French.⁷⁷ Disingenuously, Clement pledged to support a general council, and should the Medici-Valois marriage occur, he promised to use his influence with Francis I to aid the war against the Turks, to further the council, and to maintain the status quo in Italy.⁷⁸

After recently being the emperor's prisoner, Clement had rebounded by re-establishing Medici power in Florence and a degree of papal independence from Charles. Clement continued to delay the general council and celebrated the marriage of his niece Catherine to Henry of Valois on 28 October 1533. A week later he created four new French cardinals.⁷⁹ The following May the Lutheran seizure of Württemberg (encouraged by France) gave the pontiff an excuse to postpone the general council indefinitely.⁸⁰ Clement rewarded Juan's service with a glowing recommendation that he receive all the lucrative prebends of his recently deceased brother Diego.⁸¹ As will be seen, Charles also valued and rewarded Juan's work at Bologna.

In the middle of his negotiations at Bologna, Juan wrote the Polish ambassador at the imperial court asking his aid in gaining more of Alfonso's responsibilities.⁸² The request is puzzling, unless Juan knew that his appointment as imperial secretary would lapse if he did not return to Spain with the court. The previous month Valdés had gained one of Alfonso's minor appointments, archivist of Naples, but he did not intend keeping it, as he ended his letter to the ambassador saying henceforth he would 'be near the person of the pope.'⁸³ Apparently he did not want to leave his position in Rome for appointments in either Spain or Naples.

Unfortunately, Cobos so ravenously picked Alfonso's political bones that little remained to share. Alfonso's position in the Neapolitan Chancellery fell to Alonso Idiáquez, a man 'who possessed neither letters nor talent.'[84] But he hailed from Cobos's small home town, Úbeda, and had been in Cobos's service since 1523. Many of Alfonso's responsibilities at court fell to Idiáquez and to Juan Vázquez, Cobos's second cousin, who could neither read nor write Latin. The only university-trained member of Cobos's entourage was Gonzalo Pérez, Alfonso de Valdés's clerk. In his testament Alfonso left Pérez a horse, two hundred ducats, and his papers to do with as 'the High Commander of León [Cobos] commands. And for this reason I beg His Lordship to make use of his services and to consider him as recommended.'[85]

After strategically placing his clients, Cobos proceeded to transfer control of the Neapolitan Chancellery from the Aragonese Chancellery, Gattinara's old bailiwick, to the Chancellery of Castile. By the time the imperial court left Italy for Spain, Cobos had completed the administrative reorganization. Martín de Salinas, Ferdinand's ambassador at Charles's court, notified the King of the Romans of the realignment.

> The High Commander Cobos, is, as they say, much favoured by His Majesty and this entire Kingdom knows ... that everything is under his command. ... Idiáquez has received the habit of Calatrava [and] they have given him Valdés's office of state in Naples, which was possible due to the influence of the High Commander [Cobos]. In this manner all correspondence and administration is under his authority. Thus the people are afraid of his power and on his skill and suavity depends all reward and punishment.[86]

Valdés remained with the court until it left Genoa to return to Spain on 9 April 1533. The language of Charles's letter of appointment of Juan as imperial secretary indicates that Juan was to take Alfonso's position at court permanently, because the emperor instructed his accountants to pay Juan each year and not to expect a subsequent letter.[87] But in February 1532 the Inquisition began questioning theologians at Alcalá about Valdés's *Dialogue on Christian Doctrine*.[88] Juan had reason to fear a return to Spain. Rome became less hospitable as well. With the Turkish threat averted, Cobos's faction replaced ambassador Miguel Mai with the Count of Cifuentes.[89] Valdés thoroughly despised and mistrusted Cifuentes, who favoured accommodation with the French and a hard line against the Lutherans.

In June 1533 Juan's salary records indicate that he was to receive 66,500 maravedies: 6,500 for his 1532 salary, and 60,000 for the year 1533.[90] But he was not paid his 1532–3 secretarial salary for six years. The numerous alterations made in Juan's salary records for 1532–3, and the long delay in payment, raise the suspicion that Cobos had Juan's appointment cancelled to help secure positions for Idiáquez and Vázquez. As Alfonso's universal heir, Juan was a threat to those who had gained Alfonso's responsibilities. The decision to remove Juan from the payroll occurred in June 1533, as the letter of payment for 66,500 maravedies was drafted that month but not acted upon. The same month Juan de Vergara was arrested by the Spanish Inquisition and quickly told inquisitors that Juan had refused to return to Spain to defend his damaged honour.[91]

Alfonso's success with the Peace of Nürnberg gave him the political clout to aid the appointment of an important ally as Viceroy of Naples. Pedro de Toledo, the Marquis of Villafranca, attended the imperial court at Nürnberg to lobby for the position.[92] Toledo's father, Fadrique de Toledo, had been an influential member of the Council of State prior to his death in 1531 and had supported Gattinara's Italian policies against the Cobos faction.[93] Toledo's influence at court was strengthened with the arrival of his nephew, the young Duke of Alba, who commanded Spanish troops sent to aid the Hungarian campaign. As Chancellor of Naples, Alfonso signed Pedro de Toledo's letter of appointment as viceroy, thereby gaining Juan an influential patron after Alfonso's death.[94]

In December of 1532 Charles appointed Juan archivist of Naples, a position Alfonso had obtained four months earlier to complement his authority over the Neapolitan chancellery.[95] But the assignment had to be confirmed by the Neapolitan Collateral Council, a group of Spanish and Italian representatives who shared governing responsibilities with the viceroy. The council accepted thirty of the forty-three nominations Charles requested, but preferred filling the other thirteen, including the archivist position, with its own candidates. Viceroy Toledo advised Charles to do as the council asked.[96]

Because of his 'respect for that city,' Charles allowed the council to do as it wished with twelve of the thirteen positions, but he demanded that Valdés be given the office of archivist 'by my act.'[97] On 9 March 1533 the viceroy thanked Charles for his concession to the council. 'The matters of Juan de Valdés are returned [to the council] for recommendation as you ordered me to do,'[98] but he claimed that he could not resolve their opposition. Less than a week later he wrote Charles that he had talked firmly with the city's officials about Valdés' appointment without success.[99]

Charles would not easily be dissuaded. In late July the viceroy notified him that he was talking with Valdés and the Collateral Council to reach a compromise. He promised 'to do all that is in my power to get them to give him some compensation.'[100] Evidently Charles continued to press for the office because in October Toledo wrote that even after he told the council the emperor considered the appointment of Valdés to be 'for the universal good of the kingdom ... there is no way to give him the office.'[101] The viceroy again vowed to get Valdés a good compensation by making the council 'understand how it serves Your Majesty.'[102] Finally Charles relented and commented in the margin of the letter, 'I am entrusting you to make it so.'[103]

In December 1533 Valdés accepted a thousand ducats as payment for the office.[104] Two months later Toledo informed Charles that Valdés was 'very content as corresponds with Your Majesty's service.'[105] Charles gratefully replied to Toledo's assurance of Juan's satisfaction: 'I am pleased by what you say because of the service of his brother *and for the services this one has rendered*.'[106] In spite of the contemporary investigation of Valdés for heresy, Charles demonstrated his loyalty to the family and his respect for Juan's abilities.

Though it is doubtful that Juan intended to keep the archival office, he did not want to sell it cheap, hence the long negotiation. News of the death of Juan's brother Diego in November 1533 probably hastened the settlement, as Valdés needed to be in Rome to use his connections to obtain Diego's valuable prebends. On 16 January 1534 Clement wrote a glowing reference to the Bishop of Cartagena for Juan to obtain Diego's benefices in his diocese.[107] The letter indicates that Juan continued to serve as a valued secret chamberlain, a position he kept until Clement's death in September 1534. Clearly Diego expected Juan to remain in Rome. Knowing his brother was well placed for acquiring his prebends, he asked Juan to give his servant Perico the benefice of a church in Lorca.[108] Even with the pope's blessing, acquiring prebends was no easy matter, particularly outside Italy. Local clergy and other prebend-hungry curialists would often make the process long and expensive.[109] There is no evidence to date that Valdés acquired any prebend in Cartagena, but some horse trading may have ultimately contributed to his acquisition of the nice prebend of San Clemente in Cuenca in 1536. At a minimum, he would have gained some compensation, given the pope's recommendation.

Valdés's return to Rome gave Viceroy Toledo a good ally in his unending dispute with Ambassador Cifuentes. Cifuentes wrote in cipher to Cobos 12 January 1534 that he was withholding information from the viceroy about matters in Rome in order to facilitate his negotiations.

Cifuentes claimed that 'there are differences between me and the said señor viceroy.'[110] In response Toledo refused to pay Cifuentes's salary, and when he did Cifuentes claimed the viceroy shorted his wage.[111]

The clash of personalities within the diplomatic corps came at an inopportune moment as a Turkish hydra arose from the depths. In June 1534 Sultan Suleiman appointed Kheireddin Barbarossa, the famous Turkish pirate, Grand Admiral of the Turkish fleet. With over a hundred ships and ten thousand soldiers he ravaged the coasts of Sicily, Naples, and the Papal States, carrying off thousands of Christian slaves, before seizing the strategically vital port of Tunis in August. The imperialists knew Francis I was now in alliance with the Turks and encouraged the attack.[112] Charles also knew that Francis had given subsidies to the Protestant leader Philip of Hesse in January 1534 to seize Württemberg.[113] After Württemberg fell in May, Cifuentes warned Charles that the Lutherans had no other intention than 'coming to Italy and removing the pope from his seat.'[114] Cifuentes refused to believe the French had aided Hesse.

Meanwhile Toledo urged Charles to focus on the 'common enemy' (the Turks) who threatened to subject all of Christendom, and reported that he would not share information with Cifuentes for the good of the planned campaign against Tunis.[115] Toledo had a different opinion of Württemberg: 'If the Lutherans persist it is best to give them what they want for it has been in the service of God.'[116] The viceroy agreed to work closely with Granvelle, Charles's primary negotiator with the Lutherans, and expressed his longing for the days of the 'Regensburg support' (i.e., Peace of Nürnberg) when Christian forces were unified.[117]

After Clement VII's death in September, Cifuentes successfully worked for Cardinal Farnese's election and hailed the new pope, Paul III, as a 'great prince.'[118] The Farnese had estates in the Papal States as well as Naples. The former meant that he would protect Rome; the latter meant that he threatened Naples and the viceroy. Further, Paul III had been the candidate favoured by the French cardinals. Other Spanish diplomats concluded that the new pope had aligned himself with Francis I and correctly assumed that he would not join Charles's defensive league.[119] Viceroy Toledo sent Cifuentes a blistering note of disapproval.[120] Less than two weeks after the election Toledo informed Charles that the pope's nephew claimed authority over a Neapolitan castle which controlled 'one of the principal routes of the Kingdom, and as Your Majesty knows the popes have always had an eye on this Kingdom.'[121]

Bickering between Toledo and Cifuentes escalated, each condemning the other as uncooperative.[122] With France supporting the Lutheran seizure of Württemberg, and France's Turkish ally holding the vital port of Tunis, Charles's hold on Italy was seriously threatened. The new pope refused to join the imperial alliance, as did the new Duke of Ferrara, who had succeeded his father in November. As a war brewed between Paul III and Urbino over Camerino, the Duke of Ferrara sought to avoid the conflict by entering into negotiations with the papacy and France to settle the problem of Modena.[123]

The Camerino Crisis

Camerino was a heavily fortified city in the Papal States near the border of Urbino.[124] In 1527 the death of the Duke of Camerino, Giovanni Maria Varano, left a disputed succession between his kinsman Ercole Varano and his four-year-old daughter Giulia. The legacy escalated into a diplomatic crisis in 1534 when the duke's widow, Caterina Cibo, strengthened her daughter's claim by negotiating her marriage to Guidobaldo della Rovere, son and heir of the Duke of Urbino, Francesco Maria della Rovere. Since no pope would sanction such a union, the parents hastily arranged the matrimony immediately after Clement VII's death.[125] The new pontiff quickly forbade the union of Camerino and Urbino, and ordered that the marriage not be consummated. To keep the pope occupied the Duke of Urbino not-so-secretly encouraged a revolt in Perugia that led to the murder of the papal legate.[126]

These actions troubled Charles V. He had determined to strike Tunis, but his advisers warned that he could not fight two major wars at once. When the emperor first learned of the marriage negotiations in September, he urged Cifuentes to talk the Duke of Urbino out of making any changes in the status quo.[127] Charles was not obliged to defend Camerino, as it was not a party to the treaties of Bologna, but Urbino was a member of his defensive league and therefore under imperial protection. Venice and the Duke of Florence, Alessandro de' Medici, a leading member of the Italian league, staunchly supported the Roveres. To maintain his alliance, Charles had to honour his commitment to Urbino, but he had to do so without alienating Paul III, who promised to convoke the general council Charles desperately needed to pacify his Lutheran vassals. In January 1535 Charles informed the Duke of Urbino that he could be confident of his aid if Urbino was the victim of aggression, but he was to keep this commitment a secret. Further, he should move the matter of Camerino to the courts and end his support of the Perugia revolt. The duke obeyed all these demands except keeping Charles's support a secret. Rather, he openly boasted about it. Meanwhile Paul III sought to gather a war chest by demanding that the Duke of Ferrara pay him two hundred thousand ducats for Modena.[128]

The viceroy of Naples had the dual responsibility of raising troops for Tunis, and of protecting members of the Italian league. He needed accurate information about papal ambitions in order to prepare effective military contingencies, but mistrusted Cifuentes. He warned Charles that 'His Holiness is his sovereign as I have written Your Highness many times before.'[129] In September 1534, just days prior to Clement's death, the viceroy asked Cobos to reinstate Valdés in Charles's service.

> Juan de Valdés, brother of Secretary Valdés, is a good person and I certify that he served Your Majesty there [at the imperial court] as much as anyone. For us he has more importance because he has intelligence of many secrets and always I am advised by him. He is totally diligent in offering information without fail. Your Majesty has written me that they are not paying his salary as a gentleman [of court] or *contino* which Your Majesty granted him because of his absence [from court]. I ask that your Lordship consider that although he has it [his salary] from Your Majesty's court, note how he is capable of serving as I have said.[130]

Toledo did not mention Juan's appointment as imperial secretary, but rather his position as *contino*. The way the Valdés transferred the honour within the family implies a hereditary claim to the position. To date no document of transfer from Alfonso or Diego to Juan has been discovered. But *regidor* Andrés de Valdés certainly considered that Juan held the position perhaps by family inheritance. On 29 January 1534, a month after Juan surrendered his archival office, Andrés entered two documents into the notarial record of Juan del Castillo about Juan's transfer of his authority to administer the *mayoralia* of San Lázaro to Andrés including a re-copy of the original transfer of 22 September 1529. Somewhat suspiciously, Castillo's records from late 1529 through 1533, the period of Alfonso and Juan's inquisitorial investigation, have disappeared.[131] Perhaps this explains the re-entry of the documents in the record in 1534. Whatever the reason for their filing, Andrés refers to Juan in these legal documents as 'my brother *contino* of Your Majesty.'[132] Though it is not clear when Juan became a *contino*, that position reflected the personal nature of his past and future service to Charles.

With Clement on his deathbed, Valdés needed employment. As a member of the papal *familia*, he would lose his chamberlain position with the pope's demise. Because of his treatment by Cobos and the Spanish Inquisition, he was probably considered primarily as a Medici client, i.e., he would have been viewed as a trusted insider at the papal court at the time of Clement's death. In mid-December the viceroy repeated his request to Cobos for Valdés's reappointment. 'All the reward and favour Your Lordship may grant Juan de Valdés will return to your credit because he is a prudent man and he is residing in the Roman court aiding Your Majesty's service with his good intelligence.'[133] Valdés had excellent sources of information in Cardinal Ercole Gonzaga, the brother of the Duchess of Urbino, and the Duke of Ferrara. With Valdés in place, the viceroy proceeded to attack Ambassador Cifuentes.

> The count of Cifuentes never dispatches anything of importance here. Since he is not able to say what is happening he is not being paid because not one quatrin is owed him. And it seems to be a matter of vengeance that he does not inform us of these matters that relate to His Majesty's service with reasonable speed ... it is not my custom to grumble about anyone [but] ... I am no longer able to live with the count.[134]

Three documents contain summaries of ten letters Juan de Valdés wrote Viceroy Toledo concerning the Camerino crisis between 30 January and 13 March 1535. The first document is a deciphered letter from the viceroy sent directly to Charles rather than Cobos.[135] Toledo began by questioning the latest news from Cifuentes. The ambassador claimed that the pope granted Francis I the *décima* from French churches in order to outfit thirty-six galleys to aid Charles in his campaign on Tunis. But Charles had long suspected an alliance between France and the Turks, so Toledo knew the emperor would doubt Cifuentes's information. Toledo editorialized, 'From this you are able to judge what most serves Your Majesty, on the one hand and the other. Whether he [Francis I] prostitutes himself and caresses Barbarossa, or whether he will use his galleys against him.'[136]

In what became a pattern, Toledo then presented Valdés's contrasting opinion. Valdés's letter of 30 January stated that the proposed French *décima* would total 600,000 to 800,000 ducats and that the pope would get a third of it. He also certified that Francis had offered the pope additional funds to wage war for Camerino. Most distressing,

Valdés suspected that the French king had sent funds to the Lutheran leader Philip of Hesse to divert Charles from Camerino in the event of war. Toledo added that 'if it is true, they do not have entirely good intentions' for the use of the *décima*. On 6 February Valdés reported that papal courtiers talked about Camerino as if 'they were captains on campaign and the matter goes forward quickly.'[137]

The second document containing Valdés's letters is titled 'Relation of News From All Parts For the Most Serene King of the Romans and Other Ministers of Your Majesty.'[138] It is an intelligence report formulated by the Council of State evaluating whether or not the French would make war in Germany or Italy while Charles attacked Tunis. This document is particularly interesting since it mentions letters from Ferdinand, the King of the Romans. On 19 February Valdés reported that the previous day the pope read the bull granting the *décima* to France to the cardinals in consistory praising Francis I and Charles and expressing his intention to keep a balance between the two powers. That night the pope announced his sentence against Guidobaldo to prevent the union of Camerino and Urbino.

On 21 February Valdés informed the viceroy that Ferdinand advised the pope about three issues. First the German nation favoured a national council to bring order to their affairs and if the pope did not remedy the situation by quickly calling a general council, 'all of Germany might lose obedience.'[139] Second, Ferdinand informed the pope that the heretics who preached against the 'Holy Sacrament' (Zwinglians) had given up their error and joined with the Lutherans. And finally, he was going to Bavaria to discuss matters of marriage. Valdés believed the letter 'has put spurs to His Holiness' as the pope dispatched his nuncio to Germany to inquire about the time and place for the council. But Valdés pessimistically added, 'some say that he does it more for courtesy than for will.'[140] In regard to Camerino, Valdés heard from a good source 'that the pope has said if the emperor will aid Urbino, the King of France will aid me.'[141]

Cifuentes proved increasingly inept in the Camerino negotiations. In late January he claimed that papal threats against Camerino were merely a bluff. Unfortunately for Cifuentes's credibility, papal forces were already being gathered to block the movement of food, munitions, or troops into the disputed territory.[142] By starving Camerino into submission, the pontiff would force the Duke of Urbino to become the aggressor, thereby nullifying the purely defensive treaty between Charles and Urbino. Perhaps angry over his error in judgment, Cifuentes now supported a Venetian scheme to have Charles declare Camerino imperial territory and then transfer it to Urbino, just as he had transferred Modena to Ferrara.[143] Not only would this plan risk a general war in Italy, it would have ruined any hope for papal cooperation in conciliar negotiations.

The quality of Juan's information at this crucial diplomatic juncture apparently motivated Charles to employ him as his personal secretary. On 1 March Charles sent a letter to his accountants reappointing Valdés as an imperial secretary. A copy of the same letter went to *Residencias*, the body responsible for reviewing the service records of royal officials. 'He [Juan] serves us in whatever I shall order ... they [the accountants] are to pay him without asking him about or inquiring into matters of our service or any other review.'[144] The letter came directly from Charles, as it is signed *'yo el rey.'* Henceforth, all Valdés's reports from Rome were delivered anonymously. He would be identified in the viceroy's summaries simply as 'a particular in Rome,' or a 'courtier in Rome.' Juan's anonymity may have resulted from suspicions of his orthodoxy in Spain. But two years later the Council of Castile claimed to know Valdés and the nature of his work in Italy well.[145] Perhaps Charles thought Valdés could operate better if his employment remained secret, thus allowing Valdés to continue to appear as a trusted courtier at the papal court.

Close scrutiny of relevant documents and knowledge of Valdés's opinions and contacts make it possible to identify some of his work. On 19 March the Spanish ambassador to Venice noted that Cifuentes had been replaced in the Camerino negotiations. 'The latest letters that I have from Rome are the 11th of this month but they are not from the Count of Cifuentes. Others write me that the pope is very angry with the Duke of Urbino and wishes to proceed against him with complete rigour.'[146] On 21 March Toledo sent Charles a summary of four Valdés letters dated 27 February, and 6, 11, and 13 March. [147] Valdés is identified as 'a particular in Rome,' but someone later wrote Valdés's name in the margin beside his reports. Valdés conveyed timely and precise information from his connections inside the papal court. He indicated that the matter of Camerino moved quickly toward a military conflict. The pope used legal channels to annul the papal investiture of Camerino to the Varano family. He then excommunicated Giulia Varano, her mother, and her husband, Guidobaldo, and declared Giulia deposed. Afterwards he informed all the ambassadors at court of the justice of his taking arms against Camerino and asked for their support.

Valdés informed the viceroy that Juan Batista Sabelo had been dispatched with troops to aid the blockade of Camerino and listed the other commanders who were to join the enterprise soon. He repeated that the pope in secret had commented that if Charles aided Urbino, France would aid him. Valdés also quoted the Venetian ambassador's defiant response before walking out of the meeting. 'Do not bother informing me of this negotiation that I know well. By your laws you can justify anything you wish but there are also other laws very contrary to these of yours which justify us; these are those of the Gospel of Christ of which you should have more respect and which have much more importance.'[148]

Despite the strong protest of the Venetians, and the Duke of Urbino's boast that he enjoyed Charles's support, the pope proceeded with the blockade of Camerino. Since papal forces alone were no match for those of the Duke of Urbino and his allies, both the Venetians and the imperialists believed that the pope had the secret support of France.[149] Valdés ominously warned that if war could not be averted 'the major part of Italy will leave the obedience of the Church and many of the pope's territories will rise in revolt.'[150] Further darkening the atmosphere, Valdés reported on plots in the papal court to assassinate Guidobaldo and his supporters.

Charles prepared for the worst. While again assuring the Duke of Urbino and Venice of his support, he explained that they must keep it a secret.[151] Meanwhile he had the viceroy ready Ascanio Colonna for military action, as he possessed vital fortresses near Rome. Toledo informed Charles that 'The Duke of Urbino and Ascanio have made the possible arrangements. And if Ascanio has a complaint it is not because he consented to the responsibility, only that no one else wants to help defend this part of the royal patrimony.'[152] Charles planned for a local conflict, but Ascanio feared French intervention and sought the mobilization of more of Charles's allies at the outset. As war seemed imminent, Viceroy Toledo clearly indicated his preference for peace, warning Charles, 'It is a bad time for His Holiness to stir up war given his grand demonstration of wanting to convoke the council and the current state of Christendom. Our Lord has it in his hands to make peace so that all our war effort can be employed against the Infidels as Your Majesty wants to do.'[153]

In March Italy verged on the brink of a disastrous war which promised to weaken or delay Charles's strike against the Turks and also poison the prospects for a general council. Yet two months later the pope suspended his blockade of Camerino and Charles proceeded with his glorious Tunisian campaign. Two documents included under the general title 'What was discussed in Barcelona in the month of April 1535 for dispatch to Germany and Italy about the Duke of Camerino and other things'[154] provide information about the resolution of the Camerino crisis. Charles met with his Council of State in Barcelona before embarking for Tunis. The first document is a long report assessing the likelihood of war based on information from all parts of Europe. It emphasized the need for an immediate attack on the Turks, noting that 'the campaign against the Infidels has always seemed so necessary that everyone will see it as in the common interest of Christendom ... [there is] greater fear and danger of losing to the said Infidels ... and two great conflicts would be difficult if not impossible to undertake and conduct at the same time.'[155] The council was convinced that the French were incapable of initiating a campaign for another year. To keep Germany pacified, they advised Charles to declare that he would broker a fair religious settlement either through the general council or, failing that, through the Imperial Diet.

In regard to the pope, they suggested that Charles take a soft stance on Camerino in order to aid the convocation of the council and to avoid a war in Italy. They reminded the emperor of the pontiff's recent threat to the Spanish ambassador to Venice, that a situation similar to Camerino had led to the use of French troops in 1494. Finally, the council recommended that the Camerino negotiations be entrusted to someone other than Cifuentes because of his pro-French sympathies. They asked Charles to send a person 'well informed, discreet, and skilful.'[156]

The second document is an anonymous letter to Charles from that 'well informed, discreet, and skilful' person about his discussions with the papal nuncio.[157] Juan de Valdés was most likely the author. He had been a favoured courtier at the court of Clement VII and he had a good connection with the Duke of Urbino through his brother-in-law Cardinal Gonzaga. The author obviously distrusted Cifuentes, as he did not discuss any particulars with the ambassador, leaving that up to Charles. The considerable rewards Valdés received from both the pope and the emperor the following year seem to provide further confirmation of his involvement in these delicate discussions. The author's overwhelming concern that the general council be convoked immediately echoes Valdés's earlier report from Ferdinand, and his correspondence with Cardinal Gonzaga later that year.[158] No imperial representative in Rome at the time was more involved in the Camerino negotiations than Valdés, and the Duchess of Camerino would later be identified among Valdés's leading disciples. In 1539 when Charles briefed his new ambassador to Rome about Camerino, he noted that previously the matter of Camerino 'was under the authority of a particular of the Church, nevertheless a trusted person, from the vicinity of Naples.' Valdés's prebends made him a particular of the Church; Charles certainly trusted him, and he resided in Naples at the time.[159]

The letter detailed discussions with the nuncio about the general council and Camerino. The author unsuccessfully pressed the nuncio for a papal commitment to call the council irrespective of Francis I's opinion of it. He also demanded Mantua, the Gonzaga patrimony, as the site for the assembly.[160] In regard to Camerino, the author professed that Charles had no authority over the Duke of Urbino and that the Duke's Italian allies would certainly support him if war ensued. He hinted that the Lutherans would use the opportunity to stir up trouble as well. He admitted that the pope had every right to demand Urbino's obedience in the matter, but for the common good of Christendom, i.e., the council and the Turkish war, the pope should heed the pleas of Charles and the other Italian princes and agree to postpone his war against Camerino. The author emphasized that a temporary suspension would in no way be considered a surrender of papal claims to Camerino. Nothing seemed to sway the nuncio until the author spoke 'confidentially with him about enlarging the personal estates of His Holiness.' Despite the fact that the nuncio began negotiations claiming that the blockade of Camerino was intended solely 'to guard the authority and rights of the Church,' the offer to compensate the Farnese dynasty eventually had the desired effect.[161]

Two other important diplomatic documents also appear to have been written by Valdés at that time. The first is an unsigned summary of intelligence from France and Ferrara dated 9 April. The cover page curiously identifies it as a 'relation of news from France that the Count of Cifuentes sent.' The author was very anti-French and resided in Rome.[162] The report conveyed many of the same details as the summaries of Valdés's earlier letters and the same suspicions of papal-French collusion to conquer Camerino, a perspective very different from that of Cifuentes.[163] In his correspondence Cifuentes never demonstrated access to this type of intelligence in France, but Valdés did through his connection with Cardinal Gonzaga and Cardinal Medici, Pope Clement's nephew.

The author also had inside information from the court of the Duke of Ferrara because he stated that Francis I sent the Bishop of Limos to the duke demanding that he refuse to join Charles's league. The report noted that the French king told the papal nuncio that he did not want to send galleys against Barbarossa and that this did not violate his agreement with the papacy for the *décima* because 'for the defence of His Holiness and his territories, he would aid him with all his galleys and 10,000 men paid for two years.'[164] Thus it confirmed Valdés's earlier conviction that the French *décima* would be used to aid a war for Camerino rather than Charles's Tunisian enterprise. Despite this, the report concluded that France would not be ready for an offensive war for another year because Charles's captains in Germany had made it difficult for Francis to raise decent troops there. 'The said king has been unable to obtain a man worth one maravedí.'[165] Probably this document was a summary of a report from Valdés either forwarded by Cifuentes, or incorrectly attributed to him. It certainly utilized the type of contacts Valdés had in Rome, Ferrara, and Germany.

On 3 April Cifuentes wrote Charles describing a discussion he had with the pontiff about the Tunisian enterprise and the lack of papal and French support for it. Paul III argued that if Charles would redirect his fleet to Constantinople then he and the King of France would aid the enterprise with all their resources. In fact, the pope offered to sail with Charles in the fleet. Despite the lack of papal support for Charles's enterprise in terms of *décimas, cruzadas*, or subsidies, Cifuentes was still convinced that the pontiff 'without doubt truly wishes to take part and aid Your Majesty in it, and thus if it becomes necessary, he will ally with Your Majesty and not aid the King of France.'[166]

After the two-page summary of Cifuentes's letter is a single-page relation written in a different hand but included in the same folio. The cover page of the folio identifies the letter of Cifuentes, but below that a notation refers to the second document as 'advice from France/ of what passed between the pope and French ambassadors about Ferrara/ of the settlement.'[167] It appears to be a summary of a report from Valdés filed in contrast to Cifuentes's information. The report emphasized that the pope considered Camerino the most important matter in all his negotiations with the emperor, and that the pontiff was grateful for the 'pleasant audience' given his nuncio about the matter.[168] The author boldly informed the pontiff that some people at the imperial court suspected that the pope 'leans toward France because of the concession of *décimas* unreasonably made prior to attaining the objective [of Tunis] which conflicts with His Majesty's desire not to grant them because it would cause the King of France not to give the galleys he promised against Barbarossa.'[169]

The next topic of the report was a discussion of a letter from Charles dated 2 February delivered directly by Charles's 'mayordomo mayor.' The summary indicated that the emperor's letter was primarily 'advice about the commission he carried,'[170] probably a reference to Juan's reappointment to Charles's service. Though Charles's letter to his accountants reinstating Valdés was dated 1 March, Juan was paid for the full year, indicating that he was already on the job before it became official.[171] In reference to Charles's letter, the summary only responded 'to the matter of the Duke of Ferrara.'[172]

As noted previously, Valdés possessed the documents concerning imperial claims to Modena. Through his contacts in Ferrara he had just learned of the agreement whereby the duke would pay the pope 150,000 ducats over three years for Modena. The author believed the settlement certain and advised both the duke's ambassadors and the pope not to prejudice any of the emperor's rights in the agreement. In regard to the pope's suggestion to attack Constantinople, the author told the pope that Tunis had to be taken first regardless. The pontiff argued that Barbarossa would have to leave Tunis once Constantinople was threatened. The author replied that Barbarossa was a pirate and would ignore the sultan's orders if an opportunity arose to raid Charles's undefended realms. The document ends with the author asking Paul III whether or not Charles would see him and Francis I in the enterprise against Tunis. The pontiff replied that he did not know, and that he had 'first to make certain that its purposes would result in the general good.'[173]

As a result of these secret negotiations, the pope agreed to a temporary suspension of his blockade of Camerino in May. The Venetians thanked Charles for his intervention, as did the Duke of Urbino.[174] No one expressed greater relief than the Viceroy of Naples.[175] In early August he recommended the pope's grandson for the Bishopric of Jaen. 'I ask that Your Majesty give this pleasure to His Holiness and favour to Cardinal Farnese because I know it will be returned. ... Your Majesty knows the great importance of having His Holiness obliged and grateful so Your Majesty's ministers can more easily perform their duties.'[176]

The Camerino crisis was a pivotal event in the political career of Juan de Valdés. While it is impossible to determine if Paul III engaged in a bluff, the replacement of Cifuentes with Valdés in the negotiations enabled Charles to smooth relations with the papacy, and increase his credibility as the protector of the Italian league without giving up anything. Charles never committed himself to defending Camerino and four years later pressured the Duke of Urbino's heir to sell the province to Paul III for his grandson Ottavio. Not only did Valdés reap reward for his service, he soon had the additional pleasure of learning from Charles himself that Cifuentes would be removed as ambassador to Rome.[177] However, before greeting the emperor in Naples to receive his rewards, Juan had to deal with two troublesome cardinals closely connected to imperial interests: Benedetto Accolti, the old friend of the Valdés brothers, and Ippolito de' Medici, Clement VII's nephew.

4 Cardinal Relations

In Clement VII's Rome, Juan de Valdés achieved success as a courtier, not as a religious reformer. At the time he left Rome for Naples, he served three ambitious cardinals: Benedetto Accolti, the Cardinal of Ravenna, Ercole Gonzaga, the Cardinal of Mantua, and Cardinal Ippolito de' Medici, the pope's nephew. These associations provide insight into Valdés's career shift from Roman curialist and imperial agent to leader of his own humanist sodality in Naples. As a Secret Chamberlain, Valdés was a member of the papal *familia*, the most important social circle for Roman humanists. The *familia* of cardinals ranked second in the hierarchy of humanist patronage. Aside from events sponsored by the pope and cardinals, there were academies, and the less formal sodalities hosted by wealthier humanists employed in the curia like Angelo Coloccio.

All three cardinals had reason to court imperial support. As has been discussed, Accolti aided Alfonso de Valdés's negotiations in Germany, and apparently recommended Juan's appointment as Secret Papal Chamberlain. With such ties, Juan would have attended Accolti's court when he first arrived in Rome. Cardinal Accolti's humanist patronage won him recognition in Ariosto's *Orlando Furioso*, and a defence in Valeriano's *The Ill Fortune of Learned Men*.[1] Juan returned Accolti's favour by successfully serving as his solicitor in a messy murder case, helping Accolti escape with a fairly light punishment.

The young and dashing Cardinal Medici outshone all contemporaries as the greatest humanist patron in Rome. Pietro Aretino advised a fictional courtier to 'stay in Rome, for, if for no other reason than the example which the court must take from the liberality of Ippolito da' Medici, that refuge of the virtuous, the good old days must come back again.'[2] Through Ippolito's sodality Valdés met Giulia Gonzaga, who would further his career in Naples. Here too surviving documents show that Valdés's association with the cardinal involved a possible murder, in this case the murder of the cardinal himself.

Cardinal Gonzaga did not have the humanist pedigree of Accolti or Medici, but his dynastic ambitions tied Valdés and Gonzaga interests together for several years. He became Valdés's best informant in Rome, but by 1537 he fled the city in fear of his life because of his support for the imperialists.[3] All three cardinals were bitter enemies of the Farnese family and Pope Paul III. One barely escaped a murder charge with his life, another died under mysterious circumstances presumably poisoned, and the third was forced into a temporary, self-imposed exile from Rome. A couple of months after moving to Naples, Valdés complained to Cardinal Gonzaga, 'None of those near the pope and none of my Roman friends have come to visit me.'[4] One need not ask why.

A Dirty Cardinal

No episode in Juan de Valdés's career casts more doubt on his pure reputation than his involvement in the intrigue surrounding the March of Ancona, a papal legation and fortress governed by Benedetto Accolti, the Cardinal of Ravenna. Ancona was a heavily fortified citadel that the Venetians tried to wrest from papal control after the sack of Rome, but which was returned to direct papal authority by the 1529 Treaty of Bologna. Held by the Cardinal of Ancona until his death in 1532, the prebend was a major plum, and the cardinal's nephew Benedetto set about acquiring it. Though a majority of cardinals held more than one bishopric, Accolti already possessed four.[5]

Wayward cardinals elicited poignant characterizations from the great papal historian Ludwig Pastor, but few are as damning as Benedetto Accolti's.

> Having entered holy orders without a vocation, this polished humanist ... won the good graces of Leo X by his poetic talent. Under Clement VII his rise was swift ... in 1532 he purchased ... the governorship of Ancona ... [where] the tyrannical character of this genuine product of the Renaissance, steeped to the core in all the corruption of his age, reached its rankest development. ... Accolti, whose cruelty and immorality passed all bounds, carried things to such a pitch that even the patience of Clement VII was worn out.[6]

Accolti succeeded in purchasing the governorship of Ancona and the Legation of the March for the sizeable sum of 19,000 ducats. Perhaps to recoup his expenses, he excessively squeezed Ancona for revenues, creating opposition to his rule.[7]

Meanwhile Clement VII's dysfunctional family threatened to undo his dynastic plans. In the first Treaty of Bologna, Charles had agreed to support Clement's nephew Alessandro as ruler of Florence and sealed his alliance with Clement by agreeing to the engagement of his ten-year-old, illegitimate daughter Margaret to the notoriously libidinous Alessandro.[8] Clement gave his other nephew, Ippolito, a cardinal's cape in January 1529, and to keep him from plotting against his cousin, sent him to Hungary in 1532 with 50,000 ducats to support Charles's crusade against the Turks.[9]

After his return Ippolito schemed with the republican exiles in Rome led by the Florentine banker Filippo Strozzi. Clement then attempted to buy off his problems by making Strozzi treasurer of the marches, and using a loan from Strozzi to obtain Ancona from the Cardinal of Ravenna so he could transfer it to Ippolito. As Clement grew ill in the last weeks of his life, Ravenna refused to relinquish Ancona, so Clement deprived him of the legation and initiated an investigation of Accolti's governorship.[10] Ravenna still refused to resign.

In October 1534 Paul III appointed a new governor for the March of Ancona and reserved for himself the decision of the legation. In March he deprived Strozzi of his treasury of the marches, and the next month shocked all of Rome by throwing Ravenna into the prison of Castle Saint Angelo. Ignoring pleas from the College of Cardinals, the new pope sought to use Accolti's corruption as a warning to other would-be imperialist cardinals. Accolti was guilty of pluralism, simony, and innumerable personal indiscretions, but so were other cardinals. Some cardinals so feared that they might be the next target of papal wrath that they thought of fleeing Rome. Meanwhile Accolti languished in prison, refusing to eat for fear of papal poisoning.[11]

The Count of Cifuentes realized that the emperor had to mitigate Accolti's punishment, but tried not to dirty his hands with the matter. The ambassador reported that the pope provided many reasons for Ravenna's imprisonment, and the need for him to provide justice in the matter. The ambassador clearly doubted Ravenna's innocence, but understood the importance of showing other cardinals that the emperor would stand by his allies. He asked Charles 'to send a person from your house to the pope ... to moderate the punishment so that it appears that Your Majesty has done a great favour for the cardinal.'[12]

Juan de Valdés's role in the case can be inferred from his letters to Cardinal Ercole Gonzaga, a friend of Ravenna and an imperialist sympathizer. Soon after Ravenna's arrest, Gonzaga sent a long letter to Cobos defending Ravenna against wrongful imprisonment.[13] After eventually gaining his freedom, Accolti sought temporary refuge in Gonzaga's palace in Rome.[14] Ravenna asked Juan de Valdés for 3,000 ducats in early August to aid the negotiation of his release.[15] These funds were probably used as bribes to facilitate the financial settlement made later that month.

From his letters to Gonzaga, it is clear that Valdés left Rome for Naples in late August to meet the imperial court, and remained there as an adviser to the viceroy. In September Valdés reported that Ravenna's servant informed him about the latest news in the case.[16] Three weeks later a friend of Ravenna appeared at the viceroy's court and publicly thanked Valdés for his service to Ravenna.[17] The viceroy, no doubt briefed by Valdés, told Paul III's son that Ravenna had been wronged, and that if anyone but Cifuentes had been ambassador the pope would know 'how he must treat the servants of His Majesty.'[18] Valdés wrote Cardinal Gonzaga, 'I believe he [Cifuentes] knows much less about the matter than I.'[19] Valdés was still at work on the case on 18 October when he informed Gonzaga: 'I am now solicitor for Giulia Gonzaga, in addition to discussing the cause of the Cardinal of Ravenna with Jacobo Cortes, or *descortes* [impolite], and with another friend who is as cold as Christmas.'[20] Cortes was one of Ravenna's lawyers, so the friend was probably another lawyer in the case. Valdés continued to receive information about Ravenna from Rome, and knew of the cardinal's freedom three days after his release from prison at the end of October.[21]

These letters indicate that Juan acted as Ravenna's solicitor. In the Spanish legal system a solicitor was the client's agent who knew the ins and outs of a particular court and could thereby exert political influence or resort to bribery to help ensure a successful outcome.[22] Solicitors did not need a law degree and were typically the highest-paid member of a legal team. In the first letter Valdés wrote to Gonzaga from Naples, Juan alluded to a memorial he wrote about Accolti's case before he left Rome in late August.[23] In a letter to Charles dated 30 August, Cifuentes mentioned agreeing with a memorial that he sent along with his letter, but which was not attached.[24] However, there is an undated and unsigned memorial of the case, archived separately, written by someone who acted as Ravenna's solicitor before the case's resolution.[25] The author knew specifics about the evidence and witnesses against Ravenna, and met with the pope in an attempt to gain the cardinal's release.

The memorial focuses entirely on the depositions of two unnamed witnesses and the related evidence. One of the witnesses testified that the other had bribed him to give false testimony against five Anconans whom the cardinal accused of fomenting rebellion. The alleged conspirators were subsequently executed. By inference both witnesses agreed on the fact of the subornation.[26] According to Pastor the accused perjurer was Vicenzo Fanelli.[27] Clement VII had Fanelli arrested during his initial investigation. Ravenna removed Fanelli from prison, offering 12,000 ducats in security, took him to Rome, and made him swear an oath before a notary that his previous testimony had not been suborned. Ravenna responded to the latest testimony of the two witnesses by saying that he could prove both were horribly depraved and therefore should not be believed. Of course, if they were so depraved one has to wonder why Ravenna would have them as servants. Further, Ravenna claimed he freed Fanelli because of his earlier 'good work in uncovering the treason' in Ancona. As for his testimony in Rome, Fanelli had asked to give it because he had heard about the accusations of subornation and wanted to set the record straight.[28]

The author of the memorial, presumably Valdés, told the pope that 'neither the testimonies, nor the evidence were sufficient to arrest a cardinal, and particularly the crime did not merit imprisonment in Castle Saint Angelo.'[29] The pope responded that he had taken his action on the advice of his lawyers and that they would give a full explanation. Valdés noted that many people advised Ravenna that if 'he felt that he had committed a venal sin in this case, not to fear placing it in the pope's hands solely to free himself.'[30] The cardinal initially refused the offer, professing his complete innocence and expressing his belief that God would not continue to let him suffer this outrage. Evidently God thought otherwise.

Valdés believed the cardinal had been mistreated because the pope ignored his station, and in so doing struck fear into other cardinals. He also noted that the alleged subornation occurred during the pontificate of Clement VII, and that Ravenna would have been tried then if the case had merited it. Further, no torture was employed on the witnesses even though their testimony was suspect on the grounds that they were both servants of Ravenna. 'Thus it appears that these servants have some indignation against the cardinal because never has a servant spoken against his lord, except these, unless they already had indignation against him.'[31] Valdés obviously strained to make the best of a weak case.

On 27 August Ravenna publicly confessed his guilt, and paid 'nine or ten thousand ducats' to fund dowries for the daughters of the five deceased Anconans, and to pay 'officials and ministers of His Holiness' (i.e., bribes).[32] He paid an additional fine of 34,000 ducats and gave up Ancona, which had cost him 19,000 ducats. The fine took all his ready cash: thus his need for the 3,000 ducats from Valdés to help complete the settlement. The Florentine Cardinal Salviati also loaned Ravenna money, but unlike Valdés, secured the debt by assuming control over Ravenna's prebends in Cremona and Ravenna until he gained repayment.[33] Valdés's unsecured loan was probably crucial to the settlement because as late as 22 August the pope was still insisting on stripping Ravenna of his prebends as well as demanding a huge fine.[34] According to a later memorial on the final judgment, the pope was ultimately convinced that he should not let Ravenna die in Castle Saint Angelo.[35]

A stiff judgment, but Ravenna had his life, liberty, cardinal's cape, and all his prebends except Ancona. A recent historian has noted the 'interesting fact' that throughout the investigation Paul III seemed intent on taking Accolti's life, but in the end let him keep his prebends.[36] Without imperial intervention Accolti would not have fared so well.[37] Cifuentes wrote Charles that Ravenna was 'exceedingly grateful for the Emperor's interference, and remains forever bound to the imperial service.'[38] However, Valdés was outraged at the judgment, calling it 'the greatest cruelty,' and indirectly sent advice to Ravenna to appeal it. He wrote Cardinal Gonzaga, Ravenna's host at the time, that if he were Accolti he would immediately come to Naples to see Charles, and 'afterwards all would be fine, but he does not have enough confidence in me to do it if I dared to counsel it.'[39] Ravenna wisely decided not to challenge Paul III's decision immediately, but later rescinded his confession. With papal permission the cardinal left Rome for Ferrara in 1536 and eventually found safe exile in his native Florence.[40]

Death of a Cardinal

Valdés's service to Cardinal Medici is rather enigmatic, as the only documentation comes from Valdés's intelligence reports to Viceroy Toledo shortly before and at the time of the cardinal's mysterious death at age twenty-six. Aside from them, the association must be inferred from Valdés's past and future relationships. First, he had gained favour and reward from Clement VII. Many humanists who served Clement also found favour with Ippolito, making Valdés's gravitation toward Ippolito a natural career course. Florentine Cardinals Niccolò Ridolfi and Niccolò Gaddi cooperated with Ippolito's plan to oust his cousin Alessandro as ruler of Florence just before Medici's death in August 1535. In October Gaddi obtained Valdés's aid in gaining an office from the viceroy, and the following month Ridolfi passed information to Valdés.[41] Since they had worked against imperial interests, it seems likely they sought Valdés's help in regaining imperialist favour. Valdés's connections to the Medici and Florence later made Florence the third most important centre of the Valdesian heresy behind Naples and Sicily.[42]

Valdés had no firm office between Clement's death in September 1534 and his own reappointment as imperial secretary in March 1535. One of Valdés's *Divine Considerations* discusses the theological concept of hope, using the story of an officer whom Charles had promised a commission in Italy. Though the emperor delayed the appointment, and other princes sought the officer's services, the officer refused, 'fearing lest, if he [the emperor] should come to find him in the service of another, he would be unwilling to employ him.'[43] The story is too close to Valdés's biography to be dismissed. Though documentation is limited, it appears that Valdés had a firm association with Ippolito and his sodality. Juan occasionally visited Fondi as a guest of the cardinal,[44] and he must have known Giulia Gonzaga fairly well prior to having a daylong visit with her in September 1535.[45] Giulia was the central icon of Medici's sodality just as her cousin Elisabetta Gonzaga inspired the court of Urbino in Castiglione's *Courtier*. After Ippolito's death she would play a similar role in the rise of Valdés's sodality in Naples.

The Gonzagas had ruled Mantua for two centuries, but Giulia was the daughter of Lodovico Gonzaga, who headed a secondary branch of the family in Lombardy. Giulia was the youngest surviving child of Lodovico. With two older brothers and five older sisters it seemed she might have to join a convent, as did two of her sisters, 'but the cloister had no attraction for Giulia.'[46] Her tutor wrote that she was 'ever ready with comic sayings, yet ever full of courtesy.'[47] In 1526 Isabella Gonzaga, Giulia's older cousin, arranged the marriage of her thirteen-year-old cousin to Vespasiano Colonna, the Duke of Trajetto and Count of Fondi, Giulia's senior by some twenty-eight years. Vespasiano showered Giulia with jewels and paid a 70,000 ducat dowry to the Duke of Mantua as head of the family. He had a daughter from a previous marriage named Isabella, about the same age as Giulia, whom he wanted to use for a good dynastic match.[48]

Enter a teenage Ippolito de' Medici prior to his donning the cardinal's cape. Isabella Colonna resisted marriage to Ippolito because she had no literary interests. She noticed that when Ippolito visited he only had eyes for Giulia and talked poetry with her all evening. In 1528 Vespasiano Colonna died defending Naples from the French invasion. He left his fifteen-year-old widow 30,000 ducats and the rents from his vast estates as long as she did not remarry. On his deathbed Vespasiano expressed his wish that Isabella marry Ippolito. Instead she married Giulia's brother Luigi, thereby strengthening Gonzaga claims to Vespasiano's disputed estate with the powerful Colonna clan. Thus Giulia was free to become the mistress of Ippolito, who became a cardinal less than a year after Vespasiano's death.[49] In March of 1531 Ippolito flooded arenas to stage mock sea battles, and held tournaments all in the name of his love Giulia. Later that year Giulia, still a teenager, moved to Fondi, two miles from the coast and half-way between Rome and Naples. Fondi quickly became the focal point of Medici's sodality.[50]

Italian poets competed in glorifying Giulia's beauty and thereby the fame of Medici's circle. In *Orlando Furioso*, Ariosto lavished excessive praise on her.

> Lo! She to whom all living dames forego ...
> Julia Gonzaga, she that wheresoe'er
> > She moves, where'er she turns her lucid eyes,
> > Not only is in charms without a peer,
> > But seems a goddess lighted from the skies[51]

Perhaps the poets went too far, as Giulia's reputation soon inflamed an enemy's desire. In September 1534 the Turkish Admiral Barbarossa invaded Fondi to kidnap Giulia for the sultan's harem. The town was looted for four hours, tombs were destroyed, and nuns massacred. Giulia escaped her castle riding a horse through the woods and scantily clad in her nightclothes. Of course the story quickly spread through Italy and a poem, 'The Fugative Nymph,' celebrated the adventure, further elevating Giulia's fame.[52]

Ippolito began to play a dangerous game with the imperialists after his return from the crusade in Hungary in 1532. He resented the fact that Charles supported his cousin Alessandro as Duke of Tuscany. Charles attempted to make amends at the second Bologna Treaty by requesting that Ippolito be appointed papal legate to Spain, but the cardinal absolutely refused. Ippolito's dazzling display at the Marseilles wedding of Catherine de' Medici and Prince Henry of Valois shadowed even the king of France and raised imperialist suspicions about his motives.[53]

Ippolito seemed to move back to the imperialists by asking for the support of Ambassador Cifuentes to obtain the Ancona legation.[54] Meanwhile, the Florentine exiles increased their pressure on Ippolito to move against Alessandro after Clement's death. The exiles needed to act before Alessandro's marriage to Charles's daughter Margaret bolstered his position with the emperor. Not wanting to alienate Charles by precipitous action, Ippolito wrote the emperor that leading Florentine families would support his seizure of power, including the Strozzi and Florentine Cardinals Giovanni Salviati, Niccolò Ridolfi, and Niccolò Gaddi.[55]

In February 1535 Valdés notified the viceroy that Cardinal Medici was working to oust Duke Alessandro as ruler of Florence.[56] For once Valdés and Cifuentes were in agreement. On 9 February the ambassador wrote a long report about the Florentine situation. Cardinal Medici warned Cifuentes that Alessandro would not last long as the ruler of Florence. Cifuentes also noted that Cardinals Salviati and Ridolfi were negotiating with Florentine exiles to oust Alessandro.[57] In effect, Ippolito sought imperial sanction for his coup.

Pope Paul III also participated in some of these anti-Alessandro discussions. Always suspicious of Paul III, the imperialists were convinced the pope had his eye on acquiring Siena and was in league with the French to remove Alessandro.[58] The pope also wanted to break the duke's engagement with Margaret so she would be free to marry his grandson Ottavio.[59] Cifuentes relayed a message to Charles from the Duke of Urbino's ambassador in Rome about Paul III's Florentine ambitions. 'If you wish to guide your affairs with His Holiness well, you should favour the exiles of Florence in order that they may enter the city and make Luigi Farnese [the pope's son] perpetual captain-general of that republic with a large salary.'[60]

The most detailed historical accounts of Cardinal Medici's last months of life are by the contemporary Benedetto Varchi, and by the twentieth-century historian Giuseppe Moretti. Both agree that Paul III supported the plans of Cardinal Medici and the Strozzi to remove Alessandro from power while at the same time looking for an opportunity to ruin Cardinal Medici. Both believe that the pope wanted to seize Medici's prestigious ecclesiastical offices and prebends for his own family, which he in fact did immediately after the cardinal's demise.[61]

In April 1535 Ambassador Cifuentes seemed convinced that Cardinal Medici had joined the imperialist camp because of his desire to attain the legacy of Ancona. Paul III had just thrown Cardinal Ravenna in prison, leaving the legacy vacant. Cifuentes wrote Charles in cipher: 'His people have informed me that he wishes to settle matters with Duke Alessandro, and with Cardinals Ridolfi and Salviati, to become servants of Your Majesty.'[62] If not for two contemporaneous murder plots, Ippolito might have had more success courting imperial support.

In early July Viceroy Toledo informed Charles of the plots. Cifuentes and Valdés provided the intelligence in letters dated 22 and 23 June.[63] Both plots involved Filippo Strozzi, the republican exile leader now a favourite of Paul III.[64] Piero Strozzi, Filippo's son, hired some thugs in Rome to seize agents of Duke Alessandro who had allegedly been sent by the duke to murder the Strozzi. As the agents denied these allegations, news arrived from Florence of a bizarre plot of Ippolito to assassinate Alessandro. Ippolito hired his cousin Giovanbattista Cibo, the Archbishop of Marseilles, to do the job because Alessandro regularly called on Cibo's sister-in-law for trysts, to the chagrin of Cibo's brother. The assassins planned to fill the strong box Alessandro usually sat on during these visits with gunpowder. Just before the explosive encounter, Cibo wrote a letter to Count Ottaviano della Genga, a key leader at Ippolito's court, detailing the plot, asking for more money to pay the assassins, and mentioning Ippolito by name. The letter was intercepted, and Cibo confessed to the plot 22 June 1535.[65]

The pope seized Genga for questioning and convoked the consistory to discuss the matter. After meeting with the consistory, Valdés reported that Cardinal Medici returned home 'very agitated.' Since Valdés usually cited his source if it was not his own observation, he must have been among an inner circle of Medici's trusted friends. Ippolito immediately fled Rome without telling the pontiff for fear of arrest. According to Valdés, Paul III begged Medici to return to Rome while Filippo Strozzi met with Cardinal Giovanni Salviati. The viceroy believed Strozzi and Salviati were hatching a foul plot. 'I am not able to find out what they discussed but you may believe the worst with those people because they do not respect either God or the world.'[66] On the basis of urgency, Toledo justified his intervention into a matter that should have been the responsibility of Cifuentes. He promised to forward additional information as soon as he could because 'from this matter many embarrassments could arise.'[67]

Cardinal Medici had fled with Piero Strozzi to a palace near Tivoli on 22 June, the date of Cibo's confession.[68] The cardinal now promised peace with Alessandro on whatever terms Charles thought just and planned to go to Tunis to speak directly with the emperor.[69] Cardinal Medici left Rome for Tunis in the summer of 1535. He always considered himself a soldier, and perhaps some military glory would aid his negotiations. He also may have considered Tunis safer than Rome after the Cibo affair. The pope had been party to anti-Alessandro discussions, making his arrest of Genga seem a betrayal of Ippolito, and perhaps indicating collusion between the pope and Alessandro. Before departing for Tunis, Ippolito wanted to visit Giulia Gonzaga in Itri on the coast near Fondi.[70] According to Varchi, after Piero Strozzi heard of the proposed peace meeting between Charles and Cardinal Medici, he visited Itri promising to support Ippolito as the rightful ruler of Florence if the cardinal would rejoin the exiles. After Strozzi left, the cardinal supposedly told a confidant, 'I do not want to have to expect their news and their jokes anymore.'[71]

Medici's Itri visit proved much less enjoyable than he anticipated. On 2 August he began to feel ill. Two days later, after eating some boiled chicken broth and pepper, he cried out that he had been poisoned and accused his chief steward of the deed. Ippolito grew continuously worse, suffering with a mild fever until he died at 3 p.m. 10 August. According to the contemporary historian Paolo Giovio, Ippolito's death 'was less bitter in that he was near to Doña Giulia, who ministered to him with all virtuous tenderness.'[72]

Before the cardinal expired, his servants tortured a confession out of the steward, Giovann Andrea. Andrea claimed to have ground the pepper with poisonous herbs between stones that were recovered and identified by Andrea. When papal forces arrived, the steward recanted the confession, saying he feared the cardinal's servants would kill him if he did not confess.[73] Papal forces took Andrea to Castle Saint Angelo, where he underwent a secret examination and torture. Soon after, Paul III declared Andrea innocent, but many suspected the examination.[74] After gaining his freedom, Andrea took up residence at Duke Alessandro's court, but was assassinated a few months later.[75]

Viceroy Toledo's response implies that either he wanted to cover for Alessandro, or he thought the pope was involved in the murder and did not trust his investigation. At the time of Medici's death Toledo was dependent solely on Valdés for information because Cifuentes was again refusing to communicate with him. The viceroy relayed to

Charles information about the supposed poisoning and noted that the pope had sent a small force to bring the cardinal's servants to Rome.[76] Toledo seemed to hint at the possibility of sending troops across the Neapolitan border to seize the steward. The viceroy urged Charles and Cifuentes to demand that the pope send the prisoners to him for questioning because 'it affects Your Majesty's authority.'[77] Toledo clearly thought Cifuentes too passive about the matter.[78]

Toledo's last reference to information about Medici from Valdés was in a letter he sent to Charles on 3 September.[79] He again complained that the pope was unjustly imprisoning and examining servants of the cardinal, but the pope responded that his investigation was in Charles's service.[80] Juan de Valdés arrived in Naples shortly afterwards, as indicated by his first letter to Cardinal Ercole Gonzaga from Naples dated 18 September.[81] Valdés began the message by mentioning that he had spent a day with Giulia Gonzaga at Fondi while on his way to Naples. The purpose of the visit must have been to obtain information about Medici's death.

Perhaps the cardinal was not assassinated. Medici was ill for eight days with a low-grade fever. Thus some contemporaries and later historians believe that Medici died of natural causes, either malaria or perhaps his Epicurean excesses.[82] However, the timing of his death and the questions surrounding the investigation invited murder rumours. Six years after the cardinal died, Geronimo of Carpi, one of Duke Alessandro's most favoured servants, told imperial diplomats at the Diet of Regensburg that Paul III had ordered the assassination of Cardinal Medici. When the news reached Rome, the pope commanded the unfortunate Geronimo-seized and brought to Castle Saint Angelo for imprisonment.[83] The circulation of this testimony in secret diplomatic papers shows the imperialists always suspected that Paul III had a hand in Medici's murder to keep him from allying with the imperialists and revealing Paul III's Florentine machinations.

It is impossible to determine whether or not Medici was murdered. However, it is safe to conclude that though the imperialists knew of Alessandro's potential involvement, they sought to cover for him by demanding a quick release of the cardinal's servants. The imperialists were not the only ones fearing the consequences of a more thorough probe into the circumstances of Medici's death. Such an examination would certainly have brought the Strozzis under the magnifying glass and no doubt their financial and political connections to Paul III. Since Ippolito apparently had abandoned the exile cause for imperialist favour, no one of any influence demanded an answer to the question of who done it, thereby leaving the cause of Cardinal Medici's death to remain a mystery.

Gonzaga Clientage

Thanks to Sepúlveda, Valdés had established a close relationship in Rome with Ercole Gonzaga, the Cardinal of Mantua. When he left Rome for Naples he entrusted some personal belongings to Gonzaga for safekeeping.[84] Ercole needed to cultivate Spanish allies because of his family's previous alliance with the French. In 1530 Ambassador Mai had written Cobos that Cardinal Gonzaga offered his support to the imperialists, but 'we are able to expect little from servants of His Majesty who professed for the French.'[85] His older brother, Frederigo, was the current Duke of Mantua, and his younger brother Ferrante served as a ferocious imperial general in Tunis. Ferrante would soon be rewarded with appointment as Viceroy of Sicily, and later became Governor of Milan. As previously mentioned, Ercole's sister Elisabetha was the Duchess of Urbino and therefore would have been involved in Valdés's Camerino negotiations.

Juan's letters to Cardinal Gonzaga provide a glimpse into how he gathered information by offering access to imperial favour. He constantly reminded the cardinal of imperial rewards for his family and stressed that he could help continue such grants. He informed Ercole of his brother Ferrante's appointment as Viceroy of Sicily, effusively praised the selection, and offered to help the new viceroy work harmoniously with Pedro de Toledo.[86] Valdés also promised to help obtain the cardinal a reward from the imperial court. 'I will not miss a point in doing all I am able with these Señors.'[87] With Valdés's support, Gonzaga obtained the Spanish bishopric of Tarazona in 1537 and appointment as the protector of Spanish churches in Rome.[88] By 1560 he collected some 6,000 ducats a year from Spanish prebends and was the most rewarded cardinal on the imperial payroll.[89]

Cardinal Gonzaga provided Valdés crucial information from Rome. Before Charles arrived in Naples, Valdés warned him that Paul III and Francis I were in the process of negotiating a marriage alliance. On 3 September 1535 Viceroy Toledo wrote the emperor:

> It is important that Your Majesty know that a particular person in Rome writes me that His Holiness is discussing a marriage between

his granddaughter, the daughter of Pier Luigi, and Monsieur de Angoulême [Francis I's third son, Charles Duke of Angoulême]. I do not give this credit because if it were so, Your Majesty's ambassador would already have written me confirming it. Whether it is so or not, with all due respect it seemed to me that I should make all that comes to my notice known to Your Majesty.[90]

Charles responded gratefully to the viceroy and his informant: 'I commend your diligence in making this known quickly ... tell him [Valdés] thanks.'[91] From Juan's correspondence with Cardinal Gonzaga, it is certain that Valdés was the source of the information about the pending marriage negotiations.[92]

Juan's intelligence became more valuable as the French prepared to fight for Milan following the death of Francisco Sforza on 1 November 1535. Later that month Juan informed Cardinal Gonzaga that all his reports were sent to Granvelle, who shared his intelligence with Charles.[93] In fact Juan orchestrated his reports to Granvelle and the viceroy to have a greater impact on the emperor. After informing Granvelle about the marriage negotiations and papal advances to the Venetians, Valdés asked him not to say anything to Charles until his next letter arrived along with a letter from the viceroy. He told Granvelle first to read the viceroy's letter to the emperor, and afterwards his own.[94] These directions demonstrate that Juan had established a close working relationship with Granvelle.

The viceroy mailed the letter Juan requested on 13 November, again without identifying Valdés as his informant. He simply stated, 'This hour, after giving Your Majesty account of other news a faithful, meritorious person who is a great servant of Your Majesty has offered information he has from Rome.'[95] According to Valdés, all the French ministers in the Roman court confirmed that Francis I would invade Italy to claim Milan. He also noted that negotiations for the marriage of Angoulême to Pier Luigi's daughter sped along. Valdés's connections enabled him to give Charles early warning about the French invasion of Italy and the potential of papal involvement. Unfortunately Charles's principal advisers, Cobos and Granvelle, did not believe the French would attack. Valdés complained to Gonzaga that 'these people do not please me at all in their designs, not wishing to believe that the French will come.'[96]

The Gonzagas hated the upstart Farneses to the point that Ferrante Gonzaga participated in the 1547 conspiracy that led to the murder of the pope's son, Pier Luigi Farnese. Cardinal Gonzaga's dynastic ambition to gain Milan for his own family led him to exaggerate the status of the papal-French negotiations. Francis I did not offer 200,000 escudos for the marriage as Gonzaga reported; Luigi Farnese, the pope's son, did not leave Naples completely embittered at the imperialists; nor did the pope oppose the Turkish war. Valdés confirmed the marriage negotiations with different sources, but discovered Gonzaga had reported falsely about the other matters. He warned the cardinal to be careful about what he said lest he add to the growing distrust of his reports at the imperial court.[97]

Despite doubts about Gonzaga's accuracy, Valdés's information helped shape imperialist views of Paul III's dynastic ambitions. According to two diplomatic memorials written in December and January, Charles believed that Paul III wanted Siena, Parma, and Milan in addition to Camerino.[98] The most immediate problem was Camerino. By all accounts the pontiff showed every intention of resuming his blockade, because 'for certain he is depending on aid from the King of France as that is the only way he would be capable of winning it.'[99] To keep the pope neutral in his war with France, Charles ordered Cifuentes to stall for time on Camerino in order to prepare the Duke of Urbino for its possible loss in the name of 'the public good of Christendom.'[100]

Valdés deceptively informed Cardinal Gonzaga that his brother-in-law had nothing to worry about. 'His Majesty considers him [the Duke of Urbino] such a friend that there is no need for me or anyone else doing anything.'[101] According to Valdés, when the papal nuncio tried to discuss Camerino, Charles became angry because 'he looks after his [the duke's] affairs more than if they were his own.'[102] Valdés purposely misled the cardinal about the duke's position with the emperor.

As discussed in the previous chapter, the imperialists pushed the Gonzaga patrimony of Mantua as the site for the general council. Unfortunately conciliar negotiations fell apart in late 1536 and early 1537. Lutheran and English opposition and French uncertainty contributed to its demise, but Paul III's growing enmity with the Gonzagas also played a significant role. The pope renewed his threat of war for Camerino though the Duke of Urbino was the brother-in-law of the Duke of Mantua and Cardinal Gonzaga.[103] Such threats did not bode well for the Council of Mantua. The pontiff then started a bitter dispute with the Duke of Mantua over the pay and control of security forces for the proposed Mantuan council. The pope wanted the duke to pay, but he wanted control of the forces. This became his excuse to prorogue the council in April 1537.[104] As negotiations for a council in Mantua collapsed, Cardinal Gonzaga fled Rome in March in literal fear for his life.[105] Valdés's last known letter to Cardinal Gonzaga was in January 1537.[106]

Valdés served Gonzaga interests most directly as Giulia Gonzaga's solicitor. The imperialists could not afford to alienate either of the two great families involved in Giulia's litigation. The Colonnas were an old Roman clan, having had thirty family members as cardinals and one pope. With vast estates in the Kingdom of Naples as well as the Papal States, they were staunch imperial allies to the point of leading the sack of Rome. Giulia's legal problems originated with Vespasiano Colonna's testament in 1528. He left Giulia control over his estates and guardianship of his daughter Isabella Colonna even though the two were the same age. He bequeathed Isabella a pension of 5,000 ducats a year for life. After Vespasiano's demise, his cousin Ascanio, the Constable of Naples, became the primary line of inheritance for the entire Colonna clan. Ascanio promptly defended Colonna turf by occupying most of Vespasiano's estate, including the strategic fortress of Paliano near Rome. Isabella refused to move to Naples to live with her cousin, and instead considered Ascanio her mortal enemy.[107]

Rather than seek an accommodation with Ascanio, Isabella secretly married Giulia's brother Luigi in 1530, thereby strengthening Gonzaga claims to the disputed inheritance. Through the marriage, Luigi became the Duke of Trajeto and Count of Fondi, and Giulia became a dowager duchess/countess, and Isabella's sister-in-law as well as her stepmother. Two years later Luigi Gonzaga suffered a mortal wound leading papal forces battling to take Ancona.[108] Luigi's deathbed testament left the guardianship of his infant son Vespasiano to Isabella provided she did not remarry. If she married, Luigi named his father, Lodovico, as Vespasiano's guardian. Isabella promptly alienated her Gonzaga in-laws by laying claim to Gonzaga estates in Lombardy even though Luigi never possessed them because his father still lived.[109]

Ascanio relinquished Fondi to Giulia and Isabella, but retained Vespasiano's territories in the Papal States and seized some of Luigi's estates in Lombardy as well. The Duke of Mantua appealed to Charles to force Ascanio off his cousin's lands in Lombardy, an evacuation that would not be completed until Giulia's case was finally settled in 1541.[110] Meanwhile at Fondi Giulia became the focus of Cardinal Medici's literary sodality.

In the spring of 1535 Isabella Colonna sued Giulia in Naples, claiming that Vespasiano's will was not binding. Simultaneously she renewed a suit against Ascanio in Rome over Colonna territories in the Papal

States, including the strategic fortress of Paliano.[111] Isabella had been cut out of both her father's and her husband's testaments, and was now determined to have her day in court. Initially Isabella demanded an astronomical annual stipend of 13,000 ducats from her father's estate as her share of the inheritance. After the Neapolitan courts nullified Vespasiano's testament, Isabella offered Giulia a paltry 500-ducat annual allowance as her part of the fortune.[112] In addition, Isabella's guardianship of young Vespasiano would give her control over the Gonzaga estate in Lombardy at the death of Giulia's father. Isabella now refused Giulia the 2,500-ducat annual stipend she had initially agreed to pay pending the litigation's completion.[113]

At this low point in the case, Valdés became Giulia's solicitor in October 1535. At first he could do little, as Isabella refused to compromise. A month after his appointment he bemoaned, 'It is a strangely difficult matter this accord of Señora doña Giulia de Gonzaga, that not even my wearying the viceroy or having the emperor send letters are sufficient to bend this Señora Isabella who is more rigid than a marble Colonna.'[114] Giulia soon followed Valdés to Naples, where she frequently attended Church with the emperor.[115] Charles tried to curtail Isabella's litigious binge by arranging a suitable marriage for her. Her matrimony would protect Gonzaga territory in Lombardy through Lodovico's guardianship of young Vespasiano Gonzaga, Isabella's son. Isabella resisted, but finally Charles succeeded in forcing her to marry the Flemish Philippe of Lannoy, the Prince of Sulmona, the son of a former Viceroy of Naples. The wedding was celebrated in grand style in Naples in February 1536 and afterwards the five-year-old Vespasiano was sent to live with grandfather Lodovico in Lombardy.[116]

The same month Charles tried to end the complicated legal claims by appointing a special panel of three judges to review the case: Juan Marcial and Galeoto de Fonseca from the supreme court of Naples, and Juan de Figueroa, Regent of the Collateral Council, the highest office in Neapolitan administration. Figueroa was a good friend of Valdés and supported Giulia in the suit.[117] In March Valdés wrote that the case proceeded well and he expected a good ending soon.[118] In early June the judges declared that Giulia should be paid 2,500 ducats annually and 1,000 ducats for the loss of revenue during the trial, but Isabella immediately appealed the decision.[119]

Though the verdict was not overly favourable to Giulia, the case was about to take a worse turn for her. In July Valdés wrote Cardinal Gonzaga that though he was gaining ground in the case, the settlement 'would not be the amount that this señora merits.'[120] Others were puzzled at Valdés's inability to bring about a successful end to the suit. In August, Pedro de Pacheco, Bishop of Mondonedo, wrote Cobos: 'About the Señora doña Giulia they say much work passes here on her suit and that the solicitation of Valdés is not enough. I do not know the cause.'[121] The cause was the war with France that began in the spring of 1536 and Charles's need of Colonna support. The emperor sent Ascanio Colonna to Italian courts to reaffirm his defensive alliance;[122] Ascanio even pledged to lead the invasion of the Papal States himself if necessary.[123] Charles wanted Ascanio to retain the strategic fortress of Paliano near Rome to help keep Paul III from siding with the French. Isabella had to be treated gingerly so she would not push her suit against Ascanio in Rome. Thus Giulia's case would drag on without resolution. Meanwhile Valdés used his relationship with Giulia to form his own literary sodality in Naples, which elevated him to a level of fame most humanists in Italy craved.

5 The Valdesian Sodality

Juan de Valdés would never have gained the notoriety and influence he sought without his famous sodality. It began as an informal group seeking advancement at the Neapolitan and imperial courts. By 1536 it gained formal sponsorship from, of all people, Francisco de los Cobos, who became Valdés's direct supervisor after 1538. It is this official sponsorship that makes Valdés's sodality a unique example of the cultural and political dialectic between Italy and Spain in the development of the Spanish global empire. As with sodalities in Rome and at other Italian courts, a display of beauty and comfort facilitated linguistic discussions. Valdés directed his efforts at teaching Spanish as an imperial language fit for the Italian cultural elite.

Arguably the dominant spirit of the Renaissance was the pursuit of beauty. This spirit increasingly became a conscious obsession in many Italian courts after Marsilio Ficino published his Latin *Commentary on Plato's Symposium on Love* (1484). Ficino's work soon became as popular with courtly women as it was with men,[1] and it sparked the Italian vernacular revival that influenced Valdés's own linguistic work. Giulia Gonzaga served Valdés as the focus of his sodality, but she needed more from her solicitor than discussions of Spanish, Italian, and classical literature. The death of her lover and the strain of her litigation with Isabella Colonna left her emotionally unstable. To bolster her spirits, Valdés returned to the dangerous waters of religious reform in spite of his previous experience in Spain. Giulia's emotional and spiritual needs shaped many of the sodality's discussions. As a result, Valdés's group became one of the first *spirituali* centres, reform groups that sprouted across Italy after the creation of the Reform Commission in 1537. Discussion of religious reform no longer threatened curial careers, and several cardinals soon formed *spirituali* groups that were interconnected with Valdés's circle. These interconnections built upon Valdés's contacts at the papal court. Construction and direction of a sodality devoted to the purity of beauty, language, and religion were the greatest accomplishments of Valdés's career.

A World of Beauty

Ficino identified love with the desire for beauty.[2] His dialogue has seven guests take turns commenting on different speeches from Plato's *Symposium*, and some of these celebrate love making in terms far from 'Platonic.'[3] However, the physical sensuality of the dialogue is made palatable by establishing the doctrine that love of the body is a step to a higher, divine love. Because of the theme's popularity, these discussions of love and beauty spurred a movement to elevate the quality of vernacular style. The respected ciceronian Pietro Bembo led the way with his 1505 publication of *Gli Asolani*, a dialogue on love that popularized the intellectual underpinnings of Ficino's *Commentary*.[4] Castiglione was so taken by Bembo's argument that he enshrined Bembo as the philosopher of love at the end of his *Courtier*,[5] where he surpassed even Bembo's praise of platonic, intellectualized love in *Asolani*.[6]

Giulia's beauty made her the ideal focal point for a humanist sodality. Ficino, Bembo, and Castiglione all agreed that love was the desire for beauty, both mental and physical.[7] Love bound the universe together by linking heaven and earth.[8] Thus beauty was 'a sacred thing,'[9] and 'a ray of the supernatural.'[10] When observed rationally, beauty naturally led the mind inward to divine contemplation and greater spiritual awareness.[11] Ficino presented the case succinctly: 'In this life we shall love God in all things so that in the next we may love all things in God. ... And anyone who surrenders himself to God with love in this life will recover himself in God in the next life.'[12] Italian platonism complemented Pedro de Alcaraz's theory that salvation was completely a matter of the proper love of God.[13] Earthly beauty fosters rational love; rational love leads to divine contemplation and the love of God; and love of God leads to salvation.

As noted on the first page of this study, Valdés thought Giulia Gonzaga so beautiful that she should rule the entire world.[14] Since female beauty was strictly defined at the time, a comparison of Giulia to the contemporary, ideal standard would indicate if any poetic licence was involved in the praise of Giulia's beauty. The poet Bernardo Tasso wrote the following description of Giulia:

Her blond, undulating locks, mischievously straying with the breeze
Crown a forehead lofty and serene, beneath whose eyebrows dark
Lucid lights permit her from the terrestrial prison to behold the wonders of the Lord.
Her lips are rubies, her slender neck white as the driven snow.
Her angelic voice and words more fit for God than man.
In her the spirits of the blest rejoice as if the gates of heaven were ajar.[15]

In 1541 Agnolo Firenzuola published the definitive treatment of pre-Tridentine beauty in his dialogue, *On the Beauty of Women*. He dedicated his book to Caterina Cibo, the Duchess of Camerino and one of Valdés's disciples.[16] Firenzuola defines beauty as 'ordered concord, akin to a harmony that arises mysteriously from the composition.'[17] It began with the breasts and ended in the perfection of the face. The rest was merely a matter of proper proportion.[18] The woman's cheeks should be the colour of ivory fading to fleshy, her lips red, her eyelashes black, her eyebrows curved, and her eyes blue or dark tan. Her nose should be narrow at the base, her forehead broad and fair, twice as wide as high, topped with long, thick, and wavy blonde hair, not yellow but leaning to the colour of gold or honey. Her neck should be long and her shoulders broad.[19] Based on Tasso's description and the surviving portraits of Giulia, she was close to the embodiment of the Renaissance ideal for beauty. She had long, wavy, blonde hair, blue eyes, and a well-proportioned hourglass figure with a long neck and beautiful, slender hands.

Platonic desire for beauty considered mind and body together. Since the education for upper-class Italian women was the same as for men,[20] Giulia and other female Valdesian disciples seem to have contributed as much to the religious discussions as the men.[21] Valdés's circle, like the *alumbrados* of Toledo, contained numerous examples of brilliant and assertive women. In commenting on First Corinthians 11: 8–10, Valdés uses the word 'equality' to describe the relation of the sexes to God five times to emphasize the spiritual equality of men and women.[22] Referring to Paul's chauvinistic comment that women should be quiet in church, Valdés wrote that this only applied to women with living Christian husbands who were so well versed in Scripture that they could teach others Christian doctrine. He excluded all other women from Paul's order.[23]

Vittoria Colonna, Ascanio's sister, certainly had the intellect and assertiveness to join in religious debates, and she became the most influential Valdesian missionary. In Rome she maintained a close Platonic relationship with Michelangelo, who loved to hear her read Valdés's writings aloud whenever she visited him.[24] Vittoria introduced Caterina Cibo, Duchess of Camerino, to Valdés's doctrines in 1538 at the famous baths of Lucca.[25] Caterina would have known Valdés as a diplomat in Rome because of his protection of Camerino and because she was related to the Medici.[26] Born near Florence in 1501 and educated in Rome, she was, as a contemporary historian wrote, 'noted alike for her beauty and for her brilliant intelligence. She learnt four languages, Hebrew, Greek, Latin, and our Tuscan, and understood them all.'[27] She moved to Florence and joined the Valdesians there who supported Valdés's controversial doctrine of justification by faith.[28]

Isabella Brísegna would spread Valdés's doctrines as well, though she eventually fled Italy to join Protestants in Zurich. Her husband, García Manrique, was the Governor of Piacenza and a brother of the former Inquisitor General of Spain who initially protected Valdés from persecution following the publication of his *Dialogue on Christian Doctrine*. Born in Spain in 1510 and reared in Naples, she was renowned for her beauty and gaiety. Her father left her a fortune and her initial contact with Valdés in 1539 involved a financial matter.[29] In spite of her husband's discouragement, she met regularly with the Valdés circle and in the 1550s told a Basel professor that 'She had been illuminated by the light from above while at Naples.'[30]

Constanza d'Avalos, a cousin of Vittoria Colonna, also attended Valdés's group. Wife of Alfonso Piccolomini, Duke of Amalfi, she devoted her time to rearing her children and writing spiritual poetry. A life-long friend of Giulia Gonzaga, she retired to the Convent of Santa Chiara in Naples following her husband's death.[31] The contrast between Constanza's orthodoxy and Isabella Manrique's heresy implies that Valdés did not teach rigid doctrines. Other illustrious female attendees who remained completely orthodox were Isabel Villamari y Cardona, the wife of Ferrante Gonzaga, the Viceroy of Sicily; María de Cardona, Princess of Sulmona, Isabella Colonna's mother-in-law; doña María de Aragon, the wife of the Marquis of Vasto, the Governor of Milan; María's sister Juana de Aragon, the wife of Ascanio Colonna, the Constable of Naples; Dorotea Gonzaga, Marquise of Bitonto; Clarisa Ursina, Princess of Stigliano; and most surprisingly, Isabella Colonna. Insightfully, Menéndez y Pelayo noted that the 'feminine influence' of these women 'gave life and charm to this theological revolution.'[32]

Valdés's group was an open discussion circle in Spanish with a good mixture of native Spanish speakers to help the Italians master the language. By 1539 the group met on Sunday morning and ate a small breakfast, then walked along the beach or in the neighbouring gardens discussing whatever they wanted. They would return to Valdés's house, where he would read aloud one of the 'Divine Considerations' that he had written during the prior week. After lunch members of the company would suggest religious topics or ask questions for open discussion.[33] Valdés wrote some of these questions and answers down, as he referenced thirteen of them by number in his *Commentary on Matthew*.[34] Giulia Gonzaga had one of these published in 1545, and Juan Sanchez's edition of the *Divine Considerations* includes three others.[35] In January 1540 the Jesuit Nicolás de Bobadilla witnessed Valdés spontaneously answering religious questions from courtiers at the viceroy's court as well.[36] One question led to a lecture on the writings of St Paul in which Valdés allegedly denied both papal authority and the sacraments. According to Bobadilla, the lecture was well received, though he considered it sugar-coated poison.[37] Even this implacable opponent of Valdés's doctrines had to credit the Spaniard's rhetorical skill. Valdés was renowned 'above all things for the irresistible charm of his manners and conversation.'[38]

The Valdesian sodality was surrounded by beauty. Giacomo Bonfadio later reminded Carnessechi of it to help him recover from an illness.

> Attend to your recovery and enjoy your wonted cheerfulness, as in the days when we were at Naples. Would that we were now in that happy company! I know your ardent longing for that fair country, and how often Chiaja and the beautiful Posilipo are in your thoughts. I cannot deny that Florence is beautiful, but the charm of Naples, with its lovely shore and eternal Spring, far excels. There Nature rules with more entrancing sway, filling the land with joy and gladness. If you were now at the windows of that lonely tower, so often praised by us, looking round upon those sunny gardens and beyond on the spacious bosom of that smiling sea, a thousand vital spirits would refresh your heart.[39]

A large number of influential clergymen and clerical advisers were drawn to Valdés's sodality: the famous humanist Marcantonio Flaminio, Valdés's old friend from Rome Pietro Carnesecchi, and perhaps the most popular preacher of the day, Bernardino Ochino. Other important members included Pietro Antonio of Capua, the Archbishop of Otranto, Mario Galeota, an academician, Pietro Paolo Vergerio, Bishop of Capo d'Istria, Vittore Soranzo, Bishop of Bergamo, Giovan Francesco Verdura, Bishop of Cheronissa, Pietro Martyr Vermigli, Prior of Santo Pietro ad Ara in Naples, Donato Rullo, a close friend of Cardinal Pole, and Germano Minadois and Sigismundo Mignoz, Governors of the Hospital for Incurables where Giulia served. Several academicians joined the group, such as Don Placido de Sanguine, Principal of the Academy of Sereni, Giulio Terenziano, a theology professor, Scipione Capece, a poet and law professor, the historian Giacomo Bonfadio, and the humanist Benedetto Cusano.[40] A few titled nobles sought the Valdesian umbrella as well, such as Ascanio Colonna, Baron Consalvo de Bernaudo, and Galeazzo de Caracciolo. Caracciolo's father, the Marquis of Vico, was a close political ally of the viceroy.[41]

Given the social stature of most of its members, Valdés's sodality was expensive to host. Valdés admitted that he liked to 'live like a king,'[42] and apparently he did just that. Despite Valdés's anti-Farnese comments to Cardinal Gonzaga, he continued to enjoy a commendable reputation at the papal court. In January 1536 Valdés received a nice prebend, the Church of San Clemente in his home diocese of Cuenca listed in 1579 as worth 1,500 ducats a year.[43] The language of the grant contains no hint of any animosity between Valdés and the pope. 'We, being well informed of your honest life and customs, laudable austerity and your other virtues and merits, wish to favour you with these goods that we consider useful for your necessities.'[44]

Additional revenue came from Francisco de los Cobos. Initially Cobos gave Valdés a lucrative position in Neapolitan finance, and he engineered various promotions that required little work so that Valdés could manage his sodality as a courtier of political influence, renowned intelligence, and considerable wealth. Valdés's primary activities included teaching Spanish, gathering information and influencing members of the Italian elite to go along with Charles's policies.

When the French war of 1536 stalled Giulia's suit with Isabella Colonna, Valdés apparently sought patronage from the Princess of Sulmona, Isabella Colonna's mother-in-law. (Valdés may have been guilty of some double dealing with his client.) Cobos and Charles agreed to Sulmona's request for the renewal of Juan's 'lodging allowance' in 1536. Cobos would have composed the request summary that indicates official sponsorship of Valdés's sodality.

Juan de Valdés requests that His Majesty should command that he be given a patent so that in Castile they pay him his cost of living for this year, 36, just like the other you gave him for last year. It seems that this ought to be given to him. ... In this matter Your Majesty should consider how he is served by thus enabling him to enjoy residence in a graceful house.[45]

Valdés's graceful house was a villa in the aristocratic residential zone of Chiaja. García de Toledo, the viceroy's son, the Colonnas, and the Marquis of Alarcón all had palaces there. Since the viceroy owned considerable property in the district, he probably helped Valdés secure his fashionable home. Gardens and parks surrounded the dwellings where one could stroll along in a leisurely manner, looking out at a wonderful view of the gulf. It was a beautiful place where beautiful people gathered to enjoy beautiful conversation: not bad for a La Manchan *hidalgo*.[46]

Cobos took Valdés into his patronage during the triumphantly festive six months that Cobos and the imperial court resided in Naples (November 1535 to April 1536). At the time Cobos held predominant influence with the emperor because of his growing control over Charles's finances. Thanks to Pizarro's conquest of Peru, Spain became Charles's most important source for funds during the Tunisian campaign.[47] Responsibility for Charles's loans naturally increased Cobos's voice in diplomacy. Cobos's influence in foreign affairs peaked with his negotiation of the 1538 Truce of Nice with France, ending the conflict over Milan.[48] Cobos disagreed with Juan's anti-French attitude, but he recognized Valdés's utility; he needed someone with Juan's intellectual credentials to aid his administration of Italy. Cobos had complete control of Italy, where humanist groups reigned supreme among the social elites, but he could not even read Latin.[49]

Cobos and Valdés had similar backgrounds and tastes. Both hailed from *hidalgo* lineage and the urban patrician class. Both were workaholics completely dedicated to serving the emperor. Both liked to live well and sought to accumulate wealth through their service. And both were attracted to beautiful women. Prior to the Council of Trent, the cult of female beauty was inextricably tied to the social influence of courtesans.[50] In art, poetry, and short stories famous courtesans were ideally praised. They often lived in sumptuous homes, composed poetry and dialogues, and played musical instruments. Some even had extensive libraries enabling them to converse about the latest literature.[51] They were the fashion setters of the day. Courtesans would have been omnipresent at

Charles's triumphal festivities attending nobles, ambassadors, and courtiers, particularly during the masquerades where more make-up and supposed anonymity made for freer association.[52]

Courtesans were also excellent spies. Aretino's 1534 *Dialogues* about a courtesan teaching her daughter the tricks of the trade includes the following advice.

> The art of entertaining your friends with a certain manner of gossiping, which never comes to the point of hatred, is the lemon squeezed into the frying pan and the pepper sprinkled over the contents of the pan. It is a gentle novelty ... which never becomes boresome ... study, spy out, anticipate and consider, be attentive to subtly analyze and sift the brains of all.[53]

Juan de Valdés was not above calling on the services of courtesans when he had trouble getting inside information in Naples. 'I want to discover what they are saying although I am unable except for the intelligence the Neapolitan ladies have from the caballero courtiers, which I will not repeat now in reverence of the ash [i.e., Ash Wednesday].'[54]

Lucrezia Scaglione was a famous Neapolitan beauty 'whose vivacity and renown had captivated the viceroy Lannoy [a former viceroy of Naples].'[55] In the winter of 1527–8 her beauty led a young courtier to attempt to climb a rope down to her bedchamber, but instead he fell to his death, thus immortalizing her reputation.[56] According to the historian Paolo Giovio, who attended the imperial court in Naples, Charles did not want to appear melancholy, so he 'has worn a mask, and paid a visit to Lucrezia Scaglione, who is more beautiful than ever.'[57] Surrounded by equally beautiful maidens, Lucrezia was the hit of the party and caused a stir by freely insulting the looks of the young Duke of Alba, the viceroy's nephew.[58] In later years Juan ended letters to Cobos by adding a special greeting from a Lucrezia, with whom Cobos must have had an association when he resided in Naples.[59] Cobos had a notorious reputation, and his eye for women probably caused him to burn all his personal correspondence.[60] Valdés's greetings from Lucrezia may well have been from the famous Neapolitan beauty Lucrezia Scaglione.

Origins of the Sodality

In his *Dialogue on Language,* Valdés mentions friends he made during his first visit to Naples with whom he corresponded from Rome.[61] The formation of his sodality was evidenced by the two dialogues he composed in 1536, the *Dialogue on Language*, and *The Christian Alphabet*. The dialogue was the primary product of a sodality and existed in a 'creative symbiosis' with the group, defining both what it was and what it aspired to be.[62] By using his own name as the Socratic master in both dialogues, Valdés announced his leadership of the sodality. It began as a discussion group about languages in general and Spanish in particular.

Soon after writing *Asolani*, Bembo started work on his *Prose of the Common Language* (1525). Known in manuscript as early as 1512, it was the first influential Italian grammar and significantly influenced Castiglione.[63] Bembo established himself as the arbiter of Italian letters and initiated a heated debate about Italian style. Though a Venetian, Bembo enshrined Petrarch as the standard for poetry and Boccaccio for prose.[64] Two groups of 'modernists' opposed the Bembisti; one favoured contemporary Tuscan as the standard (Machiavelli, Giovanni della Casa, and Agnolo Firenzuola), and the other wanted a courtly standard based on Tuscan but understandable in all Italian courts (Castiglione, Pietro Aretino).[65] Like Bembo, Valdés wanted to elevate the vernacular, but Castilian of course, and used Bembo as a model for his *Dialogue on Language*, at times following Bembo's topical pattern.[66] Valdés also identified himself with the Bembisti by bemoaning that the Castilian language lacked authors of the stature of Petrarch and Boccaccio to use as standards for 'very proper and very elegant style.'[67] Throughout the work Valdés follows Bembo's argument that great writers establish norms for language.[68]

Pierio Valeriano also advanced the integrity of vernacular style among humanists. He composed the *Dialogue on the Common Language* around 1526 while attending Angelo Coloccio's sodality.[69] Coloccio was a wealthy member of the curia who headed the most influential sodality in Rome in the 1530s. He had strong ties to Naples and was interested in Spanish, Italian, and Portuguese literature.[70] In his dialogue Valeriano praised the beauty of the Spanish language, which he considered closer to Latin than Italian.[71] Coloccio's background and interests suggest that Valdés would have attended some of his gatherings in Rome.

No vernacular work compared to the popularity of Castiglione's *Book of the Courtier*, which went through thirteen Italian editions by 1540.[72] Yet Valdés's grudge against Castiglione for insulting his brother led him to deny reading the book even in translation.[73] Valdés made a serious mistake because the *Courtier* was one of the few popular works in Italy to praise Spanish manners.[74] However, as in his denial of reading Nebrija, Valdés may not have told the truth. Like Castiglione, Valdés believed that literary works should avoid affectation and be written just as one speaks.[75]

None of Valdés's writings bear the mark of official sponsorship more than his *Dialogue on Language*, and no other work so consciously reflects a typical humanist sodality. The book was written ostensibly to help Italian courtiers in Naples learn the Spanish language and manners: a tough job after the sack of Rome with writers such as Aretino and Della Casa condemning Spanish customs.[76] Valdés rose to the occasion with a confident assertion of Spanish culture before an Italian audience that considered anyone beyond the Alps, especially Spaniards, barbaric.[77] Charles elevated the language in his famous three-hour speech in Spanish before the papal court on 17 April 1536, claiming, 'My Spanish language is so noble it deserves to be known and understood by all Christian people.'[78] Charles's speech and Cobos's practical need for correspondence in Spanish suggest that Juan's dialogue was officially commissioned.

At the beginning of the dialogue, Marcio states that 'It has been two years since you left this territory for Rome until now.'[79] This would place its composition in early 1536 before the imperial court left Naples for Rome in April.[80] Valdés not only used his surname as the Socratic master, he immodestly identified himself as a courtier 'very chivalrous and well educated in all things of the world,' whose 'principal profession is to speak freely about what I feel about things that I am asked.'[81] He wanted others to think of him as a man of great knowledge and political influence, which indeed he was. Three seekers of Valdesian wisdom questioned the master. Though it is impossible to identify the participants with complete certitude, the usual conventions for humanist dialogues suggest that they would be either the more renowned members of the group, or individuals from whom the author might obtain favour. Marcio could have been Marcantonio Magno, Giulia's secretary and later the translator of the *Christian Alphabet* into Italian, but more likely it was the famous Italian poet and humanist Marcantonio Flaminio.[82] According to the contemporary historian Giacomo Bonfadio, Flaminio 'loved and admired' Valdés 'more than any other.'[83] In the dialogue Marcio represents an Italian humanist who could speak Spanish, but who was 'curious' about the language and wanted to learn how to write it.[84] Valdés's speeches account for 50 per cent of the dialogue, and Marcio's 30 per cent.[85]

Pacheco is a Spaniard with attitudes typical of a grandee. Most likely he was Don Pedro de Pacheco, Bishop of Mondonedo and heir of

Valdés's old patron the Marquis of Villena. Pacheco arrived in Naples early in 1536 as the *visitador*. Given Valdés's office in the treasury, and its questionable accounting methods, he had good reason to court Pacheco's favour by placing him in the dialogue. Coriolano rounds out the group as a 'good courtier' just beginning to study Spanish because 'already in Italy among ladies and among gentlemen it is considered genteel and courtly to know how to speak Castilian.'[86] He was most likely the humanist Coriolano Martirano, Bishop of San Marco, who in 1548 succeeded his brother as the secretary of Viceroy Toledo.[87]

Valdés was a gifted teacher. He often taught by reciting Spanish folk sayings, usually quite humorous, that provided his listeners with memorable examples of important rules. The oral tradition was 'purer' than any particular book and underscored his general rule that Spanish should be written just as it was spoken. Consciously imitating Erasmus's *Adages*, Valdés used this folk wisdom to generate interest in Spanish culture.[88] The *Dialogue on Language* contains 177 proverbs and refers to a book of them collected by Juan.[89] The discussion frequently alluded to Nebrija's *Grammar*, which all discussants seem to have read, even though Valdés claimed he had not.[90] Throughout the work Valdés interspersed comparative examples of Spanish and Italian mutations of Latin to show their common roots.[91] In a couple of instances, he even altered Spanish linguistic irregularities to simplify learning the language.[92]

In analysing Iberian linguistic development, Valdés refuted the Italian notion that Spanish was merely a more corrupted form of Latin than Italian.[93] Thus he rejected Nebrija's position in favour of Vergara, who incorrectly argued that Greek was the true mother language of Iberia.[94] Valdés gave Castilian a direct linguistic line to the world of Homer and Plato, and more significantly, to the gospels and letters of Paul. According to Valdés, Castilian words with Latin roots pertained to things used in daily affairs, words with Arab roots pertained to unnecessary or vulgar things, but 'almost all' words with Greek roots pertained 'to religion or to doctrine.'[95] Later Valdés noted that when translating from one language to another it was difficult to convey accurately the true meaning of phrases, particularly in matters of 'religion as a science.'[96] The inference was subtle but clear; Spanish linguistic heritage made religious doctrine purer than in Italy or anywhere else.

The insults and vulgar comments in Valdés's book reflected a typical humanist sodality.[97] The comic level of his book is somewhere between Aretino's obscenity and Castiglione's more sanitized humour. The discussion begins with a meal and festive environment, and proceeds through questions and witticisms to display an acute concern with linguistic style. He repeatedly pays homage to the classics, recommending Cicero, Caesar, Sallust, and Terence as the best stylistic models for Latin, and Demosthenes, Xenephon, Isocrates, Plutarch, and Lucian for Greek.[98] To justify study of the vernacular, Valdés pretends that the topic was beneath his group's attention, as Latin was the language for 'art and books' while Castilian was only for common usage. Marcio then asked if Pietro Bembo wasted his time in his elevation of Italian prose. Valdés responded that some said so, but that he was not an authority on Italian.[99] Obviously he agreed with the vernacular supporters, except that he elevated Spanish rather than Italian as a proper language of culture, and, in the tradition of Nebrija, empire.

In the late twentieth century, Valdés's *Dialogue on Language* became required reading in graduate courses in Spanish. As such, it has been reissued in many editions and is the best-known Valdesian work. Yet in its own day it failed to attract much attention among Italians and would not be published until the eighteenth century.[100] Although it is brilliant on many levels, most of his Italian audience cared little about Spanish authors compared to their own, particularly given Valdés's insult of Castiglione and refusal to discuss contemporary Italian writers such as Aretino. The disappearance of Valdés's book of Spanish proverbs also connotes Italian disinterest in the Spanish folk wisdom contained in the *Dialogue on Language*. Valdés could not make Spanish a language 'understood by all Christian people,'[101] as Charles proposed, by using only linguistic analysis of Spanish literature.

Valdés's sodality might have faded had he not become more closely identified with Giulia Gonzaga in the *Christian Alphabet*. The *Alphabet* quickly circulated widely in manuscript form and would be the first of Valdés's works to be published after his death.[102] As a dialogue entirely between Giulia and Valdés, it established Giulia as the co-host of Valdés's circle of friends. In the discussion she is charming, witty, at times fiery in her questioning of the master's advice. She is spiritually reflective and determined to change her life though wary of clergy and simplistic sermons. Valdés needed Giulia's fame to build his sodality, but Giulia needed more than witty conversation about linguistic style, and courtly manners.

The *Christian Alphabet* is presented as a discussion following a moving sermon Giulia and Juan heard together. Scholars agree that the occasion was one of Bernardino Ochino's famous Lenten services at San Giovanni Maggiore in the spring of 1536.[103] Ochino, the General of the Capuchin order, was a friend of Valdés. According to the later testimony of Pietro Carnessechi, Ochino 'received the themes of many of his sermons from Valdés, from whom he used to get a note on the evening, preceding the morning on which he was to mount the pulpit.'[104] Since Carnessechi had not arrived in Naples in 1536, he probably referred to later sermons, but certainly Ochino and Valdés would have known each other in 1536 when Charles V claimed that Ochino's sermons could make even stones cry.[105] In 1536 Easter Sunday fell on 16 April. Valdés saw Giulia weeping out loud in the church and after the sermon tried to console her.[106] His dialogue grew out of that counselling.

Juan and Giulia were both in the midst of an emotional identity crisis. Juan had expected to return to his beloved Rome with the imperial court.[107] He wrote Cardinal Gonzaga in March that the court was preparing to leave and he hoped to see him in Rome soon.[108] The next month he satirically complained that he was left behind because Charles was 'tyrannized by two beasts.'[109] He referred to Cobos and Granvelle, for earlier in the letter he told the cardinal that he did not trust Charles's councillors, but he believed 'necessity will make them virtuous.'[110] By the time the court embarked for Rome, Milan and the French war had relegated conciliar negotiations to a secondary level of importance and Juan disagreed with both Cobos and Granvelle about Milan.[111] Given Juan's unbending anti-French opinions, he did not suit the immediate interests of the imperial court, even though Charles had the same view of retaining Milan as Valdés.[112] Valdés would not triumphantly return to his old friends at the papal court, nor would he attend the imperial court as a top adviser like his brother Alfonso.[113]

Meanwhile Giulia's experiences had left her a psychological wreck. She had been forced to marry at age thirteen, widowed at fifteen, and had been threatened by the sultan's libido as well. The love of her life had recently died in her arms under mysterious circumstances, and to add to all this misery, Isabella Colonna, her stepdaughter/sister-in-law, had just succeeded in overturning Vespasiano's testament depriving her of all her assets. Giulia's mother had died in 1530 and her father Lodovico took holy orders, withdrawing from worldly matters.[114] Giulia felt alone and suffered from depression that would recur in her life. At the beginning of the *Christian Alphabet* she tells Valdés of her sickness. 'I want you to know that ordinarily I am very unhappy with myself and with the things of this world, and so disgusted that if you could see into my heart, I am sure you would have pity, because in it you would find confusion, perplexity and anxiety.'[115]

In spite of the emotional spirituality of the *Alfabeto*, one suspects the depth of Valdés's commitment to Giulia at the time. As previously noted, in the autumn of 1536 the Princess of Sulmona, Isabella Colonna's mother-in-law, sent Charles a long list of individuals she wanted rewarded that included a successful request to renew Valdés's generous lodging allowance. She also unsuccessfully tried to obtain back pay for Juan's service to Charles in 1533 and 1534. The first sentence of the document states that the requests 'were from the salaries of her husband,' the former Viceroy of Naples, Charles of Lannoy.[116] Viceroy Lannoy died in 1527, making it impossible for the favour to have been related to any service Juan performed for him. A couple of months later Juan wrote Cardinal Gonzaga that 'the negotiations of the Señora doña Giulia are going so slowly that for all our work we are getting almost nowhere.'[117] At this stage of the case Juan knew Giulia's cause had little hope, as the viceroy and Charles needed Colonna support in the French war. The best he could do for his client was offer spiritual and philosophical consolation.

In December 1535 Giulia asked the pope to be allowed to live in a Neapolitan Franciscan convent as a lay person.[118] Nothing could be more of an anathema to Valdés's Erasmian perspective than joining a convent. The regular clergy seemed to offer certitude of salvation and Christian perfection by turning completely from worldly vanities and worries. Valdés made a counter-offer to Giulia 'in this Christian negotiation.'[119] Juan agreed to show Giulia a 'royal and seigniorial' road that would lead her to God 'without separating yourself from the world.'[120] When asked if the vows of monks and friars led to perfection, Valdés replied, 'believe me, that the friars and the non-friars have perfection to the extent that they have faith and love of God and not one bit more.'[121] To love God truly, you had to be conscious of sin and humble yourself before him. This would lead to divine grace and justification: 'If we are not justified our souls are not saved.'[122] Study of the Old Testament law brought awareness of sin, while study of Christ's sacrifice brought awareness of God's love. Over time, faith and contemplation of God's love would be incorporated into daily life with acts of charity.

Valdés taught that the concept of 'mine and yours' should give way to a concept of stewardship. The Christian would never want what he did not have, and whatever he possessed would be viewed as a loan, not as property. Thus, according to Valdés, 'if your property was taken you would not be perturbed by your luck or come to have ill will against the persons who took it.'[123] Valdés served the court and consoled a friend by dispensing sage advice from Scripture, theologians, and ancient philosophers to help Giulia cope with a massive financial loss. However, Valdés's advice was rather hypocritical, since only a few months earlier he threatened Cardinal Ravenna over a 3,000-ducat debt. 'The disgrace will be mine but the damage his, and this I am able to accomplish very easily ... I swear to God that my hands will move to evil and he will know how important it is for him to treat me well or poorly.'[124]

While the gain or loss of property should not be the basis of happiness, there was nothing wrong in using the 'loan' for a pleasant life to include things of the world enjoyed in moderation. Giulia's depression over the suit need not lead her to abandon the elegant lifestyle to which she was accustomed. Valdés's royal road would enable her

> To depreciate the world in such a manner that the world will not depreciate you; to dress your soul with Christian virtues without removing from the body the usual clothing; to maintain your soul with spiritual food without depriving the body of its accustomed fare; to seem good in the eyes of God without seeming bad in the eyes of the world.[125]

Giulia had difficulty accepting Valdés's doctrine that one served God entirely out of love. In her longest speech she replied, 'speaking freely and desiring to examine my soul, I find that I could not do anything [good] if it was not for the fear of Hell, and sometimes for the love of heaven, rather than for the pure love of God. I know myself well enough that if it were not for Hell and Paradise, I would pass through this world well living a moral and praiseworthy life in the eyes of the world, as I have lived until now, without caring to look beyond.'[126] Valdés explained his doctrine by making an analogy to a vicious slave who at first behaves only to escape punishment. In time the slave realizes his master cares for him and begins to serve him out of gratitude. Even after he is freed, the slave continues to serve the former master for his love and good will toward him. Thus fear of Hell leads to the Christian's experience of God's love. The more one experiences God's love, the more one wants to serve God with charity. As in his *Dialogue on Christian Doctrine*, Valdés discussed faith in conjunction with hope and charity, but he is a bit more explicit: 'You are not able to be just except by faith, because the just live by faith.'[127]

Still, the *Alphabet* carried a much safer message for reform than Valdés's first book.[128] The *Alphabet* focused on individual spiritual growth and largely ignored the Church's structure. Near the end of the work Valdés endorsed attending mass regularly[129] and seemingly the doctrine of transubstantiation as well. He affirmed that 'from the sacred communion we Christians partake in the precious flesh and blood of Jesus Christ.'[130] Valdés also accepted the sacrament of confession as a 'high sacrament' with some modification. Confession to God was obligatory, but to a priest only voluntary; he deemed confession to a priest useful only if the priest was spiritually experienced.[131] The Valdesian circle did not originate as a radical reform group. Rather, it was an officially sponsored humanist sodality whose mission was to make Spanish a language of culture among the Italian elite and to care for Giulia's particular needs.

From Sodality to Spirituali Centre

The Valdesian sodality evolved into a *spirituali* centre, one of many evangelical reform groups that sprang up in Italy after the formation of the 1537 Reform Commission headed by Cardinal Contarini. The next year Charles V initiated the first of several religious colloquies in the Empire between Catholics and Protestants that culminated in the Diet of Regensburg, 1541. Thus religious reform was openly debated in Italy, but nowhere as attuned to imperial interests as in Naples. Valdés continued to teach his native language, using his own Spanish translations of Scripture directly from the original Hebrew and Greek, thus playing to his philological strength. These could be easily cross-referenced to Latin versions, or Antonio Brucioli's 1532 Italian translation.

In his translation of Romans (1538) and First Corinthians (1539), Valdés prefixed to each verse the initiatory words of the Latin Vulgate. 'I thought that they would help you more easily understand which Latin words correspond to Castilian which, as I have said, come from Greek rather than Latin.'[132] Thus Valdés could show Latin cognates to Spanish, and some points of difference between the Greek original and the Vulgate. Valdés could also tie his commentaries and discussions to topics of religious reform that might aid imperial negotiations in Germany. Having established a language base emphasizing religious terminology, he moved to the more difficult task of oral expression using religious themes as reflected in the *One Hundred Ten Divine Considerations* (1539–40). Apparently he read and discussed these tracts in Spanish, and circulated them afterwards in writing. Cardinal Monreal, who knew Valdés, succinctly described him and his group. Valdés had 'a beautiful appearance, the sweetest manners and smooth and attractive speech; he made a profession of languages and sacred scripture ... he read and explained the letters of St Paul to his disciples and affiliates in his house.'[133]

Valdés's circle joined beautiful people for spiritual renewal in a beautiful setting. At its centre Giulia Gonzaga radiated, but undoubtedly in a depressed condition. In 1537 her lawsuit with Isabella Colonna seemed all but dead. The same year Valdés wrote his translation of the Psalms accompanied by his commentary on its first book (1–41). In his dedicatory letter to Giulia he mentioned his plan to translate some of Paul's letters, but he thought the Psalms should come first because there were no good Latin translations from the original Hebrew.[134] Valdés seemed to make an excuse for continuing his efforts to stabilize Giulia emotionally. Given her situation, what could possibly ease her troubled mind more than David's Psalms? Like Giulia, David was no saint and endured the temporary loss of everything he had, but he loved God with every fibre of his being and maintained God's favour. By using Jewish history to establish the context of David's verse, Giulia could not help but identify with David's frequent lapses of confidence and inner doubts. Valdés extolled David as an example for Giulia to imitate because 'his spiritual feelings serve greatly to carry one to true piety.'[135]

Juan continued to view faith, love, and charity as inextricably linked. He wrote Giulia that he wanted to expand the 'faith in your soul which consists in believing the words of God ... that you can endure suffering and still believe in the completion of those promises while increasing charity which consists in loving what you believe and having confidence in it.'[136] David's awareness of God's presence stemmed from his love of God, i.e., his desire 'for always being able to see God and how beautiful he is.'[137] Juan's work on the Psalms focused on the unconditional love of God that underlay Christianity. God did not want sacrifices or anything else to prove that love. 'When the [travelling] merchant shows his love by sending his wife letters and poems, he does not like her to demand more of them to entertain her and to keep her honest and chaste.'[138] Apart from his emphasis on the regenerative power of divine love, there are not a lot of reform doctrines discussed at length in Valdés's Psalms. This explains why neither Valdesians nor Protestants sought to publish the work in the sixteenth century.

Valdés's handling of Giulia's lawsuit with Isabella Colonna reveals a growing personal relationship between the two. The case was returned to the original panel of three judges in 1538. In 1536 Giulia's father, Lodovico, had gained custody of Isabella Colonna's son Vespasiano, the ultimate heir of Isabella's father and Giulia Gonzaga's husband. In

1539 the guardianship of Vespasiano became even more important to the Gonzagas, as Giulia's brother died leaving young Vespasiano as the sole male heir of Lodovico. At that point the Marquis of Vasto, the governor of Milan and Ascanio Colonna's brother-in-law, decided to billet troops on Lodovico's estates in Lombardy. Vasto's military pressure must have been aimed to force Giulia and Valdés to back away from their suit with Isabella because they were on the verge of victory. Valdés immediately wrote Cobos to order Vasto off the lands and to declare them under Cobos's protection.[139] Valdés would continue making this plea for more than a year.

As Isabella's suit began to turn against her, the viceroy complained that 'their solicitors are so excessively diligent that they ask for things that move away from a reasonable conclusion.'[140] He probably aimed his criticism at Valdés, who pressed for an immediate payment of 17,000 ducats (the 1536 verdict was for 1,000) in part because of the long delay in settlement, and pressed Giulia's claims to the Colonna family jewels.[141] The court finally reached a decision 10 January 1540. Isabella would get the family jewels, and Giulia would receive an immediate payment of 16,000 ducats provided she agreed not to remarry.[142]

The viceroy wrote Cobos just before the court announced its decision that 'the negotiations of doña Giulia are finished as you ordered and in such a manner that one side is satisfied and the other is not oppressed.'[143] The viceroy failed to mention that Isabella had Giulia's annual stipend of 2,500 ducats reduced, as her lawyers obtained a quick ruling from the Collateral Council during the absence of Regent Figueroa, Valdés's good friend.[144] Thus Giulia refused to hand over the family jewels,[145] and again entered a deep depression. On 12 April Toledo wrote Cobos, 'In regard to doña Giulia there is nothing more to say except that this poor señora has been ill for more than fifty days, but she does not have a dangerous illness.'[146]

Giulia's father was gravely ill and the prospects of further litigation with the viceroy opposed to her interests left her in a desperate situation. During her 'illness' Valdés must have been too busy to meet with her personally, but he responded to her distress in three letters contained in the group of Valdesian tracts Eduard Boehmer discovered in Vienna in the late nineteenth century. After his 1538 dedication of his *Commentary on Romans* to Giulia, Valdés never again used Giulia's name. These letters are not dated, but Valdés specifically refers to them as letters to a woman who is both beautiful and sick. Since cross-references are made in the letters, it is a certainty, as Boehmer indicated, that all three were written to

Giulia Gonzaga in the order Boehmer published.[147] The first is about the providence of God, the second about temptations, and the third about sickness.[148] The letter on temptation is included among the eleven additional tracts in Juan Sánchez's edition of the *Divine Considerations* (no. 7); two of the questions and answers in that edition (nos. 5 and 12) clearly relate to Giulia's particular condition as well. One other tract unique to this edition (no. 3) deals with a related topic of the correspondence.[149]

Each letter was probably a direct response to a letter from Giulia. Giulia's litigation had been going well, then suddenly turned against her, and she wanted Valdés to know her extremity. Valdés's letter on divine providence is a warning against relying on human prudence rather than the Holy Spirit in studying Scripture. Understanding of the Holy Spirit comes from Scripture, but its experience is unique. Those addicted to philosophy never really approve of the Holy Spirit no matter how much Scripture they read. Others read Scripture, approve the doctrine of the Holy Spirit, but cannot completely give up human prudence, 'so they go limping on both feet. From these are born the diversity of superstitions, the multitude of ceremonies, and the different rules and manner of life.'[150] Valdés seemed to critique Protestants who confused God's particular providence for them with his general providence, thus denying God's liberality. Only those who read Scripture and recognize that the Holy Spirit is an internal inspiration to glorify God will remain pious, patient, and humble.[151]

Valdés elaborated further in a question and answer that Giulia had translated into Italian and published as an appendix to the *Christian Alphabet* in 1545.[152] Entitled 'In What Manner Christians Ought to Study Their Own Book and What Fruits May Be Taken from the Study, and How the Holy Scripture Serves Them as a Commentary,' the tract is also included in Sanchez's edition of the *Considerations*.[153] Giulia had heard Valdés repeatedly advise his disciples to study their own book, so she asked what was her own book, how would she study it, what fruit should she get from the lesson, and how should she apply that to her Christian study. Valdés cast the Socratic injunction of self-examination to mean studying one's own soul. As a child of Adam, one becomes aware of sin, but after incorporation into the body of Christ by believing in God's promises, one becomes aware of a change of nature and little by little will seek to imitate Christ out of love. 'If I love God and Christ as much as I can, if I love them more than myself, then I will love my neighbour as much as I can and love him/her as much as myself.'[154] This of course leads to an increase in charity and humility to the point that external circumstances, such as Giulia's legal problems, become irrelevant. Leaving all other books and human prudence aside, the Scripture becomes the commentary on our own book, indicating how far we need to go to imitate 'Christ and his saints' and become more completely incorporated into the body of Christ.[155]

Valdés's advice about self-examination only seemed to make matters worse. Giulia was beautiful and still in her twenties, but because of the verdict in her litigation she had to remain unmarried the rest of her life. In a question and answer, Giulia bares the true state of her conscience. 'Whenever I enter into self-examination, I am overwhelmed with my own evil and depravity, so full of worldly sympathies ... so full of sensual appetites ... that I loathe myself.'[156] She then asks how God, who knows her better than she knows herself, could love her. 'You can imagine how much this thought disturbs me. If you know some remedy that could recover me from this illness, I beg you to teach it to me.'[157]

Valdés initially replied rather tersely that he had given her the remedy many times before, that she should not consider herself as herself, but in Christ, as a regenerated Christian rather than a 'daughter of Adam.'[158] He then used an allegory to explain. If the emperor adopted ten peasants as sons, he would treat them as sons not as peasants. Because of Christ's sacrifice, God accepts Giulia as his daughter in the same manner rather than as a daughter of Adam. Evidently Giulia pressed Valdés further with her temptations, leading to the doctrinal letter found by Boehmer. Juan warned that temptations often arise out of uncertainty, and impious people will use that uncertainty to try to destroy Christian piety. Valdés then shifted his argument and told Giulia that she should be thankful for her temptations. God allows the devil to tempt humans in order to strengthen their faith, as in the case of Job, or even David, who briefly succumbed to murder and adultery only to attain a deeper faith and love of God. Temptations certify faith, so he advises Giulia to keep her faith, keep believing in God's promises, and she would be fine.[159]

Evidently still unsatisfied, Giulia now emphasized her physical illness. In his response Valdés first advised Giulia to make sure her sickness did not result from anxiety and fear, which were contrary to piety. He cited Paul's torments as an example of overcoming physical illness with the proper spirit. He then rather coldly wrote that God sometimes brings physical illness to beautiful people who were vain. By removing the source of vanity, they could focus on their spiritual health.[160] Finally,

Giulia should be glad about her illness because God uses sickness for sanctification, to make people aware of their need to be more holy because of the fragility of life. It is easy to sanctify God when things are going well, but when one is very ill and inwardly sanctifies God 'you will recognize this sickness is for your benefit ... that you may better understand how little you are worth without him.'[161]

Giulia's letters had the desired effect on Valdés, as in the last stage of her litigation he went farther than a courtier at the viceroy's court should have gone to bring about his client's satisfaction. Isabella paid the 16,000 ducats to Giulia in September 1540, but a new round of suits and appeals had already begun. Ludovico Gonzaga had died in June leaving young Vespasiano, now Duke of Sabbionetta, completely in the charge of young aunt Giulia, and Isabella contested her guardianship.[162] Nevertheless, Giulia took control of her father's estates in the name of Vespasiano, but Ascanio Colonna's brother-in-law, the Marquis of Vasto, continued to place troops on them. Meanwhile Viceroy Toledo favoured throwing the whole case back to the courts. Valdés would not accept that, so he went over the viceroy's head and brought pressure on him from both Cobos and the emperor. Valdés wrote Cobos that the only remedy would be for him to order the viceroy to force the two sides to accept the previous settlement and prohibit any further litigation. He complained that his four years of torturous negotiations 'would seem unbearable even in Hell.'[163] He urged Cobos to have Charles intervene and uphold Lodovico's testament before conflict escalated.[164]

Toledo informed Cobos that he was doing all he could for Giulia, but 'these are matters of justice that have had several decisions that were not executed by the different parties.'[165] The response comment written in the margin of the summary of the letter indicated Cobos's strong desire to see the matter settled in Giulia's favour. 'I am not able to stop harassing you and writing you about this because of the burden that remains on her [Giulia].'[166] Valdés urged Cobos to arrange a meeting between Charles and Regent Figueroa, who was with the imperial court in Germany.[167] Figueroa, Valdés's friend, was one of the original three judges in the case and could question the Collateral Council's reduction of Giulia's stipend because he was regent over that council.

In April 1541 Cobos informed Valdés that he had written the viceroy and Charles on Giulia's behalf. 'I have written there [the imperial court] as insistently as I am able and thus I hope it turns out well; all who are there have the same attitude as I.'[168] In September, Secretary

Idiáquez informed Cobos that he had done everything he could possibly do to aid Giulia's case at the imperial court.[169] Later that month Charles decided Giulia had suffered enough and upheld Lodovico's will, thereby ending the litigation.[170] Vespasiano Gonzaga inherited all the estates of his father and paternal grandfather intact, and at the death of his mother he gained the lands of Giulia's Colonna husband as well. Perhaps as a tribute to Valdés's service, Vespasiano later established a press in Sabbionette to publish Hebrew literature.[171]

While Valdés directed his sodality, he also acquired significant positions in Spanish administration in Naples. These positions gave him a great deal of information to help save Viceroy Toledo's reputation during a harsh audit that seemed intended to remove Toledo from office. These more earthly concerns of Valdés reveal his ambition and his continued ability to use patrons with competing interests to his own advantage.

6 Offices and Audits

When Grand Chancellor Gattinara audited the Neapolitan administration in 1521 he wrote, 'I lost my mind on it.'[1] Gattinara went on to develop a blueprint for reform in Naples. He advised that officials become more concerned with local conditions, especially the administration of justice, which, if unreformed, would lead to 'perdition and ruin and total destruction.'[2] Unfortunately, persistent warfare prevented any change. The rebellious barons were bitterly divided into pro-French and pro-Spanish factions who had free rein to indulge their murderous contest when the French invaded the kingdom in 1528. By 1530 conditions in Naples had reached their nadir. Pirates raided the coast, the army's pay was in arrears, and there was a two-year delay in the assignment of a new viceroy. Pedro de Toledo finally secured the appointment in 1532, and his selection proved to be a turning point in Neapolitan history as he launched a campaign to impose Gattinara's program.[3]

With Charles's order to protect the poor and weak from the powerful, the viceroy removed all nobles from the Collateral Council and proceeded to bring tyrannical aristocrats to justice. He made nobles and burghers equal before the law and reformed the royal courts by mixing Spanish judges with Neapolitans. Nobles, who were now tried by plebeians, could be condemned to hanging. During Toledo's tenure rigorous justices sentenced thousands of people to the death penalty. Toledo shared governance with the Collateral Council that met daily in his palace. By most accounts Pedro de Toledo was the best Spanish viceroy assigned to govern Naples.[4]

Toledo's rigour created enemies, particularly among the nobility, and his administration had its weaknesses. In 1533 he had to subdue a tax revolt initiated by the aristocracy.[5] Naples had to maintain troops to defend Italian territories and to man the fleets of Andrea Doria. As a military bastion, it contributed a disproportionate share of Charles's European revenues, but Charles always wanted more. Toledo was a military man, not an accountant, so he left the treasury alone. Fiscal irregularities triggered the first *visita* of Naples, an administrative review initiated by suspicions of corruption. During the three-year investigation, 1536–9, self-seeking officials attempted to secure the removal of all the viceroy's officials and judges, not just the corrupt treasury officials.

With the aid of the viceroy and Cobos, Juan de Valdés gained several offices in Neapolitan administration: collector of taxes on official documents, overseer of castles, and ultimately personal adviser to Cobos. Valdés's offices gave him a good perspective for evaluating the *visita* of Naples. The allegations of enormous sums of lost revenue angered Charles, and Toledo's attempts to blame Cobos for the *visita*'s malevolence only worsened matters. Valdés's knowledge of the treasury and its corruption enabled him to gain Cobos's support to moderate the *visita*'s effect on the Neapolitan administration, thereby saving the viceroy's reputation and influence.

Office Hunting

Before leaving Naples, Charles rewarded Juan's service by renewing his salary as an imperial secretary for 1536 and by granting him the office of *perceptor de los significatarios* in the treasury.[6] Unfortunately, all treasury offices were then under close scrutiny. For years Charles received reports that the kingdom of Naples needed drastic financial reform. In 1529 Cardinal Colonna reported that 'the financial disorder is unbelievable ... the kingdom is so worn out and poor from the mistreatment of soldiers that most have been forced to eat weeds until the next harvest.'[7] Despite obvious problems, Viceroy Toledo recommended that Treasurer Alonso Sánchez continue in his office because 'he is one of the best and most necessary servants Your Majesty has.'[8] Others alleged that 'neither the viceroy nor the treasurer is willing to investigate rents or payments and they will continue to collect nothing.'[9] When Charles left Naples for Rome he authored a harsh memorial on the state of finance and justice in the viceroyalty and initiated the *visita*.[10]

Valdés was paid a salary as *perceptor de las significatorias* for all of 1536 and resigned the office in April 1537.[11] Its ordinary stipend was three hundred ducats, but it also carried an 'encouragement' of 4 per cent of the collection, theoretically not to exceed a total income of five hundred ducats. The office served directly under the Sommaria Court, which had jurisdiction over all fiscal affairs in the kingdom. The Sommaria sent the *perceptor de las significatorias* the amount of taxes to be assessed on official documents in each province. The *perceptor* then had provincial commissioners allocate and collect the tax. The *perceptor* made three copies of the annual tax report, one for the Sommaria, one for the treasurer, and one for himself. According to one witness, the office was useless, and its responsibilities should have been given to the General Treasurer.[12]

Since Valdés later admitted he was unqualified for the office, he probably assigned a substitute to perform most of his duties. The *visita* condemned the use of substitutes, and some judges pointed to the office Valdés had held. They advised Charles to give the office of *perceptor de las significatorias* to Juan Thommaso de Gennaro because 'he has been administering the office for some time without having the title or the concession.'[13] The intent of the judges was clear. Charles had granted the office to an unqualified person who used a substitute and therefore Charles himself was responsible for some of the problems noted by the *visita*.

The office of *perceptor de las significatorias* was lucrative and a magnet for corruption. According to Treasurer Sánchez, don Cesare de Silva, a *perceptor de las significatorias* prior to Valdés, 'Claimed his office was superior to the office of General Treasurer' and therefore refused to send Sánchez a report.[14] The amount of extraordinary salary collected was difficult to enforce, so the real income of the office seemed to have been at least 750 ducats. Worse, there were instances of *perceptores de significatorias* taking bribes not to collect taxes owed. As late as 1572 the *perceptor de las significatorias* was the only official in Neapolitan finance not required to balance his books at the end of each year.[15]

During Juan's tenure in the office, *visitador* Pedro de Pacheco appointed Dr Bartolomé de Benavente as 'Conservator of the Royal Patrimony' to carry out the audit of the viceroyalty.[16] Benavente quickly set about bringing order to the collection of taxes on documents. In September 1536 he completed an audit of all such taxes collected from 1510 to 1535 and found a shortfall of 156,056 ducats. Benavente squeezed 74,006 ducats from those responsible for the failure, mostly *perceptores* and other finance officials, but he had to write off 37,842 ducats because the debtors were either dead or unable to pay. According to the audit, that left 44,658 ducats to be collected by bringing individuals before the Court of the

Sommaria.[17] Valdés would not have relished being a party to the humiliation of other officials, perhaps even his own servants, whose only crime was continuing past practices. He requested a more suitable office.

Conveniently, the position Valdés wanted came open the month of the audit, but Benavente advised the Council of Castile against filling it to save money.

> The overseer of castles [*veedor*] for the kingdom is dead. He [Benavente] says that the office should not be given to anyone because it is of little service to Your Majesty and it would be better for the viceroy to use the salary to send a *caballero* to visit them once a year.
>
> It is advantageous that Master Portalano de Varleta is dead because there are many honourable persons who will pay 8,000 ducats for the office.[18]

In Dr Benavente's cold calculus, the crown should look to maximize its profit from the death of a loyal servant. Cobos had different plans for the position, as he explained in the margin of the letter's summary.

> The viceroy has informed me of the vacancy that some have already requested. Others say that it is unnecessary and that it would be better, in case there is need of a salary, that I bestow it for qualified services that are well known. For this reason the wage ought to be provided ... [illegible word] to Juan de Valdés because they would terminate his other office. You can consider if this seems the proper provision.[19]

Since Juan's office had not been terminated, Cobos obviously wanted to ensure Valdés's promotion.

The next step was a formal request to Charles. Unlike Cobos, Viceroy Toledo did not bend the truth and simply notified the emperor that Juan wished to resign as *perceptor* and then indicated that the 'unnecessary' office of castle overseer was vacant.

> Juan de Valdés, to whom Your Majesty granted the office of *perceptor de las significatorias*, begs to be excused from serving in this office because his profession is not of that nature. And he writes to tell you that he has nominated two other people who understand finances and have the proper qualifications for your majesty to choose.
>
> The office of *veedor* is vacant. Ordinarily the office is not necessary and it would be best to fill it temporarily when needed. Write me your opinion and if it should be filled, send the [names of] nominees.[20]

Since no response was written in the margin, Charles wanted to obtain more information before deciding what to do with the request.

The next reference to the position indicates that Cobos again pushed Juan's selection as castle overseer. The document is a summary of matters needing Charles's attention from all parts of Italy. Cobos edited the summary and wrote in Charles's response, 'Give it to Valdés.'

> The office of *veedor* that has been vacant is very necessary and should not be left vacant. The secretary who has assisted with it till now is unnecessary because a secretary from Your Majesty can go with the overseer and the inspection will be done better and the office and salary that was given to him will be saved. The persons nominated are don Juan Sarmiento, Comendador Peñalosa, Valdés, and Pedro de Carauz *contino*. Since Valdés has not accepted the office of *perceptor de las significatorias* to which Your Majesty named him, because it is an appointment in finance where he has little understanding, he is suitable for this one. The salary is four hundred ducats.[21]

An unnecessary office suddenly became 'very necessary.' Not only did Valdés receive the office, he was apparently able to name his successor as *perceptor de las significatorias*.[22]

As a military office, castle overseer was much more 'honourable' than *perceptor*. The titles of two of the other nominees indicate that it attracted individuals of high social status; Don Juan Sarmiento was related to titled nobility while Comendador Peñalosa was a member of a military order. The *veedor* ensured royal castles and fortifications were maintained with adequate weapons, munitions, and personnel, and helped to prioritize repair and construction. He also reported whether *alcaides* 'governed well' or not.[23]

Viceroy Toledo also wanted Juan to get the position, though not as much as Cobos. When he informed Toledo that Valdés had gained the office, Cobos noted that it conformed 'with your judgment.'[24] Toledo thanked Charles effusively for the 'good provision' he had made for his future service.[25] One of Valdés's closest disciples was the renowned military engineer Mario Galeota, who may have advised Valdés in his new position. As was the case with his treasury office, corruption surrounded the office of *veedor*. Fortress commanders would sell ammunition or fail to maintain the requisite number of troops and pocket their pay. Beyond that, the viceroy's frantic construction program left many forts unfinished due to lack of materials, thereby leaving the city vulnerable.[26] After eight months in office, Valdés again lobbied for a more suitable position.

Correspondence between Cobos and Toledo, and between Cobos and the Council of Castile, indicates that Valdés was a highly valued and ambitious courtier. In mid-December Toledo informed Cobos that 'I cannot help admiring Valdés's work, which you know as well as I,' but he was surprised that Juan wanted to exchange the office of castle overseer for another position that was 'more suited to him.' Toledo added that Valdés seemed to think that he should be 'the Viceroy of this Kingdom.'[27] Toledo tried to hasten the promotion, claiming he desperately needed another overseer of castles owing to the threat of a Turkish invasion.

The wheels of Spanish administration moved slowly. In summarizing Toledo's request for the Council of Castile, Cobos also favoured Valdés's promotion by adding his own editorial emphasis. 'Here [at the Council of Castile] we know well who Juan de Valdés is and the gravity of the work that we use him for there.'[28] He then listed the two 'very honourable' offices Valdés declined, and added Toledo's comment that he 'will be content with nothing less than the viceroyalty.'[29] Toledo's pleas to fill the office gained no results until the Turkish fleet went to sea in May 1538. The next month Toledo was given permission to appoint another overseer of castles, though in summarizing Toledo's final request Cobos reminded Charles, 'it is the office you gave to Valdés,' implying that Valdés still held the office.[30]

Valdés's later correspondence with Cobos indicates that he was appointed to Cobos's personal service as an adviser for Italian affairs. No records of that appointment or salary seem to have survived. However, Valdés's salary records do include a letter from secretary Idiáquez, Cobos's *criado* at the imperial court, swearing to Valdés's service at court from 22 November 1532 to 9 April 1533.[31] As head of the Treasury, Cobos must have been responsible for Valdés finally receiving his back pay. Idiáquez's letter is dated 8 March 1539. Thus Valdés entered Cobos's personal service sometime between June 1538 and March 1539. After 1536 there is no record of his salary as an imperial secretary; however, in 1559 a witness in the Carranza trial testified that Juan 'was secretary to the Emperor' when he wrote to Carranza in 1539.[32]

What was 'the gravity of the work' that Juan Valdés performed? Typical of the patronage system of the era, Valdés's offices in finance and defence were granted as a reward for other services;[33] he was not qualified for either position. His primary job was to lead a Spanish-oriented humanist circle that included members of the Italian elite, gather intelligence, and advise Toledo and Cobos on Italian affairs. He rejected lucrative offices that apparently required little work because of his honour. He did not want his friends to view him as a petty administrator no matter how easy the job. Valdés wanted a position that reflected his influence.

Valdés's political ambition stands in stark contrast to his frequent assaults on 'worldly honour.' In his *Commentary on the Psalms*, written in 1537 while he was pursuing his promotions, he addressed the issue of why a spiritual Christian should wield political power. The Christian king governed for 'the glory and honour of God' by searching for the most perfect Christians he could find to appoint to office.[34] Care in selection of such individuals was more important than enacting good laws and constitutions. Lower-quality officials would abuse their authority to fatten themselves 'with the blood of the people.'[35] They would afterwards turn against their superiors whenever they wanted. Such a situation created the most vicious and worst possible form of tyranny even if the prince himself was good.[36]

The prince should employ men 'who govern themselves,' meaning those with interior spiritual control.[37] In essence Valdés advised selection of men like himself, knowledgeable about politics and the world yet clearly among the spiritual elite. The ruler must search out the most perfect ministers, who would discharge their political responsibilities without feeling their work either promoted or obstructed their development as Christians. Good government absolutely required leadership by the spiritual elite, an opinion that was in stark contrast to the assessments of Machiavelli and Luther, both of whom considered an amoral, efficient prince preferable to a virtuous fool.[38] Valdés could not make such a distinction between political and religious thought. Like St Augustine, he believed that the Holy Spirit perfected human reason, and without the Spirit one could not properly understand purely secular affairs.[39] 'Being illuminated with the interior light of the Holy Spirit we see and understand not only spiritual things that are in God, but also the being, the virtue and the efficacy of created things. ... Little by little we will come to know the proper order of things.'[40]

Clearly Valdés did not view the exercise of political authority as antithetical to a spiritual life. The two complemented each other in such a way that honour derived from interior control based on faith paved the way for political success.[41] When a Christian courtier rose to a position of influence, his office would be an outward recognition of his interior virtue. The office did not give honour, but it reflected the courtier's honour.

While Valdés emphasized spiritual qualifications for office, he was not above using his offices to augment his income and lifestyle. Some historians have argued that Valdés had very little money prior to his acquisition of the prebend of San Clemente in 1536,[42] but he had the rather large sum of 3,000 ducats in ready cash to help free Cardinal Ravenna from prison in the summer of 1535. He had been paid a thousand ducats as compensation for his archival office, and he would have earned some income from his position as Papal Chamberlain. Valdés needed considerable funds because, in his own words, he liked to 'live like the king.'[43]

Family inheritance may have accounted for some of Juan's funds. Fernando de Valdés died in 1530, but his testament has not been found. Juan acquired some property in Cuenca from his father, as indicated in his testament, but his own assistance in building the family's *mayorazgo* in that testament indicates that he would not have sold any of it.[44] His brother Diego left him 530 ducats in cash,[45] and Juan may have earned some compensation from Diego's prebends because of Clement's support. Juan would also have come into considerable wealth as Alfonso's universal heir. In addition to the 50,000 maravedis from Alfonso's secretarial income, he may have obtained at least another five hundred ducats from Alfonso's salary as Chancellor of Naples.[46] Alfonso's will indicates that he had amassed a considerable fortune, and anything not distributed in the testament went to Juan. Juan's apparent wealth explains his ability to gather delicate intelligence in Rome and mingle socially with cardinals. Juan de Valdés was clearly not a poor courtier in Rome.

With the acquisition of the prebend of San Clemente (1,500 ducats a year) and these various offices, Valdés must have been quite wealthy. He had to be in order to host his sodality. Valdés's testament shows him earning 600 ducats a year from rental properties, owning 1,000 ducats worth of moveable gold and silver, holding 1,000 ducats of debt notes, and distributing 700 ducats to friends and servants in Naples. He left his unspecified property in Cuenca and several silver objects to family members. His family also retained his prebend of San Clemente in spite of the heretical allegations made against him after his death.[47] Valdés could afford to circulate with the fashionable elite.

An Unwelcome Visit

In February 1536 Charles sent Pedro de Pacheco, the Bishop of Mondonedo and later Pamplona, to preside over the *visita* of Naples. He was elected cardinal in 1545 and in 1553 succeeded Toledo as Viceroy of Naples.[48] From the beginning Pacheco portrayed Toledo as both incompetent and corrupt. He asserted that judges openly bought their offices and then committed extortion to recoup the high price they had to pay. *Alguaciles* robbed those arrested, accepted bribes, and used other criminals as spies. In particular he castigated the Sommaria court, which he claimed collected less than a third of the taxes due.

Pacheco frequently complained of Toledo's refusal to cooperate. He wrote Cobos that when he tried to discuss problems the viceroy would reply that he did 'not have time because he was leaving Naples for the garden of Cardinal Colonna,'[49] i.e., the gardens beside Valdés's villa. According to Pacheco, rather than carrying out the reforms recommended in the emperor's memorial Toledo allowed the situation to deteriorate after Charles left the kingdom in 1536. Officials were so corrupt that he asked Cobos for authority to replace them immediately to stop their robbery.[50]

Aside from his concern for the rigorous enforcement of law, Toledo left most domestic matters to the Collateral Council.[51] Pacheco's assault on the viceroy and his administration could not have succeeded without Bartolomé de Benavente's uncovering evidence of widespread corruption in the treasury. Concluding his audit in 1539, Benavente wrote that all the reports about Neapolitan poverty and the kingdom's inability to provision Andrea Doria's fleet were lies, and if he could not prove it, he literally offered his head to the chopping block. Benavente claimed the treasury collectors and judges on the Sommaria were party to a giant scam whereby royal rents were initially assessed low and later reassessed at their true value before fees were collected.[52] If judges on the Sommaria were corrupt, other judges could be implicated in a call for a clean sweep of the entire administration. Thus Pacheco could place his own *criados* in positions of influence.

In addition to the Sommaria, Benavente blamed the Treasurer of Naples, Alonso Sánchez, the Collateral Council, and the viceroy. The Sommaria needed a complete overhaul, and he, of course, asked for appointment as its chief justice to ensure the reforms were enacted. He also asked for the authority to fire other investigators if they did not agree with him. With over fifty pages of detailed calculations, Benavente figured that the current annual rent on the royal patrimony was at least 30,000 ducats short, and he found evidence of 190,000 ducats shorted the treasury in unpaid past obligations. With a more thorough review he estimated the total loss might reach 300,000 ducats.[53]

Pacheco and Benavente fuelled Charles's suspicions about Neapolitan administration. During his visit to Naples, the emperor encouraged the viceroy to intervene in administration to improve justice and expedite cases involving royal finance.[54] In particular, he advised raising the salaries of financial officials, and prohibiting them from taking gifts.[55] Six months after the *visita*'s report was published, Charles continued to view the problem in Naples as a matter of individual avarice.[56] Initially Charles told the viceroy that the *visita* had nothing to do with his performance; he merely wanted to hasten needed reform.[57] However, Pacheco and Benavente, holding out the promise of hundreds of thousands of ducats in additional revenue, convinced Charles that the entire administration needed cleansing, including the Vicaria, the primary criminal and civil court, and the supreme court of Santa Clara. They linked the corruption in the treasury to judicial corruption. Only after the replacement of all Toledo's judges could the guilty be brought to justice.

The viceroy admitted that some reforms were needed, but he rejected the shock treatment proposed by Pacheco and Benavente. Naples's financial problems were well known. In 1533 Viceroy Toledo claimed the Sommaria treated everyone as a criminal and asked for help to review its accounts;[58] but he had little time to devote to fiscal reform due to military priorities.[59] Toledo did cooperate with the *visitadores* to a degree. As early as 1537 he agreed that the chief justice of the Sommaria, Hieronimo Severino, should be replaced.[60] He began remodelling the palace of Capuana to house all three courts, Sommaria, Vicaria, and Santa Clara, in order to prevent delays and avoid duplication in trials.[61] And he agreed with Benavente's reform in the collection of *significatorias*.[62]

Benavente went too far for the viceroy. He had made himself the *de facto* chief justice of the Sommaria and refused to hear any suits except those he brought against officials, thus creating a backlog for all other cases. Benavente claimed to be able to recover more than 100,000 ducats in revenues, but two years into the *visita* little of that additional revenue had been realized. In the words of Toledo, 'he offers much but gives little.'[63]

Charles and his viceroy waged a continuous battle over Neapolitan taxation after the emperor's visit to the kingdom. In 1536 Charles demanded more revenues from Naples, but the viceroy responded by claiming that the last parliamentary grant had not yet expired, and that Charles's brother Ferdinand was illegally collecting 50,000 ducats each year.[64] Even with Charles's increased demands, Neapolitan taxation barely kept up with inflation. The historian Antonio Calabria concluded in his study of Neapolitan finances that 'Naples, like Castile, was probably taxed beneath its capacity to contribute. But that was no doubt more than offset by the rapacity and unscrupulousness of His Majesty's officials.'[65]

Charles never realized that the problem in Naples was a flawed system rather than individual avarice. Officials were often paid a ridiculously low ordinary salary. Hieronimo Severino, the chief justice of the Sommaria, claimed that he had not received a salary in fifty years of service.[66] Many judges had salaries listed at a hundred or a hundred and fifty ducats. Treasurer Sánchez received a hundred ducats in ordinary salary and 8 per cent of the collection up to a maximum of four hundred ducats.[67] The unprecedented inflation combined with the failure to increase salaries encouraged corruption and dishonesty on the part of imperial officials. Treasurer Sánchez actually defended the system, saying the extraordinary salary, a percentage of the collection, made gathering funds quicker, as officials would be anxious to get their cut.[68] Viceroy Toledo did not create the system, nor did Charles ease his fiscal demands so that salaries could be raised.

Given Charles's perception, someone had to be held responsible. Though the *visita* led to the removal of many officials, the primary blame fell on Severino, the chief justice of the Sommaria, and Treasurer Sánchez. Both men faced criminal charges. The viceroy imprisoned Severino and might have done the same to Sánchez had he not appealed his case to the imperial court.

Toledo turned his anger about the *visita* on Cobos and threatened a full disclosure of Cobos's creatures in the treasury. *Visita* reports were normally kept secret, but Toledo had it published and afterwards wrote Cobos a letter dripping with bitter sarcasm uncharacteristic of the viceroy.

> I take great pleasure in knowing that don Pedro de Pacheco, Bishop of Pamplona, in the seven or eight months he was in Naples, better understands the affairs of this kingdom than I, having been in it eight years; and that His Majesty gives him more credit than I because he is a more loyal and true servant. ... Thank you for your favour and for ordering secretaries Juan Vázquez and Ydiáquez to help me in Flanders [at the imperial court]. I am such a bad man and poor servant of His Majesty that I believed you would keep them from taking my property because then His Majesty might examine yours.[69]

Toledo's wife had died in October and he had petitioned for a licence to leave Italy, i.e., to resign as viceroy.[70] He now renewed his petition so he could go to Flanders and defend himself in person. In the meantime, he threatened to execute the *visita*'s report completely.

> In regard to the *visita*, I have seen it and agree to its execution to the letter without missing a point. ... In the matter of the treasurer I see that you have written me that he has your recommendation and that I should give him my pardon. But you ought to think about it. I swear that in this negotiation I am not able to pardon anything ... I ask you to consider that it is one matter in the general offence to many.[71]

Treasurer Sánchez remained confident that Cobos would ensure his exoneration. Sánchez seemed unconcerned about the investigation in August 1539 when he asked Charles for a reward.[72] When the report was pronounced, he asked Cobos to write 'as briefly as possible my defence and justifications.' He requested that Cobos send the defence to Granvelle and Secretary Idiáquez, who were with Charles in the Netherlands, and to the viceroy and Regent Figueroa.[73] At first Idiáquez's lobbying produced few results at the imperial court, as Charles insisted upon reviewing Sánchez's case before deciding the treasurer's fate.[74] To grease the wheels, Sánchez mailed Idiáquez a moneybox hidden in a bundle to be forwarded to Cobos.[75]

Others enlisted Cobos's aid as well. Severino, the chief justice of the Sommaria, sent Cobos a diamond ring, 'requesting that you deign wearing on your hand the affection with which it is sent to you.'[76] Another judge on the Sommaria identified himself as having favoured Cobos's 'party in this city' and asked him to write a reference for him to Granvelle and Idiáquez.[77] It appears that Cobos's cronies were at the heart of the financial corruption.

In Toledo's sarcastic letter to Cobos there is a rather cryptic mention of Valdés and a personal matter. In the body of the letter he wrote: 'My solicitor has agreed to ask Your Lordship on my behalf about certain grievances that are made over Matilla and other territories of the marquisate and other matters that they propose. I ask that you treat it all very privately.' On the address cover of the letter Toledo added, 'I ask Your Lordship to order one of yours [servants] enclosed to correspond with my solicitor.'[78] Also on the cover is 'a Valdés' and beneath it Severino. The reference to Severino is puzzling. Why would the viceroy want the disgraced Severino, whom he had imprisoned, to handle a delicate personal matter? Given the tone of the letter, this may have been a cynical joke.

These personal matters probably related to Toledo's nominees for prebends in his marquisate in Spain. In his private papers there are references at this time to a suit in Rome about Toledo's appointment of a cleric named Noguero to a church in his Spanish domain. Valdés's contacts in the Roman curia apparently helped Toledo win the suit.[79]

Obviously Valdés had Toledo's confidence, so Cobos took Toledo's letter as a cue to seek Valdés's advice on the *visita*. Of the seven surviving letters that Valdés wrote to Cobos, the first two, 22 November 1539 and 3 February 1540, do not mention the *visita*. The third letter was a delayed response to Cobos's inquiry. Cobos ordered Juan to write him in a letter he sent 27 February, but Juan did not do so until 25 March, claiming he wanted to wait until Giulia Gonzaga could write him about her suit. After discussing her case, he moved to the *visita*.

> In regard to the *visita*, Your Lordship may be certain that what has resulted has not served God, nor has His Majesty gained anything. Rather I believe the opposite from what I see. God grant that in the future you will be able to say that I had been mistaken. If the *visita* was primarily to examine His Majesty's ministers and officials in order to punish those that appear to deserve it, I do not know why those who merit it are not given raises. If some are deprived of their offices for being unqualified and others for corruption, I do not know why the persons put in their places are less qualified and have less ability. I see in this *visita* that many are punished by chance and without cause. I do not see anyone getting a raise, which I marvel at because there are many who deserve it. ... I do not wish to speak about the case of the Treasurer, who seems hideous to Benavente and Estinga. I will say this, that it is very charming to pretend to reform the courts and to make good use of His Majesty's patrimony by removing from the treasury the man that I know for certain has done nothing wrong and has provided many services to Your Majesty. ... The result is this. The *visita* appears bad here; His Majesty has been too rigorous. This being the first true *visita*, His Majesty should have provided for more mature deliberation with less rigour. The intent to take the property of some [officials], as many have been judged, looks bad. The condemnation of men without hearing them, something never heard of in this Kingdom, looks bad. That His Majesty has affronted his ministers, officials, and servants in public, destroying their reputation, which is very important for the administration of their offices, looks bad. ... This provision was made without consulting the viceroy, who knew nothing about it, and in truth it appears a strange thing that a matter of such importance as this was done without giving the viceroy any part in it nor any others that are here. ... Naples is

not Valladolid. ... I know for certain there is not one of those suspended who after a private reprimand for the past would not serve better than any of those put in their place. ... This *visita* threw justice out of the land by placing it in the hands of those who do not understand it and crushing those who do.[80]

Valdés knew Cobos was particularly concerned with the treasurer, so he made clear his support for him. However, he tied Sánchez's fate to a general moderation of the whole *visita* and subtly implied that Bishop Pacheco undermined the viceroy's patronage with arbitrary appointments. Cobos wanted to protect Sánchez; Valdés wanted to protect the viceroy's authority. Valdés also intimated that low salaries had caused much of the corruption.

Juan de Figueroa, Regent of the Collateral Council, joined in the viceroy's defence.[81] His correspondence with Cobos also indicated that Cobos's primary interest was Sánchez. Days after the *visita* was announced, Figueroa wrote Cobos that he would do what he could for Sánchez as Cobos requested, but the treasurer and his file had already left Naples as Sánchez appealed his case to the imperial court.

Figueroa was more concerned with the judicial purges than Sánchez's arrest.

> The city felt and feels that some articles [of the *visita*] violate their rights and those of the city and I believe they are going to send someone to His Majesty [to appeal]. The best persons they sent to the Court of Santa Clara have refused to accept their offices after seeing the judgment on their predecessors. The others named, they say confidentially, do not have the necessary qualifications. These have entered the council and, as much as can be judged, it [the court] is not reformed and those who are judged by it are in danger of being cheated. Time will tell for certain.[82]

Figueroa claimed the replacement of all the Vicaria judges was even more damaging. These judges implemented the rigorous enforcement of Toledo's reforms. 'In my judgment those [new appointees] of the Vicaria like those of the Santa Clara will cause notable disturbances of the public good and the good administration of justice and bring about the universal discontent of the kingdom.'[83]

In the spring and early summer of 1540 the correspondence between Charles and Toledo centred on finance. Charles wanted money from Naples to help defend Germany while the viceroy requested money from Charles because he could not pay his own troops. Of course the viceroy placed the blame on the *visita*. 'The Sommaria and the Treasury, the two principal instruments in this kingdom for raising money, are not what they ought to be.'[84] Toledo swore to Cobos 'by the life of my sons I say without emotion that the *visita* has caused more harm to His Majesty than if the Turkish fleet had come to this city.'[85]

The viceroy's initial strategy was to force a moderation of the *visita* by publishing its report and implementing it to the letter, thereby creating chaos in both the courts and treasury. (Both Valdés and Figueroa complained of the viceroy's initial rigour.) By May Toledo realized his tactic had failed. He now refused to replace the judges on the Vicaria. He removed only one and was determined not to let his authority be diminished further with Pamplona's appointments.[86] The Collateral Council sent Regent Figueroa and the Prior of Naples to the imperial court to argue for a moderation of the *visita*.[87] In addition Toledo sent ten or twelve thousand ducats to be distributed at court 'to bring to good terms the negotiation.'[88]

Still the viceroy seemed to be waging a losing battle. At first Charles claimed he was too busy with other matters to review the files of the *visita*.[89] On 11 May he wrote the viceroy that he had started reviewing the *visita*, but 'many serious and inconvenient passions' were stirred by the viceroy's publication of the report, and he ordered the viceroy to be more discreet with the matter in the future.[90] In July Charles placed Benavente in charge of Neapolitan finances to find money for troops. The viceroy exploded, 'I have asked him [Benavente] two or three times [how he would find funds] and until now he has told me nothing.'[91]

The emperor had heard enough and adjusted his viceroy's attitude with a stern letter. Toledo should expect no financial aid from outside Naples, and he had to keep troops prepared for Andrea Doria's fleet. In regard to the *visita*, Charles wrote that while some considered it unconstitutional, most accepted it: 'I will respond to all in time.'[92] Charles ordered Toledo to appoint a substitute for the treasurer and to proceed with Benavente's reform of the Sommaria. Toledo felt dishonoured. 'These particular negotiations I am unable to resolve and they are conducted without any respect to my person nor of my celebrated and well known services.'[93] The viceroy needed help.

Juan de Valdés knew how to ingratiate himself with powerful men like Cobos. 'I am always molesting Your Lordship, but seeing that you receive it so well I am as assured as if I had been a servant in your house my entire life.'[94] Valdés became a conduit of hope for Neapolitan officials.

> With the letter of Your Lordship of 30 July I received much favour and credit in regard to the results of that saintly *visita*. Your Lordship may know for certain that all with one voice say it is good that Your Lordship did not understand [the *visita*]. We are sure that if you had understood it there would have been a very different outcome more useful to the kingdom, of more service to His Majesty, and less prejudicial to individuals. Of this, as I say, all are certain, and the treasurer is particularly certain because Your Lordship knows how he has served.[95]

Valdés absolved Cobos of any responsibility for the *visita* and played to Cobos's sympathy for Sánchez. He then reminded Cobos that the courts were a disaster. 'Never have the tribunals of this kingdom had more need of reform than they have now after the provision of the *visita*, because I know that all are in confusion due to the lack of experience and poor letters of those who have been placed in them.'[96]

With subtle rhetoric Valdés finally persuaded Cobos to intervene in the *visita*. 'Of matters here I am unable to say much to Your Lordship except that these councillors are beginning to be content that the report of the Bishop of Pamplona will be moderated, otherwise God grant that we do not see ourselves attacked by the Turks.'[97] In mid-April 1541 Cobos thanked Valdés profusely for his advice about the *visita*.

> I know well that your counsel and industry have helped to reduce the weariness and weight of these negotiations.
>
> I am pleased that these councillors are appeased and contented with the good hope that you have given them about the report [of the *visita*].
>
> At least if His Majesty follows the opinion that I have sent about it, they should be totally satisfied that it was never my opinion that the matter be carried to the extremes it was.[98]
>
> I hope that you will attend to settling this in a manner satisfactory to all.[99]

Cobos had indeed finally taken the viceroy's side on the *visita*. Cobos wrote Pacheco in December 1540 a couple of months after Toledo had begun hearing appeals from dismissed officials.[100] The appeals were held up because Pacheco had the files and was slow to send them to Naples, leading Cobos to send a harsh letter to Pacheco:

> The viceroy writes of nothing else except his need of the files on those suspended and you ought to know more than anyone that here [in Valladolid] there are no files. I ask Your Lordship to see what is the problem and then to

send me the file on Treasurer Alonso Sánchez as soon as possible so that these poor officials do not receive more damage from the delay.

Your Lordship ought to have known the complaints your *visita* would engender among those officials in Naples. Particularly those in the kingdom complain that it undermined the regent of the Vicaria for two years and the judges for three, and judges on the Santa Clara have resigned.[101] His Majesty has finally written me about it as you can see from the copy of the letter I send with this one ... God grant that I can do what Your Lordship merits and what I desire.[102]

In February 1541 Cobos wrote Toledo that he wanted 'to remedy what was done to the judges of the Vicaria and I hope His Majesty will order the provision that I have written about it.'[103] Of course he ended his letter giving Sánchez his highest recommendation.

Sánchez would be saved. In May Juan Vázquez reported that Charles 'showed good will about aiding him [Sánchez] because it certainly seems the bishop had been very rigorous with him.'[104] Despite Sánchez's acquittal, Toledo asked that Charles not return him to Naples as treasurer because of his 'ill service.' He reminded Charles that Severino was also 'a good man and good servant but he was replaced.'[105] Thanks to Cobos, Sánchez would continue as treasurer till the eve of the next *visita* in 1552. From reading his formal defence in that *visita*, it seems that little changed in Neapolitan finance. Sánchez blamed incompetent collectors, the Sommaria, and military emergency for apparent problems. When these excuses did not suffice, he defended himself by claiming that he had been absolved of similar charges in the earlier *visita*.[106]

Charles's response to the *visita* was mixed. Some members of the imperial court blamed the rigour of the *visita* on a desire to free up offices. Idiáquez believed there were many 'persons who may obtain good offices by damaging him [Toledo].'[107] Benavente lobbied for a seat on the Collateral Council, but failing that he was satisfied with appointment as chief justice of the Sommaria.[108] Benavente had promised too much and delivered too little. In 1543 Toledo initiated his investigation, and in 1547 ordered his execution.[109] Aside from these appointments, Charles allowed the viceroy to select his own candidates for all other court positions, and Toledo's new judges had the responsibility of sentencing the officials accused of crimes in the *visita*.[110] Even Severino escaped punishment. He was appointed a judge on the court of Santa Clara, though Cobos instructed him to help re-establish order in the treasury as well.[111]

The viceroy's judicial authority was restored and his reforms aimed at taming the barony endured.[112]

Charles continued to press for the increased revenues Benavente promised. As early as February 1540 Toledo wrote there was no money to provision Doria's fleet, and in April he claimed that many civilians were dying due to the lack of grain.[113] The 1539 parliamentary grant of 285,000 ducats was difficult to collect and he doubted another could be passed before the grant's two-year term had ended. The viceroy then itemized his current expenses in support of the war, including artillery, construction or repair of fortifications, and the lodging of 6,000 troops. After listing the latter he added, 'It occurs to bring to your memory the 9,000 ducats promised to this Kingdom to pay people for having fed the Spanish infantry.'[114] The only non-military or non-diplomatic expense was the cost of the *visita*, 3,000 ducats a year. When Charles urged him to create new types of taxes, Toledo responded that parliamentary leaders considered it unconstitutional.[115] Charles pressured him into convoking the parliament in July 1540, but it denied additional aid for another year.[116]

Toledo wrote Charles in August 1540 that he was content with Charles's provisions for the *visita*. He even admitted that merchants rejoiced because in past years they had to pay thousands of ducats in excess taxes.[117] Yet he had refused to allow the scandal in the treasury to force him into shorting the pay of soldiers or arbitrarily increasing taxation. The viceroy offered his resignation again in February 1541. Rather than resenting his viceroy's strong will, Charles rewarded it by refusing the resignation and sending him a 'present' of 30,000 ducats. Toledo needed the funds, as he used 8,000 ducats of his own money to make ends meet until the next parliamentary grant in August 1541: an impressive 800,000 ducats.[118] For all the usual descriptions of Toledo as a stern master, he was very respectful of local institutions and concerned not to over-burden his subjects with taxes. Soon after he retired in 1553, his successor, Cardinal Pacheco, imposed a number of new extraordinary taxes.[119] Toledo deserved his nickname, 'the Great Viceroy.'

Without Valdés's intervention, Toledo might never have gained such a reputation. The viceroy was politically vulnerable in 1539, the year of the *visita*'s publication. His primary enemy among the Neapolitan barony was Alfonso d'Avalos, the Marquis of Vasto, brother-in-law of Ascanio Colonna. Vasto's appointment as governor of Milan in 1538 threatened Toledo's position in Italy. The following year Toledo's wife died and the fifty-nine-year-old viceroy began an association with the sister-in-law of his daughter. Threats from young Vincenza's irate husband were followed by his sudden demise, after which she moved into the viceroy's palace. The murder rumours emboldened Toledo's baronial enemies, who referred to his cold-blooded tyranny.[120] The *visita* gave Toledo's enemies a chance to unseat him, but Valdés's knowledge of the treasury enabled him to gain Cobos's support to moderate the *visita*'s effect on Neapolitan administration, thereby saving the viceroy's reputation and influence.

Valdés's service helped to establish the Toledo dynasty firmly in Italy. In late 1551 or early 1552 the viceroy's second son, García, married Ascanio Colonna's favourite daughter, Vittoria.[121] García would succeed the Bishop of Pamplona as Viceroy of Naples; Toledo's oldest son Pedro would later became Governor of Milan; and his third and youngest son, Luis, became *lugarteniente* of Siena. Two descendants of the viceroy's nephew, the Duke of Alba, would also serve as viceroys in Naples.[122] It is easy to understand why the viceroy gave Valdés's sodality a great deal of support.

Privanza and Clientage under Charles V

Prior to Castiglione's idealization, late medieval literature portrayed the courtier as a corrupt and vice-ridden individual in pursuit of anything but virtue.[123] Castiglione defended the ingratiating skills of the courtier by taking a cue from Machiavelli: the end would justify the courtier's means. The courtier should aspire to win the complete trust of the prince in order to be able to speak honestly to him and thus lead the prince to virtue.[124] However, influencing the prince required working through court factions and favourites, i.e., *privados*. With the reign of Ferdinand and Isabel, the Spanish crown began monopolizing most sources of patronage.[125] Access to royal favour meant aligning with a *privado*.[126] The misgovernment attributed to the fifteenth-century *privado* Alvaro de Luna and the aristocratic anarchy that followed his fall led Ferdinand and Isabel to remove the titled nobility from their governing councils. Thus an aspiring *privado* could not dominate both 'persons' of the king, i.e., the king as head of state, and the king as a person. Royal administration and the royal household would not again be dominated by a single *privado* until the rise of Ruy Gómez de Silva under Philip II.[127] Nevertheless, Cobos emerged as Charles's *privado* for administration and held a firm grip on royal patronage in Spain and Italy.[128]

Studies of royal favourites and patronage during the reigns of Philip II and Philip III shed light on Cobos's more limited *privanza*. According to James Boyden, Ruy Gómez de Silva became Philip II's *privado* in part because of Philip II's shyness and feelings of inferiority when he ascended the throne. In essence the outgoing Ruy Gómez helped correct a character flaw in the ruler.[129] Compared to previous Spanish rulers, Charles V was a spendthrift. His lavish court, constant travel, and ambitious foreign policies required vast amounts of money. The more Charles relied on Cobos to find the necessary resources, the tighter Cobos's hold on patronage became.

In his analysis of the Duke of Lerma's *privanza* under Philip III, Antonio Feros argues that *privados*, especially Lerma, furthered royal centralization.[130] Certainly the concentration of patronage in Cobos's hands led to a greater *esprit de corps* and efficiency in Spanish administration.[131] Like later *privados*, Cobos tried to remove potential rivals from Charles's presence and appointed his own relatives and *criados* to positions near him. However, in Valdés's case Cobos succeeded in removing him from court, but not from influence. How Juan survived Cobos's enmity to become his *criado* shows Cobos's adaptability in maintaining his *privanza*.

The bifurcation of the king's two persons did not make Charles schizophrenic. His court always included members from both his household and administration, and some individuals had positions in both. Like other rulers of the era, Charles had to have support from those who wielded power in local government.[132] Three of Juan's brothers were appointed *continos* in Charles's household because of the family's service to the Habsburg dynasty. Access to the king facilitated Diego's and Alfonso's appointments outside the royal household. Though Alfonso gained several administrative offices, his secretarial position was to Charles's person.[133]

Offices were often regarded as private property,[134] and in Juan's case Charles obviously had a sense of loyalty to his family. Juan inherited one of Alfonso's administrative posts, Archivist of Naples, but his acquisition of Alfonso's secretarial post implied that he also had inherited Alfonso's household position as a *contino*. Since Juan could not return to Spain, Cobos seized the opportunity to get rid of a potential threat to his *privanza*. However, even as Cobos engineered Juan's removal from the payroll as imperial secretary, Charles personally intervened to obtain satisfactory compensation for his archivist office. Valdés needed an avenue around Cobos to remind Charles of their relationship and his own abilities.

The Council of State was the only council of Charles dominated by aristocrats. Viceroy Toledo's father, Fadrique de Toledo, and his nephew, the Duke of Alba, were among this select group of advisers for foreign policy.[135] They naturally viewed Cobos, a poor *hidalgo* from Ubeda, as a usurper of their authority. Valdés gained Viceroy Toledo's support through his effective clientage to a number of influential Italian families, particularly the Medicis and the Gonzagas. Though Valdés was not always loyal to any of his patrons other than Charles, he certainly gained their trust and proved effective in promoting most of their interests. Thus Valdés avoided removal from imperial service by erecting a web of intelligence contacts and skilfully forwarding his information to Charles through the viceroy. The references to Juan's appointment as *contino* were probably reminders that Cobos did not control his service. Juan's reappointment as imperial secretary was unique in that it was not tied to service at court, nor could it be reviewed. Despite his subsequent disappearance from the imperial payroll again, Valdés seems to have held this shadowy position in Charles's personal service for the rest of his life. Celio Secondo Curione's letter, included in the first edition of Valdés's *Divine Considerations* (1550), identifies Valdés as a noble Spaniard 'of honoured office and illustrious knight [Cavaliere] of the Emperor.'[136] The various administrative offices he obtained were primarily intended to support his personal service to Charles.

Unable to remove Valdés, Cobos decided to make use of his extraordinary abilities and recommended his promotions even more strongly than Viceroy Toledo. Cobos's elevation of Juan to his direct service in late 1538 or early 1539 requires further explanation. Cobos did not seek Valdés's advice about the *visita* until February 1540, making the promotion unrelated to Neapolitan administration. After his negotiations at the Truce of Nice in 1538, Cobos no longer travelled with the court or advised the emperor about foreign policy.[137] However, he kept informed through his clients at court, and he sent directions to ambassadors in Italy to help carry out Charles's policies. Between 1538 and 1541 the emperor increasingly pressed for a religious compromise in Germany much like that advocated by Gattinara and Alfonso de Valdés. Granvelle led these negotiations, but as will be seen in the next chapter, Viceroy Toledo played a crucial role in preparing the ground for papal cooperation at the Diet of Regensburg in 1541. Cobos knew that Valdés's Italian connections and religious doctrines made him an important asset in these negotiations. Favourites and courtiers were painfully aware of factional strife that could erode their positions.[138] Since Charles had departed from Cobos's advice on foreign policy, bringing Valdés into Cobos's direct service may have been aimed at self-preservation. Though he initially viewed Valdés as a political enemy, Cobos came to realize that favouring Juan would strengthen his *privanza* rather than weaken it. Thus Cobos's favour of Giulia Gonzaga in her litigation with Isabella Colonna helped secure Valdés's allegiance to Cobos's *privanza*.

7 Regensburg Justification

The Diet of Regensburg was the nearest Charles V ever came to a religious settlement between his Lutheran and Catholic vassals in Germany, yet historians have almost universally dismissed it as an exercise in futility, a meeting 'significant only for what it failed to accomplish.'[1] Because it came close to a religious compromise, its objectives have been elevated beyond contemporary expectations. Charles's immediate goal was to re-establish religious peace in Germany in order to marshal his resources for defence against another massive Turkish invasion. After significant theological concessions from both sides, the diet agreed to supply Charles's brother Ferdinand with 10,000 infantry and 2,000 cavalry immediately, and to provide an additional 20,000 infantry and 4,000 cavalry for the next three years.[2] As a result, the Turkish invasion was repelled at Buda and Charles scraped together half a million ducats for an offensive assault on Algiers. Though storms turned the Algerian expedition into a disaster, the enterprise led Suleiman to withdraw to Constantinople, thereby relieving pressure on Hungary.[3]

Rather than considering Regensburg a failure, contemporaries expressed surprise at the diet's success, given the dismal results from previous diets and colloquies. After adjourning the diet, Charles wrote the Cardinal of Toledo that he 'had good negotiations about matters of faith which were placed in a good state and peace in Germany was established ... and also the aid given by the Empire to fight the Turks is very good.'[4] Secretary Idiáquez had no reason to colour the outcome of the diet when he wrote Cobos that 'good negotiations have been completed in the diet as there was little hope of accomplishing anything, particularly the emperor has gained some Lutheran princes.'[5] Given the nature of Valdés's service, his contributions to the Regensburg negotiations were subtle.

Neapolitan Diplomacy

Imperialists owed the limited success at Regensburg to the shrewd actions of Viceroy Pedro de Toledo. When Toledo recommended Valdés's reappointment as imperial secretary, he claimed that he was 'always advised by him.'[6] After Valdés returned to Naples in the autumn of 1535 he bemoaned the fact that the viceroy was very 'ill informed' about foreign affairs and he knew that Charles wanted Toledo to play a greater role in his diplomacy.[7] 'His Majesty wants the viceroy to have more understanding in all matters of state that may arise. ... I have no doubt that he will remain here with more authority than before.'[8] Juan assumed the responsibility of advising the viceroy on foreign policy to the extent of reading him ambassadors' reports for his response.[9]

The value of Valdés's advice to Toledo can be measured in the Florentine crisis of 1537. Alessandro de' Medici married Charles's daughter Margaret in February 1536, but he was assassinated on 5 January 1537. The Strozzi and the republican exiles quickly seized the opportunity to regain influence in Florence and initiated a revolt. By the terms of the 1529 Treaty of Bologna, should Alessandro die without a male heir Florence would escheat to Charles. Desiring to avoid foreign rule, the Florentine senate quickly elected Cosimo de' Medici from the younger branch of the family as the new head of state.[10]

In a letter to Cardinal Gonzaga six days after Alessandro's murder, Valdés expressed concern at Toledo's immediate response.

> This death of Duke Alessandro has great, evil stains on it, meaning it had to come from the most corrupt source. After the Señor Viceroy learned of the news he called together the Collateral Council to determine what should be done. ... The count [of Cifuentes, now envoy to Florence] writes that it would be a good thing to have people [soldiers] in case the outlaws of Florence wish to disturb the state ... and it seems that there are people in Rome who are collecting money for this. This señor [the viceroy] does not think that it is his responsibility to provide for Florence but rather Vasto [the commander of imperial forces in Lombardy]. Thus he does not wish to prepare men or to give money, saying that his only obligations are to defend the kingdom [of Naples]. I do not think this is good counsel; I do not know how it seems to Your Excellence.[11]

The viceroy's future would have been very different had he allowed Vasto, his arch-enemy among the Neapolitan barons, to dominate the Florentine succession. Valdés quickly changed Toledo's attitude about Florence, and on 16 February the viceroy expressed his support for Cosimo while Vasto, the governor of Milan, envoy Cifuentes, and the new Ambassador to Rome, the Marquis of Aguilar, all opposed him. Afterwards the viceroy, and no doubt Valdés, did all in their power to ensure Cosimo's succession.[12] Charles eventually decided to support Cosimo as well.

Spanish troops helped defeat Filippo Strozzi and the exile army in April. The next month Charles had Cifuentes recognize Cosimo as head of state. Paul III unsuccessfully pleaded with Charles for Strozzi's life, but placed greater emphasis on negotiating a marriage between Charles's daughter (Alessandro's widow) and his own grandson, Ottavio Farnese.[13] The pope's quick move on Margaret of Habsburg left Cosimo free to marry the viceroy's youngest daughter, Eleanor de Toledo. As a result, Florence became the viceroy's most important Italian ally and also a major centre of the 'Valdesian heresy.'[14]

Valdés cultivated anti-Farnese allies for the viceroy. The Medici, the Gonzagas, and the Colonnas all detested Paul III's marriage alliance with Charles because of their own dynastic ambitions. Valdés's ties to the Medici and Gonzaga have already been discussed, but his relationship with the Colonna merits closer inspection. No doubt Ascanio Colonna was aware of Valdés's work on Giulia Gonzaga's litigation with his troublesome cousin Isabella, and how that case affected his own suit with Isabella over the fortress of Paliano and other Colonna properties in the Papal States. Ascanio's sister, Vittoria Colonna, was a good friend of Giulia Gonzaga and attended Valdés's sodality when she visited Naples. The Colonna palace was very near Valdés's home in Chiaja. Vittoria won fame for her poetry and spirituality, and she used her influence in Rome to help the great humanist Pietro Bembo obtain a cardinal's cape in 1539.[15] She also spread Valdés's doctrines to the *spirituali* centre in Viterbo headed by Cardinal Pole, with whom she maintained a close association.

Perhaps Vittoria's influence led Ascanio Colonna to enter the Valdesian ranks as well. Diego Hurtado de Mendoza, the Spanish ambassador at the Council of Trent, singled out Ascanio as one of Valdés's leading disciples who 'always had the books of Valdés and read from them.'[16] Valdés's spiritual bonds with the Colonna illustrate the diplomatic significance of his sodality.

Valdés's standing with the viceroy continued undiminished at the time of the Regensurg diet. Giovanni Morone, the papal nuncio at Regensburg, testified before the Papal Inquisition that Valdés 'was not reputed heretical, in fact he was in great favour and very close to the Viceroy of Naples as I understood, that is don Pedro de Toledo.'[17] The memoirs of one of the founding members of the Jesuits, Nicolás de Bobadilla, also indicate Valdés's stature at the viceroy's court.[18] In January 1540 Bobadilla observed Valdés giving courtiers instruction on courtly behaviour, and freely answering theological questions.[19] Charles himself alluded to his trust in Valdés as late as July 1539. In briefing Ambassador Aguilar about Camerino, he identified Valdés's earlier service, noting that previously the matter 'was under the authority of a particular of the Church, nevertheless *a trusted person*, from the vicinity of Naples.'[20]

Charles's marriage alliance with the Farnese soon proved disappointing. The pope never provided the funds he promised for the Holy League, an anti-Turk naval alliance of Charles, the pope, and Venice, and it accomplished little more than a ten-month occupation of a fortress on the Dalmatian coast. Of course the cost of supplying, fortifying, and later ransoming the survivors of that ill-fated venture fell on Naples.[21] Similarly, Charles's attempt to buy papal cooperation by forcing the Duke of Urbino to sell Camerino to the pope as a dowry for Ottavio and Margaret bore little fruit in his religious negotiations in Germany.[22] As the Turkish threat intensified and the Holy League dissolved, Charles had to re-establish the religious peace in Germany broken by the Lutheran seizure of Württemberg in 1534.[23] To the pope's chagrin, the colloquies of Leipzig and Frankfurt in 1539 and Hagenau and Worms in 1540 edged slowly toward such a settlement. The pontiff blamed the colloquies for delaying the general council, condemned the Frankfurt Recess, and accused Charles of following Henry VIII's example of legislating religion.[24] He warned Charles against allowing his fear of the Turks to cause him to sanction Lutheran variations in Germany, 'because it is not easy to judge those who are the more contrary to Christ.'[25]

The chances for any imperial success at Regensburg seemed bleak. Ambassador Aguilar and imperialist cardinals pushed the nomination of Cardinal Contarini as papal legate to the diet, though there seemed little chance of his appointment. Having served as the Venetian ambassador to Spain, Contarini knew Charles well. He led the 1537 Papal Reform Commission and was a shrewd diplomat who opposed the use of force in religious matters. He was also a *spirituali* leader like Valdés.[26] Aguilar pointed out the advantage of Contarini vis-à-vis the Turks, but the pontiff refused to mention the Turkish war to the College of Cardinals. In dismay the ambassador wrote Charles that it was a certainty that Cardinal Neocastro would be appointed legate instead of Contarini.[27]

Given Paul III's staunch opposition to the German negotiations, historians have long puzzled over his selection of Contarini as legate to the Diet of Regensburg. Peter Matheson declares, 'the very fact of his [Contarini's] presence at the Diet cannot be wondered at enough.'[28] Heinz Mackensen goes so far as to suggest divine intervention: 'That he [Contarini] was placed at the very spot where the optimum conditions for concord came to prevail seems providential indeed.'[29] In this case providence assumed the form of Viceroy Pedro de Toledo.

Payments for Camerino and the cost of his army drove Paul III to raise the salt tax in the Papal States and to increase the levy on ecclesiastical benefices to two-tenths. The communes of the Papal States looked to Perugia's lead on the salt tax because they had always jealously defended their privileges. Perugia refused to pay the new salt tax in September 1539, citing a papal concession granted a century earlier.[30] Paul III intended to make an example of Perugia. The mobilization of papal troops to invade Perugia was a tremendous gamble, as Cosimo de' Medici openly supported the rebels. The viceroy restrained his son-in-law and surprisingly agreed to loan the pontiff Spanish troops to carry out the enterprise.[31] Once the troops were engaged, Charles demanded that his viceroy withdraw them without letting anyone know it was his order.[32] Twenty days after entering papal service, Toledo withdrew the forces for lack of payment even though the original agreement stated that the pope would pay the troops later.[33] After complying with Charles's command, the dutiful viceroy wrote the emperor that he wanted to be 'a true servant and vassal' as Charles spent 'time adjusting the affairs of Flanders and Germany in matters of faith that are so necessary.'[34]

Toledo withdrew the troops just as Paul III was selecting the papal legate for the Diet of Regensburg. Three weeks after the withdrawal of Spanish troops, Aguilar informed Charles that the pope had nominated Contarini as his legate.[35] On 27 May Toledo boasted to Cobos about his 'good dissimulation of the pope.'[36] On 20 June he reported that, with the exception of Ambassador Aguilar, 'all Your Majesty's ministers' thought the enterprise had gone well.[37] Charles now ordered his ambassador not to be 'so mild' in his discussions with the pope about Germany.[38] He should remind the pope that Charles had aided him in 'completing all that His Holiness wanted in temporal matters so afterwards all his attention would be occupied in spiritual matters ... [for the] common good of Christendom.'[39] After Contarini's nomination, Toledo sent his troops back into papal service in Perugia and suppressed the revolt. When Aguilar announced Contarini's nomination, he revealed a sense of papal anxiety by letting the emperor know the pope expected Charles to speak to the diet 'as a very Catholic prince who would look to the honour and authority of this Holy See.'[40]

The Perugia revolt demonstrated the unpopularity of new papal taxes, and Paul III's dependence on imperial troops to enforce those taxes. Since Charles's manipulation of the Perugian revolt succeeded in getting Contarini appointed legate, another tax revolt could be used to pressure Paul III to accept theological compromise at the diet. In February 1541 some of Ascanio Colonna's vassals refused to pay the salt tax in Rome, leading to their imprisonment. Ascanio responded by stealing 8,000 sheep and 101 cattle from papal lands neighbouring the papal salt pits in Ostia, and by fortifying Rocca di Papa in the hills south of Rome.[41] The pope demanded that Ascanio return the livestock, pay the salt tax, and appear before him within three days. Ascanio agreed to return the spoils and pay the tax if the pope would suspend his suit with his cousin Isabella Colonna, but he refused to go to Rome, offering his son's presence instead.[42]

Ascanio had no hope for success without imperial support.[43] He asked Viceroy Toledo to send him troops and to seek an official statement of imperial protection from Charles.[44] The viceroy sent troops, but it is not clear when he first gave the order. The pope believed that Toledo paid Ascanio's troops from the outset and that the rebellion would end if Toledo cut their pay and refused to let more troops leave Naples.[45] Aguilar tried to delay the conflict by asking the pope to give him three months for peace negotiations.[46] Instead he had only a week to convince Ascanio to surrender Rocca di Papa and submit to the pope's initial demands.

The viceroy claimed the pope's use of force against Ascanio 'is not conducive to the service of God, of His Holiness, His Majesty, nor the universal good of Christendom'; Paul III responded that his only motive was 'the security of the apostolic see.'[47] Aguilar complained to Charles that the viceroy had allowed troops to leave Naples and that they carried a message to Cardinal Farnese saying 'they would give to

Ascanio as many people as he wanted.'[48] Soon after, Aguilar must have been informed of Charles's support for Ascanio, as two weeks later he wrote the emperor in cipher that though the pope claimed that Ascanio's fortress of Paliano was about to fall, 'I do not believe he will take it if the viceroy of Naples has provided it as he has written. ... It will be very difficult and cause the pope to double what he has.'[49]

Charles wanted to keep Paliano from the pope, at least for the time being. On 7 April Ascanio asked Antonio de Bijar for money to raise more troops.[50] Bijar notified Toledo, who had already written Charles asking permission to aid Ascanio.[51] Before Charles could respond, six hundred soldiers arrived by sea to join Ascanio; according to Aguilar, they were vassals of the viceroy.[52] Ascanio claimed to have a letter from the viceroy that 'counselled him not to surrender his forces to the pope in any manner.'[53] Fortunately for the viceroy, Charles supported the reinforcement of Ascanio. Paliano was to be placed in Charles's hands before being sent to the courts for final adjudication. Ascanio should pay a moderate indemnity for damages and recognize the authority of the pope, who would in turn pardon Ascanio. To achieve these goals the viceroy was ordered 'to have a hand in the conservation of the said house [of Colonna].'[54]

Aguilar felt that the viceroy was not keeping him informed: 'I am begging you to advise me your view of this ... and not to treat me in this as you did the Count of Cifuentes.'[55] Toledo responded that he was just following orders; Charles had instructed negotiators with Ascanio not to report to the ambassador.[56] Toledo hinted at the actual reason for reinforcing Paliano:

> Considering the state the affairs of Christendom are in, from the advice returned by his [the pope's] legate near His Majesty, and from the congregation of the princes of Germany, His Holiness will submit to what His Majesty orders. And you and I, for our part, are thus to deliver Paliano to His Majesty for consideration as to how it would be made into total obedience to His Holiness, as is reasonable, with the securities discussed.[57]

Because of the threat of imperial intervention and another sack of Rome, Charles and Contarini were free of papal interference at Regensburg. After Charles had selected moderate members for the theological colloquy, the pope congratulated the emperor on his 'good management' of the diet.[58] When discussions bogged down in mid-May, Contarini asked the pope for advice should Charles leave the diet in

Ferdinand's hands to prepare his assault on the Turks. According to Aguilar, the pope left the decision entirely up to Charles. 'If the diet remained in terms that might give hope for a good conclusion he [Contarini] should remain with Your Majesty's consent and if it is different then he should return with Your Majesty and in whatever case he should act with the consent of Your Majesty.'[59] By mid-May Charles had wrung all the concessions out of Contarini and the diet that he could get. Ascanio surrendered Paliano on 26 May and Contarini received a papal reprimand for his negotiations two weeks later.

In 1539 Charles appointed Cobos Contador Mayor, i.e., Chief Accountant, and most of his energy afterwards was employed in refinancing loans to fund Charles's wars and avoid Castilian bankruptcy.[60] More than anyone, Cobos knew Charles could ill afford a religious war in Germany. He wrote Aguilar in February 1541 that the negotiations at Regensburg were of 'utmost importance.'[61] He also seemed well informed about the relationship between Ascanio's war and the negotiations. At a crucial moment in the conflict in mid-April, he ordered Ambassador Aguilar to be more cooperative and to send him information about the course of the revolt because it affected 'negotiations of the faith [i.e., the Diet of Regensburg].'[62]

Because of the hostility caused by the *visita*, the viceroy would not have shared such delicate information with Cobos, and Charles kept very quiet about the matter. Though the correspondence has not been uncovered, it seems likely that Valdés provided Cobos information connecting the negotiations in Regensburg with Ascanio's revolt. After Ascanio's surrender, Cobos wrote both Ambassador Aguilar and the Marquis of Vasto, the governor of Milan since 1538, to use their influence to gain clemency for the Colonna leader.[63] The same day Cobos wrote a conciliatory letter to the viceroy effusively praising his service, particularly his work with Ascanio.[64]

The Valdesian Sodality and Double Justification

Through interconnected sodality members, Valdés's influence extended to the *spirituali* beyond Naples. Among the most influential *spirituali* were Cardinals Contarini, Jacobo Sadoleto, Reginald Pole, Pietro Bembo, Frederigo Fregoso, Abbot Gregorio Cortese, Master of the Sacred Palace Tomasso Badia, and the papal nuncio at Regensburg, Giovanni Morone. By the time the Regensburg Diet convened, Contarini was in regular communication with many of Valdes's closest disciples, particularly Vittoria

Colonna, Marcantonio Flaminio, and Pietro Martyr Vermigli. Vermigli and Flaminio served Contarini as theological advisers.[65] Contarini read some of Valdés's writings and was impressed with them.[66] Valdés also continued to have influence in Rome, as Cobos asked him in April 1541 to use his clout in the ecclesiastical courts to protect Gonzalo Pérez's prebends from a lawyer for the Roman curia. Perez kept the disputed prebends, indicating both Valdés's influence and the close relationship he had established with Cobos.[67]

Between 1538 and 1541 Valdés produced a massive body of religious writing, ostensibly to help teach Spanish, but also to complement and support Charles's religious colloquies in the north. First he composed a translation of and commentary on Romans, the Pauline letter that led Luther to his doctrine of justification by faith alone.[68] In his dedication to Giulia he lays out his scheme for Giulia's approach to God first by seeing how David imitated God, and then how Paul imitated Christ. Afterwards she could more easily comprehend the gospels.[69] Valdés wrote his commentary for a wide circulation, not just for Giulia. 'I also want this work to be helpful to all persons who will read it, and not to offend any, even in the smallest matter.'[70]

His desire not to offend anyone indicated his role as a religious conciliator. Immediately after announcing his intention, Valdés related his favourite story about rebellion and reconciliation. A king banished several of his vassals for rebelling against him.[71] The king decided to forgive them so he sent his son to proclaim the pardon even though the rebels had taken service with the king's enemy. Some of the former vassals did not recognize the son; some refused to believe the pardon; others rejected it, not wanting to admit their former guilt; while one group took gifts and presents back to the king because of their uncertainty about the indulgence. None of these vassals gained forgiveness. Only those who completely trusted in the king's love and confidently returned were pardoned: the king rewarded these vassals as if they had never rebelled. Like his brother Alfonso, Juan characterized Charles's offers to return Protestant princes to the fold as providentially inspired.

Valdés focused nearly all his attention on the doctrine of justification by faith, and apparently did not venture too far from orthodox Catholicism beyond that doctrine. Niccolo Balbani's *Life of Galeazzo Caracciolo*, published in Geneva in 1587, presents a Protestant view of Valdés and his disciples. He noted that Valdés was a Spanish knight who came to Naples with 'some knowledge of the truth of the Gospel, and especially of the Doctrine of justification.'[72] However, Valdés and his disciples 'knew as yet no more in religion but the point of Justification, and misliked [sic] and eschewed some abuses in Popery and nevertheless still frequented Popish Churches, heard Masses, and were present ordinarily at vile idolatries.'[73]

Valdés's interpretation of justification in his commentary on Romans is closer to Cardinal Contarini's Regensburg doctrine of double justification than to Luther's justification by faith alone. The crucial passage for Luther was Romans 1:17, 'the just will live by faith.' Valdés interpreted this passage to mean that only those who truly believe are just and come to a comprehension of God, but it was not a one-time experience. 'Accordingly as the man goes on to increase his faith, he increases mortification and invigoration, coming to understand the justice of God through the acceptance of the gospel, understanding that faith in faith means increasing and confirming the faith.'[74] In the equally crucial chapter 3, Valdés appears to move closer to Luther's interpretation. 'Only to those who believe does he [God] communicate his justice, which makes them just as he is just; not because of works, but only because by truly believing rather than works are they accepted by God as just.'[75]

However, Valdés clarifies his position in chapter 4. God 'imputed' faith to Abraham before his circumcision, making his circumcision a 'certification of his justification by faith.'[76] Those who imitated Abraham's belief in God also imitated the circumcision. This imitation was the same as 'walking in the steps of faith.'[77] The profession of belief had to be followed by 'steps of faith.' Valdés refused to give up free will. 'If [as Paul wrote] those who love God are aided by all things for the good, they are also aided by the forces and labours of their free will.'[78] Later in the same work he clearly alludes to the ability of free will to advance the Christian to a greater level of faith. 'The regenerate, those renovated by the Holy Spirit, in using their free will are able to increase themselves in faith, and increase themselves in the love [of God].'[79] If they were heedless then they would decline in faith and perfection.

Valdés's *Commentary on Romans* must have achieved the wider circulation he sought, as henceforth none of his works would have a dedicatory letter to Giulia Gonzaga by name. He had established a position independent of her fame. His 1539 *Commentary on First Corinthians* is introduced with a letter 'To The Christian Reader' in which he stresses the duty of all Christians to know what God expects of them by reading and studying Scripture.[80] The work complemented his frequent discussion of rebellion and reconciliation with a critique of Protestant sectarianism, a significant departure from the *Dialogue on Christian Doctrine* and the *Christian Alphabet*. He stressed the need for Christian unity by developing the Pauline/Erasmian concept of the mystic body of Christ. According to Valdés, Paul's letter to the Corinthians clearly laid down 'rules and precedents for returning to the obedience of truth those who have left, or are about to leave the unity of the Church by giving ear to false prophets.'[81] True Christians were members of the same body. 'Since you are members of the same body, keep in mind that there is in you but one will and one opinion; and one language with which that will and that opinion is expressed.'[82]

Elsewhere in this commentary Valdés penned his most virulent criticism of sectarianism.

> These same partialities, which engender envying, and contentions, are seen to be very widespread in our days, and more among those who make the greatest profession of spirituality. But actually these prejudices derive from their being men of the world, which they hide under a species of religion and piety; which is all the more pernicious as it is the mortal enemy of Christian piety, which is all love and charity, all union and conformity.[83]

Valdés suspected that sectarianism had as much to do with worldly matters as with religion. His emphasis on love and charity rather than faith in his criticism of sectarianism is quite revealing. According to Valdés, all who followed a mere mortal on all points of theological debate (like Lutherans and Calvinists) violated Christian liberty and were unworthy of being considered free men.[84]

Commenting on Corinthians chapter 13, Valdés developed his view of the inextricable nature of faith, love, and charity in great detail. He begins by identifying love and charity as the same thing. 'By charity he [Paul] means the loving affection you have for God, and for Christ, and for the things of God and Christ that you have accepted from the grace of the gospel, loving God as yourself, and loving things that are of God, not for themselves, but for God. I understand this loving affection in the man is from the Holy Spirit, and it is as great as his faith. ... between them there is no more difference than between the root and the fruit of a tree. Faith is the root, and charity is the fruit.'[85] Even if he had the faith to move mountains, Valdés wrote that without charity, 'I will not be anything, nor would I be of any worth.'[86] He continued to extol the effects of divine love: 'No one is moved by the love of God without exercising charity: and this is the reason why Paul gives such great glory to charity.'[87]

Valdés's two commentaries on Paul's letters gained widespread recognition just after the Diet of Regensburg, suggesting they were among the works Flaminio sent to Morone and Contarini during the Regensburg negotiations.[88] In December 1541, Vittoria Colonna wrote Giulia Gonzaga, 'I understand that your Ladyship has sent the Commentary on St Paul, which was very much wanted, and especially by me who have most need of it.'[89] Vittoria was in Viterbo and the language of the letter indicates that Cardinal Pole's group wanted to study Valdés's work. Later in Carnesecchi's trial Vittoria was identified as having received a copy of Valdés's *Commentary on Romans*.[90] These commentaries remained popular in Italy throughout the era of the Council of Trent and were translated into Italian and published in Venice in 1556 and 1557 respectively.

Valdés's *One Hundred Ten Divine Considerations* were not compiled until after his death. Two different Italian versions circulated in manuscript with different enumeration of the considerations.[91] However, Boehmer's discovery in Vienna of thirty-nine 'Divine Considerations,' the only ones known in the original Spanish, along with seven additional doctrinal letters suggests that these works may have been sent to Germany during the Regensburg diet. The three letters to Giulia, including his critique of Protestant prudence in studying Scripture, have already been discussed. Other tracts continued his argument for the inextricable nature of faith and charity, i.e., love, and the pre-eminence of the latter. In fact that is the title of one tract, 'Of the Nature of Those Three Gifts of God, FAITH, HOPE, and CHARITY ... and the Pre-eminence of Charity.' Faith is the belief in the promises in Scripture; hope is the patience to await the fulfilment of those promises; and charity consists in love of God and Christ, and the things of God and Christ. But of the three gifts, love is pre-eminent because one cannot truly have faith or hope unless he finds pleasure in them; thus charity 'maintains and sustains the other two.'[92]

Valdés rarely mentioned papal authority, but one consideration uncovered by Boehmer has a defence of the papal office. Valdés likened the pope's position in the body of Christ to the role of the soul in man. The body's mode of existence derived from the soul that governed the members, making sure each one performed the particular service for which it was created. 'It is quite enough for me to see and consider the presence of the pope, his careful provision, his goodness, liberality and justice, so far as he keeps his establishment in good order and well regulated.'[93] Valdés makes a point of justifying the papal office with 'human reason,' implying it was a human creation, and a rational necessity for the proper administration of the Church. He also includes a personal reflection, saying that just as when the soul leaves the body, the body is no longer of service, so when a pope or cardinal dies, all the officials of their house no longer have service.[94] Scholars who claim Valdés completely denied papal authority should consider that the prebend system depended on that authority, and Valdés enjoyed the comfortable life his prebends helped support.

In other *Divine Considerations*, Valdés continued to stress the union of works and faith. He focused on the issue most clearly in the one entitled 'In What Way That It Is to Be Understood which Holy Scripture Declares, Attributing Condemnation at One Time to Unbelief, and at Another to Wicked Works; Attributing Salvation at One Time to Faith, and at Another to Works.'[95] In it Valdés cites numerous verses on each side of the works-versus-faith argument, then denies their inconsistency. Unlike Luther, Valdés would not rank Scripture. Only individuals dependent on the Holy Spirit could comprehend the consistency because faith and works could not be separated.

Only after the Christian accepts the covenant of justification secured through Christ's death would he be capable of good works not aimed at self-interest or self-glorification. After the onset of the experience of regeneration, individuals will pursue Christian charity 'in order to confirm their calling and work out their salvation.'[96] The key to Valdés's doctrine in this consideration is love: 'In working they work purely for the love of God.'[97] In another consideration he wrote, 'the love they have to God is as great as is the knowledge they have of God.'[98] Thus faith and charity are both manifestations of the love of God. 'I understand it to be from this yearning affection that it comes to pass that a man loves God beyond everything, loving everything for God's sake; all creatures in general because they are his creatures; all mankind, because they are God's creatures, and because it is His will that man should love his neighbour.'[99]

In 1545 Giulia Gonzaga arranged for the publication of three of Valdés's works in Italian translation. The *Christian Alphabet* with the tract on self-examination as an appendix was published in Venice. Both were written specifically for Giulia, so her affection for Juan may have prompted their selection. The third work was a small collection of Valdés's writings completed just before his death and was therefore attentive to Regensburg negotiations. The five tracts were published in Rome under the title of the first tract, *The Mode of Teaching and Preaching the Principle of the Christian Religion*.[100] Only the fifth tract is taken from another work, *Commentary on Romans*.[101] Eduard Boehmer discovered an earlier hand-written manuscript of the same under the general title 'On Christian Penitence, Christian Faith and Christian Living.' In the first tract of the work Valdés included the longest version of his favourite allegory, the king's pardon of rebellious vassals. It seems unlikely he would have written such a tract just for Giulia, as she would have heard and read it many times before. The publication of the entire work in Rome suggests that Giulia thought it could influence the discussion of justification at the Council of Trent.

The first tract of the work emphasizes loving God and incorporation into the body of Christ. Valdés then adds a confusing statement about faith and works: 'Justification and glorification are through faith, and the better treatment, as well in this life as the other, is for works; not for all, but for those which are the fruit of faith.'[102] Apparently works aided the Christian both on earth and in the heavenly hierarchy. In order to emphasize that works mattered, Valdés focused on the issue in the next two tracts, 'Upon Justification By Faith Without Works' and 'A Second Tract Upon Justification By Faith Without Works.' The former is a letter addressed 'To my most worthy master in Christ.'[103] The form of address seems to imply it was sent to someone well versed in Scripture and of higher social rank. Perhaps Valdés initially wrote it to someone at Regensburg, or Rome, to help support Contarini's doctrine of double justification. In the tract Valdés wrote that the gift of faith cannot be realized without works just as light cannot be separated from a flame.[104] In the second treatise on justification, he defines faith as 'the instrumental cause of justification,'[105] but it is still inseparable from charity; otherwise you have the absurdity of Paul refuting James's claim that faith without works is worthless. Just as Abraham's offering up Isaac 'concurred' his faith, so charity validated the Christian's faith.[106]

In the fourth tract, Valdés asserts that 'faith of itself is sufficient for our salvation,'[107] but 'it is by the path of good works that one walks to the inheritance of glory and immortality.'[108] The last tract, 'Tract Upon Christian Assurance, Upon Justification and Glorification,' clarifies these confusing statements by emphasizing the love of God. Valdés criticizes 'New Testament authorities' (Calvinists?) for teaching that doubt and fear are commendable. Fear represents the Jewish spirit, but knowledge of the Gospel brings assurance of divine love. Though there is always room for improvement and one can never be completely righteous, one need not fear. Salvation is like an inheritance from a loving father; works will not merit it because if all our works were judged we would all be damned. Thus, 'the bad works our frailty commits, are not imputed to us ... and our good works, though imperfect and blemished, are grateful to and accepted of God, and are remunerated by him, because He considers us, not for that which we are in ourselves, but for what we are in Christ.'[109] Taken as a whole, this publication presented Valdés's strongest argument for a compromise position between Protestants and Catholics on the relation of works and faith.

Opposition to sectarian division did not hinder Valdés from criticizing the Church hierarchy. Valdés's *Commentary on Matthew* was probably only in draft form at the time of his death. At least a couple of copyists worked over it, violating some of Valdés's linguistic rules,[110] and it remained unpublished until its discovery in the late nineteenth century. Yet it is an important complement to his earlier works, clarifying Valdés's view of the ideal Church. The true leaders in the body of Christ should be those who evidenced the greatest degree of perfection by imitating Christ. These leaders would distribute 'the mysteries of God' to the ability of each person who had accepted the pardon offered in the gospel.[111] They would not be worldly but humble. They would not make a show of their spiritual dignity; rather they would present themselves as equals to other men.[112] Whenever two or more of the faithful met to discuss Christ, the 'power of the keys' was present in the congregation.[113] This was a purely spiritual power to communicate the treasures of divinity. The divinely inspired would offer instruction free of charge because Christ told the disciples to work for a living.[114]

With this criterion Valdés lambasted the hierarchy of the Church. He noted that the leaders of the Jewish religion arrested Christ. 'And here I understand how little I can give credit to those who are the leaders of the Christian religion among men who are not also leaders of God.'[115] In his view, a worldly hierarchy produced worldly clergy who could not move the hearts of men because God had not sent them.[116] Although Valdés accepted the necessity of papal authority for administrative purposes, he rejected the Petrine Theory by interpreting Matthew 16:18 in an Erasmian mode.[117] Christ established his Church on the 'rock' of faith exemplified by Peter's confession of faith.[118] The papacy was created by human reason, and therefore subject to human reason for reform.

According to Valdés, God communicated his secrets to men slowly and forced them to strive harder through study and contemplation.[119] 'God had placed reason in man, in order that he, by it, may know

God.'[120] Human reason, aided by God's grace, must be employed in the pursuit of perfection. Concluding his *Commentary on Romans*, Valdés wrote that his understanding of Scripture came primarily from prayer and consideration, aided by the Holy Spirit, personal experience, and daily reading.[121] He commented that the statement in Jeremiah 31: 33–4, that the law would be 'written in their hearts,' resembled Plato's doctrine of innate ideas at birth being awakened later by study. Juan went on to postulate that an initial calling by faith would be more fully revealed afterwards by studying and imitating the life of Christ.[122]

Historians are divided in their opinion of Valdés's influence on Contarini. Some say Contarini drew much of his theology directly from Valdés,[123] while others emphasize Contarini's personal experience and the general influence of the *spirituali*, including Valdesians.[124] Valdés had been searching for a compromise position on faith and works since his *Dialogue on Christian Doctrine*, and given his stature among the *spirituali*, Contarini must have been quite familiar with his doctrines before Regensburg. As previously noted, Flaminio sent Morone some of Valdes's writings and he passed them on to Contarini during the diet.[125] Contarini also knew his appointment as legate was due to the imperialists. That Valdés's writings were taken to Regensburg and examined by Contarini at that crucial juncture argues for the cardinal's use of Valdés's works in his formulation of the Regensburg doctrine of double justification. Later the Papal Inquisition would view Valdés's position on justification and the Regensburg doctrine as one and the same.[126]

On 21 April the Diet of Regensburg agreed to Charles's selection of three Catholic and three Protestant theologians for a colloquy to discuss religious doctrine.[127] Contarini met daily with the Catholic theologians, and he crafted the Regensburg doctrine of double justification.[128] The core of the doctrine was the inextricable nature of faith and love, just as in Valdés's writings. Christ's crucifixion 'imputes' righteousness to those who have faith in God's promises. This leads to Christian love and charity, 'inherent righteousness,' through which we partake of the divine nature.[129] Works were rewarded 'to the degree that they flow from faith.'[130] Thus moral indifference was avoided as well as any contractual notion of binding God to reward merit. The double justification doctrine won unanimous acceptance by the colloquy on 3 May. For a brief moment it appeared that the pivotal doctrinal issue separating Catholics and Lutherans had been resolved. Even John Calvin accepted the article as containing 'the essence of true doctrine.'[131]

As soon as the doctrine passed, Contarini sent a copy of it to Cardinal Gonzaga in Rome to build support for it in the College of Cardinals.

Almost simultaneously a number of Valdés's disciples left Naples for Rome. Carnesecchi, Flaminio, and Donato Rullo went to Cardinal Gonzaga's palace, and Marcantonio Villamarina appeared at Morone's home, even though Morone was still in Germany.[132] On 8 June Paul III criticized double justification for being unclear, providing a 'mere semblance of concord.'[133] The pontiff reprimanded Contarini for his lack of secrecy and his failure to defend papal authority. The pope was so concerned about the potential appeal of double justification to reform-minded cardinals that he refused to have it read in consistory.[134] Contarini admitted the doctrine might appear ambiguous to some, but that it was entirely Catholic. He also wrote to Cardinals Bembo and Pole about the doctrine and his views of justification.[135]

The price of Paul III's military victory over Ascanio Colonna was the awkward legacy of the Regensburg agreements. The pope wanted neither compromise with nor toleration of Protestantism, but the recess of the diet provided for a little of both. Religious discussions were remitted to a future general council. If the council was not convoked these matters were to be discussed at a national council or imperial diet within eighteen months. In the latter case, the pope was to send a legate with 'sufficient power.' The general council was to meet in Germany and 'the emperor ought to have a hand in it with His Holiness.'[136] The Lutherans consented to be bound by the agreed-upon articles, including double justification, in return for the continuation of the Peace of Nürnberg's legal toleration of Protestantism.

Alonso Sánchez, who was with the imperial court at Regensburg, wrote Cobos on the first of July that Charles planned to go to Naples after the diet adjourned.[137] On the twelfth Charles informed the diet that the Turks planned to attack Italy and that he would go there, departing no later than the twenty-fourth.[138] He did not go to Naples, but six days after he arrived in Italy Cardinal Gonzaga visited him in Modesta on the sixteenth of August. Eleven days later Gonzaga and Contarini met with Charles at Mantua.[139] Since Carnessechi, Flaminio, and Rullo were at Gonzaga's palace in Rome, it seems likely that Valdés's doctrines and Regensburg were part of their discussions. Unfortunately, Valdés had died the first of August at the peak of his fame and influence.

Epilogue: Valdés's Death and the Valdesian Heresy

The activity of Valdés's leading disciples just before and soon after his death suggests that their master prepared to use his influence in Rome for the justification debate. In his biography of Giulia Gonzaga, Christopher Hare claimed that Viceroy Toledo broke up Valdés's circle shortly before Juan's demise after being warned by his brother Juan de Toledo, the Cardinal of Burgos.[140] Circumstantial evidence seems to corroborate the assertion.

Close analysis of the official references to Valdés's death shows that the viceroy was uncharacteristically laconic about Valdés and his service. In early December of 1541 Cobos wrote the viceroy just as Charles returned to Spain from his disastrous expedition against Algiers. He thanked the viceroy for his provision of the armada, then noted that he had just been informed of Valdés's death in August. He made the viceroy aware that he knew when Valdés died, who was his executor, and who was his primary heir, the son of *regidor* Andrés de Valdés. He asked the viceroy to have Juan's executor forward the memorial to him. Cobos effusively praised Valdés's service and clearly wanted to ensure that Valdés's last wishes were carried out. Toledo had written Cobos on 20 September, a month and a half after Valdés's death.[141] Since both Cobos and Toledo valued Valdés's service, one must wonder why the viceroy did not inform Cobos of his passing in that message.

Toledo replied to Cobos's request on 7 January, 'With this I send Your Lordship the testament of Juan de Valdés, how he ordered matters of his estate and his soul, it is all completed.'[142] The next day Alonso Sánchez also wrote Cobos, 'With this I send to Your Lordship the memorial that you ordered me to send to you about the affairs of Valdés who is in glory.'[143] Given all Valdés's accomplishments, the viceroy's terse reply seems suspicious. Obviously Cobos did not trust the viceroy to implement Valdés's last wishes, as he had Sánchez send him a copy of the testament as well.

Valdés died after suffering from a fever. Soon afterwards, one of his disciples, Benedetto Cusano, died of fever as well. Pietro Martyr Vermigli barely survived it, but left Naples as soon as he recovered, perhaps fearful for his life.[144] Vittoria Colonna wrote Giulia Gonzaga in December 1541 urging her to leave Naples for the security of Gonzaga estates in Lombardy. 'It would assuredly be fitting that your Ladyship should revisit your country in Lombardy for a little, now that you are so well instructed about the celestial country.'[145] Between the lines Vittoria indicated that Naples might be unsafe.

The viceroy clearly had withdrawn his protection of Valdés's disciples. After Giulia Gonzaga abandoned her convent in the spring of 1541 to take charge of young Vespasiano, she moved into her spacious Neapolitan palace, Borgo delle Vergine, and presided over a court focused on artistic and literary discussions. Though she maintained contact with Carnesecchi, Vittoria Colonna, and other reform friends, she made no attempt to re-establish a *spirituali* group in Naples.[146] In 1542 Giulio Terenziano, a Neapolitan theology teacher and disciple of Valdés, was thrown into prison for his religious views. Ochino and Vermigli now made plans to flee to safer, Protestant lands.[147] Before leaving, Ochino visited Contarini, only to find him on his deathbed, rumoured to have been poisoned. Ochino wrote Vittoria Colonna of his intentions on 22 August 1542, and Ascanio Colonna loaned him a horse and a servant to aid his escape the next day.[148] Valdés's writings and his followers were under investigation. An agent of Cardinal Gonzaga wrote in September 1542 that 'the Inquisition may examine the writings of Valdés through and through, but concerning Pole and his companions the best opinion prevails.'[149]

Cardinal Pole had great stature in Rome and would come within four votes of the papal throne in 1549.[150] He refused to defend Contarini's double justification in Rome and left the city in May 1541, avoiding the controversial doctrine.[151] The next month Contarini wrote Cardinal Bembo that Pole 'could not have been absent at a more inopportune moment.'[152] Valdés's disciples remained in Rome, and their placement reveals that their master was calling in favours for the justification debate. In addition to those in the homes of Gonzaga and Morone, Bonfadio suddenly appeared as a favourite of Cardinal Ridolfi, and Vittore Soranzo became a familiar of Cardinal Bembo. Cardinals Bembo, Ridolfi, and Fregoso would support Contarini's doctrine.[153]

Cardinals opposed to any compromise on the doctrine of justification were led by Gian Pietro Carafa, after 1549 Pope Paul IV, and Juan de Toledo, the viceroy's brother. One has to suspect some political posturing over double justification, as Pole, Carafa, and Toledo were the three leading contenders in the 1549 conclave.[154] According to Carafa and Toledo, heresy had begun to flood Italy, and there was only one remedy for Contarini and his ilk, re-establishing the Papal Inquisition. They first trumpeted the call for inquisitorial action in July 1541, just prior to Valdés's death, and within a year Carafa and Toledo became co-leaders of the Inquisition.[155] After Contarini's demise in 1542, only Cardinal Bembo continued to champion double justification at the papal court.[156]

Valdés's disciples found themselves in a difficult situation. Their master was dead; Naples was no longer safe; a majority of cardinals opposed compromise on justification; and the Inquisition was coming. Pole's home was a logical place for them to regroup. A month after

Valdés's death his leading disciples began gravitating to Pole's home in Viterbo. Flaminio, Carnessechi, Rullo, Soranzo, and Vittoria Colonna eventually convinced Pole to accept Valdés's position on justification.[157] Pole's stature gave them protection, and they succeeded in encouraging him to rejoin the justification debate. Pole's group was actually more responsible for the Valdesian heresy than Valdés, as they employed mass propaganda rather than the 'cautious' and personal methods for which Valdés was famed.[158]

The rapid spread of Valdés's doctrines beyond Spanish-speaking members of the Italian elite began only after his death. It started with the 1543 publication of *The Benefit of Christ*, a work co-authored by Flaminio prior to the Diet of Regensburg. It was the first Valdesian work published in Italy and it was the first written in Italian. The book garnered the praise of Contarini, Pole, Morone, and Cortese.[159] It presented Valdesian justification in its simplest form. Faith enables the will to be capable of good works and permits the Christian to come to knowledge of Christ. The nuance of the union of faith and works is referred to as clothing oneself in Christ, i.e., studying and imitating Christ's life to achieve 'the perfections through which we regain the image of God.'[160] In Pole's home Valdés's writings were read and discussed in conjunction with the works of Luther and Calvin. The 'Valdesianism' of Pole's circle was doctrinally more radical and more inflexible than Valdés's Neapolitan sodality.[161]

Whether Valdés's position on justification was closer to Contarini's or Pole's matters less than the fact that Valdés was labelled as the primary culprit in the justification heresy in Italy. The Papal Inquisition did not investigate, try, and execute individuals for Pole-ism, or Contarini-ism, but it certainly did for Valdesianism. Since he was dead, Valdés could not defend himself. He was not a cardinal; he was not even an Italian. According to Massimo Firpo, 'the crisis of Italian evangelism' occurred between May of 1541 and July 1542, between Contarini's doctrine of double justification and the establishment of the Papal Inquisition.[162] With Valdés dead and his writings and followers under inquisitorial scrutiny, the die was already cast for Valdés's notorious reputation as a heretic even though the final verdict awaited the Council of Trent.

Giulia Gonzaga corresponded with members of Pole's group, but she did not attend it. Instead she sought the favour of Charles V and simultaneously arranged for the publication of Valdés's writings. In November 1544 Giulia wrote Charles asking him to employ her nephew

Vespasiano in his service, and the emperor agreed to make him a page of Prince Philip. Philip also favoured Vespasiano, and he would serve the Spanish crown with some distinction until his retirement in 1557.[163] About the same time as she requested Vespasiano's appointment, Giulia sent some of Valdés's writings to Marcantonio Magno for translation into Italian, and other tracts to Flaminio to do the same. As a result, the *Christian Alphabet* (1545), *The Mode of Teaching and Preaching the Principle of the Christian Religion* (1545), *Commentary on Romans* (1556), and *Commentary on First Corinthians* (1557) were all published in Italian translation during the first two sessions of the Council of Trent.[164]

At the first session Bartolomé de Carranza joined Pole's and Valdés's disciples.[165] A brief review of Carranza's relationship with Valdés suggests that despite allegations of heresy, Valdesianism had support among imperial representatives during the first session of Trent. Born in 1503, Carranza attended the University of Alcalá, joined the Dominican order in 1520, and studied arts and theology at the College of St Gregory's in Valladolid. He taught at St Gregory's in the 1530s and early 1540s, and in 1545 Charles included him among the three theologians he sent to the Council of Trent.[166] Carranza admitted to meeting Valdés in 1526 or 1527 at the home of his uncle, Sancho Carranza de Miranda, a former professor at the University of Alcalá and later a canon in Seville. He met Valdés again in 1528 in Valladolid when Juan went to meet with his brother at the imperial court.[167] Carranza's trial began a year after the Papal Inquisition condemned Valdés and his doctrines; thus he had good reason to minimize his contacts with Valdés as mere chance encounters.[168] However, would someone who only had a single, chance introduction bother to look that person up a year later? Carranza's uncle bulk-ordered copies of Valdés's *Dialogue on Christian Doctrine* for use by his clergy in Seville, and he was one of the primary defenders of the book during its review in 1529. Carranza claimed that when he knew Valdés in Alcalá and Valladolid he was not suspected of heresy,[169] but given Valdés's stature and relation to Carranza's uncle, he must have known about the controversy surrounding Juan's first book.

In 1539 Carranza went to Rome for the general chapter meeting of his order, where he was awarded his Master's degree in Theology. From May to September he assisted in ceremonies to induct several new cardinals, and he presented two conclusions against Protestant doctrines in open debate. According to Fray Domingo de Rojas, Carranza received an invitation to meet with Valdés in Naples. Supposedly Carranza wrote Valdés to excuse his inability to visit for lack of time and asked his advice about 'which authors would be best to read to understand Sacred Scripture.' Valdés replied with a slightly altered version of one of his considerations.[170] Carranza told a different version about the exchange. He claimed that a friend of Valdés joined in one of the debates, and afterwards gave him Valdés's invitation to meet with him in Naples. At the same time this friend of Valdés gave him the short consideration. Carranza thought the consideration of little importance, and told the friend that he could not accept the invitation to Naples.[171]

The consideration referenced in the trial as *Advice Concerning Interpreters of Scripture* advocates the use of prayer and consideration as the proper interpreters of Scripture. It is a continuation of Valdés's individualist doctrine of self-examination. Through proper prayer seeking to glorify God, one will comprehend the will of God. Consideration meant reflecting on one's personal spiritual experience to understand the work of the Holy Spirit, which leads to 'justification by the justice of God executed in His most precious flesh.'[172] Thus the consideration hinted at Valdés's controversial doctrine of justification that would be condemned at the first session of the Council of Trent.

Several witnesses claimed that Carranza had the *Advice* copied and distributed to his students after he returned to Spain, including to Luis de la Cruz, a friend of Carranza. In its search of Cruz's lodging, the Inquisition found Valdés's *Advice* among some of Carranza's books. Cruz, a friendly witness for Carranza, testified that when Carranza gave the *Advice* to him he said that it was 'given by a pious and virtuous man.'[173] Carranza denied circulating the *Advice* to his students, but admitted to using some orthodox ideas of Valdés in a course he taught in 1545.[174] He claimed that he never heard rumours that Valdés was suspected of heresy until he arrived at the Council of Trent in 1545.[175] Yet those rumours did not prevent him from close association with Valdés's followers at Trent.

Fray Rojas's identification of Valdés as 'secretary to the Emperor and who wrote the *Considerations*' further suggests that Valdés and Carranza were closer friends than Carranza admitted.[176] Given the secretive nature of Valdés's service, very few people in Spain would have known that he was Charles's personal secretary. For example, the 1540 *Ejecutoría* that established the Valdés *mayorazgo* identified Juan as the 'Chamberlain of Pope Clement VII of fond memory, after His Holiness died he left to reside in Naples, where he is to the present.'[177] In a document that is intended to impress upon the crown a family's honour, no mention is made of Valdés's service for Charles or any of his offices. Further,

Carranza knew Juan's writings well enough to declare authoritatively to an inquiring Rojas that another Valdés wrote the *Dialogue of Mercury and Charon* rather than Juan.[178] Information this accurate had to come from someone who knew Valdés rather well. Carranza seems to have preferred minimizing his relationship with Valdés rather than acknowledging the service of a condemned heretic with the dear departed emperor.

Whether or not Carranza purposely sought out Valdés's theological advice and circulated it, some facts about the relationship between Valdés and Carranza cannot be denied. Carranza had known Valdés for many years, probably was familiar with his first book, admitted to his influence in his teaching on the eve of the Council of Trent, and after he arrived in Rome sought out Valdés's supporters Morone, Pole, and Flaminio. He visited them frequently and they all supported the doctrine of double justification.[179]

The testimony of Charles's ambassador at Trent, Diego Hurtado de Mendoza, places Carranza firmly with Pole and company. Mendoza declared that he did not consider Carranza a good Christian because he had 'very close friendship with many persons, that is to say, with some persons that were heretics, and particularly the Cardinal of England [Pole], who I do not consider a good Christian, and who erred in the article of justification. ... And the Archbishop [Carranza] also had friendship with some of the house of the said cardinal who this witness considered heretics.'[180]

In a second testimony Mendoza was more specific and revealing about Valdés's influence at Trent. According to Mendoza, Carranza had friends who were 'heretics in the article of justification and they read the book of Valdés that did not discuss any other matter, like Donato Rul. ... [and] Ascanio Colonna and Monseñor Carneseca and Antonio Flaminio, and these always had the books of Valdés and read from them.'[181] 'The book' of Valdés that focused almost exclusively on his doctrine of justification was *The Mode of Teaching and Preaching the Principle of the Christian Religion*, which Giulia Gonzaga had translated and published in Rome in 1545. Mendoza must also have read *The Mode of Teaching and Preaching the Principle of the Christian Religion* in order to be so sure of its contents.

Charles had instructed his representatives at Trent to postpone discussion on the two most difficult issues, justification and communion. The majority overrode the imperialists and began a six-month discussion of justification in July 1546. Carranza unsuccessfully employed the concept of the universal mystic body of Christ to support double justification. By being incorporated into Christ, the individual's justice was also Christ's justice, thus inherent justice and the justice of Christ could not be separated.[182] Carranza pressed his interpretation of justification to the point that some considered his position Lutheran until Valdés's old friend don Pedro de Pacheco, now Cardinal of Jaén, had him make a special presentation clarifying his doctrine before Spanish, Italian, and French delegates.[183]

Cardinal Pole resigned from the Council in mid-October in protest against the majority position on justification. As in 1541, he abandoned the battle early. The Council's decision was publicly announced in January 1547, coincidentally the month of Cardinal Bembo's death. The demise of the great humanist cardinal and the defeat of a doctrine aimed at avoiding religious conflict symbolized the dawn of a new era. The creative tolerance vital to the Renaissance pursuit of beauty mattered less than doctrinal consistency and clarity in the face of the Protestant challenge. Europe's great blood-letting in the name of Christ had already begun. After the council's decision, double justification and Valdesianism became heretical pending the final ratification of the Council's decrees in 1563.[184] That condemnation cast a dark shadow over Valdés's life and accomplishments.

Because Valdés's contacts and doctrines were so important to imperial goals, the sudden change of relationship between Valdés and the viceroy may have involved more than a brotherly warning. After all, Valdés discussed his doctrines openly at the viceroy's court and near his residence for years. While Toledo may have used his religious doctrines as an excuse, more likely the viceroy suddenly became paranoid about Valdés's possible disloyalty. As previously noted, the viceroy was under a lot of pressure from the *visita* and the suspicious death of his mistress's husband. He did not trust Cobos and knew Valdés had joined his service. In late June 1541 Charles ordered Toledo to reinstate Alonso Sánchez as Treasurer of Naples.[185] Toledo despised Sánchez, and Valdés was his friend.

More significantly, Valdés had gone around the viceroy to Cobos and the emperor to end Giulia Gonzaga's litigation with Isabella Colonna. In this case the viceroy made himself vulnerable to charges that he did not administer justice fairly. Charles accepted the testament of Giulia's father in September, just weeks after Valdés's death. Knowing Valdés's influence, and perhaps hearing that Charles would act against his wishes in Giulia's case, the viceroy may have concluded that Valdés conspired with his enemies, Cobos and *visitador* Pacheco, to undermine him with Charles concerning the *visita*. The former patronage of the Pacheco family and current patronage of Cobos would make such an association logical, even though, as has been shown, Valdés defended the viceroy in all matters other than Giulia's case. A Spanish grandee would not allow a servant he had elevated to get away with such disloyalty. At a minimum, Valdés's close relationship with Giulia led the ambitious courtier to risk his career, if not his life.

Giulia responded in kind. After the Papal Inquisition began investigating Valdesians, she risked all to save his religious writings. Whatever the nature of their relationship, a strong mutual affection is evident. Aware of her own investigation by the Papal Inquisition, she refused ever to condemn Valdés's teachings as heretical, knowing others were being imprisoned and executed for holding the same position.[186] Only her death of natural causes in April 1566 saved her from a similar fate.

Conclusion

The adjectives that best describe Juan de Valdés are brilliant, spiritual, sensual, earnest, ambitious, deceptive, and egotistical. This odd mixture of conflicting qualities simply reflects the numerous contradictions between Valdés's writings and his actions. He frequently condemned the Church's materialism while living 'like a king' from the proceeds of absentee prebends. He repeatedly advised Giulia Gonzaga to ignore the loss of a family fortune even though he threatened Cardinal Ravenna over a debt of 3,000 ducats. He constantly extolled Christian humility, but represented himself as the Socratic master in two dialogues. He deprecated 'worldly honour,' yet his political ambition surprised even his patrons. He made coarse jokes about Paul III's illegitimate children, but remained in favour at the papal court.[1] Most of his secular writings contain an earthy vulgarity that contrasts sharply with the spirituality of his scriptural commentaries.

There is an obvious gulf between the ideal Church Valdés described and his behaviour and that of his associates. In one of his late religious tracts Valdés advocated a thorough cleansing of the Church. 'I would have those excommunicated and cast out of the Christian Church, after having been admonished once, twice, or thrice, according to Christ's command, viz.: the miserly, the ambitious, the blasphemous, the lustful; and those who live in hatred and quarrels, in banqueting and vanity; and those who addict themselves to ill-earned money and to illicit games; and those who attend vain and superstitious ceremonies.'[2] Could Valdés have been a member of such a Church? And how could his friends Cardinal Ravenna and Ascanio Colonna have gained admittance? Neither of these men exhibited many morally redeeming qualities. But they were staunch imperial allies who remained friends of Juan de Valdés.

Valdés's childhood in and around Cuenca is crucial to understanding his complexities. He was the youngest son of a large and influential *hidalgo* family. Within the family, he was favoured, perhaps even spoiled. But as *conversos*, members of his family were set apart from the Old Christian majority and became the targets for abuse during the violent transition to Habsburg rule in Spain. Home life must have been insecure as the Inquisition arrested members of the Valdés clan and Diego Hurtado de Mendoza threw Juan's father off the city council while seizing the family's fields.

His father's legal victory over Mendoza fuelled Valdés's egalitarianism and confidence in Spanish liberty. Valdés's frequent denunciations of inflated conceptions of dignity, along with the eclectic social composition of his Neapolitan sodality, testify to a social consciousness somewhat atypical of his era. His egalitarian thought is best expressed in an exchange with Pacheco in the *Dialogue on Language*. Valdés defined the plebeian and vulgar as 'all who have little talent and judgment.' Pacheco then asked, 'what if a person is rich and of high lineage?' Valdés responded, 'no matter how high and rich, in my opinion they will be plebes if they are not high in ingenuity and rich in judgment.'[3] Valdés linked his view of liberty with Spain by having Marcio join in the discussion, saying, 'You could not have learned this philosophy in Castile.' Valdés replied, 'You are deceived ... a large part of what you call philosophy I learned in Spain, but have forgotten in Italy.'[4]

Valdés's experiences during the Comunero Revolt seem to have triggered a spiritual awakening. Little is known for certain about his activities at the time of this experience, aside from his fascination with tales of chivalry with messianic undertones. Soon after his conversion Valdés applied to join imperial service, and three years later Charles V saved his family and hometown from Mendoza tyranny. In his *Commentary on Romans* Valdés expressed his messianic nationalism when he noted how God took the Jewish state into his hands in antiquity. He would do the same 'to a Christian nation, when he, either through himself or through the agency of an individual, or of several persons of the same nation, gives it an abundance of spiritual gifts. Thus God increases the nation's faith by its knowledge of himself and the knowledge of Christ, by increasing through charity the union that there is between it and God ... as God is all love and charity.'[5]

The traditional image of Spain as an isolated bulwark of Catholic orthodoxy must be set aside in order to appreciate that Spain abounded in spiritual gifts even before Martin Luther picked up his hammer. No other Christian nation had *converso* preachers like Pedro Ruíz de Alcaraz; no other Christian nation allowed all of Erasmus's works to circulate uncensored; and no other Christian nation had a university as dedicated to biblical philology as Alcalá. Treasuring these gifts conditioned Juan to be receptive to Protestant innovations that might aid Charles V's diplomacy. However one classifies Juan's religious views, he identified them with his Spanish background. He taught in Spanish and there is no evidence his group read and discussed the works of Luther and Calvin, whereas *spirituali* in Venice, Ferrara, and Viterbo certainly did.[6]

There is no reason to believe that Valdés ever considered himself a Protestant, and considerable evidence points to his orthodoxy. On his deathbed, Valdés declared to Pietro Antonio di Capua, the Archbishop of Otranto, that 'he died in the same faith in which he had lived.'[7] Valdés was a respected member of the Catholic clerical class; many of his friends were high-ranking churchmen and cardinals who read and recommended his writings. There is no firm evidence that either he or his writings were condemned as heretical during his lifetime.[8] In Carranza's trial, witnesses stated that they did not believe Valdés was a heretic but 'a very spiritual man.'[9] One witness even said Valdés wrote against Lutheranism.[10]

The primary reason the Papal Inquisition ordered Carnesecchi's execution in 1567 was his stubborn refusal to denounce Valdés's doctrine of justification as heretical.[11] Carnesecchi testified that not only did Valdés speak against Protestant separatism, he saved Carnesecchi from being engulfed by Lutheranism.[12] He claimed Valdés's doctrine of justification could not be considered heretical before the Council of Trent defined the Church's position on the subject. Because he was not sure of Valdés's opinion of inherent and imputed justice, he was not fully convinced that the Council of Trent's condemnation of double justification covered Valdés's doctrines, but he agreed to accept the opinion of his judges on that point.[13] By beheading Carnesecchi and other followers of Valdés who refused to recant, the papacy made Valdesianism a retroactive heresy.

Those seeking to make the case that Valdés was a heretic all along begin with his association with Pedro Ruiz de Alcaraz. The Spanish Inquisition condemned Alcaraz and his doctrines in 1529.[14] Though Alcaraz could not have been in contact with Valdés for much more than a year, the *alumbrado* made an indelible impression on his theology, as José Nieto has demonstrated. There is not a single religious work of Valdés that does not include some of Alcaraz's key doctrines: continuous mental prayer, divine love's regenerative power, and personal experience of that love.[15] By emphasizing individual spiritualism, these doctrines were tailor-made to aid a theological compromise with Protestantism. They also were appealing in the platonic literary environment of late Renaissance Italy.

Erasmus provided important elements in Valdés's religious thought as well. The flesh and spirit dichotomy, the universal mystic body of Christ, philological purity, and a degree of doctrinal toleration run through Juan's writings. Yet this Erasmian disciple never seems to have written the master humanist after he left Spain for Italy, and rarely mentioned his name after extolling him effusively in the *Dialogue on Christian Doctrine*. This reveals Juan's theological opportunism. The high-ranking churchmen Juan wanted to influence in Italy did not like Erasmus's bitter satires of the clergy.

Theological opportunism enabled Valdés to pick and choose elements from Protestantism and refashion them for his audience in Spanish. His attempts to blur the lines between Catholicism and Protestantism led to a lack of theological clarity and consistency.[16] He used Protestant terminology, such as 'calling' and 'election,' but Valdés's position on free will gave these terms totally different meanings from Luther and Calvin. Lutheran emphasis on justification by faith alone led Valdés to develop his more vague doctrine of justification that became identified with Contarini's double justification. In 1550 Celio Secondo Curione hinted at Valdés's doctrinal elasticity, writing that Valdés 'became all things to all men, that he might gain all to Christ.'[17]

Valdés's theological inconsistency is most clearly revealed in his assessments of the sacrament of communion. In his *Dialogue on Christian Doctrine* he interpreted Christ's washing the feet of the apostles prior to the Last Supper as a requirement of Christians to cleanse themselves of all sin before taking communion.[18] This implies support for the traditional confession prior to taking communion. In *The Christian Alphabet*, Valdés still retained a fairly conservative view of the sacrament: 'Under those species are the true body and blood of our Lord Jesus Christ.'[19]

In the midst of the religious discussions leading up to the Diet of Regensburg, Valdés seemed prepared to embrace a more Protestant understanding of the sacrament. In his *Commentary on First Corinthians* he discussed the subject at length. Communion was originally intended as a symbol to refresh the memory of Christ's new covenant with his members in order to increase their faith. However, over time the practice was profaned when the papal hierarchy subtracted and added things to serve the needs of the masses. This was a subtle reference to the Church's addition of the doctrine of transubstantiation and the subtraction of the cup from the laity. Valdés charged past religious leaders with sacrilege and recommended returning to the purity and simplicity of the words of Paul on the subject.[20]

As the Regensburg negotiations were under way, Valdés penned several small tracts on specific issues, including 'With What Intent You Ought to Go to Holy Communion.' In this pamphlet Valdés wrote that you go to communion:

> To refresh in your memory the death of Christ ... you will go certain in your soul that in that execution you have as much a part as you may be able to comprehend if on your own person all that rigour of justice had been executed and you had lived in total innocence as Christ lived. ... You go to proclaim by an outward symbol that you are just and holy.[21]

This spiritual union with Christ during communion goes beyond a merely symbolic ceremony and vaguely suggests some attempt to compromise with Luther's doctrine of consubstantiation. Between 1535 and 1541 Valdés moved from a fairly traditional interpretation of the sacrament to a purely symbolic interpretation and ended with an emphasis on spiritual interaction.[22] This theological fluidity forced the Papal Inquisition to classify Valdesianism as an independent heresy.

There was a continuous dialectic between honour and heresy in Juan's life. Because the Spanish Inquisition burned his uncle at the stake and forced his father and brother to do penance, Valdés could not escape his *converso* heritage. Undoubtedly he suffered humiliation and name-calling as a child. Being dishonoured naturally heightens one's desire for honour. Valdés chose service to an emperor who embodied messianic idealism as his path to honour. But his first attempt to aid Charles's propaganda efforts backfired when his *Dialogue on Christian Doctrine* proved a bit too radical and precipitated his dishonourable departure from Spain.

Juan's service at the papal court washed the dishonour of heresy from his reputation, and all such allegations were silenced until after his death. In Rome he avoided theology and studied the art of diplomacy. He developed an uncanny ability to balance the interests of competing patrons: Charles V and Clement VII; Cobos and Viceroy Toledo;

the Colonnas and the Gonzagas, to name a few. His ability to win and maintain the confidence of a variety of patrons was crucial to his ability to gather intelligence.

Valdés's administrative duties in Naples provide an interesting perspective on the operation of Charles V's composite monarchy. An obvious strength was the general desire for a powerful judiciary capable of protecting the weak from the powerful. An obvious weakness was unfair taxation and widespread bribery. Despite its flaws, Valdés defended Neapolitan autonomy much as his father defended Cuenca's liberties. That autonomy served Charles well, as the viceroy sometimes had to make key diplomatic decisions, such as sending troops to Ascanio, before receiving Charles's orders. The viceroy's independence also gave Charles a cover of deniability, as in the decision to withdraw Spanish troops from papal service in Perugia. Such a decentralized system required personal loyalty and mutual confidence between viceroy and emperor, a difficult matter given the nature of court factionalism. Valdés helped to bridge factional strife in Naples by supporting both the viceroy's judges and Cobos's *criado* Alonso Sánchez during the *visita*.

Early in his career Juan was an imperial propagandist. Alfonso de Valdés trained him in the art, and the *Dialogue on Christian Doctrine* and *Dialogue on Language* were the fruits of that training.[23] While the former was confiscated, and the latter never caught the imagination of his Italian audience, his role in elevating the Spanish language and manners at the viceroy's court contributed to the advance of both in Italy and Europe throughout the sixteenth century. That Spain became the most widely imitated nation in Europe would not have surprised Valdés.[24] Without overstating his contributions, he advanced Spanish as an imperial language and culture. His literary pursuits also enabled him to gather intelligence from influential contacts. These two aspects of Valdés's imperial service merged together in his Neapolitan sodality.

The structure of Juan's dialogues and his repeated confessions of ignorance manifest a free exchange of ideas. He preferred to speak spontaneously rather than to deliver a formal lecture. 'I know from experience that never have I spoken better in my life than when I have spoken without putting thought into what I should speak.'[25] Such spontaneous dialogues required rhetorical skill more than logical consistency. His circle was the perfect vehicle for gathering diplomatic information and influencing Italian religious thought along Ghibbiline lines.

Given that Valdés claimed his 'principal profession is to speak freely about what I feel about things that I am asked,'[26] he must have granted the same freedom of expression to his listeners. Aristocratic ladies seem to have been particularly drawn to the liberty of Valdés's discussions. Intelligent and assertive women like Francisca Hernández, Isabel de la Cruz, and María Cazalla shaped Valdés's *alumbrado* heritage. When she was informed she would be tortured, Maria Cazalla smiled and said, '*Señores*, this I merit for having defended the honour of Jesus Christ and of Spain, that had it not been for me half the kingdom would be damned.'[27] With such mentors, Valdés threw open the door of spiritual self-expression for Vittoria Colonna, Constanza d'Avalos, Caterina Cibo, Isabella Brísegna, and above all for Giulia Gonzaga.

Without Giulia, Valdés would have remained a secretive diplomatic agent long ago erased from history's memory. In a sense, she redeemed him as much as he redeemed her. Valdés travelled down an amoral career path typical of courtiers of his age. His assignment as her legal adviser, given her depression, forced him to rekindle his own spirituality and gave him the opportunity to teach what he considered proper Christian doctrine. The change of direction is reflected in Valdés's humour. After 1538 Valdés no longer employed the off-colour jokes displayed in his *Dialogue on Language*, at the University of Alcalá, and conveyed in a particularly mean-spirited tone in his correspondence with Cardinal Gonzaga. His letters to Francisco de los Cobos certainly contain humour and sarcasm, but none of the vulgarity. One assumes Cobos, as a poor *hidalgo* from Ubeda, would have been at least as receptive to such humour as Cardinal Gonzaga.

Juan's years of attention to Giulia gave her the legal right and the psychological strength to manage the estates of Vespasiano until he came of age. Despite her luxuriant court attended by philosophers, poets, and musicians, there is no record of Giulia succumbing to the sensual temptations she confided to Valdés. The poet Tasso, who had extolled her beauty in her youth, also extolled her spirituality after her death.

> Giulia Gonzaga ... who dwelt in Holy light
> And whose thoughts, like arrows to the mark,
> turned to God; in Him she lived, in Him she died,
> by no other was she nourished, with no other did she abide.[28]

Whether or not one agrees with José Nieto's argument that Pedro Ruiz de Alcaraz was a pre-Lutheran Protestant, there is no doubt that Valdés's

Conclusion   167

circle shared many similarities with Alcaraz's group at Escalona.[29] Most importantly, religion was fun. A lack of hierarchy, joking, free expression, unfettered association of men and women, scriptural concentration, and the deification of love characterized both groups. This association apparently cured Giulia of her illness forever.

It is beyond the scope of this study to resolve the debate about what Juan de Valdés 'really' believed. His doctrines may forever remain in the eye of the beholder, a compliment to his rhetorical and diplomatic skills. But with a high degree of certainty his heterodoxy was inextricably related to his political service. In this regard three documents previously cited deserve particular emphasis. In 1538 Cobos declared before the Council of Castile that it knew 'well who Juan de Valdés is and the gravity of the work that we use him for there [in Naples].'[30] The President of the Council of Castile was none other than Cardinal Juan de Tavera, the Archbishop of Toledo and one of the leaders of the purge of Erasmians at Alcalá.[31] Undoubtedly he knew the past charges against Valdés's *Dialogue on Christian Doctrine*, yet he acknowledged Valdés's merit in Italy.

The second document is Charles's July 1539 briefing of Ambassador Aguilar about Camerino. Charles indicated that previously the matter 'was under the authority of a particular of the Church, nevertheless *a trusted person*, from the vicinity of Naples.'[32] Charles announced his trust of Valdés long after his sodality had gained fame for its free religious discussions. Finally, the Jesuit Nicolás Bobadilla observed first hand Valdés's discussion of his religious doctrines openly at the viceroy's court in 1540.[33] The viceroy, Cobos, and Charles were all well aware of 'the nature' of Valdés's work.

Limitation of papal authority and pursuit of religious peace in Germany were goals shared by many in the Spanish diplomatic corps who may not have understood Hebrew or Greek, but could count the number of Turkish and French troops. Grand Chancellor Gattinara and Viceroy Toledo were not heretics, but skilled practitioners of power politics. Spain was a country poor in resources, and its dominion depended in no small part on the crafty diplomacy manifested in Valdés's career. Valdés's service exemplifies the speed and quality of intelligence-gathering that made the Spanish diplomatic corps the best in Europe.[34]

Martín Pérez de Ayala was the only Spanish representative to attend all three sessions of the Council of Trent. Ayala had worked closely with Carranza to defend the doctrine of double justification. Less than a week before his death in 1566 he finished a brief autobiography. He did not consider Trent a true general council; rather, it was a meeting of Italians jealous of the emperor's power and therefore opposed to reformation.[35] Charles had asked Ayala to delay discussion of justification and communion in order to gain Lutheran acceptance of the council. According to Ayala, Paul III pushed these issues to the front in order to maintain papal authority. He called the pope a tyrant for destroying the independence of councils and prelates and for determining issues that should have been left open.[36] Ayala embraced the same view of papal authority as Juan de Valdés, though he was never labelled a heretic.

In March of 1542 Andrés de Valdés, serving as Cuenca's *procurador* to the Cortes, received a royal favour from Charles for the city.[37] Would Charles show favour to the brother of someone he considered heretical? Similarly Charles rewarded Giulia Gonzaga after she initiated the printing of Valdés's works by promoting her nephew Vespasiano in imperial service. He never questioned favouring Valdés's closest disciple.

This study began with a reference to Cobos's observation that he considered Juan's service more valuable than Alfonso's. Beginning the letter, Cobos made an interesting correction. Originally he wrote, 'now I have been informed that at the beginning of the month of August Juan de Valdés, brother of the secretary, died.'[38] On second thought Cobos decided to mark through 'brother of the secretary.' Juan's services merited praise independent of the more renowned Alfonso. It was a fitting gesture.

Appendices

Appendix 1

AMC leg. 1493, ex. 52, Fernando de Valdés to the City Council of Cuenca, 25 June 1506.

Muy nobles señores,
A vuestras mercedes suplico me perdona porque no les quiero __ parte las nuevas a Cuenca para que espero su desear __ seculo que suela tener los que les quieren otros y que querrán tenerlo por bien y que a que noble ciudad la y puesto en más fama y honra según en lo que a __ está este reino que ninguna otra ciudad esté porque Suylla y yo fuimos a besar las manos de sus altezas y darles la obediencia que se les debía ante que otras ciudades del Reino y nosotros fuimos causa que algunos y otros caballeros y consejo fue se a hacer lo mismo y Juan de Valdés, mi hijo, lo quiero como en presencia pública, que lo pueda decir a vuestras mercedes, suplico que lo vean __ suya y me quieren que mandarán que haga en servicio de esta ciudad y lo que __ hizo en lo del fundamento de los más y sosos para mi paga, que bien lo merezco y gasto que juro al Dios y a esta __ que y traído y traigo cuatro bestias y como ____ a mi costado como se ve. Es un lledo el pan a tan grande precio que es de no creer el __ que 21 a fyba el __ burra así el ____ y no se sabe lo que se hará __ obtener __ estas __ se da __ a vuestras mercedes a tenemos Rey el más noble, llano, amistoso __ que nunca __ y __ las Repúblicas. Y __ el muy noble estado de vuestras mercedes de Benavente 25 de junio, a servicio y mando de vuestras mercedes.

Appendix 2

AGS: Estado, leg. 9, f. 77, Governors of Castile to Charles, 20 December 1521.

Juan de Valdés es sobrino de Alonso de Valdés, difunto, capitán que fue de Vuestra Magestad, de los ordinaries de infantería, que facellió en Pamplona residendo en la defensa de ella. Y otro tío suyo, que se decía Hernando de Valdés, fue capitán de la guarda de pie del Rey Católico, abuelo de Vuestra Majestad, que le mataron en Valdeconcal en una batalla contra franceses. Y este dicho Juan de Valdés es buen servidor de Vuestra Majestad y persona hábil para cualquier oficio o cargo. Suplicamos a Vuestra Majestad le mande recibir por contino de su casa en remuneración de los servicios de los dichos sus tíos ...
Cover page
A su majestad de los gobernadores. 20 de diciembre por Juan de Valdés por contino. A la sacra cessarea y católica Majestad del emperador y Rey nuestro señor.

Appendix 3

AGS: CC, leg. 196, f. 98, Fernando de Valdés to Charles, 4 May 1529. This folio also includes the letter of Fernando's appointment in 1525.

Hernando de Valdés, vecino de la ciudad de Cuenca y mayoral de las Casas de San Lázaro de la ciudad de Cuenca y su obispado por merced que Vuestra Majestad me hizo, beso los pies y las maños de Vuestra Santa Cesárea Majestad. Digo que yo estoy enfermo de la gota y no tengo habilidad para ejercitar y proveer las cosas que soy obligado hacer en el dicho cargo de mayoralía como yo quería y sería razón, y tengo un hijo que se dice Juan de Valdés, persona de letras, que hará lo que debe en mi lugar en el dicho su cargo para servicio de Dios Nuestro Señor y de Vuestra Majestad, mirando las cosas cumplideras a las ermitas y hospital y pobres y enfermos de la enfermedad. Por tanto suplico humildemente a Vuestra Majestad mande proveer del dicho cargo y mayoralía al dicho Juan de Valdés, mi hijo, en quien renuncio el dicho oficio, en lo cual Vuestra Majestad hará servicio a Dios Nuestro Señor y a mí y al dicho mi hijo bien y merced. Y si por caso Vuestra Majestad no fuere servido de proveer y hacer merced del dicho cargo al dicho Juan de Valdés, mi hijo, retengo en mí la merced que Vuestra Majestad me tiene hecha del dicho cargo. Y siempre quedo rogando a Nuestro Señor la imperial y real persona de Vuestra Majestad guarde y prospere por largos tiempos con mucho acrecentamiento de reinos y señoríos. Hecha en Cuenca a cuatro días del mes de mayo de mil y quinientos y veintinueve años. De Vuestra Sacra Cesárea Católica Majestad.
Muy humilde servidor y vasallo que sus reales pies y maños humildemente beso. Fernando de Valdés
[reverse]

Que informe de la persona y muestre el título que tiene.
Información de la persona y muestre del título que tiene.
cover page of folio
Hernando de Valdés, vecino de la ciudad de Cuenca, mayoral de la Casa de San Lázaro de ella, renuncia el dicho oficio en Juan de Valdés, su hijo, porque por ser ya muy viejo no le puede bien servir, y es persona en que encabe su por xxx pase la dicha remuneración presenta el traslado autorizado del título que de dicho oficio tiene, 6 de julio 1529.

Appendix 4

AHN: Inquisición, leg. 223, no. 7, ff. cclxxxiii–cclxxxiiii, Proceso de Juan de Vergara, presentado en 6 de marzo de 1534 por el doctor Vergara ante el señor inquisidor Vaguer. (Vergara's response to the testimonies of Dr Alonso Sánchez and Dr Juan de Medina.)

A estos dos testigos últimos digo que de más de no estar ratificada ninguna cosa dicen en mi perjuicio, porque si sobre este libro les hablé yo (de que no me acuerdo) más que al uno, que es el posterior, fue porque sin haber yo leído el dicho libro, ni tenido espacio para ello, había entendido del doctor Miranda que era buen libro, y que él había comprado muchos dellos y los enviado a su tierra, salvo que después dicen que leyéndole sobre aviso se hallaban en las cosas no bien dichas, las cuales decía el dicho doctor, que en otro tiempo pasaran sin que nadie las notara, mas que se podían fácilmente enmendar y que su voto era que la enmendasen, y el libro se tornase a imprimir y aunque el dicho doctor es muerto pero público es y notorio en la facultad de teología en Alcalá haber sido éste su voto, y así lo debe ser en el consejo de la Inquisición, donde él también sobre esta materia dijo su parecer, y casi lo mismo que esto me acuerdo haber oído al doctor Coronel según que de su parecer, debe también constar en el dicho consejo, y porque siendo la materia de tal calidad estaba en libertad de los doctores cuando lo examinaban hacer condenaciones infames, o enmendaciones modestas y caritativas. Parecía me a mi que había lugar de conformarme yo en cosa que no había leído con el voto de tales dos personas como el doctor Miranda y doctor Coronel, y conforme a esto hablé a este último testigo porque se acertó a hallar en mi posada, que de otra manera no fuera a buscarle, ni se me acordara dello, y por ser tal la materia le protesté como él aquí confiesa que no se disimulase en ninguna manera cosa que tocase en error, sino que todo se mirase y enmendase muy bien. A otro no me acuerdo haber hablado más si lo hice sería con la misma protestación, y de la misma manera que a éste lo que dice el dicho último testigo que le pareció que me pesara a mí de cualquiera afrenta que Valdés recibiera, digo que de cualquier persona me pesaría que recibiese afrenta, y lo contrario no es de cristiano, y por esta generalidad me pesara de Valdés, y porque le tenía por mancebo virtuoso, y no por otra particularidad ninguna.

Appendix 5

AGS: Quitaciones de Corte, leg. 30, f. 310–14, Quitación Juan de Valdés hermaño del Señor Alonso de Valdés.

f. 310
año de 1532
Nos el emperador de romanos y Augusto rey de Alemania, de España, de las dos Sicilias de Italia etc., hacemos saber a vosotros nuestros contadores mayores, que acerando lo que Alonso de Valdés, nuestro secretario, ya difunto nos sirvió y que falleció estando en nuestra corte y servicio y la habilidad y suficiencia de Juan de Valdés, su hermano, para nos poder servir de nuestra merced y voluntad es de tomarlo y recibirlo por nuestro criado para que nos sirva en lo que le mandaremos y que haya y tenga de nosotros sesenta y mil maravedís de quitación en cada un año porque vos mandamos que los pongáis y asentéis así en los nuestros libros que vosotros tenéis y le libráis los dichos sesenta mil maravedís este presente año lo que de ello hubiere de haber por renta desde el día de la fecha de este nuestro albalá hasta en fin de el y dende en adelante en cada un año enteramente en las neomenias y en la persona y a los tiempos y según y de la manera que se librarán sus quitaciones y salarios a los de nuestro consejo secretarios y otros oficiales de nuestra corte solamente por virtud deste dicho nuestro albalá sin esperar en ningún año otra nuestra carta ni mandamiento alguno y asentado el traslado de este dicho nuestro albalá en los dichos nuestros libros y volver este original sobre esperton de vosotros al dicho Juan de Valdés para que él lo tenga fecha en Mantua a veinte y dos de noviembre de mil y quinientos y treinta y dos años.
Yo, el rey; yo, Francisco de los Cobos, contador mayor de Leon, secretario de sus cesáreas y catolicas majestades, la facer escribir por su mandado etc.
Tal sobre esperton como es asiento.
f. 310v
En virtud del cual dicho albalá suso incorporado se ponen asentar que al dicho Juan de Valdés los dichos 60,000 para le ser librados en cada un año en esta manera.
Años de 1532 y 1533
Item: Librados al dicho Juan de Valdés porción en Madrid a 30 de junio

de 1533 66,500 y que hubo de haber
desde 22 días de noviembre del dicho año
pasado del 1532 hasta el fin del   66,500
mes de diciembre de este año de 1533 en   23,000
Cristóbal Suárez para que se lo pague
de su cargo de 1533 lleno la carta castañeda.
    Margin
    Item: Bájase esta libranza en 23,000
    que el dicho Juan de Valdés
    hubo de tener desde 22 de
    noviembre que se hizo el dicho asentamiento
    por la nonio el año de
    1532 hasta 9 de abril
    de 1533 que residió
    en la corte sino parece
    por fe del secretario Ydiaquez
    que a su ___ ___.
ojo
Rasgo se la dicha libranza de los dichos 23,000 y a librar en el cargo del
dicho Suárez de el viii por carta contada 28 marzo de 1539 que ___ ___.
Año de dxxxv
Item: Librados al dicho por nómina de su majestad fecha en Madrid el primero de
marzo de 1535 cuesta al comienzo del libro de quitaciones de la al 60,000
que ha de haber deste dicho año en el dicho Cristóbal Suárez en su cargo del
dicho año.
Año de 1536
Item: Librados al dicho por nómina de su majestad cuesta en el libro de quitaciones de la fecha en Madrid el 30 de marzo de 1536 los dichos 60,000 que ha de
haber este dicho año en el dicho Cristóbal Suárez en su cargo de este dicho año
con cargo conforme a su residir.
f. 311 an altered version of f. 310v
Por virtud del cual dicho albalá suso incorporado se ponen asentar que al dicho
Juan de Valdés los dichos lxU para serle librados en cada un año en esta manera.
Años de 1532/1533
Librado por carta en Madrid 30 de junio de 1533 al dicho Juan de Valdés viUd que
___ ___ ___ por rato de los dichos 60,000 desde 22 noviembre de 1532 hasta a fin
de diciembre del y los 60,000 que ___ de haber en este año de 1533 que son por
autos 60,000 en Cristóbal Suárez, contador y pagado de las cuentas desta corte
de 1533 se los pague habiendo residido desde que aserto hasta fin de diciembre
de 1533 y sino por ratuelvo la carta castañedo el de Ribera los dichos años.

Margin:
Bajase este libramiento en
23,000 que hubo de haber desde
22 de noviembre de 1532
hasta 9 de abril de 1533 que
por fe del secretario Ydiáquez
que éste a de parece que lo residió.
ojo
Se rasgó este libramiento y
Se le libraré a los herederos
del dicho Juan de Valdés como
de suso se contiene.

next paragraph
Libro por carta envía el 28 de marzo de 1539 a los herederos del dicho Juan de Valdés los dichos xxiiiU que hubo de haber en los dichos dos años de 1532 y 1533 en el dicho Cristóbal Suárez pagador de las quitaciones de la corte el año pasado de 1538 ___ al dicho Juan de Valdés por cuanto ___

Margin:
Por mandamiento de contadores que
___ se me remitió a Lope
de Ra. ojo
Esta libranza antes
que le acabase de despachar
y el 29 de marzo de
1539 se dio/ otro para
que se diese con éstos.

f. 312, copy of the same letter is in AGS: Residencias, leg. 4, f. 604.

Al Rey

Nuestros contadores mayores, yo vos mando que los sesenta mil maravedís que de nosotros tiene de quitación en cada año Juan de Valdés, hermano de Alonso de Valdés, nuestro secretario ya difunto, para que nos sirva en lo que le mandare se los libráis este presente año de quinientos treinta y cinco según y como le están mandados librar por el asiento que de ellos tiene para que le sean pagados sin pedirle como entiende en cosas de nuestro servicio ni otra residencia alguna y para la cobranza de ello dadle las cartas de libramientos y otras provisiones que fueren necesarios. Fecha en Madrid el primero día del mes de marzo de quinientos treinta y cinco años. Yo el Rey por mandado de su majestad. Cobos, Comendador Mayor

ff. 313–14, two copies of same letter

Yo, Alfonso de Ydiáquez, secretario de su majestad digo que Juan de Valdés, su criado, residió personalmente en su corte desde el día que se hizo su asiento con

salario de sesenta mil maravedís que fue según parece por él en Mantua el veinte y dos días del mes de noviembre de mill quinientos treinta y dos años hasta que su majestad se embarcó en Génova para venirse en España a nueve días del mes de abril del año siguiente de mil quinientos treinta y tres. Fechada en Toledo a 7 de marzo 1539. Ydiaquez, Diego Lopez
In bottom corner upside down:
El dicho Juan de Valdés del secretario Ydiaquez de cómo residió desde el 22 de noviembre de 1532 hasta el 9 de abril de 1533 años.

Appendix 6

AGS: Estado, leg.1015, f. 107, Relation of Viceroy's letters of 29 December 1532, and 4, 25, and 29 January 1533.

Que de 43 capítulos que Vuestra Majestad concedió al príncipe de Salerno en nombre de aquella ciudad los 30 están en servicio de Vuestra Majestad y provecho de la ciudad y los otros 13 en perjuicio de ella y en deservicio de Vuestra Majestad según que se ha visto en el Colateral Consejo. Y que allí les pareció a todos que él les aceptase los dichos capítulos con tal que pudiesen dejar de ejercitar los 13 hasta tanto que tuviesen recurso a Vuestra Majestad. Y que los de aquella ciudad tornan en mucho que Vuestra Majestad mande quitar aquellos 13 de los 43 sin que en bien persona a ello. Y que vean que él ha tenido cuidado de dar aviso a Vuestra Majestad desto y que se les ha hecho la merced sin venir o pedirla y que con hacerse esto les quedarán las bocas de tales para hacer de ellos todo lo que fuere menester, mayormente en lo del monte y galeras. Y que así conviene al servicio de Vuestra Majestad según les parece a todos los que en aquel caso han hablado.
   Margin:
   Que se acepten y quiten estos y enviando
   los otros para que si gusten rasguen
   y se haga así por respecto de
   aquella ciudad y afirma doce
   con su parecer.
   A mi hecho doce; el de Valdés.

Appendix 7

AGS: Estado, leg. 1015, f. 17, Viceroy to Charles, 9 March 1533, excerpt.

Beso las manos a Vuestra Majestad por la merced de haber hecho a esta ciudad de los doce capítulos de los trece que enviaron a suplicar a Vuestra Majestad les quitase por que el treceno. Que es el oficio de archivero desta ciudad de que Vuestra Majestad hizo merced al secretario Alfonso de Valdés y por su fallecimiento, lo goza Juan de Valdés su hermano. Pues, tiene adquirido derecho y no se puede quitar ni revocar y Vuestra Majestad es servido esta ciudad. No sé cómo lo sentí. Yo se lo diré de parte de Vuestra Majestad como me lo envían a mandar y la voluntad que tiene de hacerles merced y que enviado los dichos treinta y tres capítulos que Vuestra Majestad mandó despachar. Se tornará luego a hacer y despachar los veinte y uno. Quita los doce como está dicho. Las cosas de Juan de Valdés torne por tan encomendadas como Vuestra Majestad me lo mandó.

Appendix 8

AGS: Estado, leg. 1015, f. 103, Viceroy to Charles, 6 October 1533, excerpt.

Vuestra Majestad manda que en el oficio de archivo de que hizo merced a Juan de Valdés por sucesión de la muerte del secretario, su hermano, le favorezca de manera que se efectúe la como que Vuestra Majestad le ha hecho. Yo entiendo en ello para hacerle dar alguna recompensa porque para que dar con el oficio no hay medio porque allende de lo que dicen los deste colateral consejo que no tiene justicia. Me informado de otros letrados particulares y afirman lo mismo, no embargante, que se alegué por su parte ser el capítulo en utilidad universal del Reino. En esto yo trabajaré lo a mi posible para que haya alguna recompensa como digo, haciéndoles entender que Vuestra Majestad es servido que se cumpla y obedezca lo que en este artículo la ciudad suplicó y Vuestra Majestad concedió.

Appendix 9

AGS: Guerra y Marina, leg. 6, f. 119, Viceroy to Cobos, 15 September 1534, excerpt.

Juan de Valdés, hermano del secretario Valdés, es buena persona y certifico a Vuestro Señor que fue a Su Majestad allí lo que puede y tanto como otro nosotros de más calidad porque tiene inteligencias de las muy secretas y siempre soy avisado del de lo que se ofrece con toda diligencia sin falta fue hallado. Su Majestad en lo que digo, a me escribió que no le pagan salieron de cierta plaza de gentil o contino de que Su Majestad le hizo merced por su ausencia. Certifico a Vuestro Señor que aunque la tenga de la corte de Su Majestad, nota hace en servir lo que puede en lo que dicho.

Appendix 10

AGS: Estado, leg. 1021, f. 30. Markings on this document indicate that it was deciphered material from a letter. The context indicates that Viceroy Toledo wrote it to Charles V in early February 1535.

Por letras del conde de Cifuentes de 30 de enero se entiende como el rey de Francia había enviado a decir a Su Santidad que para esta empresa ayudara con 36 galeras y otras naves y galeones con que Su Santidad le conceda las décimas ansí dice que se las concedió porque dice que si no se las daba él se las tomaría como ha hecho muchas veces. De aquí se puede considerar lo que más fuere servido Vuestra Majestad, por una parte putañear y hacer caricias a Barbarroja y por la otra decir dar a sus galeras contra él. Dios le tenga de su mano para que persevere en su servicio.

Por diversas vías se entiende las pláticas que el rey de Francia tiene en Alemania y ahora más que nunca con los duques de Gueldres y de Wurtenburg y Langrave y también se publica por toda Francia la venida en Italia.

Por letra de Juan de Valdés del mismo día se entiende como a los 29 en consistorio Su Santidad propuso que el rey de Francia le demandaba la décima para las iglesias de Francia para ayuda de las galeras que quiere poner en orden para defensión de la Cristiandad y que decía que llegaría toda la décima a la suma de 100,000 ducados y que desto será contento, se cogiese la tercia parte para Su Santidad y ansí se efectuó el negocio en que dice se estima sacará de 600 hasta 800,000 ducados.

Dice que en el mismo consistorio se propusieron las iglesias de Gaeta y Lanchano y no las quisieron pasar poniendo dolencia en las capitulaciones que Vuestra Majestad hizo con Papa Clemente. Y en todo lo que más tiene para esta presentación que parece materia de mala digestión.

Dice más que el negocio de Camerino va creciendo y que le habían certificado que el rey de Francia había enviado a ofrecer al Papa dineros para esta guerra y que en ella si ganase sería para Pero Luis Farnese sospechase que quien dio dineros a a Langrave para contra el duque de Urbino. Si es verdad, no tienen todos buena intención.

Por letra del dicho Valdés de 6 de febrero se entiende como en el negocio del duque de Urbino se esperaba cada día sería sobre el negocio de Camerino contra las duquesas y nuevo duque y que por otra parte se platicaba en los que han de ser capitanes en la empresa y que la cosa va muy adelante.

Dice que hasta aquel día Su Santidad no había tomado resolución para proveer de dineros para las tres galeras que compra en Génova para el armada y tiene sospecha que son palabras.

Por letra de Andalot de 15 de enero se entiende como venía con los siete mil alemanes a Trento para seguir el camino que el príncipe Andrea Doria les ordenase. Y ansí mismo escribe que por parte del rey de Francia se hacía gente en Alemania y daban un florín por hombre y habían de ir a tomar la muestra a Mobelart que es en el condado de Borgoña. No parecen buenos pasos para dar sus galeras contra el turco, mas significa querer estorbar la santa intención de Su Majestad en lo cual Dios no le dará tal poder y le lloverá en casa su ruin intención si la tiene.

Appendix 11

AGS: Estado, leg. 1021, ff. 42–51, Relación de nuevas de todas partes no embargante que así el Serenísimo Rey de Romanos como los otros ministros de Su Majestad lean y han dado cuenta de ellas. Excerpt.

Juan de Valdés por cartas de 19 de febrero escribe que a los 18 [días] se tuvo consistorio y que a las 24 horas de la tarde no era acabado, y que hasta las 21 horas los reverendísimos, cada uno por sí, hablaron en sus negocios particulares y que después se leyó la bula de la concesión de la décima al rey de Francia, y que Su Santidad, para a mostrar que era bien hecha la concesión, hizo una oración en loor del rey de Francia, acudiendo siempre a loar a Vuestra Majestad, y dice que parecía los estaba pesando teniendo al uno en una balanza y al otro en otra. Más dice que el Cardinal Campeggio propuso una iglesia de Flandes que fue muy alterada porque dice que Papa Clemente a instancia de Vuestra Majestad la despojó y dice no pasó hasta otro consistorio. Dice que tras esto luego Su Santidad mandó se refiriese si se había hallado la bula de la capitulación de Barcelona para proponer la iglesia de Gaeta, y le dijeron que sí, y luego Su Santidad mandó se despacha lo contradijó el Cardenal de Roma, diciendo que porque en aquella capitulación el Papa Clemente perdonaba a Vuestra Majestad los 7,000 ducados del fondo de Nápoles, no se debía admitir la presentación porque parecía confirmar la capitulación por el papa no nuestra de lo que decía y así se despachó la iglesia. Más dice que aquella noche Su Santidad en su cámara pronunció la sentencia contra Guidobaldo y duquesas de Camarino, los condenando etc. por la rebelión de no haber comparecido, etc.

El dicho Juan de Valdés por cartas de 21 de febrero dice que lo que había traído una posta que había venido dos días había del serenísimo rey de Romanos. Entendía eran tres cosas principales: la una, que la majestad del dicho rey avisa al papa como la nación alemana está para hacer un concilio particular y dar orden en sus cosas por no estar en el desasosiego que están, diciendo que si

Su Santidad no remedia brevemente con la convocación del concilio general se pone a peligro que toda Alemania le quite la obediencia; la otra, que aquellos herejes que predicaban y escribían contra el santo sacramento han dejado en este caso su error y en lo demás se han juntado con los luteranos. La otra que el dicho serenísimo rey iba emborronado a verse con los duques de Baviera para tratar ciertas cosas de casamiento, etc., y dice que la venida de aquel correo ha puesto espuelas a Su Santidad para despachar el nuncio que había de ir al serenísimo Rey de Romanos, el cual partía otro día y dice lleva breves para todos los príncipes del imperio en que les intima el concilio y les pide su parecer en lo que toca al lugar donde y al tiempo que se debe hacer. Algunos dicen que lo hace más por cumplimiento que por voluntad. Dice que ha entendido de buen lugar que el papa ha dicho si el emperador ayudará a Urbino, el rey de Francia me ayudará a mí con dineros, que hacen él caso y veremos cual podrá más.

Appendix 12

AGS: Estado, Guerra y Marina, leg. 6, f. 156, Razón de lo que escriben particulares de Roma al virrey de Nápoles sobre la causa de Camerino. Excerpt.

Por cartas de 27 de febrero y antes escriben cómo se guardaban sus términos jurídicamente para venir a la descomunión y que Su Santidad después de haber anulado el proceso que el papa Alejandro hizo contra el padre o abuelo del duque Macías a quien dio la investidura de Camarino, mando de nuevo se viese si se pudo hacer o no.
Margin: Valdés
Por letras de 6 de marzo se entiende como Su Santidad apretaba el negocio de camarino con mucha pasión y color diciendo que en todo caso había de proceder por censura y después con mano armada hasta salir con su intención y que se decían había dicho en secreto que si Su Majestad favorecía al duque de Urbino con gente o en otra cosa que el rey de Francia le favorecería a él con dineros.
Margin: Valdés
Por letras de 6 de marzo se entiende cómo su Santidad había enviado al auditor de la cámara y así moneta auditor de Rrota por todos los embajadores de príncipes y señorías residentes en esa corte para informarles de la mucha justicia que tiene de tomar las armas contra el duque y duquesa de Camarino y pedirles favor y ayuda y que con esta demanda ha mandado de casa en casa de Vuestra Santidad estuvieron dos horas.
Margin: Valdés
Escriben debajo desta dacta de la respuesta que les dio el embajador de Venecia y dicen que con otros dos auditores hubieron propuesto a lo que

venían y querían comenzar sus testos y glosas. Les dijo no tomáis trabajo en informarme deste negocio que yo sé bien que por vuestras leyes lo justificaréis cuanto quisiérades pero también sé que hay otras leyes muy contrarias a las vuestras por las cuales no os podrían justificar que son las del Evangelio de Cristo. Ved vosotros a cuales habéis de tener más respeto y cuáles son de más importancia y gobierna os según aquellas y de mí no esperéis otra respuesta y que dicho, acuesto se levantó y los despedía y así escriben procede Su Santidad en su propósito con descomuniones. Y dice que envía a Juan Batista Sabelo en la marcha con algunos caballos y que se cree son para hacer estar en Cerbelo a Urbino y a Camarino uno para sacarlos a barrera por ver si se podrían hacer que de ellos saliese el comer rompimiento y escriben se tiene sospecha que en comenzar esta guerra la mayor parte de Italia quitará la obediencia a la y iglesia y que muchas de sus tierras del papa se le levantarían.

Por letras de 13 de marzo se entiende cómo Su Santidad ha publicado la descomunión contra el duque y duquesas de Camarino y que se habían de poner por las calles la domínica inpasione y que Juan Batista Sabelo llevaría más gente en la marcha de la cual se crea y comenzaría a impedir las vituallas que suelen ir a Camerino y que a Fonova vendrá conde y que Arramino es venido el çepontino y que Estefano de Palestrinia será lugarteniente general en la empresa por Pedro Luis que está enfermo.

Margin: Valdés

Appendix 13

AGS: Estado, leg. 1458, ff. 107–8, Unsigned letter to Charles V, n.d. Transcribed by Sara T. Nalle. The author originally published this document as an appendix to 'Juan de Valdés y la crisis de Camerino, 1534–1535,' in *Aspectos históricos y culturales bajo Carlos V*, ed. Christoph Strosetzki (Frankfurt: Velvuert, 2000), 115–18.

Sire, nosotros estuvimos ayer largamente con el nuncio al cual dijimos las razones y consideraciones acordadas sobre el negocio del concilio y la necesidad que hay del, presuponiendo largamente y loando la buena voluntad del papa en ello, y mayormente el quererlo convocar y celebrar quiera o no el rey de Francia. Tocando incidentalmente es que el dicho rey ha escrito por su letra a los alemanes para les persuadir que lo que el dicho santo padre se inclinaba era por su medio y no por el motivo propio de su santidad, lo cual el dicho nuncio notó bien. Razonando también lo que importaba para que el lugar del dicho concilio fuese en Mantua y que lo declarase Su Santidad de sí mismo para dejar menos ocasión al dicho rey de Francia de malignar para le estorbar y atravesarse en él, y para que Vuestra Majestad tanto mejor pudiese inducir todos los de la dicha Germanía así católicos como desviados para lo apropiar. Juntado así mismo lo que nos pareció poder convenir para justificar el dicho lugar de tal manera que en fin el dicho nuncio lo apropió. Cuanto a lo que concernía a Su Santidad solamente poniendo dificultad cuanto al dicho rey de Francia que podría pretender ser la dicha ciudad de Mantua muy lejos, allende de ser ciudad imperial, sobre lo cual se le respondió que él había aprobado otras ciudades imperiales así de ésta como de la otra parte de los montes y no osaría persistir según lo que últimamente ha escrito a la dicha Germania por la dicha letra, y en fin que si quería allegar alguna cosa contra la dicha Mantua aquello se podría ver y examinar cuando el dicho concilio estuviese junto, porque de otra manera no hay apariencia de le poder contentar con éste ni con otro ningún lugar, ni menos de la seguridad del. Y presupuesto que por este camino tenía color para estorbar el dicho concilio como se lo habemos por diversos actos mostrado y que estando hecha la dicha convocación se vería entonces bien el fundamento que el dicho rey podría tener para contradecir y se hallaría expediente o que él enviase sus procuradores o según que se miraría y vería la disposición se podría poner delante para les cumplir de razones de mudar el dicho concilio ahora fuese a una de las ciudades de la iglesia o a otro lugar de Italia, lo cual el dicho nuncio halló ser bueno con tal que este último punto de translación fuese tenido secreto. Lo cual como él dice podrá confundir al dicho rey de Francia, con lo que nos parece que el dicho nuncio lo toma a ataja de Su Santidad y por le satisfacer, prometiendo maravillas de la voluntad de Su Santidad cuanto al dicho concilio, mostrando gran deseo de venir al punto siguiente.

Cuanto al negocio de Camarino, nosotros trabajamos mucho en le persuadir la suspensión y vía amigable declarándole el estado de los negocios públicos, la necesidad inminente y urgente contra los infieles y la armada que Vuestra Merced hace para les resistir y la buena afección por que su santidad muestra, conociendo cuanto esto importa, los inconvenientes y estorbos que podrían suceder señaladamente a Italia continuando a lo menos en esta sazón la exención, la adherencia que el dicho duque de Urbino podría tener y procurar de sus aliados parientes y deudos, y por aventura por desesperación, de otros que no fuesen de Italia que no buscan sino color y ocasión, y que la dicha suspensión no quitaba ni perjudicaba al derecho que Su Santidad podía tener. Y que por lo que el dicho nuncio sustentaba reciamente que lo que Su Santidad hacía era solamente para hacer el deber para guardar el autoridad y los derechos de la iglesia, le declaramos que la razón quería que Su Santidad considerase junto con esto por su gran prudencia y experiencia lo que más importaba, y que si Su Santidad se quería parar en la injuria que pretendía haber sido hecha a la autoridad eclesiástica, que sería cosa de gran estima y muy convenible a su calidad y de muy buen ejemplo señaladamente en este principio de su pontificado, de usar en esto de clemencia, y a lo menos comportar y suspender la prosecución por algún tiempo para dar medio al dicho duque de se reconciliar y reconocer en que debía. Si se hallaba en culpa, y también su hijo y las dos duquesas, madre y hija de Camarino, atento así mismo que el proceso había sido hecho contra ellos por contumacia, y que si en el dicho proceso se había considerado el interés, se podía también o mejor y más prestamente conocer por árbitros y medianeros y así se evitarían los inconvenientes antedichos, y que si Su Santidad no lo quería hacer por el respeto de los susodichos ni a su suplicación a lo menos se debería mover por la suplicación de Vuestra Majestad y de los otros potentados de Italia que todos se lo suplicarían por lo que importa al bien público de la cristiandad, y señaladamente de Italia que es su propia patria por la cual ellos han tratado la liga defensiva que Su Santidad sabe. Y que Vuestra Majestad pendiente la dicha suspensión se emplearía de muy buena gana en lo que convendría para dar un buen fin en el dicho negocio, y aunque tuvimos convencido de razones al dicho nuncio sin réplica, y que una vez nos demandó por cuanto tiempo debería ser la dicha suspensión, y nos respondió le que por un año o a lo menos por medio año para hacerle la cosa más fácil y hallar principio a la dicha suspensión, después él tornó a decir que no pensaba que Su Santidad condescendería en ello, y que el dicho duque de Urbino no era tan gran cosa como se pensaba y que no tenía medio de mover nada, y que era recia cosa que el señor no pudiese castigar su vasallo, y que si Vuestra Majestad le mandaba obedecer a la sentencia, él no osaría contradecir, y que habían dicho los venecianos que ellos harían lo que Vuestra Majestad y no más, a lo cual se le respondió que Vuestra Majestad no quería razonar sobre la sentencia ni de lo que la otra parte pretendía al contrario mas que Vuestra Majestad tenía por muy cierto que mandando lo que arriba está dicho al dicho duque no haría nada sino solamente se despertaría para hacer peor. Junto con esto que Vuestra Majestad no le podrá mandar nada cuanto al dicho Camarino que el dicho duque fuese obligado de obedecer, y lo tendría por especie de desconfianza lo cual no podía convenir tanto menos estando los negocios públicos en los términos antedichos, y Vuestra Majestad tan impedido en ellos. Por las cuales consideraciones entre otras parecía a Vuestra Majestad hacer buen deber para con Su Santidad y ser lo mejor el suplicarle por el dicho sobreseimiento y via amigable, y que los dichos venecianos persistían en lo mismo con la obligación que tienen al dicho duque, y que se ha visto diversas veces sobreseer ejecuciones de sentencias de importancia por buenas causas, mayormente concernientes el bien público y por evitar inconveniente, rogando al dicho nuncio que hiciese buen oficio, y que Vuestra Majestad escribiría sobre esto al conde de Cifuentes, y fue la conclusión después de muchas declaraciones y pláticas que hablaría aun a Vuestra Majestad una palabra sobre esto. A la cual avisamos de lo que arriba está dicho para que le responda en conformidad o cómo será servido, mostrándole confianza de que hará en esto buen deber.

Allende de esto nosotros le hablamos de las alianzas de casamientos de que un cardenal sin le nombrar había hablado al dicho Conde de Cifuentes, y por tanto que nosotros entendimos que el dicho nuncio quería en gran manera justificar al dicho Santo Padre de que no pretendía nada en lo de Camarino por su particular. Hablamos de otros dos puntos y le apartamos cuanto pudimos de este punto, tomando fundamento que después de haber hablado al dicho nuncio de lo que tocaba al Su Santidad cuanto a la dignidad pontifical tanto del espiritual a la fe y al concilio como de la temporalidad de la iglesia en lo que toca a Camarino, nos queríamos hablar particular y confiadamente con él de lo que tocaba a la casa de Su Santidad y al engrandecimiento de ella. Y aunque él nos dijo que había entendido nada de lo que el dicho conde había escrito conocimos que no gustaba mal de ello, mas bien dudaba que se hubiese de facilitar el negocio de Camarino por el medio de las dichas alianzas, lo cual nosotros guiamos por otro camino, por dar a entender a Su Santidad la buena voluntad que Vuestra Majestad le tiene, y la confianza que puede tomar de Vuestra Majestad y el respeto a la admonición de hijo y buen consejo de ella, y que ningún otra cosa movía a Vuestra Majestad sino la razón, honestidad, y deber al bien público, y lo que Vuestra Majestad veía convenir a Su Santidad y a su dignidad, y lo que él debe a su propia patria y a la tranquilidad de ella, y lo puede bien entender por su gran prudencia y experiencia, y no le hicimos memoria del secuestro porque que primero sería menester saber la voluntad de la parte y que basta haber primero hecho esto remitiendo lo demás al conde de Cifuentes.

Sire, es verdad que esta escritura es larga prolija, más las pláticas han sido muy largas y servirá así mismo de memoria para escribir al dicho conde de Cifuentes lo que ha pasado y avisar a don Lope de Soria, y hablar a los embajadores de Venecia y de Urbino.

Appendix 14

AGS: Estado, leg. 863, f. 12, Relación de nuevas de Francia 9 April 1535.

Lo que últimamente se sabe de Francia es que pidiendo le el nuncio al rey las galeras que había ofrecido contra Barbarossa respondió que no las daría para contra el dicho Barbarossa ni quería usar de la dicha concesión de Su Santidad sino tomar los bosques y tierras de las iglesias de Francia que son fuera de décima por lo cual habría más de seiscientos mil ducados y que esto no era contra la sede apostólico ni contra lo con la Iglesia que para defensión de Su Santidad y de sus tierras que él le ayudaría con todas sus galeras y 10,000 hombres pagados por dos años y

Illegible line _____

También dicen que ha enviado 3,000 escudos a Suiza y que en Alemania por tener los capitanes de Su Majestad prevenido toda la mejor gente que hay en Alemania no puede haber el dicho Rey hombre que valora un maravedi.

Asimismo escriben que ogaño más atenderá el rey a defenderse que no ha ofender y que ha publicado el dicho rey que ha venido. Otro mensajero a el de Barbarosaa que dice que el Turco envía grueso socorro a Barbarossa, lo cual se contra dice por la nueva que yo tengo por via de Venecia, lo cual le envía a llamar para que vaya a guardar aquellos mares de Constantinopla.

Asimismo he entiendo que envía el dicho rey al Obispo de Limos al duque de Ferrara para que no venga en la liga y después se vendrá aquí a solicitar el Capelo del Obispado de París.

Appendix 15

AGS: Estado, leg. 863, f. 14, Avisos de Francia/y de lo que pasó el papa con los embajadores de Francia sobre lo de Ferrara/ del concierto, n.d.

Que Su Santidad le dijo la grata audiencia que Vuestra Majestad había dado a su nuncio y lo que mostraba favorecer su justicia en lo de Camerino. Y que este negocio es el que Su Santidad siente mas que otro ninguno.

Que también le dijo Su Santidad que en esta corte algunos tenían que Su Santidad inclinaba a Francia tomando fundamento por la concesión que hizo al Rey de Francia de las décimas en lo cual no tenían razón porque antes para los fines que el tiene y conviene a Vuestra Majestad no quisiera dejar de haberlas otorgado por ninguna cosa porque será causa no haciendo el Rey de Francia lo que tiene prometido de dar las galeras para contra Barbarossa de coligarse y hacer todo lo que Vuestra Majestad quisiera.

Que después de escrito lo de arriba recibió la carta de Vuestra Majestad de 2 de febrero que llevó a Genova el mayordomo mayor a la cual por ser todo de avisos de la comisión que llevaba no tiene que responder por solo a lo del Duque de Ferrara. Porque demás de lo que esto tiene escrito el día de pasivo supo que el dicho duque se había declarado en dar a Su Santidad clU ducados en tres años cual no hizo hasta ahora y que por esto y por la ocasión desta empresa y otras causas cree que se concentraran y ha prevenido a los embajadores del duque que tengan la mano en el concierto que no se perjudique el derecho y autoridad de Vuestra Majestad y hará la misma diligencia con Su Santidad en general hasta saber la particularidad de lo que a Vuestra Majestad tiene ____.

Que hablando con Su Santidad en lo de la empresa dijo a Su Santidad que toda era una empresa, la de Túnez y Constantinopoli; pues no se podía hacer la una sin haber hecho la otra y Su Santidad le dijo que se podía dejar la de Túnez porque yendo en Constantinopoli de necesidad Barbarossa había de ir allá. Y el respondió que no le parecía buena consecuencia porque como Barbarossa es cosario, estará en deservir del turco cuando a él le importará y su ve que no le estará bien ir a Constantinopoli, no irá aunque el turco se lo mande y quedaría poderoso para hacer daño en los reinos de Vuestra Majestad.

Que en esta misma platica le preguntó Su Santidad si Vuestra Majestad holgaría de verse con él y con el Rey de Francia y él le respondió que no lo sabia, más que en lo pasado había entendido que moviéndolo a Vuestra Majestad algunas veces no lo había querido si ya primo no se tuviese certinidad que había de resultar bien general de las vistas.

Appendix 16

AGS: Estado, leg. 863, f. 13, La relación del caso que envía el Conde de Cifuentes de lo del Cardinal de Ravenna.

Lo que deponen dos testigos contra el Cardinal de Ravena es que queriendo el cardinal por pasión particular justiciar unos cinco anconitaños que fueron justiciado mientras fue legado de Ancona soborno al uno de estos dos testigos por medio del otro para que acusase a los cinco hombres de una conjura que hacían contra el Cardinal y la Iglesia para levantarse con la tierra y que para esto le dio dinero.

Los indicios son que siendo preso el un testigo el cardinal pensando que le podría deponer trabajó de sacarlo de la prisión y ofreció 12,000 ducados de seguridad.

El otro indicio es que viniendo este testigo mismo a Roma el cardinal por su seguridad le hizo hacer un testimonio ante un notario ratificando lo que había dicho en Ancona y diciendo que no había sido sobornando este es el cargo y lo que siguiente es el descargo – estos son los que hasta ahora se han publicado.

Cuanto a lo primero de los testigos se responde por el (damage) _____ es infame y omiso y hombre que en un tiempo mismo tuvo dos mujeres y que confesando su fealdad no se le ha de dar crédito y por derecho es de probado y que el otro que es un su maestre sala es infame y público ceñido y estaba en desgracia del cardinal por sus ruines maneras, lo cual todo se probará.

Cuanto al primero indicio se dice que es de ningún momento por lo que el cardinal negocia y prometía por el testigo era por la buena obra que en descubrir la traición que le tenían armada en Ancona le hizo y porque había sido preso en su casa y espiado de los enemigos que son ciertos Anconitaños, parientes de los muertos.

Cuanto al segundo indicio del testimonió ello pasa así que ligué dicen el mismo Aconitaño vino a ofrecerse de querer hacer esto porque decía que había entendido que los de Ancona decían que el había sido sobornado desto, cómo al cardinal no le tocase no se caro de ello sino remitir lo a sus criados, los cuales como mal pláticas en cosas de puntos de justicia fueron en que hiciese el testimonio ratificando lo pasado, no lo haber hecho por sobornación.

Ahora estando la cosa desta manera al papa se le dice que ni los testigos ni los indicios eran bastantes aprender un cardinal y que cuando lo fuera, el delito no era de calidad que por él se debiese meter en prisión del castillo de San Angel. El papa responde que lo que ha hecho ha sido consejo y parecer de sus letrados y que ellos darán cuenta de si.

Damaged line _____

Se publicado luego que el Aconitaño fue preso, lo que se hacía contra él. No procuró como pudiera de ausentar a su maestre sala de Roma, mas que después de preso el maestre sala siendo el cardinal por muchos personas aconsejado que si se sentía haber pecado venialmente en este caso no esperase a ponerse en manos del papa sino se ausentarse. El cardinal no lo quiso hacer diciendo que así como él estaba inocentísimo en este caso así esperaba en Dios que no permitiría que le fuese hecho agravio y asegurado en su inocencia se fue a consistorio donde fue preso.

Más hay otra señal de importancia que habiendo sido este caso en tiempos Papa Clemente ya no haberse hecho en tiempo de Su Santidad parece ser que tanto lugar de castigo. En caso que se le probase lo que le acusaron parece que los testigos dicen contra el cardinal son criados suyos, los cuales sin ninguno tormento dijeron su dicho por donde parece que tenían alguna indignación contra el cardinal los dichos criados, que es cosa que nunca criado dijo contra su señor sino estos sí ya estuviese indignado contra el.

Appendix 17

AGS: Estado, leg. 1021, f. 120, Avisos de diversos partes, n.d.

Por letras al Conde de Cifuentes y otros particulares cortesanos Romanos de 22 y 23 de junio 1535 se entiende que pocos días antes pasando por moneda el hijo de Filipo Strozi hizo pretender ciertos hombres que por mandado del Duque de Florencia estaban allí para matarlo. Ellos confesaron de si y los soltaron. Venido a Roma este hijo de Strozi fueron presos otros dos que dice que estaba para matar al Filipo por el mismo orden. Estos no han confesado y habiéndose aclarado que la cosa no era verdad. El papa los mandaba soltar. El Filipo exclamó y están presos. Estando esta cosa en esto vino a las manos del Duque de Florencia una letra que el Obispo de Marsella, hermano del Cardinal Cibo que está en Florencia, escribía al Conde de Genga, capitán muy favorito de Medici, en la cual se comprendía que había puesto a la guardia contra el dicho Duque seis o siete soldados y busca para poner otros vi que fuesen doce con los cuales pensaba poner en ejecución su deseo de todos ellos que era matar el Duque y preso el obispo, confesó como esto era verdad y luego el Duque dio dello aviso al papa y Su Santidad hizo luego prender al dicho Conde de Genga en el palacio de San Marco mientras las cardinales estaban con Su Santidad en consistorio que fue a los 22 del dicho. Acabado el consistorio y venido el Cardinal de Medicis a su casa mostró gran sin finito de su capitán y muy enojado sin dar noticia al Papa se salió aquella noche de Roma. Unos escriben que a un castillo suyo llamado San Angelo 20 millas de Roma y otros que a Venecia y en Roma la mayor parte dice que es huído aunque algunos piensan que volverá. Luego otro día fueron a palacio el Cardinal Salviati y Filipo Strozi y otros a quien puede tocar este caso; lo que entre ellos se platica no se sabe. No se puede nada averiguar pero pudiese creer todo mal de aquella gente que ni a Dios ni al mundo tienen respeto. El Papa procura por muchos medios hacer tornar al Cardinal Medici en Roma y se estima que los florentines de la parte francesa sienten de hacerlo ir en Francia. De lo que en esto caso más suceden y en sabiendo daré dello aviso a Vuestra Majestad porque es cosa de donde pueden nacer muchos embarazos.

Appendix 18

AGS: Estado, leg. 1026, f. 131, Viceroy to Cobos and the Council of Castile, 18 December 1537.

Muy ilustrísimo señor,
Como yo tengo a vuestra señoría por tan señor hablo en todas las cosas que se ofrecen, así del servicio de Su Majestad como de vuestro señor tan abiertamente como es razón. Yo no puedo sino estar admirado de lo que con Valdés se hace, conociéndole vuestro señor tan bien como yo y como le conocía. Pero González que haya gloria que habiéndole Su Majestad dado el oficio de exactor de las significatorias que es muy honrado y de provecho no le quiso aceptar: y que después le haya hecho merced del oficio de veedor de los castillos que también es muy honrado: y que no le acepte y dijo que espera de ahí y han de proveer de otra cosa que más le cumple. Estoy muy maravillado que esto se pase así sabiendo como he dicho quien él es. Y cuando ahora veo que no quiere aceptar este otro oficio, pienso que debe de esperar que le envíen la provisión de virrey deste reino y porque los castillos tienen gran necesidad que el veedor ande por ellos: y los visite por los muchos bastimentos que en ellos se pusieron

el año pasado para la invasión de los enemigos. Conviene al servicio de Su Majestad que se provea luego el dicho oficio, y porque Valdés no le acepta envío dentro desta una memoria de mi mano de las personas que me ocurren para el dicho oficio que me parece son cuales se requieren para que su Majestad sea bien servida. Suplico a vuestro señor tenga por bien proveer que luego se nombre persona que ejercite el dicho oficio porque como he dicho hay necesidad que no se dilate más. Nuestro Señor guarde la muy ilustrísima persona de vuestro señor como desea. De Nápoles a 18 de diciembre.
del 1537 años
Servidor de vuestro señor
Item: Francisco de Barrahina
Item: Pedro de Solys
Item: Pero Ortiz de Valderrama
Cover Page: Al muy ilustrísimo señor, el señor don Francisco de los Cobos, comendador mayor de y del consejo de Su Majestad.

Appendix 19

AGS: Estado, leg. 1026, f. 134, Cobos's summary of the above letter for the Council of Castile.

El virrey de Nápoles escribe al comendador mayor y dice que puede dejar de hablar libremente en las cosas que tocan al servicio de Su Majestad y de aquí viene a decir que acá conocen bien quien es Juan de Valdés y la gravedad y términos que allí usa con él, y que cuando los días pasados Su Majestad le proveyó del oficio de las significatorias que es muy honrado no le quiso aceptar, ni ahora lo ha querido el oficio de veedor de los castillos de que Vuestra Majestad le hizo merced, y hablándole él en ello para que usase el dicho oficio por lo que conviene, le respondió que de acá esperaba otra cosa que mejor le estuviese y anda en estas puntas con él y cree que no se contentará con menos del virreinado, dice que este oficio de veedor de los castillos conviene que este en persona de cualidad y confianza por lo mucho que importa de servicio de Su Majestad, y que al presente hace muy gran falta la tal persona porque no andando sobre ello no habrá el recaudo que conviene en las provisiones que hay en los castillos y corre grandísimo interese en esto y para adelante es de mucha consecuencia. Suplica que Vuestra Majestad comande proveer como conviene con toda brevedad, envía en una relacioncilla de su mano nombradas tres personas que dice te parece son convenientes para ello y son Francisco de Barrahina, Pedro de Solis, Pedro Ortiz de Valderama.

Appendix 20

AGS: Estado, leg. 54, f. 7, Cobos to Valdés, 16 April 1541. Transcribed by Sara T. Nalle. The author originally published this document as an appendix to 'Juan de Valdés and the Comunero Revolt: An Essay on Spanish Civic Humanism,' in the *Sixteenth Century Journal* 22, no. 2 (Summer 1991): 252.

Señor:

La carta de vuestra merced de 20 de diciembre es la última que he recibido y con ella, la señora doña Julia, a la cual respondo, la que irá con ésta. En sus negociaciones de ahí no sabría qué decir porque me parece que de mi parte, con suplicar al señor virrey los favorezco—no se puede hacer más. En lo que ha de despachar por Su Majestad: yo he escrito allá tan encarecidamente cuanto he podido y así lo haré siempre y espero que harán bien, pues todos los que están allá entenderán en ellos con la misma voluntad que yo. Por lo demás que vuestra merced dice en su carta, le beso las manos, que bien sé que vuestro consejo e industria no puede dejar de ayudar mucho a llevar con menos fatiga el peso de los negocios.

Huelgo de que esos señores consejeros estén algo más sosegados y contentos con la buena esperanza que se les ha dado de la pragmática.

The following paragraph was marked through: A lo menos si Su Majestad sigue el parecer que sobre ello le he enviado, tendrán causa de estarlo del todo, que nunca fui de parecer que la cosa se llevase por los extremos que fue, Nuestro Señor su magnífica persona y casa guarde y prospere como desea. De Madrid a de abril, 1541.

Espero que su merced lo proveerá de manera que estén satisfechos del todo.

Gonzalo Pérez me ha dicho que un Alonso Díaz le ha movido pleito en Roma sobre unos beneficios que tiene en Villena y que vuestra merced sería mucha parte para que se desistiese de ello. Ya sabe lo que merece y ha servido y sirve y la voluntad que yo le tengo, y la razón que hay para que se le haga toda buena obra. Pido por merced a vuestra merced que haga en ello lo que él le suplicaré, que toda la merced que se le hiciere a él, recibiré yo por propia.

Nuestro Señor. De Madrid, a 16 de abril, 1541

Abbreviations

Alcaraz Proceso	AHN: Inquisición, leg. 106. Proceso de Pedro Ruiz de Alcaraz.
Carranza Documentos	Tellechea Idígoras, Ignacio. *Fray Bartolomé Carranza, Documentos Históricos*, 5 vols. Madrid: Real Academia de Historia, 1962–76.
Cartas inéditas	Valdés, Juan de. *Cartas inéditas de Juan de Valdés al cardenal Gonzaga*. Edited and introduced by José F. Montesinos. Madrid: Saguirre Impressor, 1931.
Croce, 'Cartas'	Croce, Benedetto, ed., appendix II, 'Lettere Inedite di Juan de Valdés al Segrtario di Stato Cobos Riguardanti Giulia Gonzaga e L'Amministrazione Spagnuoli di Napoli,' of *Alfabeto cristiano: dialogo con Giulia Gonzaga*. Bari: Guis, Laterya and Figli, 1938.
Erasmus, 'Epistolario'	Erasmus, Desiderius. 'Epistolario con Españoles.' In *Erasmo: Obras Escogidas*. 2nd ed. Translated and edited by Lorenzo Riber. Madrid: Aguilar, 1964.
Longhurst, 'Vergara Trial'	Longhurst, John. 'Alumbrados, erasmistas y luteranos en el processo de Juan de Vergara.' *Cuadernos de historia de España* 27 (1957): 99–163; 28 (1958): 102–65; 29–30 (1959): 266–92; 31–2 (1960): 322–56; 35–6 (1962): 337–53; 37–8 (1963): 356–71.
Sarpi	Polano, Pietro Soave. *The History of the Council of Trent Containing Eight Books*. Translated by S. Nathaniel Brent. London: J. Macock, 1676.
Valdés Suit	AGS: CR, leg. 73, no. 2, 'Pleito de García Fernández y Andrés de Valdés *regidores* de Cuenca con el canónigo Diego Manrique primo hermano de

Diego Hurtado de Mendoza sobre los atropellos y excesos que los cometian en dicha ciudad, son muchos y notables.'

Vergara Proceso AHN: Inquisición, leg. 223, no. 7 (2), Proceso de Juan de Vergara.

Notes

Introduction

1 Juan de Valdés, *Cartas inéditas de Juan de Valdés al cardenal Gonzaga*, ed. and intro. José F. Montesinos (Madrid: Saguirre Impressor, 1931), 3, no. 1, 18 Sept. 1535. Henceforth cited as *Cartas inéditas*.
2 Don Fermín Caballero, *Alonso y Juan de Valdés* (Madrid: Oficina Tipográfica del Hospicio, 1875), appendix no. 83, pp. 469–71, Jacobo Bonfadio to Pietro Carnesechi, n.d., but late 1541 or 1542.
3 AGS: Estado, leg. 1460, f. 138, Cobos to the viceroy, n.d. This document is transcribed in Benedetto Croce, ed., 'Il Testamento del [Juan de] Valdés,' appendix 3 of *Alfabeto cristiano: dialogo con Giulia Gonzaga* (Bari: Guis, Laterya e Figli, 1938), 174–5.
4 Gordon Kinder, 'Juan de Valdés,' *Bibliotheca Dissidentium* 9 (1988): 162–69. Following a very brief biography, Kinder has an extensive bibliography of works by or about Valdés from the sixteenth century to the 1980s. This is an invaluable tool for anyone beginning research on Valdés. Kinder also includes the frontispieces of Valdés's works published in the sixteenth century. Throughout this study I use this work for the chronology of Valdés's writings and publications.
5 Marcel Bataillon, *Erasmo y España: estudios sobre la historia espiritual del siglo XVI*, trans. Antonio Alatorre (Ciudad de México: Fondo de Cultura Económica, 1966, orig. 1938), 342–43.
6 'Lettere inedite di Juan de Valdés al segretario di stato Cobos reguardanti Guilia Gonzaga e l'amministrazione spagnuola di Napoli (1539–1540),' appendix 2 of *Alfabeto cristiano*, 152–73, henceforth cited as Croce, 'Cartas.' The original letters are AGS: Estado, leg. 1030, f. 161, and AGS: Estado, leg. 1032, ff.18–23.

7 Bataillon, *Erasmo*, 418.
8 The following list by no means exhausts the scholars who have generally followed Bataillon's interpretation of Juan de Valdés. José Luis Abellán, *El erasmismo español: una historia de la otra España* (Madrid: S.A. Editorial Graficas Esejo, 1976); Eugenio Asensio, 'El erasmismo y las corrientes espirituales afines,' *Revista de filología española* 36 (1952): 31–99; Marcel Bataillon, *Erasmo y el erasmismo*, trans. Carlos Pujol (Barcelona: Editorial Crítica, 1977); Américo Castro, 'Lo hispánico y el Erasmo,' *Revista de filología hispánica* 4 (1942): 1–66; Theodore Merrill Haggard, 'The Church and Sacraments in the Theological Writings of Juan de Valdés' (PhD diss., Emory University, 1971); John Longhurst, *Erasmus and the Spanish Inquisition: The Case of Juan de Valdés* (Albuquerque: University of New Mexico Press, 1950) and *Luther's Ghost in Spain* (Lawrence, Kansas: Coronado Press, 1969); José Antonio Maravall, *Carlos V y el pensamiento político del renacimiento* (Madrid: Instituto De Estudios Políticos, 1960); Francisco Eguiagary Bohigas, *Los intelectuales españoles de Carlos V* (Madrid: Instituto de Estudios Políticos, 1965); Miguel de la Pinta Llorente, *El erasmismo del doctor Juan de Vergara y otras interpretaciones* (Madrid: n.p., 1944); Domingo Ricart, *Juan de Valdés y el pensamiento religioso europeo en los siglos XVI y XVII* (México: El Colegio De México, 1958); Domingo de Santa María, *Juan de Valdés 1498 (?)–1541: su pensamiento religioso y las corrientes espirituales de su tiempo* (Rome: Apud Uedes Universitatis Gregorianae, 1957).
9 José Nieto, *Juan de Valdés and the Origins of the Spanish and Italian Reformation* (Geneva: Libraire Droz, 1970), 65–76, 132–6, 164, 169, 239, and 323–4; the mask aspect is developed more fully in his 'El Espectro de Lutero y las Máscaras de Erasmo en España,' appendix 2 in the Spanish edition of his book, *Juan de Valdés y los orígenes de la reforma en España e Italia* (Mexico City: Fondo de Cultura Económica, 1979), 543–63.
10 Carlos Gilly, 'Juan de Valdés, traductor y adaptador de escritos de Lutero en su *Diálogo de Doctrina Cristiana*,' in *Miscelánea de estudios hispánicos; Homenaje de los hispanistas de Suiza, Ramón Sugranyes de Franch*, ed. Luis López Molina (Montserrat: Grafiques Badalona, S.A., 1982), 85–106; and Gordon Kinder, 'Spain,' in *The Early Reformation in Europe*, ed. Andrew Pettegree (Cambridge: Cambridge University Press, 1992), 215–37.

1. Rebellion's Child

1 Carla Rahn Phillips and William D. Phillips, *Spain's Golden Fleece: Wool Production and the Wool Trade from the Middle Ages to the Nineteenth Century* (Baltimore: Johns Hopkins University Press, 1997), 252.

2 Joseph Pérez, *La revolución de las comunidades de Castilla (1520–1521)*, trans. Juan José Faci Lacasta (Madrid: Siglo Veintiuno de España Editores, S.A., 1977), 5–7.
3 Richard Kagan, *Lawyers and Litigants in Early Modern Castile 1500–1700* (Chapel Hill: University of North Carolina Press, 1981), 4.
4 José Martínez Millán et al., ed. *La corte de Carlos V*, vols. 1–2, *Corte y gobierno* (Madrid: Sociedad Estatal para la Conmemoración de Felipe II y Carlos V, 2000), 1: 105–10, and 222–3.
5 The Valdés genealogy has been clarified by Miguel Jiménez Monteserín's 1995 publication of excerpts from the 1540 *ejecutoría* that established the Valdés *mayorazgo*, or entailed estate. See Miguel Jiménez Monteserín, 'La familia Valdés de Cuenca,' introduction to the facsimile edition of *Alonso Y Juan de Valdés* by Fermín Caballero (Cuenca: Instituto de Juan de Valdés, 1995, orig. edition 1875), xxv–xxviii, xliv. Jiménez Monteserín provides a family tree in 'La familia Valdés de Cuenca: nuevos datos,' in *Los Valdés: Pensamiento y literatura* (Cuenca: Instituto de Juan de Valdés, 1997), 88–9.
6 Jiménez Monteserín, 'Familia Valdés,' xxv–xxviii, xliv.
7 Miguel Martínez Millán, *Los hermanos conquenses Alfonso y Juan de Valdés: Su ambiente familiar y la clasificación social de su familia* (Cuenca: Imprenta de Falange, 1976), 73.
8 Nieto, *Valdés*, 101–2; A witness testified to the Inquisition that Pedro Ruiz de Alcaraz taught his doctrines to *mochachos*. Following the accusation, the witness listed numerous individuals who frequented Alcaraz's sermons, including the Marquis of Villena, who was certainly not a *mochacho*, as well as Valdés. Other Valdés scholars have dismissed the inference that Valdés was a *mochacho* on the basis of this reference. For a more detailed critique of Nieto's chronology see Antonio Márquez, 'Juan de Valdés, teólogo de los alumbrados,' *La Ciudad de Dios* 84 (1971): 215–20 passim; and Jiménez Monteserín, 'Familia Valdés,' xlvii–xlviii.
9 Dorothy Donald and Elena Lazaro, *Alfonso de Valdés y su Época* (Cuenca: Excma. Diputación Provincial, 1983), 101, 114. Donald and Lazaro did not include it in the documentary appendices of their book, and José Nieto has claimed the document did not mention Juan. See Nieto, *Two Catechisms*, 104, n. 12. The document is written in a very difficult hand, but it clearly mentions Juan de Valdés, as Donald and Lazaro stated. See appendix 1, AMC leg. 1493, ex. 52.
10 Miguel Jiménez Monteserín, 'Los hermanos Valdés y el mundo Judeo converso conquense,' in *Política, religión e inquisición en la España moderna*, ed. P. Fernández Albadalejo, J. Martínez Millán, and V. Pinto Crespo (Madrid: Universidad Autónoma de Madrid, 1996), 395, n. 53.

11 J. Tellechea Idigoras, 'Juan de Valdés y Bartoloméo de Carranza: La apasionante historia de un papel,' *Revista española de teología,* 20 (1961): 307. The term *juvenis* in sixteenth-century Castile was elastic enough to cover young men in their mid-twenties. For example, in a 1520 letter Pedro Martyr de Angleria referred to Juan's older brother Alfonso as a *juvenis*. See Donald, 22.
12 AHN: Inquisición, leg. 223, no. 7 (2), Proceso de Juan de Vergara: Respuestes a los testigos, f. cclxxxiiii, 6 March 1534. Henceforth cited as Vergara Proceso.
13 Vergara's birth date is firm, as it is taken from his sepulchre. See Antonio de la Torre y del Cerro, 'La Universidad de Alcalá: Datos para su Historia,' *Revista de archivos, bibliotecas y museos* 21 (1909): 281, n. 8.
14 Jiménez Monteserín prefers a 1495 birth date for Juan based on the probable age of María, who, according to Jiménez Monteserín, must have been thirty-nine or forty by 1500. See Jiménez Monteserín, 'Familia Valdés,' xlviii.
15 In 1975 Miguel Martínez Millán first identified Fernando's illegitimate son. See *Los hermanos,* 70. References to the two Fernandos in Cuenca led one historian to identify the *regidor* and the Captain of the Guard as the same person. See Pedro Luis Lorenzo Cadarso, 'Esplendor y decadencia de las oligarquías conversos de Cuenca y Guadalajara (siglos XV y XVI)' *Hispania* 54/1, no. 186 (1994): 71.
16 AGS: CC, leg. 129, fol. 170, and AGS: Estado, leg. 28, f. 168, Lo que sea de consultar a Vuestra Majestad tocante particulares.
17 Appendix 2, AGS: Estado, leg. 9, f. 77. My emphasis.
18 AHPC: Protocolos, leg. P-13, f. clxxiii.
19 See Jiménez Monteserín, 'Familia Valdés,' xlviii.
20 AGS: CC leg. 196, f. 98.
21 Caballero, appendix 1, 20 April 1520.
22 Martínez Millán, *Los hermanos,* 44, 71–2, 75; Donald, 34, 335, appendix 12.
23 AGS: CSR, leg. 125, f. 231. This document is a request by Diego for payment of his 1519 stipend as a *contino*.
24 Martínez Millán, *Los hermanos,* 71–2.
25 AGS: CSR, leg. 125, f. 229. This appointment of a Diego de Valdés and his salary record lists payment only for 1529. The facts that Diego was listed as a member of the clergy, and resided at the royal court, make it likely that this was Juan's brother rather than another Diego de Valdés. Diego's acquisition of prebends in 1530 probably led to his departure from court and his position as chaplain.
26 Jiménez Monteserín, 'Familia Valdés,' xli; Juan Meseguer Fernández, 'Nuevos datos sobre los hermanos Valdés: Alfonso, Juan, Diego y Margarita,' *Hispania* 18, no. 67 (1957): 385–90, docs. 3–5.

27 Both Alfonso and Diego intervened with Charles on behalf of their brother-in-law Luis Salazar. Luis had falsified documents in an attempt to cheat his aunt out of part of her inheritance. In November 1528 the royal court in Granada sentenced him to pay a fine of 100,000 maravedís, to serve a year in Oran with his own horse and sword, and to be banished from Cuenca for four years. At first his in-laws pleaded for a complete pardon, but only attained a reduction of the fine to 80,000 maravedis the following May. They claimed that two years in Granada prison during the trial had left Luis too sick to serve in Oran. Finally Alfonso convinced Charles to pardon the military service. The reduced fine and the period of exile were apparently enforced. See AGS: CC, leg. 192, f. 61, leg. 197, f. 78, leg. 198, f. 65.

28 Julián Zarco y Cuevas, ed., 'Testamentos de Alfonso y Diego de Valdés,' *Boletín de la Real Academia Española* 14 (1927): 679–85 passim; Donald and Lazaro also provide transcriptions of Alfonso and Diego's testaments, 345–53, appendices 21, 23; Croce, ed., 'Il Testamento de Juan de Valdés,' 174–5.

29 Lorenzo Cadarso, 59.

30 Donald, 63, 327, appendix 3, Como Otorgaron Poder a Valdés, 1 March 1493; Martínez Millán, *Los hermanos*, 16–17. The appointment may have been reward for Fernando's military service during the War of Succession, as the city council selected Fernando as Cuenca's representative for the reorganization of the urban militias into the *Santa Hermandad* under royal jurisdiction. See Jiménez Monteserín, 'La Familia Valdés,' xxvii. A *regidor* was a city councilman, and the *ayuntamiento* was the city council.

31 Donald, 68–70, 327.

32 Caballero, 59, 66; Martínez Millán, *Los hermanos*, 39; Donald, 53.

33 Donald, 68–9. Royal cities like Cuenca had to be constantly on guard against encroachment from neighbouring aristocrats. Loss of these lands meant loss of taxpayers and a reduction in the city's grain supply. Such seizures reduced the royal patrimony and tax base, but during periods of monarchical weakness the crown often ignored such thefts in order to garner aristocratic support.

34 Juan de Pacheco, the Marquis of Villena, helped oust the Mendoza from Cuenca in bitter fighting between 1447 and 1449. During the reign of Henry IV (1454–74) Pacheco's vast estates and numerous vassals in Aragón and Castile enabled him to broker war and peace between the two states. His son Diego inherited the marquisate and leadership of the aristocratic faction opposing the joining of the two kingdoms and the succession of Isabel to the crown of Castile. Although defeat in the War of Succession reduced Villena's territories and influence in the region, the grandee eventually regained favour with the crown by his faithful service in the Granada Wars

and his later support for the Habsburg succession. See Juan de Mata Carriazo, gen. ed., *Colección de crónicas españolas*, 9 vols. (Madrid: Espasa-Calpe, S.A., 1940–6), vol. 2: *Crónica de don Alvaro de Luna; Condestable de Castilla, maestre de Santiago*, 223–9 and vol. 8: *Crónica del halconero de Juan II de Pedro Carrillo de Huete*, 482–516; Juan Torres Fontes, 'La conquista del Marquisado de Villena en el reinado de los Reyes Católicos,' *Hispania: revista española de historia* 50 (1973): 37–42.

35 D. Trifón Muñoz y Solivo, *Historia de la muy noble, leal e impertérrita ciudad de Cuenca, y del territorio de su provincia y obispado, desde los tiempos primitivos hasta la edad presente*, 2 vols. (Cuenca: El Eco de Cuenca, 1866–7), 1: 468.

36 Felix G. Olmedo, *Diego Ramírez Villaescusa (1459–1537): Fundador del Colegio de Cuenca y autor de los cuatro diálogos sobre la muerte del Príncipe don Juan* (Madrid: Editorial Nacional, 1944), 107–9.

37 AGS: CR, leg. 73, no. 2, 'Pleito de García Fernández y Andrés de Valdés *regidores* de Cuenca con el canónigo Diego Manrique primo hermano de Diego Hurtado de Mendoza sobre los atropellos y excesos que los cometian en dicha ciudad, son muchos y notables,' passim, henceforth cited as Valdés Suit. Some excerpts from this suit are printed in Manuel Dánvila y Collado, ed., *Historia crítica y documentada de los comunidades de Castilla*, 6 vols. (Madrid: La Real Academia de Historia, 1897–9), 5: 519–31; Lorenzo Cadarso (79) identifies Rodrigo Manrique as a *regidor* of Cuenca, but all the documents I have seen refer to him only as an *aguacil* and *Comendador* of Salamanca. His frequent appearance at the city council meetings possibly explains the confusion.

38 AGS: CR leg. 45, no. 6.

39 AMC, leg. 12, f. 2.

40 Olmedo, 146–7.

41 AGS: CR leg. 9, no. 3, leg. 39, no. 1, leg. 40, no. 9, leg. 60 no. 9. The latter is a 1522 suit of the city against Diego Hurtado and includes a document from a 1509–10 case against the grandee.

42 José Martínez Millán, *Corte*, 1: 108.

43 Peggy Liss, *Isabel the Queen: Life and Times* (New York: Oxford University Press, 1992), 347. An insightful revision of Juana the 'Mad's' supposed passivity is presented by Bethany Aram. Though she does not try to answer the question of Juana's sanity, many of her odd behaviours are given logical explanation. Aram believes that Juana's 'incapacity' stemmed from her refusal to accept the advice of her mother and her advisers. Most importantly Aram shows that Juana actually negotiated her retirement from political power with Philippe and later Ferdinand in order to ensure the succession of her son Charles to the throne. See *Juana the Mad: Sovereignty*

and Dynasty in Renaissance Europe (Baltimore: Johns Hopkins University Press, 2005), 67, 74, 86, 87, 89, 102–3.
44 William H. Prescott, *History of the Reign of Ferdinand and Isabella the Catholic* (Philadelphia: David McKay, 1893), 3: 190–3.
45 Pedro de Alcocer, *Relación de algunas cosas que pasaron en estos reinos desde que murió la reina catolica doña Isabel, hasta que le acabaron las comunidades en la ciudad de Toledo* (Seville: Imprenta y Libreria Española y Extrangera, 1872), 12–13.
46 Donald, 101.
47 Appendix 1, AMC, leg. 1493, ex. 52. After the Cortes adjourned, Fernando wrote the crown that Cuenca was withholding its *corregidor*'s pay for neglect of his duties and non-residence in the city, a tactic used by *corregidores* who feared hearing cases involving territorial disputes between cities and powerful nobles. Philip appointed a new *corregidor* nominated by Villena, Martín Vázquez de Acuña. See AGS: CC leg 7 f. 73, Petition of Fernando de Valdés to the Royal Council, 12 August 1506, and José Martínez Millán, *Corte*, 1: 105.
48 Prescott, 3: 261.
49 Valdés Suit, ff. 2–3; On 15 February 1507 the city council met in Infantado's presence. The *regidores* declared that because of the absence of the *corregidor* and his lieutenant the city 'is without justice ... [and] receives much damage' and proceeded to select new *alcaldes* (judges) and *alguaciles*. Only eight of the twenty-four *regidores* were present, as Mendoza personally placed the names of nominees in a hat and then drew out and announced the new officials. See AMC, leg. 222, f. 18.
50 Donald, 106–7.
51 Donald, 75–6. Fernando had been removed from office for a month in 1498 for collecting an excess salary and had to repay the amount. The 1509 charge refers to his alleged over-taxation of nobles, which probably refers to his 1508 appointment as collector of royal subsidies in the provinces of Cuenca and Huete. A 1512 document indicates that Fernando continued collecting these revenues even while he was banished from the city council. See Martínez Millán, *Los hermanos*, 71.
52 Lorenzo Cadarso, 70.
53 Benjamin Wiffen, *Life and Writings of Juan de Valdés, Spanish Reformer in the Sixteenth Century* (London: Bernard Quartich, 1865), 6, 12–13; Alfonso de Valdés, *Diálogo de las cosas ocurridas en Roma*, ed. and intro. José F. Montesinos (Madrid: Espasa-Calpe, S.A., 1928), introduction, xiv; Caballero, 50; Donald, 120.
54 Martínez Millán, *Los hermanos*, 37–8.

55 Juan de Valdés, *Diálogo de la lengua*, 5th ed., notes by Rafael Lapesa (Zaragoza: Editorial Ebro, S.I., 1965), 51.
56 Ibid., 115–16.
57 Sara Nalle poignantly portrays the unbearable poverty of the village of about two hundred families in her analysis of the Inquisition trial of Bartolomé Sánchez, 'the Secret Messiah of Cardenete.' The villagers of Cardenete did not believe Moya had a legal right to his jurisdiction over them so they threw him out during the Comunero Revolt. Calculating his losses at 24,000 ducats, the marquis sucked the very life out of Cardenete. See Sara T. Nalle, *Mad for God: Bartolomé Sánchez, the Secret Messiah of Cardenete* (Charlottesville: University Press of Virginia, 2001), 58, 61.
58 AHPC, Protocolos, leg. P-14, ff. xvi–xviii, Obligation for Payment to Juan and Francisco de Valdés, 21 Jan. 1523. Martínez Millán mentions this document (17), but he incorrectly identified the Juan and Francisco named as uncles of Juan de Valdés. Prior to Monteserín's citation of the Valdés *mayorazgo* document, Francisco was an unrecognized Valdés. The obligation is for payment of 228,300 maravedís to Juan and Francisco by Gregorio Álvarez de Chinchilla, a *regidor* of Cuenca. The debt was owed from the dowry of the recently deceased Ana de Valdés, Chinchilla's wife and the sister of Juan and Francisco. Ana must have been the given name of the oldest Valdés daughter mentioned in the Valdés *mayorazgo* as having died soon after marriage. If the marrige between Gregorio and Ana had been of long duration, or produced children, it seems unlikely Juan and Francisco would have inherited the dowry.
59 Benjamin Wiffen asserts that both Juan and Alfonso were trained by Angleria. See *Life and Writings*, 13.
60 *Lengua*, 70–1.
61 Fernando, Andrés, and Mathias de Valdés, another *criado* of Luis Carrillo, testified on their kinsman's behalf. Given Moya's status, Alonso's penalty was light; he was fined 2,000 maravedís and obliged 'not to seduce my wife in any time.' AHPC, Protocolos, leg. P-13, f. 164, Juan del Castillo for Alonso de Valdés, 18 June 1521. Mathias de Valdés's service for Luis de Carrillo is noted in the same notarial book, f. 161, in a document dated 17 April 1521. Martínez Millán transcribes the former document about uncle Alonso's indiscretion (18), but he was unable to identify him as Juan's uncle.
62 Martínez Millán, *Los hermanos*, 49.
63 Since the nineteenth century, Valdesian scholars have been divided about Fernando de Valdés's support of the revolt. Benjamin Wiffen believed there was a significant link between Fernando de Valdés and the comuneros 'when they rose to assert the liberties of the people.' Ten years after

Wiffen's pioneer study, Fermín Caballero rejected any connection between the comuneros and the Valdés family, writing that the revolt in Cuenca was completely a lower-class uprising. Caballero's opinion prevailed to such an extent that Bataillon castigated the comuneros as anti-Erasmian and therefore as anti-Valdesian. Dorothy Donald and Elena Lazaro's biography of Alfonso de Valdés minimized the issue by suggesting that the revolt in Cuenca did not last long, and that Fernando's name did not appear on the list of comuneros punished after the revolt ended. Among twentieth-century scholars only the present author and Miguel Jiménez Monteserín have indicated that the Valdés family may have joined the rebellion, in Monteserín's view purely for self-preservation. See Wiffen, *Life and Writings*, 4; Caballero, 68–9; Marcel Bataillon, *Erasmo*, 224; Donald, 70–2; Miguel Jiménez Monteserín, 'La Andadura humana de Juan de Valdés,' appendix to *Diálogo de doctrina cristiana*, ed. Javier Ruiz (Madrid: Editora Nacional, 1979), 172; Dan Crews, 'Juan de Valdés and the Comunero Revolt: An Essay on Spanish Civic Humanism,' *Sixteenth Century Journal* 22, no. 2 (Summer 1991): 233–52, passim.

64 Dánvila, 1: 411.
65 For the constitutional interpretation, see Henry Latimer Seaver, *The Great Revolt in Castile: A Study of the Comunero Movement of 1520–21* (New York: Octagon Books, 1966). For analysis of the revolt as modern class conflict, see José Antonio Maravall, *Las comunidades de Castilla; una primera revolución moderna*, 3rd ed. (Madrid: Alianza Editorial, 1979, orig. 1963), passim.
66 Valdés Suit, f. 3. Studies of the Comunero Revolt by Stephen Haliczer and Juan Gutiérrez Nieto have focused attention on the anti-señorial nature of the revolt and the leading role Cuenca played in the anti-señorial movement. In August Cuenca became the first comunero city to instigate anti-señorial uprisings in order to recover lands usurped by neighbouring grandees. See Stephen Haliczer, *The Comuneros of Castile: The Forging of a Revolution, 1485–1521* (Madison: University of Wisconsin Press, 1981), 77–8; Juan Ignacio Gutiérrez Nieto, *Las Communidades como movimiento antiseñorial; la formación del bando realista en la guerra civil castellana, 1520–1521* (Barcelona: Editorial Planeta, 1973), 188.
67 AGS: PR, leg. 1, f. 84, 26 Oct. 1520.
68 Pérez, 425.
69 Dánvila, 3: 161.
70 Ibid., 4: 453. In Guadalajara Diego Hurtado de Mendoza at first seemed to support the rebellion, but then played a double game throughout the summer between the city and Governor Adrian of Utrecht. See Pablo Sánchez León, *Absolutismo y comunidad: Los orígenes sociales de la guerra de los comuneros de Castilla* (Madrid: Siglo XXI de España Editores, S.A., 1998), 204–8.

71 As quoted in Miguel Jiménez Monteserín, 'La andadura humana,' 172–3.
72 AGS: PR leg. 1, f. 84, Andrés de Valdés to Charles, 10 April 1521.
73 AGS: CC, leg. 139, f. 237.
74 Dánvila, 3: 319; Julián Zarco y Cuevas, ed., *Relaciones de pueblos del obispado de Cuenca; hechas por orden de Felipe II*, 2 vols. (Cuenca: Imprenta Del Seminario, 1927), 1: 63.
75 Martínez Millán, *Los hermanos*, 49–50.
76 At an initial investigation of the Valdés complaints, Canon Manrique read to over two hundred people 'an infamous lampoon that said many injurious, ugly and dishonest things about caballeros, *regidores*, citizens and their lineage ... creating a great scandal' (Valdés Suit, ff. 4–5). Slander, *palabras injuriosas*, was a major source of litigation in sixteenth-century Castile, as individuals defended their perceived honour in an era of increased social tension. See Kagan, *Lawyers*, 90–1.
77 Jiménez Monteserín, 'Familia Valdés,' xxxviii–xxxix.
78 Real Academia de la Historia, ed., *Cortes de los antiguas reinos de León y de Castilla*, 4 vols. (Madrid: Successores De Rivadeneyra, 1861–3), 4: 353–64.
79 AGS: CC, leg. 150, f. 57; The request is also the subject of Andrés's letter to Secretary Castañeda. See AGS: CC, leg. 175, f. 101.
80 Juan de Valdés, *El Evangelio según San Mateo, declarado por Juan de Valdés* (Madrid: Librería Nacional y Extranjera, 1986, orig. 1880), 439.
81 Ibid., 226.
82 Erika Rummel, *Jiménez de Cisneros: On the Threshold of Spain's Golden Age* (Tempe: Arizona Center for Medieval and Renaissance Studies, 1999), 42–5.
83 Otis H. Green, *Spain and the Western Tradition: The Castillian Mind in Literature from El Cid to Calderón*, 4 vols. (Madison: University of Wisconsin Press, 1965), 3: 165. Felipe Fernández-Armesto concluded that while Cisneros 'may have helped to make Spain's soil inhospitable to Lutheranism, he also sowed the seeds or stimulated the growth of more radical spiritual heresy ... [because he] overstimulated readers inclined to ill-disciplined piety.' See his essay, 'Cardinal Cisneros as a Patron of Printing,' in *God and Man in Medieval Spain: Essays in Honour of J.R.L. Highfield*, ed. Derek W. Lomax and David Mackenzie (Warminster: Aris and Phillips, 1989), 168.
84 José Martínez Millán, *Corte*, 1: 224–5.
85 Melquiades Andrés Martín, *Nueva visión de los 'alumbrados' de 1525* (Madrid: Fundacióen Universitaria Española, 1973), 13, 24; Antonio Márquez, *Los alumbrados: orígenes y filosofía (1525–1559)*, 2nd ed. (Madrid: Taurus Ediciones, S.A., 1980), 15, 194, 219, 222.
86 The Admiral of Castile to Charles, 25 April 1521, as cited by Márquez, *Alumbrados*, 195.

87 As quoted in Márquez, *Alumbrados*, 145.
88 Charles V, *The Autobiography of Charles V*, trans. Leonard Francis Simpson (London: Longman, Green, Longman, Roberts and Green, 1862), 8.
89 Henry Kamen, *The Spanish Inquisition: An Historical Revision* (London: Weidenfeld and Nicholson, 1997), 76–7.
90 Norman Roth, *Conversos, Inquisition and the Expulsion from Spain* (Madison: University of Wisconsin Press, 1995), 184, 314; Alastair Hamilton, *Heresy and Mysticism in Sixteenth-Century Spain: The Alumbrados of Toledo* (Toronto: University of Toronto Press, 1992), 71; Kamen, *Inquisition*, 87.
91 Rummel, *Cisneros*, 42–5; Kamen, *Inquisition*, 5, 87. According to a seventeenth-century author, Cuenca was a particularly fertile soil for 'supernatural resources, miraculous springs and relics, famous shrines, [and] saintly men and women.' See Sara T. Nalle, *God in La Mancha: Religious Reform and the People of Cuenca 1500–1650* (Baltimore: Johns Hopkins University Press, 1992), 6. For insight into the mixture of *alumbrado*, comunero, and messianic ideas in the theology of a humble wool carder in the territory near Cuenca, see Nalle, *Mad for God*, passim.
92 Márquez, *Alumbrados*, 71–3, 131–5.
93 Hamilton, *Heresy and Mysticism*, 15, quotation from Francisco de Osuna's *Tercer abecedario espiritual*.
94 Mary Elizabeth Perry, *Gender and Disorder in Early Modern Seville* (Princeton: Princeton University Press, 1990), 98.
95 Lu Ann Homza, *Religious Authority in the Spanish Renaissance* (Baltimore: Johns Hopkins University Press, 2000), 7.
96 Henry C. Lea, *A History of the Inquisition of Spain* (New York: Macmillan Co., 1922), 4: 7–9.
97 Mary Giles, who defends Francisca against the Inquisitorial patriarchy, concludes that she used her looks and charm 'to push against the bounds of decorum and convention.' See Mary E. Giles, 'Francisca Hernández and the Sexuality of Religious Dissent,' in *Women in the Inquisition: Spain and the New World*, ed. Mary Giles (Baltimore: Johns Hopkins University Press, 1999), 96.
98 Proceso de Vergara, f. xxxxiv; John Longhurst, 'Alumbrados, erasmistas y luteranos en el processo de Juan de Vergara,' *Cuadernos de historia de España* 28 (1958): 118–19. Henceforth cited as Longhurst, 'Vergara Trial.'
99 Alfonso de Valdés, *Diálogo de Mercurio y Carón*, ed. and intro. José F. Montesinos (Madrid: Espasa-Calpe, S.A., 1929), appendix, Censure of Doctor Vélez, 241–6.
100 Garci Rodríguez de Montavo, *Amadis of Gual*, 2 vols., trans. Edwin B. Place and Herbert C. Behm (Lexington: University of Kentucky Press, 1974–5), 1: 24–31.
101 *Lengua*, 107–8.

102 Ibid., 122–3.
103 Ciriaco Morón Arroyo, *Celestina and Castilian Humanism at the End of the Fifteenth Century*, Occasional Papers no. 3 (Binghamton, NY: Center for Medieval and Renaissance Studies, 1994), 15, 20, and 29.
104 Ibid., 37–8.
105 *Lengua*, 122.
106 Antonio Paz y Melia, 'Otro erasmista español. Diego Gracián de Alderete, Su correspondencia,' *Revista de archivos bibliotecas y museos* 5 (1901): 130, Gracián to Francisco de Vergara, n.d.
107 Ibid., 130, Gracían to Juan de Valdés, 1 Jan. 1529.
108 Some historians consider that this intense missionary fervour may have been the cause for the Inquisition's fear of the movement. See A. Selke de Sánchez, 'Algunos datos nuevos sobre los primeros alumbrados; el edicto de 1525 y su relación con el proceso de Alcaraz,' *Bulletin Hispanique* 54 (1952): 144; John E. Longhurst, 'La beata Isabel de la Cruz ante la Inquisición 1524–1529,' *Cuadernos de historia de España* 25–6 (1957): 283.
109 AHN: Inquisición, Proceso de Pedro Ruiz de Alcaraz, leg. 106, f. cccli, questioning of Alcaraz prior to torture, 19 July 1527. On a very few pages prior to folio 370 arabic numbers appear beside roman numerals which do not match. After folio 370 only arabic numerals are used for pagination. I cite only the roman numerals written on the folio referenced, and after folio 370 I cite only the arabic numeral. Henceforth cited as Alcaraz Proceso.
110 Near the end of the trial, inquisitors listed 136 charges against Alcaraz beside the names of witnesses, immediately followed by a similar list of charges against Isabel. See ibid., ff. 411–20.
111 Ibid., f. xxix, letter of Alcaraz to inquisitors, 10 Jan. 1526.
112 Ibid. Nieto holds that Alcaraz's doctrine of experience is a distinguishing characteristic in Valdés's writings. See Nieto, *Valdés*, 256–90, passim.
113 Alcaraz Proceso, f. xviii, letter of Alcaraz to inquisitors, 31 Oct. 1524.
114 Hamilton, *Heresy and Mysticism*, 15.
115 A. Gordon Kinder, '"Ydiota y Sin Letras": Evidence of Literacy among the Alumbrados of Toledo,' *Journal of the Institute of Romance Studies* 4 (1996): 37–48.
116 Alcaraz Proceso, f. xxix, letter of Alcaraz to inquisitors, 10 Jan. 1526.
117 Miguel Ángel Pérez Priego, 'Estimaciones literarias de Juan de Valdés,' in *Los Valdés: Pensamiento y literatura* (Cuenca: Instituto de 'Juan de Valdés,' 1997), 150–2; The works of Augustine were probably the Spanish translations of *Meditaciones* and *Doctrina cristiana* attributed to him. See Clive Griffin, *The Crombergers of Seville: The History of a Printing and Merchant Dynasty* (Oxford: Clarendon Press, 1988), 148.
118 Griffin, 145–52.

119 Manuel Serrano y Sanz, 'Pedro Ruiz de Alcaraz, iluminado alcarreño del siglo XVI,' *Revista de archivos, bibliotecas y museos* 7 (1903): 6–7.
120 Melquiades Andrés Martín has shown that the terms *recogimiento* and *dejamiento* employed by Eduard Boehmer to describe the factions were sometimes used interchangeably by the *alumbrados* themselves. Nevertheless the labels are a convenient way of distinguishing the two different religious approaches. *Nueva visión*, 8–11.
121 Lea, 4: 7. Olmillos gained widespread fame for his ecstatic contortions when preaching.
122 Alcaraz Proceso, f. vii, letter of Alcaraz to inquisitors, 10 Oct. 1524. This letter immediately followed a very brief letter of Alcaraz stating his innocence on 22 June 1524. These two initial letters of defence by Alcaraz are transcribed in the PhD dissertation of Angela Sánchez-Barbudo, 'Algunos aspectos de la vida religiosa en la España del Siglo XVI: los alumbrados de Toledo' (PhD diss., University of Wisconsin, 1953), 278–86. Sánchez assumes the two were actually one letter and dates them together as 22 June 1524.
123 Alcaraz Proceso, f. vii, 10 Oct. 1524.
124 Serrano y Sanz, 9.
125 Vicente Beltrán de Heredia, 'El edicto contra los alumbrados del reino de Toledo,' *Revista española de teología* 10 (1950): 130.
126 Alcaraz Proceso, ff. xii–xiii, initial list of errors and heresies of Alcaraz, 31 Oct. 1524, and ff. xxiii–xxiiii, second list of errors and heresies of Alcaraz presented 10 Dec. 1525.
127 Ibid., f. xiii, initial list of errors and heresies of Alcaraz, 31 Oct. 1524.
128 Ibid., f. xxv, second list of errors and heresies of Alcaraz presented 10 Dec. 1525.
129 Ibid., xxvii.
130 All three are transcribed in Márquez, 'Teólogo alumbrado,' 215–18.
131 Alcaraz Proceso, lxxx, testimony of Francisco de Azevedo, 28 Dec. 1525.
132 Alcaraz Proceso, f. ccxlvi, testimony of Antonio Baeca, 16 Nov. 1526.
133 Márquez was the first scholar to identify this reference to Alcalá. See Márquez, 'Teólogo alumbrado,' 218.
134 Alcaraz Proceso, f. cciii, letter of Alcaraz's wife to inquisitors, 4 Dec. 1526.
135 Lea, 4: 8.
136 Martínez Millán, *Los hermanos*, 22, 27–8, 33–4, 41.

2. Reform School

1 Karl Brandi, *The Emperor Charles V: The Growth and Destiny of a Man and of a World-Empire*, trans. C.V. Wedgwood (London: Jonathan Cape, 1965), 240–1.

2 John Headley, 'Gattinara, Erasmus, and the Imperial Configurations of Humanism,' *Archive for Reformation History* 71 (1980): 80. For a supporting interpretation of Alfonso's use of the printing press for propaganda see Augustín Redondo, 'La "prensa primitiva" ("relaciones de sucesos") al servicio de la política imperial de Carlos V,' in *Aspectos históricos y culturales bajo Carlos V*, ed. Christoph Strosetzki (Madrid: Iberoamericana, 2000), 246–76, passim.
3 The widespread use of the term stems from Bataillon's historiographic influence. In the next chapter we will see how the 'Erasmian' imperial policy evolved in the 1530s while distancing itself from Erasmus and his writings. The term is problematic, as it implies a degree of influence over imperial policy that neither Erasmus nor his doctrines ever wielded. For an extensive critique of Bataillon's historiographic influence see Homza, *Religious Authority*, passim.
4 Ramón González Navarro, 'El impresor navarro Miguel de Eguía, en Alcalá de Henares,' *Príncipe de Viana* 42 (1981): 315.
5 Américo Castro, 46.
6 I have briefly explored Juan's education and his contributions to Charles's imperial ideology in two earlier publications. See 'Intellectual Sources of Spanish Imperialism: The Education of Juan de Valdés,' *Proteus: A Journal of Ideas 9*, no. 1 (Spring 1992): 38–43; and 'Juan de Valdés and Spanish Imperial Humanism,' *Explorations in Renaissance Culture* 11 (1986): 43–51.
7 No doubt some Spaniards favoured Erasmus to gain favour with Erasmus's Burgundian countrymen at Charles's court.
8 Alastair Hamilton, 'Humanists and the Bible,' in *The Cambridge Companion to Renaissance Humanism*, ed. Jill Kraye (Cambridge: Cambridge University Press, 1996), 107. Nebrija wanted to publish a corrected Latin translation of the New Testament and apparently resigned from the project in 1514 in frustration. See Jerry Bentley, *Humanists and Holy Writ: New Testament Scholarship in the Renaissance* (Princeton: Princeton University Press, 1983), 89–90.
9 Melquiades Andrés Martín, 'Evangelismo, humanismo, reforma y observancias en España 1450–1525,' *Missionalia Hispania* 23 (1967): 16; Antonio de la Torre y del Cerro, 'La Universidad de Alcalá: Datos para su historia,' *Revista de archivos, bibliotecas y museos*, 21 (1909): 270.
10 Hamilton, 'Humanists and the Bible,' 112.
11 Antonio de Nebrija, *Gramática Castellana* (Madrid: Talleres de D. Silverio Aguirre y de Gráficas Reunidas, 1946), 5.
12 Ibid., 8–11.
13 Though he used the work, Valdés criticized Nebrija for using his Andalusian dialect rather than Castilian. See Valdés's *Lengua*, 36.
14 Antonio Alvar Ezquerra, *La Universidad de Alcalá de Henares a principios del siglo XVI* (Alcalá: Universidad de Alcalá, 1996), 45.

15 Headley, 'Imperial Humanism,' 80; Ramón González Navarro, 'El impresor navarro Miguel de Eguiá, en Alcalá de Henares,' *Príncipe de Viana* 42 (1981): 315.
16 Bataillon, *Erasmo y España*, 209. Variants of the Bataillon thesis can be found in Eugenio Asensio, 'El erasmismo y las corrientes espirituales afines,' *Revista de filología española* 36 (1952): 78; and Beltrán de Heredia, 'Erasmo y España,' 571.
17 The most insightful critique of Bataillon's merger of *alumbrados* and Erasmians is presented by Alvaro Huerga, 'Erasmismo y Alumbradismo,' in *El erasmismo en España: Ponencias del coloquio celebrado en la Biblioteca de Menéndez Pelayo del 10 al 14 de Junio de 1985*, ed. Manuel Revuelta and Ciriaco Morón Arroyo (Santander: Menéndez Pelayo, 1986), 339–56 passim. He notes that un-Erasmian *alumbrados* continued to exist in Spain after 1525 and that the dogmatic over-identification of the two glosses over what in his view are two very different phenomena: one an expression of popular mysticism, the other a product of elite humanists.
18 Valdés, *Lengua*, 113.
19 Vicente Beltrán de Heredia, 'La teología en la Universidad de Alcalá,' *Revista española de teología* 5 (1945): 408, 422.
20 AHN: Universidades, leg. 555, ff. 1–6, 'Visitación hecha por los Magnificos Señores El Obispado Don Pedro del Campo y Pedro Suarez de Guzman por Comisión de la Santa Iglesia de Toledo.'
21 Antonio Marín Ocete, 'Pedro Mártir de Angleria y su *Opus Epistolarum*,' *Boletin de la Universidad de Granada* 15, no. 73 (1943): 222; John Headley, *The Emperor and His Chancellor: A Study of the Imperial Chancellery under Gattinara* (New York: Cambridge University Press, 1983), 62.
22 Pere Molas Ribalta, 'Los concilleros de CarlosV,' in *Carlos V y la quiebra del humanismo político en Europa (1530–1558)*, vol. 1, ed. José Martínez Millán and Ignacio J. Ezquerra Revilla (Madrid: SDAD Estatal Felipe II, 2001), 231; However, Charles had a contentious relationship with his chancellor, with whom he often disagreed. See John Headley, 'The Emperor and His Chancellor: Disputes over Empire, Administration, and Pope (1519–1529),' in ibid., 21–35 passim.
23 Headley, *Gattinara*, 32–3, 71, 78.
24 AGS: GA, leg. 3140; This important document was discovered by doña Isabel Aguirre Landa, head of the Reading Room at the General Archive of Simancas. She kindly provided me a copy of it.
25 Caballero, 489–504, appendix 87, 'Relación de las nuevas de Italia.'
26 Erika Rummel has presented compelling evidence that a 1528 tract published anonymously in Antwerp was actually an imperial propaganda tract written by Alfonso de Valdés. The work was a satire of official statements

made by the English ambassador to Spain, Edward Lee. Alfonso's tract exposed Lee's treachery and struck a blow against Lee's support of the anti-Erasmians in Spain who had attempted to ban Erasmus's works the previous year. See Erika Rummel, 'Political and Religious Propaganda at the Court of Charles V: A Newly-Identified Tract by Alfonso de Valdés,' *Historical Research* 70, no. 171 (Feb. 1997): 23–33 passim; Brandi, 278–9.
27 Alfonso de Valdés, *Roma*, 2.
28 Ibid., 63–4, 75.
29 Ibid., 155.
30 Alfonso de Valdés, *Mercurio*, 183–4.
31 Francisco de Enzinas, *Memorias de Francisco de Enzinas*, trans. Adam F. Sosa (Buenos Aires: Librería Aurora, 1943), 43.
32 Nieto emphasizes this point in order to stress Juan's dependence on the thought of Alcaraz. See *Valdés*, 171.
33 Paz y Melia, 'Otro erasmista Español,' 130, Gracían to Juan de Valdés, 10 Jan. 1529.
34 Caballero, 331, appendix 15.
35 Ibid., 434, appendix 58, Alfonso de Valdés to Maximiliano Transilvano, 22 April 1529.
36 Tellechea Idigoras, 'Valdés y Carranza: papel,' 307.
37 Eduard Boehmer, ed., 'Alfonsi Valdesii literae XL ineditae,' in *Homenaje a Menéndez y Pelayo* vol. 1 (Madrid: Librería General de Victoriano Suárez, 1889), 400, Alfonso de Valdés to Juan Dantiscus, 1 Feb. 1529. A Spanish translation of the letter is in Antonio Fontán and Jerzy Axer, eds., *Españoles y polacos en la Corte de Carlos V: Cartas del embajador Juan Dantisco* (Madrid: Alianza Editorial, 1994), 217.
38 Torre y del Cerro, 'Alcalá Datos,' 50 and 58.
39 Alvar Ezquerra, 45 and 61.
40 Torre y del Cerro, 'Alcalá Datos,' 50.
41 Alvar Ezquerra, 38, 46, and 49.
42 Richard Kagan, *Students and Society in Early Modern Spain* (Baltimore: Johns Hopkins University Press, 1974), xx, 6, 81.
43 Valdés, *Lengua*, 77.
44 Alcaraz Proceso, ff. ccxlvi; Erasmus, 'Epistolario con Españoles,' in *Erasmo: Obras Escogidos*, 2nd ed., ed. and trans. Lorenzo Riber (Madrid: Aguilar, 1964), 1747, Erasmus to Juan de Valdés, 13 Jan. 1530. Henceforth cited as Erasmus, 'Epistolario.'
45 Tellechea Idigoras, 'Valdés y Carranza: papel,' 307.
46 Valdés, *Lengua*, 115–16.
47 Alcaraz Proceso, lxxx, testimony of Francisco de Azevedo, 28 Dec. 1525.

48 The previous chapter noted the testimony of an Inquisition witness who claimed that he saw Fernando de Valdés praying with his sons in Hebrew. See Jiménez Monteserín, 'Los hermanos,' 395, n. 53.
49 Caballero, 353, appendix 25, letter of Erasmus to Juan de Valdés, 3 Jan. 1528.
50 Beltrán de Heredia, 'La teología en Alcalá,' 425.
51 Antonio de la Torre y del Cerro, 'La Universidad de Alcalá, estudio de la enseñanza según las visitas de cátedras de 1524–1525 a 1527–1528,' in *Homenaje a Menendez y Pelayo* (Madrid: Librería y Casa Editorial Hernando, S.A., 1925), 3: 376–7.
52 José López Rueda, *Helenistas españoles del siglo XVI* (Madrid: Institute Antonio de Nebrija, 1973), 238–41.
53 Valdés, *Lengua*, 124.
54 López Rueda, *Helenistas*, 371, 416; Juan Urriza, *La preclara facultad de artes y filosofía de la Universidad de Alcalá de Henares en el siglo de Oro 1509–1621* (Madrid: Consejo Superior de Investigaciones Científicas, Instituto Jerónimo Zurita, 1941), 335.
55 Vergara Proceso, f. cclxvi.
56 Ibid., f. cclxxxi.
57 Julio Melagres Marín, ed., 'Proceso de María Cazalla,' in *Procedimientos de la Inquisición* (Madrid: Imprenta de Enrique Rubinos, 1886), 2: 3, 8, 23, 27–8, 30, 35–9, 45, 50, 59, 62, 86; Vergara Proceso, ff. cclvii–cclxxxv, passim.
58 Erasmus, 'Epistolario,' 1674–6, 24 April 1522.
59 Bataillon, *Erasmo y España*, 248, 262–4. Lu Ann Homza argues that Bataillon's work has created a false dichotomy between humanism and scholasticism in the council's deliberations. See her *Religious Authority*, chapter 2, passim.
60 Don Antonio Rodríguez Villa, ed., *Memorias para la historia del asalto y saqueo de Roma en 1527 por el ejército imperial; formadas con documentos orginales, cifrados e inéditos en su mayor parte* (Madrid: Imprenta de la Biblioteca de Instrucción y Recreo, n.d.), 236, 253.
61 Caballero, 352, appendix 24, Charles to Erasmus, 13 Dec. 1527.
62 Erasmus, 'Epistolario,' 1737, 23 Dec. 1527.
63 Alfonso de Valdés, *Alfonso de Valdés and the Sack of Rome: Dialogue of Lactino and an Archdeacon*, trans. John E. Longhurst (Albuquerque: University of New Mexico Press, 1952), 111, appendix 3, letter of Castiglioni to Alfonso de Valdés, Aug. 1528.
64 Headley, *Gattinara*, 123–7.
65 Caballero, 434–6, appendix 58, Alfonso de Valdés to Maximiliano Transilvano, 22 April 1529; Fontan, 217, Alfonso to John Dantiscus, 14 Feb. 1529.
66 Alfonso de Valdés, *Roma*, 114.

67 Jacqueline Ferreras Savoye, 'Géneros literarios en el Siglo XVI: el diálogo humanístico, crisol de experimentaciones literarias,' in *Aspectos históricos y culturales bajo Carlos V*, ed. Christoph Strosetzki (Madrid: Iberoamericano, 2000), 288–94.
68 José C. Nieto, *Juan de Valdés: Two Catechisms*, 2nd ed., trans. William B. and Carol D. Jones (Lawrence, Kansas: Coronado Press, 1993), 271, n. 2.
69 Erasmus, *Ten Colloquies*, trans. Craig R. Thompson (New York: Library of Liberal Arts, 1957), 130–74, passim.
70 Juan de Valdés, *Diálogo de doctrina cristiana*, notes by B. Foster Stockwell (Buenos Aires: Editorial 'La Aurora,' 1946), 51–2, 175.
71 Ibid., 152.
72 Erasmus, 'The Godly Feast,' in *Ten Colloquies*, 158.
73 Saint Augustine and Jean Gerson are mentioned twice, and Saints Jerome, Gregory, Cyprian, and John of Chrysostom are each cited once. See *Doctrina cristiana*, 47, 90, 97, 137, and 175.
74 As noted earlier, Nieto believes that even though Valdés used an Erasmian mask in the work, it was still primarily rooted in *alumbrado* doctrine. See Nieto, *Valdés*, 162.
75 When the priest asks for recommendations about devotional prayers for recitation, the archbishop says he was only dealing with 'what is essential for all Christians to know; I will not meddle in other matters.' See *Doctrina cristiana*, 36. After scoffing about Christians who wear beads from their daggers and keep prayer books up their sleeves to assure their salvation, the archbishop again cuts the discussion off. 'Because to discuss this I would have to have more patience than I have here, it is best to leave this. ...' Ibid., 71.
76 Ibid., 141.
77 Ibid., 83 and 173.
78 Ibid., 173.
79 Gilly, 'Valdés, traductor de Lutero,' passim.
80 Milagros Ortega-Costa, *Proceso de la Inquisición contra María de Cazalla* (Madrid: Fundación Universitaria Española, 1978), 137, Response of María Cazalla to the Accusations, 17 June 1532.
81 Valdés, *Doctrina cristiana*, 106–7.
82 Ibid., 107–8.
83 John Barton Payne, *Erasmus: His Theology of the Sacraments* (Richmond: John Knox Press, 1970), 202.
84 Valdés, *Doctrina cristiana*, 124.
85 Ibid., 125–6.
86 Ibid., 129.

87 Ibid., 132.
88 Bataillon, *Erasmismo*, 28; Melquiades Andres Martín, *La teología española en el siglo XVI* (Madrid: La Editorial Católica, 1976), 2: 292.
89 Valdés, *Doctrina cristiana*, 64.
90 Ortega-Costa, *Proceso de Cazalla*, 118.
91 Homza, 13.
92 Ibid., 15.
93 Vergara Proceso, f. clxxxi; Longhurst, 'Vergara Trial,' 28: 113.
94 Ibid.
95 Vergara Proceso, f. clxxxii; Longhurst, 'Vergara Trial,' 28: 115.
96 Ibid.
97 Ibid.
98 Ibid.
99 'Vergara Proceso,' f. cci.
100 Ibid., ff. ccii–cciii.
101 Ibid., f. cciii.
102 Vergara Proceso, f. ccxxxviii; Longhurst, 'Vergara Trial,' 29–30: 282.
103 Vergara Proceso, f. cxxix; Longhurst, 'Vergara Trial,' 28: 150, testimony of Vergara, 28 June 1533.
104 Vergara Proceso, ff. ccclii–cccliii.
105 Appendix 4, Vergara Proceso, ff. cclxxxiii–cclxxxiiii.
106 Ibid.
107 Martínez Millán, *Los hermanos*, 50–1.
108 Andrés Martín, *Nueva visión*, 17.
109 Ortega-Costa, *Proceso de Cazalla*, 118, testimony of María Cazalla, 1532.
110 Ibid., 129, Accusation of the Prosecutor, 1532.
111 Ibid., 137, Response of María Cazalla to the Accusations, 17 June 1532. These were the passages Valdés lifted directly from Luther.
112 Ibid.
113 Ibid., 230, Reply of María Cazalla to testimony of witnesses, 17 March 1533.
114 Ibid., Testimony of Diego d'Aguilar, 15 May 1533. He said that he received the letter ten months earlier.
115 Ibid., 498, Original Sentence, 9 Dec. 1534.
116 Ibid., 144, n. 39. Specifically he charges Nieto with an 'insustainable exaggeration' for claiming the book was a principal charge against María.
117 Boehmer, ed., 'Alfonsi Litterae,' 400, Alfonso to Juan Dantiscus, 14 Feb. 1529; Spanish translation in Fontán and Axer, 217.
118 Longhurst, *Erasmus and the Spanish Inquisition*, 39.
119 AHN: Universidades, leg. 555, ff. 1–6, Visita of Alcalá.

120 Erasmus, 'Epistolario,' 1743, 21 March 1529.
121 The letter further evidences the close association of the two brothers.
122 Appendix 3, AGS: CC, leg. 196, f. 98.
123 AGS: CC, leg. 157, no. 14, ff. 1–2; This document refers to demands for reform of the *mayoralia* made by Fernando de Valdés to Charles shortly after he gained the prebend in 1525. Ten thousand maravedís of the salary came from the Cámara de Castilla, and 15,000 came from the rents of the *mayoralia*. Fernando did not want to take any funds from the *mayoralia*, so he requested an additional stipend from the Cámara de Castilla for 15,000 maravedís.
124 Javier Vales Failde, *La emperatriz Isabel* (Madrid: Gráficas Ultra, S.A., 1944), 319–23.
125 José Antonio Escudero, *Los secretarios de estado y del despacho 1474–1724* (Madrid: Instituto de Estudios Administrativos, 1969), 55–6, and 77; Alberto Yalí Román Román, 'Orígen y evolución de la secretaría de estado y de la secretaría del despacho,' *Jahrbuch für Geschichte von Staat, Wirtschaft und Gesellschaft Lateinamerikas* 6 (1969): 54-61; Luisa Cuesta y Florentino Zamora Lucas, 'Los secretarios de Carlos V,' *Revista de archivos, bibliotecas y museos* 64, no. 2 (1958): 427–31.
126 Headley, 'Gattinara, Erasmus, and Imperial Humanism,' 81.
127 Hayward Keniston, *Francisco de los Cobos: Secretary of the Emperor Charles V* (Pittsburg: University of Pittsburg Press, 1960), 14–15.
128 Werner Thomas, 'La creciente represión del protestantismo en la España carolina,' in *Carlos V y la quiebra del humanismo político en Europa (1530–1558)*, vol. 4, ed. Jesús Bravo Lozano and Carlos J. de Carlos Morelos (Madrid: SDAD Estatal Felipe II, 2001), 285; Doris Moreno Martínez, 'Carlos V y la Inquisición,' in *Carlos V: Europeísmo y universalidad*, vol. 2, *La organización del poder*, ed. Juan Luis Castellano and Francisco Sánchez-Montes González (Madrid: Sociedad Estatal Para la Conmemoración de los Centenarios Felipe II y Carlos V, 2001), 424.
129 Martínez Millán, *Los hermanos*, 76.
130 Erasmus, 'Epistolario,' 1747.
131 Ibid.
132 Kamen, *Inquisition*, 90–1.
133 Longhurst, *Erasmus and the Spanish Inquisition*, 48–9.
134 Juan Antonio Llorente, *Historia crítica de la Inquisición de España* (Madrid: Hiperión, 1980, orig. 1817 in French translation), 2: 217–18, and 344–5. He so garbled fragmentary references that he speculated Juan and Alfonso might have been the same person, Juan-Alfonso de Valdés. He attributed a work he entitled *Acharo* to Juan and cited the trial of Carranza as his

source. In Carranza's trial Fray Domingo de Rojas's 1559 testimony mentioned his seeing *Charon* in Carranza's home, and that Carranza told him another Valdés wrote it. Obviously the witness referred to Alfonso's *Dialogue of Mercury and Charon*. See J. Ignacio Tellechea Idigoras, ed., *Fray Bartolomé Carranza, Documentos Históricos*, 5 vols. (Madrid: Real Academia de Historia, 1962–76), 2: part 1, 117, Testimony of Fray Domingo de Rojas, 17 Aug. 1559.
135 Lea, 2: 53.
136 Longhurst, *Erasmus and the Spanish Inquisition*, 48–9; Vergara Proceso, ff. xxxxiv–xxxxv, clxxxii, cccxxix.
137 Ibid.
138 Lea, 3: 416; Longhurst, *Erasmus and the Spanish Inquisition*, 48.
139 Alfonso de Valdés, *Mercury*, appendix, 'Extract of the Censure of Dr. Vélez,' 241–6.
140 Alfonso de Valdés, *Rome*, appendix 4, 'Censure of the Dialogue on Events in Rome,' 13 Sept. 1531, 116–18; for the original Latin see Montesinos's edition, Alfonso de Valdés, *Roma*, appendix, 161–4.
141 Vergara Proceso, f. cccxxix.
142 Enzinas, 43.

3. Italian Design

1 The following works question Charles's dedication to a crusade against the Turks: M. J. Rodríguez Salgado, '¿Carlos Africanus?: el emperador y el turco,' in *Carlos V y la quiebra del humanismo político en Europa (1530–1558)*, vol. 1, ed. José Martínez Millán and Ignacio J. Ezquerra Revilla (Madrid: SDAD Estatal Felipe II, 2001), 487–531; and Peter Rauscher, 'Carlos V, Fernando I y la ayuda del Sacro Imperio contra los turcos: Dinero, religión y defensa de la Cristiandad, 'in volume 4 of the same work, ed. Jesús Bravo Lozano and Carlos J. de Carlos Morales, 363–83. According to Henry Kamen, Charles never concerned himself with 'imperialist' theory, leaving his advisers to formulate their own image. See Henry Kamen, *Empire: How Spain Became a World Power, 1492–1763* (New York: HarperCollins, 2003), 53.
2 Peter Partner, *The Pope's Men: The Papal Civil Service in the Renaissance* (Oxford: Clarendon Press, 1990), 91.
3 Julia Haig Gaisser, 'Seeking Patronage under the Medici Popes: A Tale of Two Humanists,' in *The Pontificate of Clement VII: History, Politics, and Culture*, ed. Kenneth Gouwens and Sheryl E. Reiss (Aldershot, England: Ashgate, 2005), 303.

4 'Familia' refers to a household and entourage, and 'sodalities' were the gatherings of humanists usually to share a meal and discuss topics for entertainment such as literature or archaeological work on classical sites.
5 Meseguer Fernández, 'Nuevos datos,' 381–4, doc. 1, Indulgence for Alfonso and his Relatives, 12 Dec. 1529.
6 Caballero, 441–2, appendix 64.
7 Brandi, 276; Pastor, 10: 56, 60.
8 Francisco Guicciardini, *The History of Italy*, trans. Sidney Alexander (Princeton: Princeton University Press, 1969), 387; Pietro Soave Polano [henceforth cited as Sarpi], *The History of the Council of Trent Containing Eight Books*, trans. S. Nathaniel Brent (London: J. Macock, 1676), 44; Alfred Kohler, *Carlos V 1500–1558: Una Biografía*, trans. Cristina García Ohlrich (Madrid: Marcial Pons, 2000, orig. 1999), 206; Miguel Ángel Ochoa Brun, *Historia de la diplomacia española*, vol. 5, *La diplomacia de Carlos V* (Madrid: Ministerio de Asuntos Exteriores, 1999), 211.
9 Barbara McClung Hallman, 'The "Disastrous" Pontificate of Clement VII: Disastrous for Giulio de'Medici,' in Kenneth Gouwens and Sheryl E. Reiss, eds., *The Pontificate of Clement VII: History, Politics, and Culture* (Aldershot, England: Ashgate, 2005), 38.
10 Leopold von Ranke, *History of the Reformation in Germany*, trans. Sarah Austin (New York: Frederick Ungar Publishing Co., 1966), 2: 590.
11 Leopold von Ranke, *History of the Popes: Their Church and Their State*, trans. E. Fowler (New York: P.F. Collier and Sons, 1901), 1: 78.
12 Ranke, *Reformation*, 2: 598.
13 G. Bagnatori, 'Cartas inéditas de Alfonso de Valdés sobre la Dieta de Augsburgo,' *Bulletin hispanique* 57 (1955): 360, 367, Alfonso to Cardinal Accolti, 12 July 1530, 1 Aug. 1530.
14 Ranke, *Popes*, 1: 81; Pastor, 10: 130–1.
15 Bagnatori, 368, Alfonso to Accolti, 12 Aug. 1530.
16 Ibid., 373, Alfonso to Accolti, 24 Aug. 1530.
17 Real Academia de la Historia, ed., *Colección de documentos inéditos para la historia de España*, 112 vols. (Madrid: Imprenta de Rafael Marco y Viñas, 1842–95, Kraus Reprint, 1966), 2: 266–7, 'Relación de lo que en las cosas de la fe ha hecho en la Dieta de Augsburgo en el año de 1530'; Ranke, *Reformation*, 2: 609–10; Pastor, 10: 131–40; Ranke, *Popes*, 1: 81.
18 Headley, *Gattinara*, 78. At least Alfonso sensed his enemies at work. Ambassador Mai never seemed to realize that Loaysa was undercutting him. Indeed, during the Augsburg Diet, Mai wrote a strong recommendation to Charles to appoint Loaysa's nephew to a post in Naples: 'I ask that Your Majesty make this appointment recognizing his honour and

that of the Cardinal.' See AGS: Estado 850–7, Mai to Charles, 10 Sept. 1530.
19 Erika Rummel, *Erasmus and His Catholic Critics* (Nieuwkoop: De Graf Publishers, 1989), 2: 84.
20 Caballero, 442–3, appendix 65, Loaysa to Cobos, 27 June 1530.
21 Bagnatori, 365, 1 Aug. 1530.
22 Keniston, 144.
23 AGS: Estado, leg. 850, f. 124, Mai to Cobos, 29 Nov. 1530.
24 G. Heine, ed., *Briefe an Kaiser Karl V Geschrieben von Seinem Beichvater in den Tahren 1530–1532* (Berlin: Verlag von Wilhelm Besser, 1848), 358, 378, Loaysa to Charles, 18 July 1530, 8 Oct. 1530.
25 AGS: Estado, leg. 849, f. 38, 13 July 1530; two months later Loaysa submitted a list of seven cardinals meriting pensions with the conciliarist Ravenna noticeably absent. See Real Academia de la Historia, ed., *Documentos inéditos*, 97: 267, Loaysa to Cobos, 20 Oct. 1530.
26 AGS: Estado, leg. 849, f. 106, Mai to Cobos, 21 Oct. 1530.
27 Pastor, 10: 159–62.
28 McClung Hallman, '"Disastrous" Pontificate,' 38; Cecil H. Clough, 'Clement VII and Francisco Maria Della Rovere, Duke of Urbino,' in Gouwens and Reiss, eds., *The Pontificate of Clement VII*, 98.
29 Pascual de Gayangos, ed., *Calendar of Letters, Dispatches and State Papers Relating to the Negotiations between England and Spain 1485–1553*, 12 vols. (London: Kraus Reprint 1969, orig. 1888), 4: pt. 2, 292, Mai to Charles, 20 Nov. 1531; Heine, 500–2, Loaysa to Charles, 25 Jan. 1532. By March Loaysa was even more anxious that Charles cut a deal: 'If you can not leave that nation in the grace of God, leave it at least in your own.' See Gayangos, 4: pt. 2, 406, Loaysa to Charles, 7 March 1532.
30 AGS: Estado, leg. 1456, f. 135, 2 April 1531.
31 Ibid.
32 Ibid.
33 The diet began in Regensburg and moved to Nürnberg because of an outbreak of plague. Hence it is also referred to as the Regensburg Peace, or Regensburg Recess.
34 Stephen A. Fischer-Galati, *Ottoman Imperialism and German Protestantism 1521–1555* (Cambridge: Harvard University Press, 1959), 52; Pastor, 10: 168; and Ranke, *Reformation*, 2: 688.
35 Ranke, *Reformation*, 2: 692.
36 A friend bemoaned, 'we were not permitted to see him sick, to speak with him, or to console him, nor attend the burial ... nor to make a grave-stone bearing his name.' Fontán, 238, M. Accursio to Dantiscus, 20 Oct. 1532.

37 Luigi Guicciardini, *The Sack of Rome*, trans. and intro. James H. McGregor (New York: Italica Press, 1993), 107–10.
38 Kenneth Gouwens, *Remembering the Renaissance: Humanist Narratives of the Sack of Rome* (Leiden: Brill, 1998), 6.
39 Ibid., 15, 93.
40 Julia Haig Gaisser, introduction to Piero Valeriano, *Pierio Valeriano on the Ill Fortune of Learned Men: A Renaissance Humanist and His World* (Ann Arbor: University of Michigan Press, 1999), 68.
41 Valeriano, *Ill Fortune*, 258–9.
42 Gouwens, *Sack*, 36–8.
43 Myron P. Gilmore, 'Erasmus and Alberto Pio, Prince of Carpi,' in *Action and Conviction in Early Modern Europe: Essays in Memory of E.H. Harbison*, ed. Theodore Rabb and Gerrold Seigel (Princeton: Princeton University Press, 1969), 301, 306, 313.
44 John F. D'Amico, *Renaissance Humanism in Papal Rome: Humanists and Churchmen on the Eve of the Reformation* (Baltimore: Johns Hopkins University Press, 1983), 140.
45 As quoted in Johan Huizinga, *Erasmus and the Age of Reformation: With a Selection from the Letters of Erasmus*, trans. F. Hopman and Barbara Flower (New York: Harper and Row, 1957, orig. 1924), 173.
46 J.A. Fernández Santa-María, *The State, War and Peace: Spanish Political Thought in the Renaissance, 1516–1559* (Cambridge: Cambridge University Press, 1977), 163–168; Rummel, *Erasmus and His Catholic Critics*, 2: 115–28.
47 Baltasar Cuart Moner, 'Juan Ginés de Sepúlveda, cronista del Emperador,' in *Carlos V y la quiebra del humanismo político en Europa (1530–1558)*, vol. 3, ed. Jesús Bravo Lozano and Félix Labrador Arroyo (Madrid: SDAD Estatal Felipe II, 2001), 351.
48 Caballero, 447, appendix 69, Sepúlveda to Alfonso, n.d.
49 Erasmus, 'Epistolario,' 1759, Sepúlveda to Erasmus, 1 April 1532.
50 Ibid.
51 Caballero, 449–51, appendix 71, Sepúlveda to Alfonso, 26 Aug. 1531.
52 Ibid., 461–2, appendix 75, 16 Oct. 1531.
53 Ibid., 449–51, appendix 71, Sepúlveda to Alfonso, 26 Aug. 1531.
54 Erasmus, 'Epistolario,' 1761, Erasmus to Sepúlveda, 14 Oct. 1532. How Erasmus would have reacted without the Valdés intervention we will never know. Certainly Sepúlveda anticipated the worst when he wrote Alfonso that 'already I expected a response from Erasmus to the *Anti-Apology*, given his readiness or facility to write books.' See Caballero, 464–7, appendix 77, 30 June 1532.
55 Caballero, 456, appendix 73, Sepúlveda to Juan, 5 Sept. 1531.
56 Ibid., 457.

57 Partner, *Pope's Men*, 119.
58 Charles L. Stinger, 'The Place of Clement VII and Clementine Rome in Renaissance History,' in Gouwens and Reiss, eds., *The Pontificate of Clement VII*, 175.
59 Valdés, *Doctrina Cristiana*, 51, 152, 175.
60 Peter Partner, *Renaissance Rome 1550–1559: A Portrait of a Society* (Berkeley: University of California Press, 1976), 224. In early 1534 Charles's ambassador wrote that Carnessechi was 'the man most in favour with the pope just now.' See Gayangos, 5: pt. 1, 105, Cifuentes to Charles, 2 April 1534.
61 Eduard Boehmer, *Spanish Reformers of the Two Centuries from 1520: Their Lives and Writings According to the Late Benjamin B. Wiffen's Plan and With the Use of His Materials*, 3 vols. (New York: Burt Franklin, 1874–1904), 1: 74.
62 AGS: Estado, leg. 849, f. 38, 13 July 1530.
63 AGS: Estado, leg. 857, f. 196, Mai to Charles, 28 Feb. 1532.
64 D'Amico, 42; Partner, *Pope's Men*, 20.
65 Partner, *Rome*, 60, 142; Partner, *Pope's Men*, 61.
66 Partner, *Pope's Men*, 29–30.
67 Safe conduct granted to Juan de Valdés by Clement VII, Oct. 3, 1532, as cited in Angel Castellán, 'Juan de Valdés y el círculo de Nápoles,' in *Cuadernos de historia de España* 37/38 (1963): 258.
68 Meseguer Fernández, 389–90, document no. 5, Clement VII to the Bishop of Cartagena, Mateo Lang, 16 Jan. 1534.
69 AGS: Estado, leg. 857, f. 164, 16 Oct. 1532.
70 Appendix 5, AGS: QC, leg. 30, f. 310.
71 Pastor, 10: 204; Ranke, *Reformation*, 2: 695.
72 AGS: Estado, leg. 1457, f. 132, 'To the royal council, points for meeting between Charles and the Pope,' 22 Oct. 1532.
73 Christopher Hare, *Men and Women of the Italian Reformation* (London: Stanley Paul and Co., 1914), 219.
74 T.C. Price Zimmerman, *Paolo Giovio: The Historian and the Crisis of Sixteenth-Century Italy* (Princeton: Princeton University Press, 1995), 107.
75 *Cartas inéditas*, 31, 67, nos. 11, 28, 29 Oct., 10 Dec. 1535.
76 Ochoa Brun, 227; Kohler, 252; Manuel Fernández Álvarez, *Carlos V, el César y el hombre* (Madrid: Espasa Calpe, S.A., 1999), 463.
77 Zimmerman, 128.
78 Castellán 37/38: 258; Pastor 10: 218–19; Brandi, 350; Stephen Ehses, ed., 'Clemens VII. Und Karl V Zu Bologan 1533,' *Römische Quartalschrift für Christliche Alterhumskunde und für Kirchengeschicte* 5 (1891): 299–307.
79 Christopher Hare, *A Princess of the Italian Reformation: Giulia Gonzaga 1513–1566, Her Family and Her Friends* (New York: Charles Scribner's Sons, 1912), 132.
80 Sarpi, 61, 63, 67.

81 Meseguer Fernández, 389–90, document no. 5, Clement VII to the Bishop of Cartagena, Mateo Lang, 16 Jan. 1534.
82 Letter of Juan de Valdés to John Dantiscus, 12 Jan. 1533, as cited in Eduard Boehmer, *Lives of the Twin Brothers Juan and Alfonso de Valdés*, appended to *Juan de Valdés' Commentary on the Sermon on the Mount*, trans. John T. Betts (London: Ballantyne Press, 1882), XI. The original Latin version of the letter is included as an appendix to Montesinos's edition of *Cartas inéditas*, 94, no. 42.
83 Ibid.
84 Keniston, 147, 336.
85 Donald, 345–8, appendix 21, Testament of Alfonso de Valdés. Perez became Cobos's Latinist, though he did not gain appointment as an imperial secretary until 1543. See Keniston, 336.
86 Antonio Rodríguez Villa, ed., *El emperador Carlos V y su corte; según las cartas de don Martín de Salinas embajador del infante don Fernando 1522–1539* (Madrid: Establecimiento Tipográfico de Fortanet, 1903), 532, 20 June 1533. There seems to be an error in the citation of this letter. It is listed as having been written to the Secretary of Castile, i.e., Cobos. It obviously was not written to Cobos. Since Salinas was in Valladolid with the court, I believe that it was originally written to Ferdinand. Someone else may have copied the letter and sent it to Cobos.
87 Appendix 5, AGS: QC, leg. 30, f. 310.
88 Vergara Proceso, clxxxi; Longhurst, 'Vergara Trial,' 28: 113–15.
89 Miguel Angel Echevarría Bacigalupe, 'La occidentalización de la diplomacia imperial bajo Carlos V,' in *Carlos V: Europeísmo y universalidad*, vol. 2, *La organización del poder*, ed. Juan Luis Castellano Castellano and Francisco Sánchez-Montes González (Madrid: Sociedad Estatal Para la Conmemoración de los Centenarios Felipe II y Carlos V, 2001), 177.
90 Appendix 5, AGS: QC, leg. 30, ff. 310–11.
91 Vergara Proceso, cxxix.
92 Carlos José Hernando Sánchez, *Castilla y Nápoles en el siglo XVI: el virrey Pedro de Toledo linaje, estado, y cultura 1532–1553* (Madrid: Junta de Castilla y León, 1994), 191.
93 Martínez Millán, *Corte*, 2: 30; José María Cordero Torres, *El consejo de estado: su trayectoria y perspectivas en España* (Madrid: Instituto de Estudios Políticos, 1944), 50. The Toledo family's crusading zeal was fuelled by the 1510 death of Fadrique's oldest son at Gelves. Thenceforth Fadrique tempered his clan for ferocious vengeance. See William Maltby, *Alba: A Biography of Fernando Alvarez de Toledo, Third Duke of Alba, 1507–1582* (Berkeley: University of California Press, 1983), 9–13.
94 Hernando Sánchez, 194.

95 Benedetto Croce, 'Una datta importante nella vita di Juan de Valdés,' *Archivo Storico per le Provincie Napoletane* 27 (1902): 151–3.
96 Appendix 6, AGS: Estado, leg. 1015, f. 107, Relation of letters from the Viceroy, 29 Dec. 1532, 4, 25, 29 Jan. 1533. I use 'Relation' to indicate a summary of one or more letters with a wide margin where a response is written for return.
97 Ibid. Of course Charles would not actually write the response. Cobos would have been the usual author, which makes it difficult at times to determine whether the response is actually Cobos writing what Charles said, or making his own response. In this case it is clear from the context that Charles pressed for Juan's appointment as archivist.
98 Appendix 7, AGS: Estado, leg. 1015, f. 17, viceroy to Charles, 9 March 1533.
99 AGS: Estado, leg. 1015, f. 22, viceroy to Charles, 14 March 1533.
100 AGS: Estado, leg. 1015, f. 70, viceroy to Charles, 28 July 1533.
101 Appendix 8, AGS: Estado, leg. 1015, f. 103, viceroy to Charles, 6 Oct. 1533.
102 Ibid.
103 AGS: Estado, leg. 1017, f. 127, Relation of viceroy's letters of 6 and 7 Oct. 1533.
104 Croce, 'Una datta importante,' 153.
105 AGS: Estado, leg. 1017, f. 18, viceroy to Charles, 9 Feb. 1534.
106 AGS: Estado, leg. 1017, f. 26, Relation of letter from the viceroy, 9 Feb. 1534. My emphasis.
107 Meseguer Fernández, document 5, 389–90.
108 Zarco y Cuevas, 'Testamentos,' 684.
109 Partner, *Pope's Men*, 63.
110 AGS: Estado, leg. 861, f. 24, Cifuentes to Cobos, 12 Jan. 1534.
111 AGS: Estado, leg. 862, f. 11, Cifuentes to Cobos, 23 March 1534; AGS: Estado, leg. 862, f. 51, Cifuentes to Cobos, 1 Sept. 1534.
112 Some feelers may have been extended to the Turks as early as 1526, but the first definite agreement was not signed until 1532. A comprehensive treaty of alliance was signed in 1536. See Brandi, 344, 359; Roger Bigelow Merriman, *The Rise of the Spanish Empire in the Old World and in the New*, vol. 3, *The Emperor* (New York: Cooper Square Publishers, 1962, orig. 1918), 291.
113 Brandi, 330.
114 AGS: Estado, leg. 862, f. 32, Cifuentes to Charles, 6 June 1534.
115 AGS: Estado, leg. 1017, f. 28, 14 Feb. 1534.
116 AGS: Estado, leg. 1017, f. 9, viceroy to Charles, 21 Jan. 1534.
117 AGS: Estado, leg. 1017, f. 29, viceroy to Cobos, 8 March 1534.
118 AGS: Estado, leg. 862, f. 86, Cifuentes to Charles, 25 Nov. 1534; Gayangos, 5: pt. 1, 281, Aves to Cobos, 13 Oct. 1534.
119 AGS: Estado, leg. 1180, f. 3, Relation of letter from Antonio Leyva, 7 Nov. 1534.

120 The ambassador whined to Charles, 'why would one of your servants write this way?' See AGS: Estado, leg. 862, f. 71, 3 Oct. 1534.
121 AGS: Estado, leg. 1017, f. 76, 26 Oct. 1534.
122 AGS: Estado, leg. 862, f. 39, Cifuentes to Charles, 27 June 1534.
123 Ibid; AGS: Estado, leg. 1180, f. 11, Juan Baptista Gastaldo to Antonio de Leyva, 28 Dec. 1534.
124 I published an earlier article on Valdés and the Camerino crisis; 'Juan de Valdés y la crisis de Camerino, 1534–1535,' in *Aspectos históricos y culturales bajo Carlos V*, ed. Christoph Strosetzki (Frankfurt: Velvuert, 2000), 106–18.
125 Pastor, 11: 304–5
126 AGS: Estado, leg. 1180, f. 87, Relation of Leyva letters of 8, 27 Nov. and 5 Dec. 1534; AGS: Estado, leg. 1311, ff. 118–20, Lope de Soria to Charles, 19 Dec. 1534.
127 AGS: GM leg. 6, f. 109, Relation of letters from Cifuentes, 24 and 26 of Sept. 1534.
128 AGS, Estado, leg. 1311, f. 27, Soria to Charles, 30 Jan. 1535; and AGS: Estado leg. 1311, f. 71, Relation of letter from Soria to Charles, 23 Feb. 1535.
129 AGS: Estado, leg. 1021, f. 18, viceroy to Charles, n.d.
130 Appendix 9, AGS: GM, leg. 6, f. 119, viceroy to Cobos, 15 Sept. 1534.
131 Martínez Millán, *Los hermanos*, 76.
132 AHPC, P-20; a partial transcription of these documents is in Martínez Millán, *Los hermanos*, 74–6.
133 AGS: GM leg. 6, f. 123, viceroy to Cobos, 15 Dec. 1534.
134 AGS: GM, leg. 6, f. 153, 23 Jan. 1534.
135 Appendix 10, AGS: Estado, leg. 1021, f. 30, no date, but the last date of a cited letter was 6 Feb. 1535.
136 Ibid.
137 Ibid.
138 Appendix 11, AGS: Estado, leg. 1021, ff. 42–51; the latest letter mentioned is 25 Feb. 1535.
139 Ibid.
140 Ibid.
141 Ibid.
142 AGS: Estado, leg. 1311, f. 11, Relation of letter from Soria, 30 Jan. 1535.
143 AGS: Estado, leg. 1311, f. 62, Relation of letter from Soria to Charles, 6 April 1535.
144 Appendix 5, AGS: QC, leg. 30, f. 312; and AGS: Residencias, leg. 4, f. 604. The wording of the Residencia document is the same as Charles's letter to his accountants.
145 Appendix 19, AGS: Estado, leg. 1026, f. 134, Cobos's summary of viceroy's letter for presentation to the Council of Castile.
146 AGS: Estado, leg. 1311, ff. 83–5, Soria to Cobos, 19 March 1535.

147 Appendix 12, AGS: GM, leg. 6, f. 156, 'Razon de lo que escriben particulares en Roma al Visorey de Napoles sobre la causa de Camerino,' addressed to Charles from Viceroy Toledo, 21 March 1535.
148 Ibid.
149 AGS: Estado, leg. 1311, f. 74, Relation of letter from Soria, 30 Jan. 1535.
150 Appendix 12, AGS: GM leg. 6, f. 156, 21 March 1535.
151 AGS: Estado, leg. 1311, ff. 79–82, Lope de Soria to Charles, 13 March 1535.
152 AGS: Estado, leg. 1021, f. 70, 16 March 1535.
153 AGS: GM, leg. 6, f. 151, viceroy to Charles, 21 March 1535.
154 AGS: Estado, leg. 1458, ff. 102–6, ff. 107–8.
155 Ibid., ff. 102–6.
156 Ibid. The report noted that Cifuentes supported the nomination of the Bishop of Paris as Cardinal. Charles and the advisers agreed with 'others in Rome' that the nomination would be totally against Charles's interests.
157 Appendix 13, AGS: Estado, leg. 1458, ff. 106–8, unsigned letter to Charles V.
158 *Cartas inéditas*, 41, no. 16, 8 Nov. 1535.
159 See AGS: Estado, leg. 868, f. 124, Charles to Aguilar, 3 July 1539.
160 In the intellegence report discussed above, Mantua was one of three preferred cities.
161 Appendix 13, AGS: Estado, leg. 1458, ff. 106–8.
162 Appendix 14, AGS: Estado, leg. 863, f. 12, Relación de nuevas de Francia, 9 April 1535. At the end of the report the author states that the Bishop of Limos would 'come here to solicit the [cardinal's] cape for the Bishop of Paris.' Thus the author must have been in Rome.
163 Ibid. The author mentions the value of the French *décima* as 'more than 600,000 ducats,' whereas the viceroy relayed Valdés's earlier report that the *décima* would generate 600,000–800,000 ducats.
164 Ibid.
165 Ibid.
166 AGS: Estado, leg. 863, f. 14, Relation of the letter from Cifuentes, 3 April 1535.
167 Appendix 15, AGS: Estado, leg. 863, f. 14, avisos de Francia/y de lo que passó el papa con los embajadores de Francia sobre lo de Ferrara/ del concierto. The first sentence of the relation of Cifuentes's letter states that it is in reply to letters from Charles dated 26 February and 8 March. A sentence in the middle of the second document mentions replying to a letter from Charles dated 2 February. The summary of the letter of Cifuentes refers to 'the count,' i.e., Cifuentes, three times, but the second document does not mention Cifuentes. The topics discussed and the attitudes expressed identify Valdés as the source of the report. Further marking this document as belonging to Valdés is its placement. The cover of AGS: Estado, leg. 863, f. 12 has '12 a 14' written on it. Folio 12 has already been

identified as a Valdesian tract, and later in this study folio 13 will be identified as a report from Valdés as well. See chapter 4, pages 76–8, and appendix 16, pages 185–6.
168 Valdés was not above praising his own service.
169 Appendix 15, AGS: Estado, leg. 863, f. 14, avisos de Francia/y de lo que passó el papa con los embajadores de Francia sobre lo de Ferrara/ del concierto.
170 This could be a reference to Charles's reappointment of Valdés to his service a month before the letter to his accountants.
171 See the records of Valdés's pay as secretary, appendix 5, AGS: QC, leg. 30, ff. 310–11.
172 Appendix 15, AGS: Estado, leg. 863, f. 14, avisos de Francia/y de lo que passó el papa con los embajadores de Francia sobre lo de Ferrara/ del concierto.
173 Ibid.
174 AGS: Estado, leg. 1311, ff. 52–5, Soria to Charles, 5 June 1535; AGS: Estado, leg. 1458, f. 202, Duke of Urbino to Charles, 1 Aug. 1535.
175 AGS: Estado, leg. 1021, f. 87, viceroy to Charles, 24 May 1535.
176 AGS: Estado, leg. 1021, f. 130, viceroy to Charles, 6 Aug. 1535.
177 *Cartas inéditas*, 65, no. 27, 6 Dec. 1535.

4. Cardinal Relations

1 Ludovico Ariosto, *Orlando Furioso*, trans. Guido Waldman (London: Oxford University Press, 1974), 558; Valeriano, *Ill Fortune*, 105–6.
2 Pietro Aretino, *The Works of Aretino: Dialogues*, trans. Samuel Putnam (New York: Covici-Friede Publishers, 1933), 221.
3 Montesinos, introduction to *Cartas inéditas*, xxxiv–xxxvi, xcix, c.
4 *Cartas inéditas*, 56, no. 24, 26 Nov. 1535.
5 Barbara McClung Hallman, *Italian Cardinals, Reform, and the Church as Property* (Berkeley: University of California Press, 1985), 16, 21, and 28.
6 Pastor, 11: 310.
7 Ibid., 11: 310–11.
8 Eric Cochrane, *Florence in the Forgotten Centuries, 1527–1800* (Chicago: University of Chicago Press, 1973), 10.
9 Pastor, 10: 39–40, 200.
10 Melissa Meriam Bullard, *Filippo Strozzi and the Medici Family: Favor and Finance in Sixteenth-Century Florence and Rome* (Cambridge: Cambridge University Press, 1980), 152, 160, n. 36, and 171, n. 81.
11 Pastor, 11: 310–11.
12 AGS: Estado, leg. 864, f. 149, 9 April 1535.
13 AGS: Estado, leg. 861, f. 75, 7 April 1535.

14 Pastor, 11: 312.
15 *Cartas inéditas*, 16–17, 65, nos. 5, 27, 9 Oct. 1535, 10 Dec. 1535.
16 Ibid., 6, no. 2, 24 Sept. 1535.
17 Ibid., 20, no. 6, 14 Oct. 1535.
18 Ibid., 22, no. 7, 18 Oct. 1535.
19 Ibid.
20 Ibid., 23–4, no. 7, 18 Oct. 1535.
21 Ibid., 37, no. 14, 3 Nov. 1535.
22 Kagan, *Lawyers*, 52–6.
23 *Cartas inéditas*, 4, no. 1, 18 Sept. 1535.
24 AGS: Estado, leg. 864, f. 84, Cifuentes to Charles, 30 Aug. 1535.
25 Appendix 16, AGS: Estado, leg. 863, f. 13, The Relation That the Count of Cifuentes Sent about the Cardinal of Ravenna. Also see chapter 3, note 167.
26 Ibid.
27 Pastor, 11: 311.
28 Appendix 16, AGS: Estado, leg. 863, f. 13, The Relation That the Count of Cifuentes Sent about the Cardinal of Ravenna.
29 Ibid.
30 Ibid.
31 Ibid.
32 AGS: Estado, leg. 863, f. 96, n.d., no signature.
33 Ibid.
34 AGS: Estado, leg. 863, f. 22, Cifuentes to Charles, 22 Aug. 1535.
35 AGS: Estado, leg. 863, f. 96, n.d., no signature.
36 Hallman, *Cardinals*, 70.
37 Pastor, 11: 311.
38 Gayangos, 5, pt. 1, 561–2, Cifuentes to Charles, 31 Oct. 1535.
39 *Cartas inéditas*, 44, no. 17, 12 Nov. 1535.
40 Pastor, 11: 312.
41 *Cartas inéditas*, 23, 42, nos. 7, 16, 18 Oct., 8 Nov. 1535.
42 Hernando Sánchez, 539; Caponetto, 83–93.
43 Juan de Valdés, *One Hundred and Ten Divine Considerations*, trans. John T. Betts, appended to *Life and Writings of Juan de Valdés, Spanish Reformer in the Sixteenth Century* by Benjamen Wiffen (London: Trubner and Co., Ludgate Hill, 1882), 413.
44 Hare, *Princess*, 140.
45 *Cartas inéditas*, 3, no. 1, 18 Sept. 1535.
46 Hare, *Princess*, 19.
47 Ibid., 8.
48 Ibid., 59, 61–2.
49 Ibid., 74, 76–9, 97.

50 Zimmermann, 113.
51 Ludovico Ariosto, *Orlando Furioso*, trans. William Stewart Rose (London: George Bell and Sons, 1905), 2: 457.
52 Hare, *Princess*, 113–18.
53 Ibid., 130–2; Aretino was proud of Ippolito's display. 'If it were not that the pomp of Cardinal Medici covers everything, we [i.e., Italians] should be like a crowd of bankrupt tradesmen.' See Aretino, *Dialogues*, 229.
54 Gayangos, 5: pt. 1, 257, Cifuentes to Cobos, 20 Sept. 1534.
55 John R. Hale, *Florence and the Medici: The Pattern of Control* (London: Thames and Hudson, 1977), 124.
56 AGS: Estado, leg. 1021, f. 18, Relation of viceroy's letters of 14 and 22 Feb. 1535.
57 AGS: Estado, leg. 863, f. 3, Relation from the Count of Cifuentes, 9 Feb. 1535.
58 AGS: Estado, leg. 1458, f. 141, Relation of letters from the Duke of Melfi, 10 and 22 June 1535.
59 Hale, *Princess*, 126.
60 AGS: Estado, leg. 863, f. 3, Relation from the Count of Cifuentes, 9 Feb. 1535.
61 Giuseppe Moretti, 'Il cardinale Ippolito dei Medici dal tratto di Barcelona alla morte (1529–1535),' *Archivo Storico Italiano* 1 (1940): 169–70; Benedetto Varchi, *Storia Fiorentina* (Florence: Salani Editore, 1963), 2: 407, 438. Varchi began writing his history between 1527 and 1531 and was given a stipend by the Medici family. Ibid., 1: 5.
62 AGS: Estado, leg. 864, f. 150, Cifuentes to Charles, 9 April 1535.
63 Appendix 17, AGS: Estado, leg. 1021, f. 120, 'Advice from Various Parts'; AGS: Estado, leg. 1021, f. 121, Relation of letters from the viceroy, 4 and 12 July 1535.
64 Partner, *Rome*, 85–6.
65 John Stephens, 'Giovanbattista Cibo's Confession,' in *Essays Presented to Myron P. Gilmore*, ed. Sergio Bertelli and Gloria Ramakus (Florence: La Nuova Italia Editrice, 1978), 256–7.
66 AGS: Estado, leg. 1021, f. 121, Relation of letters from the viceroy, 4 and 12 July 1535.
67 Ibid.
68 Moretti, 172; Varchi, 2: 422.
69 Moretti, 176; Varchi, 2: 427.
70 Varchi, 2: 434–5; Moretti, 177.
71 Varchi, 2: 428.
72 As quoted in Hare, *Princess*, 130.
73 Varchi, 2: 435.

74 AGS: Estado, leg. 864, f. 84, Cifuentes to Charles, 30 August 1535; Varchi, 2: 439.
75 Varchi, 2: 439; G.F. Young, *The Medici* (New York: Random House, 1930), 370.
76 AGS: Estado, leg. 1021, f. 142, viceroy to Charles, 18 Aug. 1535; and AGS: Estado, leg. 1021, f. 82, Relation of viceroy's letters of 17 Aug., 3 and 4 Sept. 1535.
77 AGS: Estado, leg. 1021, f. 142, viceroy to Charles, 18 Aug. 1535.
78 AGS: Estado, leg. 1021, f. 135, viceroy to Charles, 20 Aug. 1535.
79 AGS: Estado, leg. 1021, f. 150, viceroy to Charles, 3 Sept. 1535.
80 AGS: Estado, leg. 1021, f. 82, Relation of viceroy's letters of 17 Aug., 3 and 4 Sept. 1535.
81 *Cartas inéditas*, 3, no. 1, 18 Sept. 1535.
82 Pastor, 11: 312; Moretti, 178.
83 AGS: Estado, leg. 52, f. 256. This letter was included in a pack of small, tightly folded, anonymous, undated, and obviously secret papers written at the time of the 1541 Regensburg Diet.
84 *Cartas inéditas*, 86, no. 38, 19 April 1536.
85 AGS: Estado, leg. 850, f. 102, Mai to Cobos, 30 Oct. 1530. Those contacts in France provided Valdés valuable information.
86 *Cartas inéditas*, 26, 61, nos. 8 and 26, 19 Oct. and 1 Dec. 1535.
87 Ibid., 41, no. 16, 8 Nov. 1535.
88 AGS: Estado, leg. 866, f. 150, Ambassador of Lucca to Cardinal Gonzaga, 2 March 1537; Montesinos, introduction to *Cartas inéditas*, xxxiii.
89 Hallman, *Cardinals*, 57–8.
90 AGS: Estado, leg. 1021, f. 150, viceroy to Charles, 3 Sept. 1535.
91 AGS: Estado, leg. 1021, f. 82, Relation of letters from the viceroy, 17 Aug. and 3, 4 Sept. 1535.
92 Montesinos, 'Introduction' to *Cartas inéditas*, xxxii.
93 *Cartas inéditas*, 51, no. 21, 20 Nov. 1535.
94 Ibid., 39, no. 15, 7 Nov. 1535.
95 AGS: Estado, leg. 1021, f. 203, viceroy to Charles, 13 Nov. 1535.
96 *Cartas inéditas*, 54, no. 22, 23 Nov. 1535.
97 Ibid., 62, 64–5, 72, nos. 26, 27, 31, 1, 6, and 18 Dec. 1535.
98 AGS: Estado, leg. 1024, f. 26, Charles's Memorial on Negotiations, 31 Dec. 1535; AGS: Estado, leg. 1459, f. 2, 'The State of Public Things of Christendom and Particulars of His Majesty,' Jan. 1536.
99 Ibid.
100 AGS: Estado, leg. 1024, f. 26, Charles's Memorial on Negotiations, 31 Dec. 1535.

226   Notes to pages 87–91

101 *Cartas inéditas*, 12, no. 3, 1 Oct. 1535.
102 Ibid., 32, no. 11, 29 Oct. 1535.
103 Gayangos, 5: pt. 2, 299, Cifuentes to Charles 26 Nov. 1536, and 304, Cifuentes to Charles, 26 Dec. 1536.
104 AGS: Estado, leg. 1459, f. 93, 'What Will Be Discussed in Council,' 18 May 1537. In rejecting the council the Lutherans violated their *Augsburg Confession*, which had insisted upon a general council. Pastor blames the Duke of Mantua for the ultimate failure of the Mantua council, while Sarpi claims that most Italians blamed the pope. See Pastor, 9: 90–9; Sarpi, 77–8.
105 Montesinos, introduction to *Cartas inéditas*, xxxiv–xxxvi, xcix, c.
106 *Cartas inéditas*, 92–3, no. 41, 12 Jan. 1537.
107 AGS: Estado, leg. 1455, f. 128, Letter from Diego de Soto Mayor to Charles, 23 Feb. 1530.
108 Hare, *Princess*, 94.
109 Ibid., 94, 123–4.
110 AGS: Estado, leg. 1458, f. 117, Duke of Mantua to Charles, n.d., but the text of the letter indicates that it was written a few days after the death of Luigi.
111 AGS: Estado, leg. 864, f. 135, Relation of Cifuentes letter of 21 July 1534.
112 Wiffen, 'Julia Gonzaga,' trans. Adam F. Sosa, in *Alfabeto cristiano* by Juan de Valdés, ed. B. Foster Stockwell, trans. Luis Usoz y Río (Buenos Aires: Editorial 'La Aurora,' 1948), 25–6.
113 Hare, *Princess*, 126. This 24 May agreement was made before the death of Cardinal Medici, Giulia's powerful protector.
114 *Cartas inéditas*, 37, no. 14, 3 Nov. 1535.
115 Hare, *Princess*, 139.
116 Ibid., 137–8.
117 AGS: Estado, leg. 1030, f. 162, Figueroa to Cobos, 20 Dec. 1539.
118 *Cartas inéditas*, 84, no. 37, 18 March 1536.
119 Wiffen, 'Julia Gonzaga,' 25.
120 *Cartas inéditas*, 88, no. 39, 14 July 1536.
121 AGS: Estado, leg. 1025, f. 37, Bishop of Mondonedo to Cobos, 11 Aug. 1536.
122 Manuel Fernández Álvarez, *Política Mundial de Carlos V y Felipe II* (Madrid: CSIC, Escuela de Historia Moderna, 1964), 97.
123 AGS: Estado, leg. 865, f. 110, Ascanio to Charles, 7 March 1536.

5. The Valdesian Sodality

1 Marsilio Ficino, *Commentary on Plato's Symposium on Love*, trans. Sears Jayne (Woodstock, Connecticut: Spring Publications, 1985), 19.

2 Ibid., 1–4.
3 Ibid., 130.
4 Peter Burke, *The Fortunes of the Courtier: The European Reception of Castiglione's Cortegiano* (University Park: Pennsylvania State University Press, 1995), 21.
5 Baldesar Castiglione, *The Book of the Courtier*, trans. and intro. George Bull (London: Penguin Books, 1967, reprinted 1976), 324–43.
6 Pietro Bembo, *Gli Asolani*, trans. Rudolf B. Gottfried (Bloomington: Indiana University Press, 1954), xv.
7 Ficino, 41; Bembo, *Asolani*, 156–7; Castiglione, 325.
8 Castiglione, 341.
9 Ibid., 330.
10 Ibid., 334.
11 Ficino, 145; Bembo, *Asolani*, 182; Castiglione, 339–40.
12 Ficino, 145.
13 Antonio Dueñas Martínez, *Juan de Valdés: un reformador español en Italia* (Trieste: Nuova del Bianco-Industria Grafiche, 1981), 23; Nieto, *Valdés*, 66.
14 *Cartas inéditas*, 3, no. 1, 18 Sept. 1535.
15 As quoted in Roland H. Bainton, *Women of the Reformation in Germany and Italy* (Minneapolis: Augsburg Publishing House, 1971), 171.
16 Agnolo Firenzuola, *On the Beauty of Women*, trans., ed., and intro. Konrad Eisenbichler and Jacqueline Murray (Philadelphia: University of Pennsylvania Press, 1992), 5.
17 Ibid., 14.
18 Ibid., 23, 46.
19 Ibid., 15, 45–6, 49–51, 57, 60. These are very near Bembo's standards, though more detailed. See Bembo, *Asolani*, 116–17.
20 Jacob Burkhardt, *The Civilization of the Renaissance in Italy* (New York: Barnes and Noble, 1992), 240.
21 Martinez-Gongara believes Valdés was contradictory about the status of women and that women were drawn to him because he was powerless and marginal. She also thinks Giulia played a passive role and contributed little to the discussion in the *Alfabeto* and by implication in discussions in Valdés's sodality. As will be emphasized in my conclusion, Valdés was not consistent about much; he was a courtier not a theologian. Valdés was not powerless, and the fact that Giulia risked her life to publish his works seems to argue against her supposed passivity. See Mar Martínez-Góngora, *Discursos sobre la mujer en el humanismo renacentista español: Los casos de Antonio de Guevara, Alfonso y Juan de Valdés, y Luis de León* (York, SC: Spanish Literature Publication Co., 1999), 142–53.

22 Juan de Valdés, *La primera epístola de San Pablo a los Corintios,* in vol. 11 of *Reformistas antiguos españoles,* ed. Luis Usoz i Rio (Madrid: 1856; reprinted Barcelona: Librería de Diego Gómez Flores, 1982), 202–3.
23 Ibid., 267–8.
24 Hare, *Men and Women,* 39–40; Hare, *Princess,* 155.
25 Hare, *Men and Women,* 268.
26 Bainton, *Women,* 189.
27 Serdonati, as quoted in Hare, *Men and Women,* 65.
28 Ibid., 66.
29 Bainton, *Women,* 219–20; Hare, *Men and Women,* 238–9.
30 Celio Secondo Curione, a professor in Basel, as quoted in Bainton, *Women,* 225.
31 Hare, *Men and Women,* 238–9.
32 Marcelino Menéndez y Pelayo, *Historia de los heterodoxos españoles,* vol. 3, *Erasmistas y protestantes* (Santander: Consejo Superior de Investigaciones Científicas, 1947, orig. 1880), 221–2.
33 Hare, *Princess,* 144.
34 Juan de Valdés, *Trataditos de Juan de Valdés,* ed. Eduard Boehmer (Bonn: Imprento de Carlos Georgi, 1880), appendix of the editor, 192.
35 *Las ciento diez divinas consideraciones: Recensión inédita del manuscrito de Juan Sánchez (1558),* ed. J. Ignacio Tellechea Idigoras (Salamanca: Universidad Pontificia, 1975), 52–3, 56–60, 64–9.
36 Paul III ordered Bobadilla to Naples 'because of the petition of Ascanio Colonna and other persons for certain negotiations.' See letter of Bobadilla to the Duke of Ferrara, 4 July 1539, in *Bobadillae monumenta,* 16, document no. 12.
37 Ibid., 18–19, document no. 13.
38 Hare, *Princess,* 269.
39 Ibid., 149–50. Letter of Giacomo Bonfadio to Pietro Carnesecchi, n.d. but late 1541 or 1542, as quoted by Hare.
40 Hare, *Men and Women,* 52, 76, 231; Salvatorre Caponetto, *The Protestant Reformation in Sixteenth-Century Italy,* trans. Anne C. Tedeschi and John Tedeschi (Kirksville, MO: Thomas Jefferson University Press, 1999, orig. 1992), 67; Hernando Sánchez, 497.
41 Hare, *Men and Women,* 254; Caponetto, 67; Hernando Sánchez, 363.
42 *Cartas inéditas,* 62, no. 26, 1 Dec. 1535.
43 Jiménez Monteserín, 'La andadura humana,' 186, n. 71.
44 Diego Torrente Pérez, ed., *Documentos para la Historia de San Clemente,* 2 vols. (Madrid: Marsiega, SA, 1975), 1: 407, document no. 169, Paul III's Concession of San Clemente to Juan de Valdés, 4 Jan. 1536.
45 AGS: Estado, leg. 1024, f. 37, Consultation of Matters that the Princess of Sulmona Asks, n.d., but text of document indicates 1536.

46 Hernando Sánchez, 152, 449, and 520.
47 Kamen, *Empire*, 75; Cobos's agents smelted the loot taken from Atahualpa and Cobos negotiated a Fugger loan in 1536 to fund Charles's war with France. See Ramón Carande, *Carlos V y sus banqueros*, vol. 3, *Los caminos del oro y de la plata (deuda exterior y tesoros ultramarinos)*, 2nd ed. (Barcelona: Editorial Crítica, 1987), 165, 174.
48 Keniston, 333.
49 Ibid., 369.
50 The 1527 census of Rome lists 4,900 courtesans by occupation out of a population of 55,035; i.e., almost 10 per cent of the city's inhabitants were professional prostitutes. See Lynne Lawner, *Lives of the Courtesans: Portraits of the Renaissance* (New York: Rizzoli, 1987), 6; D'Amico, 5.
51 Lawner, 4, 6–8, 46.
52 Ibid., 225.
53 Aretino, *Dialogues*, 117.
54 *Cartas inéditas*, 82, no. 36, 1 March 1536: Valdés seems to be making a joke that he was giving up discussion of courtesans for Lent.
55 Zimmermann, 88.
56 Ibid.
57 As quoted in Hare, *Princess*, 133.
58 Zimmermann, 144.
59 Croce, 'Cartas,' 157 and 171, Valdés to Cobos, 3 Feb. and 15 Sept. 1540.
60 Keniston, 202–4.
61 *Lengua*, 31.
62 Gaisser, introduction to Valeriano's *Ill Fortune*, 47.
63 J.R. Woodhouse, *Baldesar Castiglione: A Reassessment of The Courtier* (Edinburgh University Press, 1978), 80.
64 Firenzuola, xvi.
65 Ibid., xvii.
66 Juan de Valdés, *Diálogo de la lengua*, introduction by José Montesinos (Madrid: Espasa-Calpe, SA, 1964, orig., 1928), xlv–xlix; Angelo Mazzocco, 'The Italian Connection in Juan de Valdés' *Diálogo de la Lengua*,' *Historiographia linguística* 24, no. 3 (1997): 271–4.
67 *Lengua*, 34.
68 Mazzocco, 272.
69 Gaisser, introduction to Valeriano's *Ill Fortune*, 17, 47, and 72.
70 Ibid., 53–7; D'Amico, 107–8.
71 Pierio Valeriano, 'Dialogo della Volgar Lingua,' in *Discussioni linguistiche del cinquecento*, ed. Mario Pozzi (Turin: Unione Tipografico-Editrice Torinese, 1988), 67–9.

72 Burke, 41.
73 *Lengua*, 113–14.
74 Castiglioni wrote, 'Look at the Spaniards, who appear to be the leaders in courtiership.' He went on to advise Italians to imitate Spanish customs and dress as well. See Castiglione, 129, 135, and 146.
75 Ibid., 75; Mazzocco, 279–80.
76 Giovanni Della Casa, *Galateo*, trans. and intro. Konrad Eisenbichler and Kenneth Bartlett (Toronto: Centre for Renaissance and Reformation Studies, 1986), xix, 55; In Aretino's *Dialogues*, they are described as cruel, cheap, over-mannered, dirty, and smelly. See 117–18, 122, 135–6.
77 Eguiagaray Bohigas, 72.
78 Manuel F. Miguélez, 'Famoso discurso en castellano de Carlos V en Roma,' *Ciudad de Dios* 94 (1913): 187–8.
79 *Lengua*, 50–1.
80 The viceroy's letter to Charles saying Valdés was content with the compensation for his archival office seems to indicate that Valdés was still in Naples in early February, 1534. See AGS: Estado, leg. 1017, f. 18, Viceroy to Charles, 9 Feb. 1534.
81 *Lengua*, 29, 125.
82 Mazzocco, 268.
83 Caballero, no. 83, pp. 469–71, Jacobo Bonfadio to Pietro Carnesechi, n.d., but late 1541 or 1542.
84 *Lengua*, 51.
85 Surles, 231.
86 *Lengua*, 31.
87 Hernando Sánchez, 491–2.
88 *Lengua*, 38.
89 Ibid., 38; H. Chanon Berkowitz, 'The Quaderno de Refranes Castellanos of Juan de Valdés,' *Romanic Review* 16 (1925): 71–6 passim.
90 *Lengua*, 61; Valdés's running criticism of Nebrija demonstrates his familiarity with the work. See ibid., 65, 93.
91 Ibid., 70.
92 For example, he preferred *salirá*, a regular form, for the irregular *saldrá*, 'porque viene de salir.' See ibid., 93.
93 Castiglione, 75.
94 Ibid., 42–3; Surles, 233; Mazzocco, 271.
95 *Lengua*, 81.
96 Ibid., 102.
97 Isaias Lerner, 'El discurso literario del *Diálogo de la lengua* de Juan de Valdés,' in vol. 2 of *Actas del VIII congresso del la Asociación Internacional de Hispanistas*,

Congress Held in Providence, Rhode Island, 22–27 August 1983, ed. A. David Kossoff, José Amor y Vazquez, Ruth H. Kossoff, and Geoffrey W. Ribbans (Madrid: Ediciones Istmo, 1986): 148–50.
98 *Lengua*, 124.
99 Ibid., 33.
100 Rafael Lapesa, 'Introduction,' *Lengua*, 17.
101 Manuel Miguélez, 'Famoso discurso,' 187–8.
102 The *Alphabet* soon circulated in manuscript as far as Siena. See Massimo Firpo, *Entre alumbrados y 'espirituales': Estudios sobre Juan de Valdés y el valdesianismo en la crisis religiosa del '500 italiano*, trans. Daniela Bergonzi (Madrid: Fundación Universitaria Española Universidad Pontificia de Salamanca, 2000), 224.
103 Caponetto, 68.
104 Boehmer, *Reformers*, 1: 74.
105 Ibid., 1: 69.
106 Hare, *Men and Women*, 225.
107 In the *Dialogue on Language* he cited a Spanish proverb illustrative of his view of Rome. 'Quien lengua ha, a Roma va.' 'Whoever knows language, goes to Rome.' The proverb illustrates the view of a curial humanist. See *Lengua*, 62.
108 *Cartas inéditas*, 84, no. 37, 18 March 1536.
109 Ibid., 87, no. 38, 19 April 1536.
110 Ibid.
111 Granvelle believed the war would aggravate the Lutheran problem and advised Charles to grant Milan to Angoulême, provided he would marry a Habsburg princess. Cobos feared that Charles did not have the finances to support such a conflict in the wake of the costly Tunisian campaign, so he wanted to neutralize Milan by giving it to the Portuguese. Of course Ferdinand's ambassador at court lobbied for the return of the imperial fief to the Holy Roman Empire. See *Cartas de Salinas*, 789, Salinas to Ferdinand, 24 Aug. 1536, and, 687, Salinas to Ferdinand, 18 Dec. 1535; Keniston, 175.
112 Valdés, following in the mould of Gattinara, saw Milan as crucial to Charles's hold on Italy, enabling German troops to enter the peninsula if needed. His initial response was to oppose 'relinquishing the state in any manner not even to the son of the King of the Romans, since he lacks the means to defend it. ... And if war results, the damage will be done to the one who starts it.' After realizing Gonzaga ambitions for Milan, Valdés wrote the cardinal that he did not think Charles had to keep Milan, but the context of the letter suggests that he used the prospect of Gonzaga control of Milan

as a lever to continue the family's cooperation during the war with France. See *Cartas inéditas*, 44, no. 17, 12 Nov. 1535, and 68, no. 29, 11 Dec. 1535.
113 Given what occurred with Cardinal Gonzaga and the failed Council of Mantua, Valdés probably could have done very little to alter the outcome of negotiations.
114 Hare, *Princess*, 82, 90.
115 Juan de Valdés, *Alfabeto cristiano*, ed. B. Foster Stockwell, trans. Luis Usoz y Río (Buenos Aires: Editorial 'La Aurora,' 1948), 41-2.
116 AGS: Estado, leg. 1024, f. 37. Consultation of Matters that the Princess of Sulmona Asks, n.d., but it is identified as being answered while Charles was in Genoa in the autumn of 1536.
117 *Cartas inéditas*, 90, no. 40, 11 Jan. 1537.
118 Hare, *Princess*, 139.
119 *Alfabeto*, 39.
120 Ibid., 65.
121 Ibid., 69.
122 Ibid., 57.
123 Ibid., 78.
124 *Cartas inéditas*, 69, no. 29, 11 Dec. 1535. Six days later Valdés had his money; he was not a man to cross. See ibid., 72, no. 31, 18 Dec. 1535.
125 *Alfabeto*, 65.
126 Ibid., 166
127 Ibid., 90.
128 Menéndez y Pelayo thought the doctrine in the *Alfabeto* was 'not so crudely Lutheran as the other works of Valdés' and in matters such as confession was orthodox. See Menéndez y Pelayo, 3: 227.
129 *Alfabeto*, 147-8.
130 Ibid., 160.
131 Ibid., 159-60.
132 Juan de Valdés, *La epístola de San Pablo a los Romanos*, in vol. 10 of *Reformistas antiguos españoles*, ed. Luis Usoz i Rio (Madrid: 1856; reprinted Barcelona: Librería de Diego Gómez Flores, 1982), xiii.
133 As quoted by Menédez y Pelayo, *Heterodoxos*, 3: 217.
134 Juan de Valdés, *Commentario a los Salmos* (Madrid: Librería Nacional Extranjera, 1885, reprinted Barcelona: Terrassa, 1987)), 6.
135 Ibid.
136 Ibid., 12-13.
137 Ibid., 149.
138 *Salmos*, 237.
139 Croce, 'Cartas,' 155, no. 1, 22 Nov. 1539.

140 AGS: Estado, leg. 1028, f. 40, viceroy to Cobos, 12 June 1538.
141 Croce, 'Cartas,' 158, no. 3, 25 March 1540.
142 Ibid., 156–7, no. 2, 3 Feb. 1540.
143 AGS: Estado, leg. 1031, f. 15, 23 Jan. 1540.
144 Croce, 'Cartas,' 158, no. 3, 25 March 1540.
145 Wiffen, 'Julia Gonzaga,' 26. In her testament Giulia left Isabella 350 ducats for the jewellery she never returned.
146 AGS: Estado, leg. 1031, f. 44, viceroy to Cobos, 12 April 1540.
147 *Trataditos*, Boehmer's appendix, 194.
148 Ibid., 135–60.
149 *Las ciento diez divinas consideraciones de Juan Sánchez*. The two questions and answers, nos. 5 and 12, are on pages 52–3 and 64–9 respectively. The letter on temptation is no. 7, but is placed on pages 309–17 at the end of the manuscript. Tellechea believes all four questions and answers were to Giulia, introduction p. 17, but the repetition of a longish allegory to make a point in nos. 5 (p. 53) and 8 (p. 56) seems to indicate responses to different questioners. Consideration no. 3 is on pages 46–9.
150 *Trataditos*, 138.
151 Ibid., 137–8.
152 Kinder, 'Valdés,' 165.
153 *Las ciento diez divinas consideraciones de Juan Sánchez*, no. 12, 64-9.
154 Ibid., 65.
155 Ibid., 68.
156 Ibid., 52.
157 Ibid.
158 Ibid.
159 *Trataditos*, 139–52, passim.
160 Ibid., 153–4.
161 Ibid., 155.
162 Hare, *Princess*, 173.
163 Croce, 'Cartas,' 166–7, no. 5, 11 June 1540; AGS: Estado, leg. 1030, f. 21.
164 Croce, 'Cartas,' 170, no. 6, 15 Sept. 1540; AGS: Estado, leg. 1030, f. 22.
165 AGS: Estado, leg. 1031, f. 152, viceroy to Cobos, 25 Aug. 1540.
166 AGS: Estado, leg. 1031, f. 156, Relation of viceroy's letter of 25 Aug. 1540.
167 Croce, 'Cartas,' 167, no. 5, 11 June 1540; AGS: Estado, leg. 1030, f. 21.
168 Appendix 20, AGS: Estado, leg. 54, f. 7, Cobos to Valdés, 16 April 1541.
169 AGS: Estado, leg. 53, f. 75, Idiáquez to Cobos, 10 Sept. 1541.
170 Wiffen, 'Julia Gonzaga,' 26.
171 Selwyn Brinton, *The Gonzaga-Lords of Mantua* (London: Methuen and Co., 1927), 176–8.

6. Offices and Audits

1. Giuseppe Galasso, 'Trends and Problems in Neapolitan History in the Age of Charles V,' in *Good Government in Spanish Naples*, ed. and trans. Antonio Calabria and John A. Marino (New York: Peter Lang, 1990), 24.
2. Ibid.
3. Ibid., 57.
4. Benedetto Croce, *History of the Kingdom of Naples*, ed. and intro H. Stuart Hughes, trans. Frances Frenaye (Chicago: University of Chicago Press, 1970, orig. 1925), 113–14; H.G. Koenigsberger, 'The Empire of Charles V,' in *The New Cambridge Modern History*, vol. 2, *The Reformation 1520–1559*, ed. G.R. Elton (Cambridge: Cambridge University Press, 1958, reprinted 1968), 327–8; Leopold von Ranke, *The Ottoman and the Spanish Empires in the Sixteenth Century*, trans. Walter K. Kelly (London: Whittaker and Co., 1843, reprinted 1975), 85; Hernando Sánchez, 276.
5. Hernando Sánchez, 250.
6. More will be said of this office later. Valdés's salary records show his 1536 pay. See AGS: QC, leg. 30, f. 311.
7. AGS: Estado, leg. 1454, f. 142, Relation of letters from Cardinal Colonna, 24, 28 Nov. 1529.
8. AGS: Estado, leg. 1015, f. 50, viceroy to Cobos, 1533.
9. AGS: Estado, leg. 1179, f. 185, Commander Valenzuela to Cobos, 17 Dec. 1533.
10. AGS: Estado, leg. 1024, f. 46, 'What Needs to be Provided for this Kingdom,' 17 March 1536.
11. AGS: Estado, leg. 1027, f. 92, Ordinary Rents and Expenditures for Naples, 1536.
12. AGS: VI, leg. 5, f. 11, Report on Pedro de Puente and his father, Antonio de Puente, who held the office of *perceptor de las significatorias* after Valdés. Most of the testimony was collected in 1572.
13. AGS: Estado, leg. 1029, f. 7, Appeal of *Visita* by Judges, n.d.
14. AGS: VI, leg. 13, f. 7, Alonso de Sánchez's defence to charges of *visitadores*, 19 Jan. 1563.
15. AGS: Estado, leg. 1027, f. 56, Audit of *Significatorias* by Benavente, 1536; AGS: VI, leg. 5, f. 11, Report on Pedro de Puente and his father, Antonio de Puente.
16. Hernando Sánchez, 218.
17. AGS: Estado, leg. 1029, f. 94, 'Brief and Clear List of all the *Significatorias* Made by His Majesty's Comissioners in Revision of the Accounts of the Royal Court of Sommaria, September 1536.' There was an error in the math in this document, as the sums listed add up to 156,506 rather than 156,056. Benavente must have been in a hurry.

18 AGS: Estado, leg. 1025, f. 49, Relation of letter from Bartholomew Benavente, 30 Sept. 1536.
19 Ibid.
20 AGS: Estado, leg. 1024, f. 44, Relation of letter from the viceroy, 15 Nov. 1536.
21 AGS: Estado, leg. 1459, f. 90, 'Matters from Italy to be Discussed in Council,' 26–7 April 1537.
22 Two nominees were submitted. Valdés had earlier indicated that he would send forth two nominees. The office was given to Antonio de Puente, a royal secretary, who held it until 1551, when evidence of financial irregularities (one witness claimed extortion) led him to renounce the office in favour of his son Pedro. Pedro, also accused of taking bribes, etc., renounced the office in 1561 in favour of Juan Luis Candido. Since both nominees were royal secretaries and Valdés was to be assisted by a royal secretary in his new office, it is likely some sort of deal was worked out in advance between Valdés and the nominees. Juan probably pocketed some money for the office. Puente's ordinary salary was reduced to two hundred ducats, a hundred ducats less than Valdés received. See AGS: Estado, leg. 1026, f. 151, Cobos to viceroy, 2 June 1537.
23 AGS: Estado, leg. 1010, f. 123, Report of Veedor Luis de Cardenas to Charles, 31 Aug. 1531. An examination of the Neapolitan documents through 1541 yields this single report of the castle overseer.
24 AGS: Estado, leg. 1026, f. 151, Cobos to viceroy, 2 June 1537.
25 AGS: Estado, leg. 1026, f. 48, 11 July 1537.
26 Hernando Sánchez, 407–8.
27 Appendix 18, AGS: Estado, leg. 1026, f. 131, viceroy to Cobos, 18 Dec. 1537.
28 Appendix 19, AGS: Estado, leg. 1026, f. 134, Cobos's summary of viceroy's letter for presentation to the Council of Castile.
29 Ibid.
30 AGS: Estado, leg. 1028, f. 14, 30 March 1538; AGS: Estado, leg. 1028, f. 36, 9 June 1538.
31 Appendix 5, AGS: QC, leg. 30, f. 313.
32 Ignacio Tellechea Idigoras, ed., *Fray Bartolomé Carranza, Documentos históricos* (Madrid: Real Academia de Historia, 1962–76), 2: p. 1, 117, Testimony of Fray Domingo de Rojas, 17 Aug. 1559.
33 H.G. Koenigsberger, 'Patronage and Bribery during the Reign of Charles V,' in *Estates and Revolutions: Essays in Early Modern European History* (Ithaca: Cornell University Press, 1971), 169.
34 *Salmos*, 127.
35 Ibid., 74.

36 Ibid., 69.
37 Ibid.
38 George Forell, 'Luther and Politics,' in *Luther and Culture*, ed. George Forell, Harold J. Grimm, and Theodore Holety-Nickel (Decorah, Iowa: Luther College Press, 1960), 37; Niccolo Machiavelli, *The Prince*, trans. Luigi Ricci (New York: New American Library, 1952), 84–5.
39 *Divine Considerations*, 335, 404.
40 *Salmos*, 208.
41 Domingo Ricart, 'El concepto de honra en Juan de Valdés,' *Revista de Filosofía de la Universidad de Costa Rica* 4 (1964): 147–64, passim.
42 Jiménez Monteserín, 'Familia Valdés,' lviii; This view makes it easier to portray Juan as a frustrated courtier who retired from political activity as soon as he could afford to do so.
43 *Cartas inéditas*, 62, no. 26, 1 Dec. 1535.
44 Zarco y Cuevas, 'Testamentos,' 679–85 passim. Donald and Lázaro also provide transcriptions of Alfonso's and Diego's testaments, 345–53, appendices 21, 23; 'Il Testamento del [Juan de] Valdés,' appendix 3 of *Alfabeto cristiano: diálogo con Giulia Gonzaga*, ed. Benedetto Croce (Bari: Guis, Laterya e Figli, 1938), 174–5.
45 Zarco y Cuevas, 'Testamentos,' 684.
46 Ibid., 680–3. My estimate of the chancellor's salary is based on the salary of other high Neapolitan offices. The list of salaries for Neapolitan offices for 1538 only cites the total expense of the Chancellory as 2,940 ducats. See AGS: Estado, leg. 1027, f. 88, Ordinances of Bartolomé de Benavente, 1538. This was compiled as part of the *visita* 1536–9.
47 Torrente Pérez, 1: 407.
48 Castellán, 37/38: 263.
49 AGS: Estado, leg. 1025, f. 26, Pacheco to Cobos, 2 June 1536.
50 AGS: Estado, leg. 1025, f. 21, Pacheco to Cobos, 4 May 1536; AGS: Estado, leg. 1025, f. 29, Pacheco to Cobos, 9 June 1536; AGS: Estado, leg. 1025, f. 37, 11 Sept. 1536; AGS: Estado, leg. 1025, f. 43, Pacheco to Cobos, 12 Oct. 1536.
51 AGS: Estado, leg. 1017, f. 80, viceroy to Charles, 6 Nov. 1534; AGS: Estado, leg. 1017, f. 9, viceroy to Charles, 21 Jan. 1534.
52 AGS: Estado, leg. 1030, f. 120, Doria to Charles, 4 July 1539; AGS: Estado, leg. 1030, f. 167, Benavente to Charles, 9 Feb. 1539; AGS: Estado, leg. 1030, f. 171, Benavente to Cobos, 21 Oct. 1539.
53 AGS: Estado, leg. 1030, f. 169, Benavente to Cobos, 23 March 1539; AGS: Estado, leg. 1030, ff. 175–9, Report of Bartolomé de Benavente to Charles, 1539.
54 AGS: Estado, leg. 1024, f. 26, Charles's Memorial on Negotiations, 31 Dec. 1535.

55 AGS: Estado, leg. 1024, f. 46, 'What Needs to Be Done in This Kingdom,' 17 March 1536.
56 When Viceroy Toledo asked Charles what he should tell judges besmirched by the *visita*, Charles replied, 'principally, prohibit presents.' See AGS: Estado, leg. 1031, f. 130, Relation from viceroy's letter of 30 June 1540.
57 ADMS, leg. 4336, Charles to viceroy, 5 Dec. 1536.
58 AGS: Estado, leg. 1015, f. 36, viceroy to Charles, 1 May 1533.
59 Not only did he brilliantly organize the defence of Naples from the French, 1536–7, he also had to supply Andrea Doria with provisions and soldiers for offensive and defensive naval actions practically every year.
60 Charles had to order Toledo to make Treasurer Sánchez and Chief Justice Severino turn their books over to Benavente. Initially these officials demanded a new royal order each time Benavente requested documents. See ADMS, leg. 4336, Charles to viceroy, 5 Dec. 1536; AGS: Estado, leg. 1026, f. 36, Relation of letters from viceroy, 20, 21, 23 June 1537.
61 AGS: Estado, leg. 1459, f. 87, Consultations for Charles from Italy, 8 Oct. 1537.
62 AGS: Estado, leg. 1028, f. 23, viceroy to Charles, 30 April 1538.
63 AGS: Estado, leg. 1026, f. 128, Relation of letters from viceroy, 30 Nov. and 4 Dec. 1537.
64 AGS: Estado, leg. 1025, f. 4, viceroy to Charles, 8 June 1536. Ferdinand had rents in Calabria, but Charles declared those null by a pragmatic in 1530. Both the viceroy and parliamentary leaders reminded Charles of this in 1536 and sent him copies of his 1530 pragmatic. See AGS: Estado, leg. 1025, f. 9, Copy of Charles's Letter to the Sommaria, 4 June 1530.
65 Antonio Calabria, *The Cost of Empire: The Finances of the Kingdom of Naples in the Time of Spanish Rule* (Cambridge: Cambridge University Press, 1991), 132.
66 AGS: Estado, leg. 1024, f. 37, List of requests to Charles, n.d.
67 AGS: Estado, leg. 1024, f. 11, List of salaries, n.d.
68 AGS: VI, leg. 13, f. 8, no. 46, Defence of Alonso Sánchez, 19 Jan. 1563. This document is Sánchez's reply to accusations made in the 1554 *visita*, but in it are a few documents from the earlier *visita*.
69 AGS: Estado, leg. 1031, f. 15, viceroy to Cobos, 23 Jan 1540.
70 AGS: Estado, leg. 45, f. 108, Relation of letter from Italy, 8 Oct. 1539.
71 AGS: Estado, leg. 1031, f. 15, viceroy to Cobos, 23 Jan. 1540.
72 AGS: Estado, leg. 1030, f. 155, Sánchez to Charles, 2 Sept. 1539. He had provisioned the city while the viceroy organized defence of the kingdom from Melfi in anticipation of a Turkish invasion.
73 AGS: Estado, leg. 1032, f. 1, Sánchez to Cobos, 27 Dec. 1539.
74 AGS: Estado, leg. 498, f. 65, Idiáquez to Cobos, 4 Aug. 1540.

75 AGS: Estado, leg. 498, f. 70, Relation of letter from Idiáquez to Cobos, 17 Sept. 1540.
76 AGS: Estado, leg. 1033, f. 155, Hieronimo Severino to Cobos, 23 March 1540. More than a year and a half later Cobos claimed he never received the diamond. See AGS: Estado, leg. 54, f. 212, Cobos to Severino, 30 Nov. 1541.
77 AGS: Estado, leg. 1032, f. 41, Doctor Baron to Cobos, 6 Feb. 1540.
78 AGS: Estado, leg. 1031, f. 15, viceroy to Cobos, 23 Jan. 1540.
79 ADMS, leg. 4335, viceroy to Mudarra, 12 July 1540; Toledo's relatives complained that the victory did him little service, as the clergy he selected were lazy and refused to say Matin prayers. See ADMS, leg. 1300, Don Fabrique Alvarez de Toledo to Viceroy Pedro II, 19 Sept. 1540.
80 Croce, 'Cartas,' 160–4, no. 3, 25 March 1540; AGS: Estado, leg. 1032, f. 19.
81 In his 1536 testimony to the *visitadores*, Figueroa gave Toledo a glowing recommendation, showing the high esteem the Collateral Council had for him. 'The viceroy has guarded well matters of justice and the administration and conservation of the royal patrimony ... always he has done what he should as a good servant of Your Majesty and prudent governor.' See AGS: Estado, leg. 1025, f. 61, Report of Regent Figueroa, 1536.
82 AGS: Estado, leg. 1030, f. 162, Figueroa to Cobos, 20 Dec. 1539.
83 AGS: Estado, leg. 498, f. 87, Figueroa to Cobos, 31 Oct. 1540.
84 AGS: Estado, leg. 1031, f. 131, Relation of letter from viceroy, 30 June 1540. In March the viceroy began complaining that he could not pay his soldiers and that the population suffered disturbances from them. See AGS: Estado, leg. 1031, f. 31, viceroy to Charles, 8 March 1540.
85 AGS: Estado, leg. 1031, f. 44, viceroy to Cobos, 12 April 1540.
86 AGS: Estado, leg. 1031, f. 51, viceroy to Bracamonte, 24 April 1540; AGS: Estado, leg. 1031, f. 52, viceroy to Bracamonte, n.d.; AGS: Estado, leg. 1031, f. 63, viceroy to Cobos, 3 May 1540.
87 After joining the imperial court, Figueroa became a primary adviser on Italian affairs, though his aloof personality reduced his influence. Bernado Navagiero, the Venetian ambassador at Charles's court from 1544 to 1546, penned the following assessment of Figueroa. 'Next to these two men [Cobos and Granvelle] the Duke of Alva and the Regent Figueroa stand highest with the Emperor as his advisers in Council. Figueroa is a Spaniard, who was brought up by the Viceroy of Naples. He is esteemed a man severe and just, and is always consulted touching affairs of Italy, but on account of his very cold and reserved manners it is not supposed that he will get on much in the world.' See 'Relatione del Clarissimo M. Bernardo Navagiero, ritornato Ambasciatore d'Alemagna da Carlo Quinto Imperator, l'anno MDXLVI, nel mese di luglio,' in William Bradford, ed., *Correspondence of the Emperor Charles V*

Notes to pages 127–9   239

and His Ambassadors at the Courts of England and France from the Original Letters in the Imperial Family Archives at Vienna; with a Connecting Narrative and Biographical Notices of the Emperor, and of Some of the Most Distinguished Officers of His Army and Household; Together with the Emperor's Itinerary from 1519–1551 (London: Richard Bentley, 1850), 445.

88 AGS: Estado, leg. 1031, f. 68, viceroy to Cobos, 10 May 1540.
89 AGS: Estado, leg. 1031, f. 34, Charles to viceroy, 11 April 1540.
90 AGS: Estado, leg. 1031, f. 130, Charles to viceroy, 6 May 1540. This is the second of two documents in this folio.
91 AGS: Estado, leg. 1031, f. 137, viceroy to Charles, 20 July 1540.
92 AGS: Estado, leg. 1031, f. 143, 31 July 1540.
93 AGS: Estado, leg. 1031, f. 117, viceroy to Cobos, 30 July 1540; As early as February Toledo bemoaned to Cobos, 'I am so disgraced.' See AGS: Estado, leg. 1031, f. 20, 24 Feb. 1540.
94 Croce, 'Cartas,' 165, no. 4, 1 May 1540.
95 Ibid., 168, no. 6, 15 Sept. 1540.
96 Ibid.
97 Ibid., 172, no. 7, 20 Dec. 1540.
98 This paragraph was marked through in the draft I examined.
99 Appendix 20, AGS: Estado, leg. 54, f. 7, Cobos to Valdés, 16 April 1541.
100 AGS: Estado, leg. 1031, f. 153, viceroy to Charles, 25 Aug. 1540; AGS: Estado, leg. 1031, f. 164, Charles to viceroy, 13 Sept. 1540.
101 Francisco Reverter wrote Cobos that good judges were refusing office because of the politically charged and vengeful atmosphere. In his view, justice was in the hands of incompetents, further alienating those qualified from service. See AGS: Estado, leg. 1032, f. 69, 12 May 1540.
102 AGS: Estado, leg. 52, f. 120, Cobos to Pacheco, 14 Dec. 1540.
103 AGS: Estado, leg. 55, f. 28, Cobos to viceroy, 1 Feb. 1541.
104 AGS: Estado, leg. 638, f. 155, Juan Vazquez to Cobos, 7 May 1541.
105 AGS: Estado, leg. 1033, f. 75, viceroy to Charles, 26 May 1541. In July Severino finally officially surrendered his office of Chief Justice of the Sommaria to Benavente. Toledo wrote Cobos in August that he was doing all he could for Severino, as Cobos requested. He even came to accept Sánchez, writing Charles in an undated letter that Sánchez's appointment 'is fine.' The rift between the viceroy and Cobos was over. See AGS: Estado, leg. 1031, f. 194, viceroy to Cobos, 30 Nov. 1540; AGS: Estado, leg. 1033, f. 154 Severino to Cobos, 30 July 1541; AGS: Estado, leg. 1033, f. 79, viceroy to Charles, n.d.
106 AGS: VI, leg. 13, f. 8, passim, Defence of Alonso Sánchez, 19 Jan. 1563.
107 AGS: Estado, leg. 498, f. 65, Idiáquez to Cobos, 4 Sept. 1540.

108 AGS: Estado, leg. 1030, f. 169, Benavente to Cobos, 23 March 1539.
109 Hernando Sánchez, 221.
110 AGS: Estado, leg. 1033, f. 72, Charles to viceroy, 20 June 1541; AGS: Estado, leg. 1033, f. 83, viceroy to Charles, 8 July 1541; AGS: Estado, leg. 1033, f. 79, viceroy to Charles, n.d.; AGS: Estado, leg. 498, f. 145, Charles to viceroy, 7 July 1540.
111 AGS: Estado, leg. 55, ff. 30–3, Cobos to viceroy, 6 July 1541; AGS: Estado, leg. 54, f. 211, Cobos to Severino, 1 Dec. 1541.
112 In the spring and summer of 1540 Charles pressured Toledo to clear up the mess in his courts by expediting cases. He sent several terse messages to the viceroy discussing a half-dozen cases, including Giulia Gonzaga's, which he believed had been mishandled or delayed. See AGS: Estado, leg. 498, ff. 137, 139–40, 143, 145, Charles to viceroy, 3 March, 24 March, 11 May, 7 July, 31 Aug. 1540.
113 AGS: Estado, leg. 1031, f. 6, viceroy to Charles, 10 Feb. 1540; AGS: Estado, leg. 1031–6, viceroy to Charles, 1 April 1540.
114 AGS: Estado, leg. 1032, f. 52, viceroy to Charles, 18 March 1540.
115 AGS: Estado, leg. 1031, f. 114, viceroy to Charles, n.d.
116 AGS: Estado, leg. 498, f. 75, Idiáquez to Cobos, 12 Nov. 1540; AGS: Estado, leg. 498, f. 66, Idiáquez to Cobos, 4 Sept. 1540.
117 AGS: Estado, 1031, 150, viceroy to Charles, 30 Aug. 1540.
118 AGS: Estado, leg. 1460, f. 144, Granvelle to Cobos, 24 Feb. 1541; AGS: Estado, leg. 1033, f. 75 viceroy to Charles, 26 June 1541.
119 Calabria, 43.
120 Hernando Sánchez, 100–1.
121 Ibid., 95; ADMS, leg. 427, Dowry Payments from Ascanio to Don García de Toledo. The document indicates some misunderstanding about the dowry payments, a total of 50,000 ducats. Though not specifically dated, this is a summary report of letters from the Toledo family to Ascanio and Vittoria Colonna on 30 Sept. 1553, 4 Aug. 1555, and 7 May 1556.
122 Hernando Sanchez, 14–15, 97.
123 Sydney Anglo, 'The Courtier: The Renaissance and Changing Ideals,' in *The Courts of Europe: Politics, Patronage and Royalty 1400–1800*, ed. A.G. Dickens (New York: Greenwich House, 1977), 34.
124 Ibid., 43.
125 Antonio Feros, *Kingship and Favoritism in the Spain of Philip III, 1598–1621* (Cambridge: Cambridge University Press, 2000), 35.
126 For a good survey of *privanzas* in early modern Spain compared to other European favourites, see John Elliott, 'Unas reflexiones acerca de la privanza española en el contexto europeo,' *Anuario de historia del derecho español* 67, no. 2 (1997): 885–99.

127 Antonio Feros, 'Images of Evil, Images of Kings: The Contrasting Faces of the Royal Favorite and the Prime Minister in Early Modern European Literature, c. 1580–c. 1650,' in *The World of the Favorite*, ed. J.H. Elliott and L.W.B. Brockliss (New Haven: Yale University Press, 1999), 206; James A. Boyden, *The Courtier and the King: Ruy Gómez de Silva, Philip II, and the Court of Spain* (Berkeley: University of California Press, 1995), 64, 118.

128 Antonio de Guevara's dedication of his *Aviso de privados y doctrina de cortesanos* in 1539 was a clear recognition of Cobos's *privanza*. See Keniston, 353. In 1565 Pedro de Navarra referred to Cobos as Charles's principal *privado*. See Elliott, 'Unas reflexiones acerca de la privanza,' 888; The limited nature of Cobos's *privanza* was reflected in Luis de Zapata's comment in the late sixteenth century that Charles had two great *privados*: Cobos was the 'king's friend' and Don Luis de Avila was 'Charles' friend.' See Antonio Feros, 'Twin Souls: Monarchs and Favorites in Early Seventeenth-Century Spain,' in *Spain, Europe and the Atlantic World: Essays in Honour of John H. Elliott*, ed. Richard Kagan and Geoffrey Parker (Cambridge: Cambridge University Press, 1995), 31–2.

129 Boyden, 64–6.
130 Feros, *Kingship and Favoritism*, 4.
131 Keniston, 334.
132 Koenigsberger, 'Patronage and Bribery,' 166.
133 For Alfonso's secretarial position see Cuesta Zamora, 437; Escudero, 1: 67; Clearly Juan's 1535 appointment was to Charles's person as well. See Appendix 5, AGS: QC, leg. 30, f. 312; AGS: Residencias, leg. 4, f. 604.
134 Koenigsberger, 'Patronage and Bribery,' 169.
135 Cordero Torres, 50.
136 Juan de Valdés, *Le Cento e Dieci Divine Considerazioni*, preface by Edmondo Cione (Milan: Fratelli Bocca, 1944), 527. The letter is dated 1 May 1550.
137 Keniston, 333.
138 James A. Boyden, '"Fortune Has Stripped You of Your Splendor"'; Favorites and Their Fates in Fifteenth- and Sixteenth-Century Spain,' in *The World of the Favorite*, ed. Elliott and Brockliss, 30.

7. Regensburg Justification

1 Hastings Eells, 'The Origin of the Regensburg Book,' *Princeton Theological Review* 26 (1928): 371.
2 AGS: Estado, leg. 638, f. 220, The Recess of Regensburg, 29 July 1541.
3 Merriman, 334.
4 AGS: Estado, leg. 638, f. 138, Charles to Cardinal Toledo, 10 Aug. 1541.

5 AGS: Estado, leg. 638, f. 179, Relation from letter of Idiáquez, 10 Aug. 1541.
6 AGS: GM, leg. 6, f. 119, Viceroy to Cobos, 15 Sept. 1534.
7 *Cartas inéditas*, 6, no. 2, 24 Sept. 1535.
8 Ibid., 61, no. 26, 1 Dec. 1535.
9 Ibid., 11 and 46, nos. 3 and 18, 1 Oct., and 15 Nov. 1535. Obviously Valdés shared information sent by the Venetian ambassador with Gonzaga.
10 Cochrane, *Florence*, 15–18.
11 *Cartas inéditas*, 92, no. 41, 12 Jan. 1537.
12 Hernando Sánchez, 120.
13 Cochrane, *Florence*, 30–2; Pastor, 11: 315; Partner, *Rome*, 86; and Merriman, 279. Under torture Strozzi confessed his disloyalty to the emperor, but denied involvement in Alessandro's murder.
14 Hernando Sánchez, 539; Caponetto, 83–93.
15 Bainton, *Women*, 202.
16 *Carranza Documentos*, 2: pt. 2, 570, Testimony of Diego Hurtado de Mendoza, 20 Oct. 1559.
17 Massimo Firpo and Domenico Marcatto, eds., *Il Processo inquisitoriale del cardinal Giovanni Morone*, 6 vols. (Roma: Instituto storico italiano per l'eta moderna contemporanea, 1981–7), 2: 573.
18 Letter of Bobadilla to the Duke of Ferrara, 4 July 1539, in *Bobadillae monumenta*, 16, document no. 12.
19 Ibid., 18–19, document no. 13.
20 AGS: Estado, leg. 868, f. 124, Charles to Aguilar, 3 July 1539.
21 AGS: Estado, leg. 1033, f. 75, viceroy to Charles, 26 June 1541.
22 During the Camerino negotiations, Charles ordered Aguilar to make the pope aware of his need of papal support in his negotiations in Germany. See AGS: Estado, leg. 868, f. 123, Charles to Aguilar, 21 June 1539.
23 Eells, 356–7.
24 AGS: Estado, leg. 637, f. 98, Papal Response to the Frankfort Recess, n.d.
25 Sarpi, 83–5.
26 Elisabeth G. Gleason, *Gasparo Contarini: Venice, Rome, and Reform* (Berkeley: University of California Press, 1993), 36, 110, 190–3.
27 AGS: Estado, leg. 869, f. 65, Aguilar to Charles, 11 May 1540.
28 Peter Matheson, *Cardinal Contarini at Regensburg* (Oxford: Clarendon Press, 1972), 181.
29 Heinz Mackensen, 'Contarini's Theological Role at Ratisbon,' in *Archiv für Reformationsgeschichte* 51 (1960): 55.
30 Pastor, 11: 329.
31 AGS: Estado, leg. 869, f. 53, Aguilar to Charles, 29 April 1540.

32 AGS: Estado, leg. 1031, f. 56, Charles to viceroy, 24 April 1540.
33 Cobos was not aware of Charles's role in the deception. On 7 May Toledo wrote Cobos that the emperor was not served by loaning the troops to the pope, but Cobos responded that he should leave the troops with the pope. See AGS: Estado, leg. 1031, f. 45, Relation from viceroy's letter of 7 May 1540. Evidently Cobos pressed for an explanation, as Toledo confessed that he had actually followed Charles's order: 'I do not have any other interest with the pope than the service of His Majesty.' See AGS: Estado, leg. 1031, f. 82, 20 May 1540. Only long after the affair was over did Toledo pen an official explanation that seems to have been put in the record to protect Charles. He said that he halted the troops after twenty days of service without pay and that he alone made the decision because there was no time to consult any other ministers. See AGS: Estado, leg. 1031, f. 47, viceroy to Charles, 12 July 1540.
34 AGS: Estado, leg. 1031, f. 58, viceroy to Charles, 11 May 1540.
35 AGS: Estado, leg. 869, f. 70, Aguilar to Charles, 28 May 1540.
36 AGS: Estado, leg. 1031, f. 109, viceroy to Cobos, 27 May 1540.
37 AGS: Estado, leg. 1031, f. 130, Relation from viceroy's letter, 20 June 1540. Either Charles or Cobos wanted Toledo to stop his bragging, because to the side of the relation was the reply, 'there is no need to reply more about this.'
38 AGS: Estado, leg. 869, f. 11, Charles to Aguilar, 8 Sept. 1540.
39 AGS: Estado, leg. 869, f. 116, Charles to Aguilar, 3 Nov. 1540.
40 AGS: Estado, leg. 869, f. 70, Aguilar to Charles, 28 May 1540.
41 Thomas J. Dandelet, *Spanish Rome 1500–1700* (New Haven: Yale University Press, 2001), 49.
42 AGS: Estado, leg. 870, f. 26, Aguilar to Charles, 4 March 1541.
43 In January Viceroy Toledo blocked the transfer of two Neapolitan fortresses to Ottavio Farnese. The pope had not paid for one and the annual rent paid the viceroy for the other was far below the stipulated amount. Charles agreed with his viceroy to prohibit the transfer until the bills were paid in full. Given the ensuing conflict, the viceroy's action may have been more than just coincidence. See AGS: Estado, leg. 1033, f. 2, 9 Jan. 1541, viceroy to Charles; AGS: Estado, leg. 1033, f. 11, Charles to viceroy, 5 Feb. 1541.
44 AGS: Estado, leg. 1033, f. 16, Ascanio to viceroy, 31 Feb. 1541.
45 AGS: Estado, leg. 1033, f. 19, Aguilar to Charles, 3 March 1541.
46 AGS: Estado, leg. 870, f. 29, Aguilar to Charles, 7 March 1541.
47 AGS: Estado, leg. 1033, f. 32, viceroy to Paul III, 3 April 1541; AGS: Estado, leg. 1033, f. 34, Aguilar to viceroy, 3 April 1541.
48 AGS: Estado, leg. 870, f. 24, Aguilar to Charles, 5 April 1541.

49 AGS: Estado, leg. 870, f. 36, 18 April 1541.
50 AGS: Estado, leg. 1033, f. 37, Ascanio to Antonio Bijar, 7 April 1541.
51 AGS: Estado, leg. 1033, f. 38, Bijar to viceroy, 26 April 1541; AGS: Estado, leg. 1033, f. 39, viceroy to Charles, 18 April 1541.
52 AGS: Estado, leg. 1033, f. 44, Aguilar to viceroy, 29 April 1541.
53 AGS: Estado, leg. 870, f. 33, Aguilar to Charles, 29 April 1541.
54 AGS: Estado, leg. 1033, ff. 197–8, Charles to viceroy, 30 April 1541.
55 AGS: Estado, leg. 1033, f. 55, Aguilar to viceroy, 21 May 1541.
56 AGS: Estado, leg. 1033, f. 35, viceroy to Aguilar, 25 May 1541. This folio is a collection of copies of several letters about the matter.
57 AGS: Estado, leg. 1033, f. 45, viceroy to Aguilar, 13 May 1541.
58 AGS: Estado, leg. 870, f. 36, Aguilar to Charles, 18 April 1541.
59 AGS: Estado, leg. 870, f. 53, Aguilar to Charles, 13 May 1541.
60 Carande, 2: 72–3, 3: 209–10.
61 AGS: Estado, leg. 55, f. 74, Cobos to Aguilar, 21 Feb. 1541.
62 AGS: Estado, leg. 55, ff. 79–80. Cobos to Aguilar, 16 April 1541.
63 AGS: Estado, leg. 55, ff. 76–8, Cobos to Aguilar, 6 July 1541; AGS: Estado, leg. 55, f. 34, Cobos to Vasto, 6 July 1541.
64 AGS: Estado, leg. 55, ff. 30–3, Cobos to viceroy, 6 July 1541.
65 Pastor, 11: 404.
66 Ibid.; George Williams, *The Radical Reformation* (Philadelphia: Westminister Press, 1962), 537.
67 Appendix 20, AGS: Estado, leg. 54, f. 7, Cobos to Juan de Valdés, 16 April 1541. 'Gonzalez Pérez has told me that one Alonso Díaz has started suit in Rome over some benefices that he [Perez] has in Villena and that you could play a big role in stopping it. ... I ask that you assist him in any way possible and I consider any favour done for him a favour for me.' Pérez was groomed by Cobos as his successor and made secretary to Prince Philip in 1543. Alonso Díaz was a lawyer for the Roman Curia who at the 1546 Diet of Regensburg shocked the imperial court by having his Protestant-leaning brother murdered in his sleep.
68 Roland Bainton, *Here I Stand: A Biography of Martin Luther* (New York: New American Library, 1955, orig. 1950), 49–50.
69 *Romanos*, x–xi.
70 Ibid., xii.
71 Ibid., xiii–xv. He repeats the story twice in his *Divine Considerations*, 236–8, 566–7. The story is also in Marcantonio Flaminio and Don Benedetto, *The Benefit of Christ*, trans. Ruth Prelowski, ed. John Tedeschi, in *Italian Reformation Studies in Honor of Laelius Socinus* (Florence: Casa Editrice Felice Le Monnier, 1965), 60. The longest interpretation of the allegory was published in Italian in 1545 under the title *The Mode of Teaching and Preaching the Principle of the*

Christian Religion. It is included in Juan de Valdés, *XVII Opuscules: Juan de Valdés' Minor Works*, ed. and trans. John T. Betts (London: Trubner and Co., Ludgate Hill, 1882), 131–5.
72 Niccolo Balbani, *The Italian Convert; News from Italy of a Second Moses; or The Life of Galeacius Caracciolous* ..., trans. from Italian into Latin by Theodore Beza, and from Latin into English by William Crashaw (London: Thomas Ratcliff and Thomas Daniel, 1668), 6.
73 Ibid., 29–30.
74 *Romanos*, 11.
75 Ibid., 44.
76 Ibid., 55.
77 Ibid.
78 Ibid., 143.
79 Ibid., 216.
80 *Corintios*, xv–xvi.
81 Ibid., xvix.
82 Ibid., 9.
83 Ibid., 53.
84 Ibid., 134.
85 Ibid., 238–9.
86 Ibid., 241.
87 Ibid., 242.
88 Firpo and Marcatto, eds., *Il Processo Morone*, 2: 572–3.
89 Ermanno Ferrero and Giuseppe Müller, eds., *Carteggio di Vittoria Colonna, Marchesa di Pescara* (Turin: Ermanno Loescher, 1889), 240.
90 Ibid.
91 *Las ciento diez divinas consideraciones de Juan Sánchez*, Tellechea's introduction, 7–30, passim.
92 *Trataditos*, 121.
93 Ibid., 109–10.
94 Ibid., 108–9.
95 *Divine Considerations*, 521–6.
96 Ibid., 525.
97 Ibid., 523.
98 Ibid., 424.
99 Ibid., 425.
100 Boehmer published the work in Italian and German in 1870 (Kinder, 'Valdés,' 167), but included only the first tract in the original Spanish in his *Trataditos* (163–84). An English translation of the entire work, i.e., all five tracts, is in John Betts's *Minor Works* of Valdés, 120–88.

101 *Trataditos*, Boehmer's appendix, 186, 192.
102 *Minor Works*, 135.
103 Ibid., 146.
104 *Minor Works*, 147, 152.
105 Ibid., 160.
106 Ibid., 160–3.
107 Ibid., 166.
108 Ibid., 168.
109 Ibid., 170.
110 Eduard Boehmer, Preface to Valdés, *Mateo*, vi–vii.
111 *Corintios*, 70.
112 *Mateo*, 51–3.
113 Ibid., 339–40.
114 Ibid., 177–8 and 224.
115 Ibid, 496.
116 *Romanos*, 194–5.
117 Payne, 28.
118 *Mateo*, 305–7.
119 *Divine Considerations*, 286–7. For this reason Valdés held that the Christian who believed with difficulty was superior to the one who believed with facility. The latter was likely to accept all sorts of superstitions and falsities unquestioningly. The former will be slower to accept the truth, but when he does he will separate it from superstition. See ibid., 231–3.
120 Ibid., 236.
121 *Romanos*, 304.
122 *Las ciento diez divinas consideraciones de Juan Sánchez*, 54–5. This is one of the eleven additional considerations included in this edition.
123 Mackensen, 49; Basil Hall, 'The Colloquies between Catholics and Protestants, 1539–1541,' *Studies in Church History* 7 (1971): 255.
124 Gleason, 190–2, 233.
125 Firpo and Marcatto, eds., *Il Processo Morone*, 2: 572–3.
126 Ibid., 2: 205.
127 AGS: Estado, leg. 638, f. 212, Approval of Religious Colloquy, n.d.
128 Herbert Jedin, *A History of the Council of Trent*, 3 vols., trans. Dom Ernest Graf (Edinburgh: Thomas Nelson and Sons, 1961), 2: 382; Hall, 262; Matheson, 107; Mackensen, 37.
129 Mackensen, 41.
130 Matheson, 108.
131 Gleason, 241.
132 Firpo, 198, 227–8.

133 Gleason, 243.
134 Ibid.; Matheson, 151–2.
135 Pastor, 11: 462.
136 AGS: Estado, leg. 638, f. 220, 29 July 1541, The Recess of Regensburg.
137 AGS: Estado, leg. 1469, f. 169, 1 July 1541.
138 See 'The Itinerary of the Emperor Charles V, Originally Written in Flemish by His Private Secretary Vandenesse. Comprising an Account of the Emperor's Journeys from the Year 1519 to 1551,' in Bradford, 522.
139 Ibid., 524–5.
140 Hare, *Princess*, 152.
141 AGS: Estado, leg. 1460, f. 138. The letter is not dated, but it mentions Cobos just receiving a letter from Charles from Majorica and the emperor's plan to go to Cartagena. Charles arrived at Majorca 26 November, and reached Cartegena 1 December. Cobos refers to the viceroy's last letter to him on 20 September at the beginning of this letter.
142 AGS: Estado, leg. 1033, f. 1, viceroy to Cobos, 7 Jan. 1541 (*sic*). The viceroy misdated this document, as Valdés did not die until August 1541. The actual date was no doubt 7 Jan. 1542.
143 AGS: Estado, leg. 1034, f. 48, Alonso Sánchez to Cobos, 8 Jan. 1542.
144 Hare, *Men and Women*, 77.
145 Ferrero and Müller, *Carteggio di Vittoria Colonna*, 239.
146 Hare, *Princess*, 176–7.
147 Hare, *Men and Women*, 169–70.
148 Maud F. Jerrold, *Vittoria Colonna: With Some Account of Her Friends and Her Times* (Freeport, NY: Books for Libraries Press, 1969 reprint, orig. 1906), 255–7.
149 As quoted by Pastor, 11: 497.
150 Pastor, 13: 12.
151 Firpo, 231, 259.
152 Ibid., 229, Contarini to Bembo, 28 June 1541, as quoted by Firpo.
153 Ibid, 198, 253–4, 257.
154 Pastor, 13: 12.
155 Ibid., 12: 505; Firpo, 228.
156 Gleason, 259.
157 Firpo, 132.
158 Ibid, 42.
159 Castellán, 41/42: 184.
160 Flaminio and Benedetto, *Benefit*, 68.
161 Firpo, 58, 216, 259.
162 Ibid., 216
163 Hare, *Princess*, 179–80, 193, 203, 205, 207, 214–16.

164 Kinder, 'Valdés,' 116; Caponetto, 68.
165 From the 1880s through the 1950s their friendship was an accepted fact in Valdesian scholarship. In the early 1960s Ignacio Tellechea Idigoras tried to exculpate Carranza of any taint of heresy by publishing extensive transcriptions of his trial to support the conclusion that Carranza told the truth to inquisitors and that his contact with Valdés was 'sporadic and insignificant.' Tellechea Idigoras, 'Valdés y Carranza: papel,' 312. While Carranza's enemies may have exaggerated their relationship, particularly in regard to the translation and circulation of Valdés's *Divine Considerations* in Spain, neither Domingo Ricart nor the present author is convinced that the relationship was merely casual and unimportant. See Domingo Ricart, 'El texto auténtico de una consideracón valdesiana,' *Hispanófilia* 23 (1965): 23–36, passim.
166 Marcelino Menéndez y Pelayo, *Historia de los heterodoxos españoles*, vol. 4, *Protestismo y Sectas Místicas* (Santander: Consejo Superior de Investigaciones Científicas, 1947, orig. 1880), 4: 11–13.
167 Tellechea Idigoras, 'Valdés y Carranza: papel,' 307.
168 In May 1558 the Papal Inquisition requested a list of all Valdés's living relatives from the Cuenca Inquisition. The Papal Inquisition's decision to proceed against Valdesianism as a condemned heresy must have been made about that date, i.e., soon after the second session of Trent adjourned. See Martínez Millán, *Los hermanos*, 53.
169 Tellechea Idigoras, 'Valdés y Carranza: papel,' 309.
170 Ibid., 117. The version sent to Carranza was referenced as 'Advice Concerning The Interpreters of Scripture.' It is almost the same as Consideration 54 in the Basel edition, and Consideration 65 in the Sánchez edition. The title of these is 'That Prayer and Consideration Are Two Books, or interpreters, for the Sure Understanding of Holy Scripture; and the Way in which Man Should Make Use of Them.' Llorente first cited the *Aviso*, but Menéndez y Pelayo was the first to analyse its role in the trial of Carranza. See Llorente, *Inquísicion*, 3: 344; Menéndez y Pelayo, *Heterodoxos*, 4: 26–28. For the parallel texts of the consideration and the *Aviso* see Ignacio Tellechea Idigoras, 'Juan de Valdés y Bartoloméo de Carranza: Sus normas para leer la Sagrada Escritura,' *Revista Española de Teología* 22 (1962): 377–82; for an analysis of the *Aviso* in comparison to the different early editions of the *Divine Considerations* see Domingo Ricart, 'Texto auténtico,' 23–36; and Tellechea Idigoras's introduction to *Las ciento diez divinas consideraciones de Juan Sánchez*, 7–29.
171 Tellechea Idigoras, 'Valdés y Carranza: papel,' 308.
172 *Considerations*, 369.

173 *Carranza Documentos,* 2: pt. 2, 754, 'Ratification of Testimony by Luis de la Cruz,' 26 Nov. 1560.
174 Ricart, 'Texto auténtico,' 34.
175 Tellechea Idigoras, 'Valdés y Carranza: papel,' 309.
176 *Carranza Documentos,* 2: pt. 1, 117, 'Testimony of Domingo de Rojas,' 17 Aug. 1559.
177 Contrast this with Alfonso's description in the *ejecutoria*: 'secretary to the emperor Carlos, our king and lord, who had charge over matters in Rome, Naples and Germany.' See Jiménez Monteserín, 'Familia Valdés,' xxviii.
178 *Carranza Documentos,* 2: pt. 1, 119, 'Testimony of Domingo de Rojas,' 17 Aug. 1559.
179 Ibid., Bataillon, *Erasmo y España,* 516; Ricart, *Juan de Valdés y el pensamiento religioso europeo,* 79; Jedin, 2: 245.
180 *Carranza Documentos,* 2: pt. 2, 530–1, 'Testimony of Diego Hurtado de Mendoza, 28 Sept. 1559.
181 *Carranza Documentos,* 2: pt. 2, 570, Testimony of Diego Hurtado de Mendoza, 20 Oct. 1559.
182 Jedin, *Trent,* 2: 256.
183 Menéndez y Pelayo, *Heterodoxos,* 4: 14.
184 Ibid., 2: 256, 279; P. Venacio D. Carro, *Los Dominicos y el concilio de Trento: estudio histórico-teológico del concilio y de la aportación de la orden Dominicana* (Salamanca: Calatrava, 1948), 179.
185 AGS: Estado, leg. 1033, f. 71, Charles to Viceroy Toledo, 20 June 1541.
186 Hare, *Men and Women,* 282–93; Menéndez y Pelayo, *Heterodoxos,* 3: 234. Carnesecchi wrote to Giulia that he was glad she had not renounced Valdés as had Cardinal Pole and Flaminio. He continued writing to her as their investigations progressed. The first Valdesians met the chopping block in Naples in March 1564. Carnesecchi was beheaded in 1567, the year after Giulia died. After seeing the correspondence between Giulia and Carnesecchi, Pope Pius IV declared that had he read it sooner 'he would have taken good care to burn her alive.' See Hare, *Princess,* 254.

Conclusion

1 After learning that the pope's son Luigi had arranged to marry off his daughter to the Prince of Bisiniano, Valdés commented: 'what she may presume of the papal lineage, he will also presume, and if she may call him the son of a mule [i.e. a bastard] he will call her the niece of a mule, and thus he will go, as they say in my country, butting as a cuckold.' See *Cartas inéditas,* 22, no. 7, 18 Oct. 1535.

2 *Trataditos*, 179.
3 *Lengua*, 71.
4 Ibid., 71.
5 *Romanos*, 202–3.
6 Nieto, *Valdés*, 148–9.
7 Boehmer, *Twin Brothers*, 26.
8 The *Dialogue on Christian Doctrine* was recalled for correction for having in it 'things not well said.' It was not condemned as heretical.
9 *Carranza Documentos*, 2: pt. 1, 119, Testimony of Fray Domingo Rojas, 17 Aug. 1559.
10 Ibid., 2: pt. 2, 756, Testimony of Luis de la Cruz, 2 July 1560.
11 *Report on the Trial and Martyrdom of Pietro Carnesecchi; Sometime Secretary to Pope Clement VII, and Apostolic Protonary*, ed. and trans. Richard Gibbings (Dublin: University Press, 1856), 42, Sentence against Carnesecchi, 16 Aug. 1567.
12 Boehmer, *Reformers*, 1: 75.
13 Boehmer, *Twin Brothers*, 29; Gibbings, *Trial of Carnesecchi*, 46–7, Sentence against Carnesecchi, 16 Aug. 1567.
14 His fate was not as bad as Carnesecchi's. He was flogged and forced to live in reclusion for ten years. See Hamilton, *Heresy and Mysticism*, 61.
15 Nieto, *Valdés*, 333–4.
16 According to Pastor, Valdés was 'wanting in clearness of thought.' See Pastor, 12: 495. Nieto believes that just before his death Valdés was moving toward a systematic approach. See Nieto, *Valdés*, 195.
17 *Le Cento e Dieci Considerazioni*, 527. The letter is dated 1 May 1550.
18 *Doctrina cristiana*, 126–7.
19 *Alfabeto*, 161.
20 *Corintios*, 215–18.
21 *Trataditos*, 161.
22 These alterations in Valdés's interpretation are reflected in historiographic debates. Castellán proposed that Valdés held a Zwinglian doctrine while Haggard, admitting a Zwinglian similarity, believed Valdés maintained a 'real presence.' See Haggard, 250, and Castellán, 40: 274.
23 José Antonio Maravall credits Sepúlveda and Alfonso de Valdés with creating the first modern theory of empire. See 'La visión utópica del imperio de Carlos V en la España de su epoca,' in *Carlos V 1500–1558; Homenaje de la Universidad de Granada* (Granada: Universidad de Granada, 1958), 41, 59, 62, 66–8.
24 Philippe Erlanger, *The Age of Courts and Kings: Manners and Morals, 1558–1715* (New York: Anchor Books, 1970), 1, 11–12.

25 *Mateo*, 185; this goes along with Bobadilla's description of Valdés spontaneously answering questions in 1540.
26 *Lengua*, 125.
27 Julio Melagres Marín, ed., 'Proceso de María Cazalla,' 2: 136.
28 As quoted in Hare, *Men and Women*, 251.
29 Nieto, *Valdés*, 164. Though I agree with Nieto on the resemblance of the two, I do not think Valdés established an independent Protestant Church in Naples, as it would contradict his political career. Aside from Giulia, Valdés always acted in his own self-interest.
30 Appendix 19, AGS: Estado, leg. 1026, f. 134, Cobos's summary of viceroy's letter of 13 Dec. 1537 for presentation to the Council of Castile.
31 Doris Moreno Martínez 'Carlos V y la Inquisición,' in *Carlos Europeanismo* 2: 424.
32 AGS: Estado, leg. 868, f. 124, Charles to Aguilar, 3 July 1539.
33 *Bobadillae monumenta*, 18–19, document no. 13.
34 Garrett Mattingly, *Renaissance Diplomacy* (Boston: Houghton Mifflin, 1955), 149.
35 Martín Pérez de Ayala, 'Discurso de la vida,' in *El Concilio de Trento*, 2nd ed. (Buenos Aires: Espasa-Calpe, 1947), 43.
36 Ibid., 29, 61–4.
37 AGS: Estado, leg. 41, ff. 87–8, Petition of Andrés de Valdés, 16 March 1542.
38 AGS: Estado, leg. 1460, f. 138, Cobos to the viceroy, n.d.

Bibliography

Archival Collections

Archivo General de Simancas (AGS)
    Cámara de Castilla (CC)
    Casas, Sitios Reales (CSR)
    Consejo Real de Castilla (CR)
    Estado
    Guerra y Marina (GM)
    Patronato Real (PR)
    Quitaciones de Corte, Escribiano (QC)
    Residencias
    Visitas de Italia (VI)
Archivo Histórico Nacional (AHN)
    Inquisición
    Universidades
Archivo Municipal de Cuenca (AMC)
Archivo Histórico para la Provincia de Cuenca (AHPC)
Archivo de los Duques de Medina Sidonia (ADMS)

Printed Primary Sources

Alcocer, Pedro de. *Relación de algunas cosas que pasaron en estos reinos desde que murió la reina católica doña Isabel, hasta que le acabaron las comunidades en la ciudad de Toledo.* Seville: Imprenta y Librería Española y Extrangera, 1872.

Aretino, Pietro. *The Works of Aretino: Dialogues.* Translated by Samuel Putnam. New York: Covici-Friede Publishers, 1933.

Ariosto, Ludovico. *Orlando Furioso*. Translated by Guido Waldman. London: Oxford University Press, 1974.
– *Orlando Furioso*. 2 vols. Translated by William Stewart Rose. London: George Bell and Sons, 1905.
Ayala, Martin Perez de. 'Discurso de la vida.' In *El Concilio de Trento*, 2nd ed. Buenos Aires: Espasa-Calpe, 1947.
Bagnatori, G., ed. 'Cartas inéditas de Alfonso de Valdés sobre la Dieta de Augsburgo.' *Bulletin Hispanique* 57 (1955): 353–74.
Balbani, Niccolo. *The Italian Convert; News from Italy of a Second Moses; or The Life of Galeacius Caracciolous.* ... Translated from Italian into Latin by Theodore Beza, and from Latin into English by William Crashaw. London: Thomas Ratcliff and Thomas Daniel, 1668, orig. 1587.
Bembo, Pietro. *Gli Asolani*. Translated by Rudolf B. Gottfried. Bloomington: Indiana University Press, 1954.
Beltrán de Heredia, Vicente. 'El edicto contra los alumbrados del reino de Toledo.' *Revista española de teología* 10 (1950): 105–30.
Bobadilla, Nicolai Alphonsi de. *Bobadillae monumenta*. Matriti: Typis Gabrieles Lopez de Horno, 1913.
Boehmer, Eduard, ed. 'Alfonsi Valdesii literae XL ineditae.' In *Homenaje a Menéndez y Pelayo*, 1: 385–412. Madrid: Librería General De Victoriano Suárez, 1889.
Bradford, William, ed. *Correspondence of the Emperor Charles V and His Ambassadors at the Courts of England and France from the Original Letters in the Imperial Family Archives at Vienna; with a Connecting Narrative and Biographical Notices of the Emperor, and of Some of the Most Distinguished Officers of His Army and Household; Together with the Emperor's Itinerary from 1519–1551*. London: Richard Bentley, 1850.
Castiglione, Baldesar. *The Book of the Courtier*. Translated by George Bull. London: Penguin Books, 1967, reprinted 1976.
Charles V. *The Autobiography of Charles V.* Translated by Leonard Francis Simpson. London: Longman, Green, Longman, Roberts and Green, 1862.
Croce, Benedetto, ed. Appendix 2, 'Lettere inedite di Juan de Valdés al segretario di stato Cobos riguardanti Giulia Gonzaga e l'amministrazione spagnuoli di Napoli,' and appendix 3, 'Il Testamento del [Juan de] Valdés,' of *Alfabeto cristiano: dialogo con Giulia Gonzaga*. Bari: Guis, Laterya e Figli, 1938.
– 'Una datta importante nella vita di Juan de Valdés.' *Archivo Storico per le Provincie Napoletane* 27 (1902): 151–3.
Dánvila y Collado, Manuel, ed. *Historia crítica y documentada de las comunidades de Castilla*. 6 vols. Madrid: La Real Academia de Historia, 1897–9.

Della Casa, Giovanni. *Galateo*. Introduction and translation by Konrad Eisenbichler and Kenneth Bartlett. Toronto: Centre for Renaissance and Reformation Studies, 1986.
Ehses, Stephen, ed. 'Clemens VII. Und Karl V Zu Bologan 1533.' *Römische Quartalschrift für Christliche Alterhumskunde und für Kirchengeschicte* 5 (1891): 299–307.
Enzinas, Francisco de. *Memorias de Francisco de Enzinas*. Translated by Adam F. Sosa. Buenos Aires: Librería Aurora, 1943.
Erasmus, Desiderius. 'Epistolario con españoles.' In *Erasmo: Obras Escogidas*. 2nd ed. Translated and edited by Lorenzo Riber. Madrid: Aguilar, 1964.
– *Ten Colloquies*. Translated by Craig R. Thompson. New York: Library of Liberal Arts, 1957.
Ferrero, Ermanno, and Giuseppe Müller, eds. *Carteggio di Vittoria Colonna, Marchesa di Pescara*. Turin: Ermanno Loescher, 1889.
Ficino, Marsilio. *Commentary on Plato's Symposium on Love*. Translated by Sears Jayne. Woodstock, Connecticut: Spring Publications, 1985.
Firenzuola, Agnolo. *On the Beauty of Women*. Translated, edited, and introduced by Konrad Eisenbichler and Jacqueline Murray. Philadelphia: University of Pennsylvania Press, 1992.
Firpo, Massimo, and Domenico Marcatto, eds. *Il Processo inquisitoriale del cardinal Giovanni Morone*. 6 vols. Roma: Instituto storico italiano per l'eta moderna contemporanea, 1981–7.
Flaminio, Marcantonio, and Don Benedetto. *The Benefit of Christ*. Translated by Ruth Prelowski. In *Italian Reformation Studies in Honor of Laelius Socinus*, ed. John Tedeschi. Florence: Casa Editrice Felice Le Monnier, 1965.
Fontán, Antonio, and Jerzy Axer, eds. *Españoles y polacos en la Corte de Carlos V: Cartas del embajador Juan Dantisco*. Madrid: Alianza Editorial, 1994.
Gayangos, Pascual de, ed. *Calendar of Letters, Dispatches and State Papers Relating to the Negotiations Between England and Spain 1485–1553*, 12 vols. London: Kraus Reprint, 1969, orig. 1888.
Guicciardini, Francisco. *The History of Italy*. Translated by Sidney Alexander. Princeton: Princeton University Press, 1969.
Guicciardini, Luigi. *The Sack of Rome*. Translated and introduced by James H. McGregor. New York: Italica Press, 1993.
Heine, G., ed. *Briefe an Kaiser Karl V Geschrieben von Seinem Beichtvater in den Tahren 1530–1532*. Berlin: Verlag von Wilhelm Besser, 1848.
Longhurst, John. 'Alumbrados, erasmistas y luteranos en el processo de Juan de Vergara.' *Cuadernos de historia de España* 27 (1957): 99–163; 28 (1958): 102–65; 29–30 (1959): 266–92; 31–2 (1960): 322–56; 35–6 (1962): 337–53; 37–8 (1963): 356–71.
Machiavelli, Niccolo. *The Prince*. Translated by Luigi Ricci. New York: New American Library, 1952.

Martínez Millán, Miguel. *Los hermanos conquenses Alfonso y Juan de Valdés: Su ambiente familiar y la clasificación social de su familia*. Cuenca: Imprenta de Falange, 1976.

Martir, Pedro. *Cartas de Pedro Martir sobre las comunidades*. Translated by P. José De La Canal. Madrid: Real Monasterio De El Escorial, 1945.

Mata Carriazo, Juan de, gen. ed. *Colección de crónicas españolas*. 9 vols. Madrid: Espasa-Calpe, S.A., 1940–6.

Melagres Marín, Julio, ed., 'Proceso de María Cazalla.' In *Procedimientos de la Inquisición*, vol. 2. Madrid: Imprenta de Enrique Rubinos, 1886.

Meseguer Fernández, Juan. 'Nuevos datos sobre los hermanos Valdés: Alfonso, Juan, Diego y Margarita.' *Hispania* 18, no. 67 (1957): 368–94.

Miguélez, Manuel F. 'Famoso discurso en castellano de Carlos V en Roma.' *Ciudad de Dios* 94 (1913): 173–88.

Nebrija, Antonio de. *Gramática castellana*. Madrid: Talleres de D. Silverio Aguirre y de Gráficas Reunidas, 1946.

Ortega-Costa, Milagros. *Proceso de la Inquisición contra María de Cazalla*. Madrid: Fundación Universitaria Española, 1978.

Paz y Melia, Antonio. 'Otro erasmista español. Diego Gracián de Alderete, Su correspondencia.' *Revista de archivos bibliotecas y museos* 5 (1901): 27–36, 125–39, 608–25.

Real Academia de la Historia, ed. *Colección de documentos inéditos para la historia de España*. 112 vols. Madrid: Imprenta de Rafael Marco y Viñas, 1842–95, Kraus Reprint, 1966.

– *Cortes de los antiguos reinos de León y de Castilla*. 4 vols. Madrid: Successores De Rivadeneyra, 1861–3.

Report on the Trial and Martyrdom of Pietro Carnesecchi; Sometime Secretary to Pope *Clement VII, and Apostolic Protonotary*. Edited and translated by Richard Gibbings. Dublin: University Press, 1856.

Rodríguez de Montavo, Garci. *Amadis of Gaul*. 2 vols. Translated by Edwin B. Place and Herbert C. Behm. Lexington: University of Kentucky Press, 1974–5.

Rodríguez Villa, Antonio, ed. *El emperador Carlos V y su corte; según las cartas de don Martín de Salinas embajador del infante don Fernando 1522–1539*. Madrid: Establecimiento Tipográfico de Fortanet, 1903.

– *Memorias para la historia del asalto y saqueo de Roma en 1527 por el ejército imperial; formadas con documentos originales, cifrados e inéditos en su mayor parte*. Madrid: Imprenta de la Biblioteca de Instrucción y Recreo, n.d.

Rojas, Fernando de. *La Celestina*. Miami: Ediciones Universal, 1972, 2nd ed.

Tellechea Idigoras, Ignacio, ed. *Fray Bartolomé Carranza, Documentos historicos*. 5 vols. Madrid: Real Academia de Historia, 1962–76.

Torrente Perez, Diego, ed. *Documentos para la historia de San Clemente*. 2 vols. Madrid: Marsiega, S.A., 1975.

Valdés, Alfonso de. *Alfonso de Valdés and the Sack of Rome: Dialogue of Lactino and an Archdeacon.* Translated by John E. Longhurst. Albuquerque: University of New Mexico Press, 1952.
- *Diálogo de las cosas ocurridas en Roma.* Edited and introduced by José F. Montesinos. Madrid: Espasa-Calpe, S.A., 1969, orig. 1928.
- *Diálogo de Mercurio y Carón.* Introduction and notes by José F. Montesinos. Madrid: Espasa-Calpe, S.A., 1971.

Valdés, Juan de. *XVII Opuscules: Juan de Valdés' Minor Works.* Edited and translated by John T. Betts. London: Trubner and Co., Ludgate Hill, 1882.
- *Alfabeto cristiano.* Edited by B. Foster Stockwell, and translated by Luis Usoz y Río. Buenos Aires: Editorial 'La Aurora,' 1948.
- *Cartas inéditas de Juan de Valdés al cardenal Gonzaga.* Edited and introduced by José F. Montesinos. Madrid: Saguirre Impressor, 1931.
- *Commentario a los Salmos.* Madrid: Librería Nacional Extranjera, 1885; reprinted Barcelona: Terrassa, 1987.
- *Diálogo de doctrina cristiana.* Notes by B. Foster Stockwell. Buenos Aires: Editorial 'La Aurora,' 1946.
- *Diálogo de la lengua.* 5th ed. Notes and introduction by Rafael Lapesa. Zaragoza: Editorial Ebro, S.I., 1965.
- *Diálogo de la lengua.* Introduction by José Montesinos. Madrid: Espasa-Calpe, SA, 1964, orig. 1928.
- *El Evangelio según San Mateo, declarado por Juan de Valdés.* Madrid: Librería Nacional y Extranjera, 1986, orig. 1880.
- *La epístola de San Pablo a los Romanos.* In vol. 10 of *Reformistas antiguos españoles,* ed. Luis Usoz i Rio. Madrid: 1856; reprinted Barcelona: Librería de Diego Gómez Flores, 1982.
- *La primera epístola de San Pablo a los Corintios.* In vol. 11 of *Reformistas antiguos españoles,* ed. Luis Usoz i Rio. Madrid: 1856; reprinted Barcelona: Librería de Diego Gómez Flores, 1982.
- *Las ciento diez divinas consideraciones: Recensión inédita del manuscrito de Juan Sánchez (1558).* Edited by J. Ignacio Tellechea Idigoras. Salamanca: Universidad Pontificia, 1975.
- *Le cento e dieci divine considerazioni.* Preface by Edmondo Cione. Milan: Fratelli Bocca, 1944.
- *One Hundred and Ten Divine Considerations.* Translated by John T. Betts; appended to *Life and Writings of Juan de Valdés, Spanish Reformer in the Sixteenth Century* by Benjamen Wiffen. London: Trubner and Co., Ludgate Hill, 1882.
- *Trataditos de Juan de Valdés.* Edited by Eduard Boehmer. Bonn: Imprento de Carlos Georgi, 1880; reprinted Barcelona: Librería de Diego Gómez Flores, 1983.

Valeriano, Pierio. 'Dialogo della volgar lingua.' In *Discussioni Linguistiche del Cinquecento*, ed. Mario Pozzi, 39-93. Turin: Unione Tipografico-Editrice Torinese, 1988.
- *Pierio Valeriano on the Ill Fortune of Learned Men: A Renaissance Humanist and His World*. Introduction and translation by Julia Haig Gaisser. Ann Arbor: University of Michigan Press, 1999.

Varchi, Benedetto. *Storia Fiorentina*. 2 vols. Florence: Salani Editore, 1963, orig. 1559.

Zarco y Cuevas, Julián, ed. *Relaciones de pueblos del obispado de Cuenca; hechas por orden de Felipe II*. 2 vols. Cuenca: Imprenta del Seminario, 1927.
- 'Testamentos de Alfonso y Diego de Valdés.' *Boletín de la Real Academia Española* 14 (1927): 679–85.

Secondary Works

Abellán, José Luis. *El erasmismo español: una historia de la otra España*. Madrid: S.A. Editorial Graficas Esejo, 1976.

Ajo G. y Sainz de Zúnigo, C. M. *Historia de las universidades hispánicas: orígenes y desarrollo desde su aparición hasta nuestros días*. 2 vols. Madrid: Imp. Lit., Ed. La Normal, San Bernardo, 1957.

Alvar Ezquerra, Antonio. *La Universidad de Alcalá de Henares a principios del siglo XVI*. Alcalá: Universidad de Alcalá, 1996.

Alexander, Paul J. 'The Medieval Legend of the Last Roman Emperor and Its Messianic Origin.' *Journal of the Warburg and Courtauld Institutes* 41 (1978): 1–15.

Andrés Martín, Melquiades. 'Evangelismo, humanismo, reforma y observancias en España 1450–1525.' *Missionalia Hispania* 23 (1967): 5–25.
- *La teología española en el siglo XVI*. 2 vols. Madrid: La Editorial Católica, 1976.
- *Nueva visión de los 'alumbrados' de 1525*. Madrid: Fundacíon Universitaria Española, 1973.

Anglo, Sydney. 'The Courtier: The Renaissance and Changing Ideals.' In *The Courts of Europe: Politics, Patronage and Royalty 1400–1800*, ed. A.G. Dickens, 33–53. New York: Greenwich House, 1977.

Aram, Bethany. *Juana the Mad: Sovereignty and Dynasty in Renaissance Europe*. Baltimore: Johns Hopkins University Press, 2005.

Asensio, Eugenio. 'El erasmismo y las corrientes espirituales afines.' *Revista de filología española* 36 (1952): 31–99.

Asensio, Manuel J. 'La intención religiosa del Lazarillo de Tormes y Juan de Valdés.' *Hispanic Review* 27 (1959): 78–102.

Bainton, Roland H. *Erasmus of Christendom*. New York: Charles Scribner's Sons, 1969.
- *Here I Stand: A Biography of Martin Luther*. New York: New American Library, 1955, orig. 1950.

– *Women of the Reformation in Germany and Italy.* Minneapolis: Augsburg Publishing House, 1971.

Bataillon, Marcel. *Erasmo y el erasmismo.* Translated by Carlos Pujol. Barcelona: Editorial Crítica, 1977.

– *Erasmo y España: estudios sobre la historia espiritual del siglo XVI.* Translated by Antonio Alatorre. Ciudad de Mexico: Fondo de Cultura Económica, 1966, orig. 1938.

Beltrán de Heredia, Vicente. 'Erasmo y España.' *Ciencia tomista* 57 (1938): 544–83.

– 'La teología en la Universidad de Alcalá.' *Revista española de teología* 5 (1945): 405–32.

Bentley, Jerry H. *Humanists and Holy Writ: New Testament Scholarship in the Renaissance.* Princeton: Princeton University Press, 1983.

Berkowitz, H. Chanon. 'The Quaderno de Refranes Castellanos of Juan de Valdés.' *Romanic Review* 16 (1925): 71–86

Boehmer, Eduard. *Lives of the Twin Brothers Juan and Alfonso de Valdés,* appended to *Juan de Valdés' Commentary on the Sermon on the Mount.* Translated by John T. Betts. London: Ballantyne Press, 1882.

– *Spanish Reformers of the Two Centuries from 1520: Their Lives and Writings According to the late Benjamin B. Wiffen's Plan and With the Use of His Materials.* 3 vols. New York: Burt Franklin, 1874–1904.

Boyden, James A. '"Fortune Has Stripped You of Your Splendor"; Favorites and Their Fates in Fifteenth- and Sixteenth-Century Spain.' In *The World of the Favorite,* ed. J.H. Elliott and L.W.B. Brockliss, 26–37. New Haven: Yale University Press, 1999.

– *The Courtier and the King: Ruy Gómez de Silva, Philip II, and the Court of Spain.* Berkeley: University of California Press, 1995.

Brandi, Karl. *The Emperor Charles V: The Growth and Destiny of a Man and of a World-Empire.* Translated by C.V. Wedgwood. London: Jonathon Cape, 1965.

Brinton, Selwyn. *The Gonzaga-Lords of Mantua.* London: Methuen and Co., 1927.

Bullard, Melissa Meriam. *Filippo Strozzi and the Medici Family: Favor and Finance in Sixteenth-Century Florence and Rome.* Cambridge: Cambridge University Press, 1980.

Burke, Peter. *The Fortunes of the Courtier: The European Reception of Castiglione's Cortegiano.* University Park: Pennsylvania State University Press, 1995.

Burkhardt, Jacob. *The Civilization of the Renaissance in Italy.* New York: Barnes and Noble, 1992.

Caballero, Fermín. *Alonso y Juan de Valdés.* Madrid: Oficina Tipográfica del Hospicio, 1875.

Calabria, Antonio. *The Cost of Empire: The Finances of the Kingdom of Naples in the Time of Spanish Rule.* Cambridge: Cambridge University Press, 1991.

Camillo, Ottavio di. 'Humanism in Spain.' In *Renaissance Humanism: Foundations, Forms, and Legacy*, ed. Albert Rabil, 2: 55–108. Philadelphia: University of Pennsyvania Press, 1988.

Caponetto, Salvatorre. *The Protestant Reformation in Sixteenth-Century Italy*. Translated by Anne C. Tedeschi and John Tedeschi. Kirksville, MO: Thomas Jefferson University Press, 1999, orig. 1992.

Carande, Ramón. *Carlos V y sus banqueros*. Vol. 2: *La hacienda real de Castilla*; vol. 3: *Los caminos del oro y de la plata (deuda exterior y tesoros ultramarinos)*, 2nd ed. Barcelona: Editorial Crítica, 1987.

Carro, P. Venacio D. *Los Dominicos y el concilio de Trento: estudio histórico-teológico del concilio y de la aportación de la orden Dominicana*. Salamanca: Calatrava, 1948.

Castellán, Angel. 'Juan de Valdés y el círculo de Nápoles.' *Cuadernos de historia de España* 35/36 (1962): 202–73; 37/38 (1963): 199–291; 39/40 (1964): 261–308; 41/42 (1965): 127–223; 43/44 (1967): 188–242.

Castro, Américo. 'Lo hispánico y el erasmismo.' *Revista de filología hispánica* 4 (1942): 1–66.

Clough, Cecil H. 'Clement VII and Francisco Maria Della Rovere, Duke of Urbino.' In *The Pontificate of Clement VII: History, Politics and Culture*, ed. Kenneth Gouwens and Sheryl E. Reiss, 75–108. Aldershot: Ashgate, 2005.

Cochrane, Eric. *Florence in the Forgotten Centuries, 1527–1800*. Chicago: University of Chicago Press, 1973.

– *Italy 1530–1630*. Edited by Julius Kirshner. London: Longman, 1988.

Cordero Torres, José María. *El consejo de estado: su trayectoria y perspectivas en España*. Madrid: Instituto de Estudios Políticos, 1944.

Crews, Daniel A. 'Intellectual Sources of Spanish Imperialism: The Education of Juan de Valdés.' *Proteus: A Journal of Ideas* 9, no. 1 (Spring 1992): 38–43.

– 'Juan de Valdés and the Comunero Revolt: An Essay on Spanish Civic Humanism.' *Sixteenth Century Journal* 22, no. 2 (Summer 1991): 233–52.

– 'Juan de Valdés and Spanish Imperial Humanism.' *Explorations in Renaissance Culture* 11 (1986): 43–51.

– 'Juan de Valdés y la crisis de Camerino, 1534–1535.' In *Aspectos históricos y culturales bajo Carlos V*, ed. Christoph Strosetzki, 106–18. Frankfurt: Velvuert, 2000.

– 'Spanish Diplomacy and the Mysterious Death of Cardinal Medici.' *Mediterranean Studies* 12 (2003): 103–10.

Croce, Benedetto. *History of the Kingdom of Naples*. Edited and introduced by H. Stuart Hughes; translated by Frances Frenaye. Chicago: University of Chicago Press, 1970.

Cuart Moner, Baltasar. 'Juan Ginés de Sepúlveda, cronista del Emperador.' In *Carlos V y la quiebra del humanismo político en Europa (1530-1558)*, vol. 3, ed. Jesús Bravo Lozano and Félix Labrador Arroyo, 341–67. Madrid: SDAD Estatal Felipe II, 2001.

Cuesta, Luisa y Florentino Zamora Lucas. 'Los secretarios de Carlos V.' *Revista de archivos, bibliotecas y museos* 64, no. 2 (1958): 415–46.
D'Amico, John F. *Renaissance Humanism in Papal Rome: Humanists and Churchmen on the Eve of the Reformation*. Baltimore: Johns Hopkins University Press, 1983.
Dandelet, Thomas J. *Spanish Rome 1500–1700*. New Haven: Yale University Press, 2001.
Della Casta, Giovanni. *Galateo*. Translated and introduced by Konrad Eisenbichler and Kenneth Bartlett. Toronto: Centre for Renaissance and Reformation Studies, 1986.
Donald, Dorothy, and Elena Lazaro. *Alfonso de Valdés y su Época*. Cuenca: Excma. Diputación Provincial, 1983.
Dueñas Martínez, Antonio. *Juan de Valdés: un reformador español en Italia*, Trieste: Nuova Del Bianco-Industria Grafiche, 1981.
Echevarría Bacigalupe, Miguel Angel. 'La occidentalización de la diplomacia imperial bajo Carlos V.' In *Carlos V: Europeísmo y universalidad*, vol. 2, *La organización del poder*, ed. Juan Luis Castellano Castellano and Francisco Sánchez-Montes González, 171–87. Madrid: Sociedad Estatal Para la Conmemoración de los Centenarios Felipe II y Carlos V, 2001.
Eells, Hastings. 'The Origin of the Regensburg Book.' *Princeton Theological Review* 26 (1928): 355–69.
Eguigary Bohigas, Francisco. *Los intelectuales españoles de Carlos V*. Madrid: Instituto de Estudios Políticos, 1965.
Elliott, John. 'Unas reflexiones acerca de la privanza española en el contexto Europeo.' *Anuario de historia del derecho español* 67, no. 2 (1997): 885–99.
Erlanger, Philippe. *The Age of Courts and Kings: Manners and Morals, 1558–1715*. New York: Anchor Books, 1970, orig. 1967.
Escudero, José Antonio. *Los secretarios de estado y del despacho 1474–1724*. Madrid: Instituto de Estudios Administrativos, 1969.
Fernández Álvarez, Manuel. *Carlos V, El César y el hombre*. Madrid: Espasa Calpe, S.A., 1999.
– *Política Mundial de Carlos V y Felipe II*. Madrid: C.S.I.C., Escuela de Historia Moderna, 1964.
Fernández-Armesto, Felipe. 'Cardinal Cisneros as a Patron of Printing.' In *God and Man in Medieval Spain: Essays in Honour of J.R.L. Highfield*, ed. Derek W. Lomax and David Mackenzie, 149–68. Warminster: Aris and Phillips, 1989.
Fernández Santa-María, J.A. *The State, War and Peace: Spanish Political Thought in the Renaissance, 1516–1559*. Cambridge: Cambridge University Press, 1977.
Feros, Antonio. 'Images of Evil, Images of Kings: The Contrasting Faces of the Royal Favorite and the Prime Minister in Early Modern European Literature,

c. 1580–c. 1650.' In *The World of the Favorite*, ed. J.H. Elliott and L.W.B. Brockliss, 205–22. New Haven: Yale University Press, 1999.
– *Kingship and Favoritism in the Spain of Philip III, 1598–1621*. Cambridge: Cambridge University Press, 2000.
– 'Twin Souls: Monarchs and Favorites in Early Seventeenth-Century Spain.' In *Spain, Europe and the Atlantic World: Essays in Honour of John H. Elliott*, ed. Richard Kagan and Geoffrey Parker, 27–47. Cambridge: Cambridge University Press, 1995.
Ferrandis, Manuel. 'El Concilio de Trento, Obra de la Diplomatica de Carlos V.' In *Carlos V 1500–1558: homenaje de la Universidad de Granada*, 373–400. Granada: Universidad de Granada, 1958.
Ferreras Savoye, Jacqueline. 'Géneros literarios en el Siglo XVI: el diálogo humanístico, crisol de experimentaciones literarias.' In *Aspectos históricos y culturales bajo Carlos V*, ed. Christoph Strosetzki, 288–94. Madrid: Iberoamericano, 2000.
Firpo, Massimo. *Entre alumbrados y 'espirituales': Estudios sobre Juan de Valdés y el valdesianismo en la crisis religiosa del '500 italiano*. Translated by Daniela Bergonzi. Madrid: Fundación Universitaria Española Universidad Pontificia de Salamanca, 2000.
Fischer-Galati, Stephen A. *Ottoman Imperialism and German Protestantism 1521–1555*. Cambridge: Harvard University Press, 1959.
Forell, George. 'Luther and Politics.' In *Luther and Culture*, ed. George Forell, Harold J. Grimm, and Theodore Holety-Nickel, 3–73. Decorah, Iowa: Luther College Press, 1960.
Gaisser, Julia Haig. 'Introduction' to *Pierio Valeriano on the Ill Fortune of Learned Men: A Renaissance Humanist and His World*. Ann Arbor: University of Michigan Press, 1999.
– 'Seeking Patronage under the Medici Popes: A Tale of Two Humanists.' In *The Pontificate of Clement VII: History, Politics, and Culture*, ed. Kenneth Gouwens and Sheryl E. Reiss, 293–309. Aldershot: Ashgate, 2005.
Galasso, Giuseppe. 'Trends and Problems in Neapolitan History in the Age of Charles V.' In *Good Government in Spanish Naples*, ed. and trans. Antonio Calabria and John A. Marino. New York: Peter Lang, 1990.
Gil Fernández, Luis. *Panorama social del humanismo español 1500–1800*. Madrid: Editorial Tecnos, S.A., 1997.
Giles, Mary E. 'Francisca Hernández and the Sexuality of Religious Dissent.' In *Women in the Inquisition: Spain and the New World*, ed. Mary Giles, 75–118. Baltimore: Johns Hopkins University Press, 1999.
Gilly, Carlos. 'Juan de Valdés, traductor y adaptador de escritos de Lutero en Su *Diálogo de doctrina cristiana*.' In *Miscelánea de estudios hispánicos; Homenaje*

de los hispanistas de Suiza, Ramon Sugranyes de Franch, ed. Luis López Molina, 85–106. Montserrat: Grafiques Badalona, S.A., 1982.
Gilmore, Myron P. 'Erasmus and Alberto Pio, Prince of Carpi.' In *Action and Conviction in Early Modern Europe: Essays in Memory of E.H. Harbison*, ed. Theodore Rabb and Gerrold Seigel, 299–318. Princeton: Princeton University Press, 1969.
Gleason, Elisabeth G. *Gasparo Contarini: Venice, Rome, and Reform*. Berkeley: University of California Press, 1993.
González Navarro, Ramón. 'El impresor navarro Miguel de Eguía, en Alcalá de Henares.' *Príncipe de Viana* 42 (1981): 307–19.
Gouwens, Kenneth. *Remembering the Renaissance: Humanist Narratives of the Sack of Rome*. Leiden: Brill, 1998.
Green, Otis H. *Spain and the Western Tradition: The Castillian Mind in Literature from El Cid to Calderón*. 4 vols. Madison: University of Wisconsin Press, 1965.
Griffin, Clive. *The Crombergers of Seville: The History of a Printing and Merchant Dynasty*. Oxford: Clarendon Press, 1988.
Guttiérez Nieto, Juan Ignacio. *Las Comunidades como movimiento antiseñorial; la formación del bando realista en la guerra civil castellana, 1520–1521*. Barcelona: Editorial Planeta, 1973.
Haggard, Theodore Merrill. 'The Church and Sacraments in the Theological Writings of Juan de Valdés.' PhD diss., Emory University, 1971.
Hale, John R. *Florence and the Medici: The Pattern of Control*. London: Thames and Hudson, 1977.
Haliczer, Stephen. *The Comuneros of Castile: The Forging of a Revolution, 1485–1521*. Madison: University of Wisconsin Press, 1981.
Hall, Basil. 'The Colloquies between Catholics and Protestants, 1539–1541.' *Studies in Church History* 7 (1971): 235-66.
Hallman, Barbara McClung. 'The "Disastrous" Pontificate of Clement VII: Disastrous for Giulio de'Medici?' In *The Pontificate of Clement VII: History, Politics and Culture*, ed. Kenneth Gouwens and Sheryl E. Reiss, 29–40. Aldershot: Ashgate, 2005.
– *Italian Cardinals, Reform, and the Church as Property*. Berkeley: University of California Press, 1985.
Hamilton, Alastair. *Heresy and Mysticism in Sixteenth-Century Spain: The Alumbrados of Toledo*. Toronto: University of Toronto Press, 1992.
– 'Humanists and the Bible.' In *The Cambridge Companion to Renaissance Humanism*, ed. Jill Kraye, 100–17. Cambridge: Cambridge University Press, 1996.
Hare, Christopher. *Men and Women of the Italian Reformation*. London: Stanley Paul and Co., 1914.

- *A Princess of the Italian Reformation: Giulia Gonzaga 1513–1566, Her Family and Her Friends*. New York: Charles Scribner's Sons, 1912.
Headley, John. 'The Emperor and His Chancellor: Disputes over Empire, Administration, and Pope (1519–1529).' In *Carlos V y la quiebra del humanismo político en Europa (1530–1558)*, vol. 1, ed. José Martínez Millán and Ignacio J. Ezquerra Revilla, 21–35. Madrid: SDAD Estatal Felipe II, 2001.
- *The Emperor and His Chancellor: A Study of the Imperial Chancellery under Gattinara*. New York: Cambridge University Press, 1983.
- 'Gattinara, Erasmus, and the Imperial Configurations of Humanism.' *Archive for Reformation History* 71 (1980): 64–98.
Hernando Sánchez, Carlos José. *Castilla y Nápoles en el siglo XVI: el virrey Pedro de Toledo linaje, estado, y cultura 1532–1553*. Madrid: Junta de Castilla y León, 1994.
Homza, Lu Ann. *Religious Authority in the Spanish Renaissance*. Baltimore: Johns Hopkins University Press, 2000.
Huerga, Alvaro. 'Erasmismo y Alumbradismo.' In *El Erasmismo en España: Ponencias del coloquio celebrado en la Biblioteca de Menéndez Pelayo del 10 al 14 de Junio de 1985*, ed. Manuel Revuelta and Ciriaco Morón Arroyo, 339–56. Santander: Menéndez Pelayo, 1986.
Huizinga, Johan. *Erasmus and the Age of Reformation: With a Selection from the Letters of Erasmus*. Translated by F. Hopman and Barbara Flower. New York: Harper and Row, 1957, orig. 1924.
Jedin, Herbert. *A History of the Council of Trent*, 3 vols. Translated by Dom Ernest Graf. Edinburgh: Thomas Nelson and Sons, 1961.
Jerrold, Maud F. *Vittoria Colonna: With Some Account of Her Friends and Her Times*. Freeport, NY: Books for Libraries Press, 1969, orig. 1906.
Jiménez Monteserín, Miguel. 'La andadura humana de Juan de Valdés.' Appendix to *Diálogo de doctrina cristiana*, ed. Javier Ruiz. Madrid: Editora Nacional, 1979.
- 'La familia Valdés de Cuenca: Nuevos datos.' In *Los Valdés: Pensamiento y literatura*. Cuenca: Instituto de Juan de Valdés, 1997.
- 'La familia Valdés de Cuenca.' Introduction to the facsimile edition of *Alonso y Juan de Valdés* by Fermín Caballero. Cuenca: Instituto de Juan de Valdés, 1995, orig. edition 1875.
- 'Los hermanos Valdés y el mundo Judeo converso conquense.' In *Política, religión e inquisición en la España moderna*, ed. P. Fernández Albadalejo, J. Martínez Millán, and V. Pinto Crespo. Madrid: Universidad Autónoma de Madrid, 1996.
Kagan, Richard. *Lawyers and Litigants in Early Modern Castile 1500–1700*. Chapel Hill: University of North Carolina Press, 1981.

- *Students and Society in Early Modern Spain*. Baltimore: Johns Hopkins University Press, 1974.
Kamen, Henry. *Empire: How Spain Became a World Power, 1492–1763*. New York: HarperCollins, 2003.
- *The Spanish Inquisition: An Historical Revision*. London: Weidenfeld and Nicholson, 1997.
Keniston, Hayward. *Francisco de los Cobos: Secretary of the Emperor Charles V*. Pittsburg: University of Pittsburg Press, 1960.
Kinder, A. Gordon. 'Juan de Valdés.' *Bibliotheca Dissidentium* 9 (1988): 111–95.
- 'Spain.' In *The Early Reformation in Europe*, ed. Andrew Pettegree, 215–37. Cambridge: Cambridge University Press, 1992.
- '"Ydiota y Sin Letras": Evidence of Literacy among the Alumbrados of Toledo.' *Journal of the Institute of Romance Studies* 4 (1996): 37–49.
Koenigsberger, H.G. 'The Empire of Charles V.' In *The New Cambridge Modern History*. Vol. 2, *The Reformation 1520–1559*, ed. G.R. Elton, 301–33. Cambridge: Cambridge University Press, 1958, reprinted 1968.
- 'Patronage and Bribery during the Reign of Charles V.' In *Estates and Revolutions: Essays in Early Modern European History*. Ithaca: Cornell University Press, 1971.
Kohler, Alfred. *Carlos V 1500–1558: Una biografía*. Translated by Cristina García Ohlrich. Madrid: Marcial Pons, 2000, orig. 1999.
Lawner, Lynne. *Lives of the Courtesans: Portraits of the Renaissance*. New York: Rizzoli, 1987.
Lea, Henry C. *A History of the Inquisition of Spain*. 4 vols. New York: Macmillan Co., 1922.
Lerner, Isaias. 'El discurso literario del *Diálogo de la lengua* de Juan de Valdés.' In vol. 2 of *Actas del VIII Congresso del la Asociación Internacional de Hispanistas, Congress Held in Providence, Rhode Island, 22–27 August 1983*, ed. A. David Kossoff, José Amor y Vázquez, Ruth H. Kossoff, and Geoffrey W. Ribbans, 145–50. Madrid: Ediciones Istmo, 1986.
Liss, Peggy. *Isabel the Queen: Life and Times*. New York: Oxford University Press, 1992.
Llorente, Juan Antonio. *Historia crítica de la Inquisición de España*. 4 vols. Madrid: Hiperión, 1980, orig. 1817 in French translation.
Longhurst, John E. 'The Alumbrados of Toledo: Juan del Castillo and the Lucenas.' *Archiv für Reformationsgeschichte* 45 (1954): 233–53.
- *Erasmus and the Spanish Inquisition: The Case of Juan de Valdés*. Albuquerque: University of New Mexico Press, 1950.
- 'La beata Isabel de la Cruz ante la Inquisición 1524–1529.' *Cuadernos de historia de España* 25–6 (1957): 279–303.

- *Luther's Ghost in Spain.* Lawrence, Kansas: Coronado Press, 1969.
López Rueda, José. *Helenista españoles del siglo XVI.* Madrid: Instituto de Antonio de Nebrija, 1973.
Lorenzo Cadarso, Pedro Luis. 'Esplendor y decadencia de las oligarquías conversos de Cuenca y Guadalajara (siglos XV y XVI).' *Hispania.* 54/1, no. 186 (1994): 53–94.
Mackensen, Heinz. 'Contarini's Theological Role at Ratisbon,' *Archiv für Reformationsgeschichte* 51 (1960): 36–57.
Maltby, William. *Alba: A Biography of Fernando Alvarez de Toledo, Third Duke of Alba, 1507–1582.* Berkeley: University of California Press, 1983.
- *The Reign of Charles V.* New York: Palgrave, 2002.
Maravall, José Antonio. *Carlos V y el pensamiento político del renacimiento.* Madrid: Instituto de Estudios Políticos, 1960.
- *Las comunidades de Castilla; una primera revolución moderna.* 3rd ed. Madrid: Alianza Editorial, 1979, orig. 1963.
- 'La visión utópica del imperio de Carlos V en la España de su epoca.' In *Carlos V 1500–1558; homenaje de la Universidad de Granada,* 41–77. Granada: Universidad de Granada, 1958.
Marín Ocete, Antonio. 'Pedro Mártir de Angleria y su *Opus Epistolarum*.' *Boletín de la Universidad de Granada* 15, no. 73 (1943): 145–257.
Márquez, Antonio. 'Juan de Valdés, Teólogo de los alumbrados.' *La Ciudad de Dios* 84 (1971): 215–20.
- *Los alumbrados: orígenes y filosofía (1525–1559),* 2nd ed. Madrid: Taurus Ediciones, S.A., 1980.
Martínez-Góngora, Mar. *Discursos sobre la mujer en el humanismo renacentista español: Los casos de Antonio de Guevara, Alfonso y Juan de Valdés, y Luis de León.* York, SC: Spanish Literature Publication Co., 1999.
Martínez Millán, José, et al., eds. *La Corte de Carlos V.* Vols. 1–2, *Corte y gobierno.* Madrid: Sociedad Estatal para la Conmemoración de Felipe II y Carlos V, 2000.
Martínez Millán, Miguel. *Los hermanos conquenses Alfonso y Juan de Valdés: Su ambiente familiar y la clasificación social de su familia.* Cuenca: Imprenta de Falange, 1976.
Matheson, Peter. *Cardinal Contarini at Regensburg.* Oxford: Clarendon Press, 1972.
Mattingly, Garrett. *Renaissance Diplomacy.* Boston: Houghton Mifflin, 1955.
Mazzocco, Angelo. 'The Italian Connection in Juan de Valdés' *Diálogo de la Lengua.*' *Historiographia linguistica* 24, no. 3 (1997): 267–83.
Menéndez y Pelayo, Marcelino. *Historia de los heterodoxos españoles.* Santander: Consejo Superior de Investigaciones Científicas, 1947, orig. 1880.
Merriman, Roger Bigelow. *The Rise of the Spanish Empire in the Old World and in the New,* vol. 3, *The Emperor.* New York: Cooper Square Publishers, 1962, orig. 1918.

Molas Ribalta, Pere. 'Los cancilleres de Carlos V.' In *Carlos V y la quiebra del humanismo político en Europa (1530–1558)*, vol. 1, ed. José Martínez Millán and Ignacio J. Ezquerra Revilla, 227–46. Madrid: SDAD Estatal Felipe II, 2003.
Montesinos, José F. 'Algunas notas sobre el *Diálogo de Mercurio y Carón*.' *Revista de Filología Española* 16, no. 3 (1929): 225–66.
Moreno Martínez, Doris. 'Carlos V y la Inquisición.' In *Carlos V: Europeísmo y universalidad*, vol. 2, *La organización del poder*, ed. Juan Luis Castellano and Francisco Sánchez-Montes González, 421–35. Madrid: Sociedad Estatal Para la Conmemoración de los Centenarios Felipe II y Carlos V, 2001.
Moretti, Giuseppe. 'Il cardinale Ippolito dei Medici dal tratto di Barcelona alla morte (1529–1535).' *Archivo Storico Italiano* 1 (1940): 137–78.
Morón Arroyo, Ciriaco. *Celestina and Castilian Humanism at the End of the Fifteenth Century*. Occasional Papers no. 3. Binghamton, NY: Center for Medieval and Renaissance Studies, 1994.
Muñoz y Solivo, D. Trifón. *Historia de la muy noble, leal e impertérrita ciudad de Cuenca, y del territorio de su provincia y obispado, desde los tiempos primitivos hasta la edad presente*, 2 vols. Cuenca: El Eco de Cuenca, 1866–7.
Nader, Helen. *The Mendoza Family in the Spanish Renaissance 1350–1550*. New Brunswick, NJ: Rutgers University Press, 1979.
Nalle, Sara T. *God in La Mancha: Religious Reform and the People of Cuenca 1500–1650*. Baltimore: Johns Hopkins University Press, 1992.
– *Mad for God: Bartolomé Sánchez, the Secret Messiah of Cardenete*. Charlottesville: University Press of Virginia, 2001.
Netanyahu, Benzion. *The Marranos of Spain from the Late XIVth to the Early XVIth Century According to Contemporary Hebrew Sources*, 3rd ed. Ithaca: Cornell University Press, 1999.
Nieto, José C. 'La Imagen Cambiente de Juan de Valdés.' In *Los Valdés: Pensamiento y literatura*, 7–41. Cuenca: Instituto Juan de Valdés, 1997.
– 'El espectro de Lutero y las máscaras de Erasmo en España.' In *Juan de Valdés y los orígenes de la reforma en España e Italia*. Mexico City: Fondo de Cultura Económica, 1979.
– *Juan de Valdés and the Origins of the Spanish and Italian Reformation*. Geneva: Libraire Droz, 1970.
Nieto, José C., ed. *Juan de Valdés: Two Catechisms*. 2nd ed. Translated by William B. and Carol D. Jones. Lawrence, Kansas: Coronado Press, 1993.
Ochoa Brun, Miguel Ángel. *Historia de la diplomacia española*, vol. 5, *La diplomacia de Carlos V*. Madrid: Ministerio de Asuntos Exteriores, 1999.
Olmedo, Felix G. *Diego Ramírez Villaescusa (1459–1537): Fundador del Colegio de Cuenca y autor de los cuatro diálogos sobre la muerte del Príncipe don Juan*. Madrid: Editorial Nacional, 1944.

Partner, Peter. *The Pope's Men: The Papal Civil Service in the Renaissance*. Oxford: Clarendon Press, 1990.
- *Renaissance Rome 1550–1559: A Portrait of a Society*. Berkeley: University of California Press, 1976.
Pastor, Ludwig. *The History of the Popes from the Close of the Middle Ages*. 4th ed., 36 vols. Edited and translated by Ralph Francis Kerr. London: Routledge and Kegan Paul, 1950.
Payne, John Barton. *Erasmus: His Theology of the Sacraments*. Richmond: John Knox Press, 1970.
Peréz, Joseph. *La Revolución de las Comunidades de Castilla (1520–1521)*. Translated by Juan José Faci Lacasta. Madrid: Siglo Veintiuno de España Editores, S.A., 1977.
Pérez Priego, Miguel Ángel. 'Estimaciones literarias de Juan de Valdés.' In *Los Valdés: Pensamiento y literatura*. Cuenca: Instituto de 'Juan de Valdés,' 1997.
Perry, Mary Elizabeth. *Gender and Disorder in Early Modern Seville*. Princeton: Princeton University Press, 1990.
Phillips, Carla Rahn, and William D. Phillips. *Spain's Golden Fleece: Wool Production and the Wool Trade from the Middle Ages to the Nineteenth Century*. Baltimore: Johns Hopkins University Press, 1997.
Phillips, Margaret Mann. *Erasmus and the Northern Renaissance*. London: Hodder and Stoughton, 1949.
Pinta Llorente, Miguel de la. *El erasmismo del doctor Juan de Vergara y otras interpretaciones*. Madrid: n.p., 1944.
Polano, Pietro Soave. *The History of the Council of Trent Containing Eight Books*. Translated by S. Nathaniel Brent. London: J. Macock, 1676.
Prescott, William H. *History of the Reign of Ferdinand and Isabella the Catholic*. 3 vols. Philadelphia: David McKay, 1893.
Prieto Cantero, Amalia, ed. *Archivo general de Simancas, catálogo V: Patronato Real*. 2 vols. Valladolid: Editorial Sever-Cuesta, 1949.
Ranke, Leopold von. *History of the Popes: Their Church and Their State*. 3 vols. Translated by E. Fowler. New York: P.F. Collier and Sons, 1901.
- *History of the Reformation in Germany*. 2 vols. Translated by Sarah Austin. New York: Frederick Unger Publishing Co., 1966 (orig. 1845–7).
- *The Ottoman and the Spanish Empires in the Sixteenth Century*. Translated by Walter K. Kelly. London: Whittaker and Co., 1843, reprinted 1975.
Rassow, Peter. *El mundo político de Carlos V*. Translated by F. González Vicen. Madrid: Afrodisio Aguado, S.A., 1945.
Rauscher, Peter. 'Carlos V, Fernando I y la ayuda del Sacro Imperio contra los turcos: Dinero, religión y defensa de la Cristiandad.' In *Carlos V y la quiebra del humanismo político en Europa (1530-1558)*, vol. 4, ed. Jesús Bravo

Lozano and Carlos J. de Carlos Morales, 363–83. Madrid: SDAD Estatal Felipe II, 2001.
Redondo, Augustín. 'La "prensa primitiva" ("relaciones de sucesos") al servicio de la política imperial de Carlos V.' In *Aspectos históricos y culturales bajo Carlos V*, ed. Christoph Strosetzki, 246–76. Madrid: Iberoamericana, 2000.
Ricart, Domingo. 'El concepto de honra en Juan de Valdés.' *Revista de Filosofía de la Universidad de Costa Rica* 4 (1964): 147–64.
– 'El texto auténtico de una consideración valdesiana.' *Hispanófila* 23 (1965): 23–36.
– *Juan de Valdés y el pensamiento religioso europeo en los siglos XVI y XVII*. México: El Colegio De México, 1958.
Rivero Rodríguez, Manuel. 'Memoria, escritura y estado; la autobiografía de Mercurino Alborio di Gattinara, Gran Canciller de Carlos V.' In *Carlos V y la quiebra del humanismo político en Europa (1530–1558)*, vol. 1, ed. José Martínez Millán and Ignacio J. Ezquerra Revilla, 199–224. Madrid: SDAD Estatal Felipe II, 2001.
Rodríguez Salgado, M. J. '¿Carlos Africanus?: el emperador y el turco.' In *Carlos V y la quiebra del humanismo político en Europa (1530–1558)*, vol. 1, ed. José Martínez Millán and Ignacio J. Ezquerra Revilla, 487–531. Madrid: SDAD Estatal Felipe II, 2001.
Román Román, Alberto Yalí. 'Orígen y evolución de la secretaría de estado y de la secretaría del despacho.' *Jahrbuch für Geschichte von Staat, Wirtschaft und Gesellschaft Lateinamerikas* 6 (1969): 41–142.
Roth, Cecil. *The Last Florentine Republic*. New York: Russell and Russell, 1968, orig. 1925.
Roth, Norman. *Conversos, Inquisition and the Expulsion from Spain*. Madison: University of Wisconsin Press, 1995.
Rummel, Erika. *Erasmus and His Catholic Critics*. 2 vols. Nieuwkoop: De Graf Publishers, 1989.
– *Jiménez de Cisneros: On the Threshold of Spain's Golden Age*. Tempe: Arizona Center for Medieval and Renaissance Studies, 1999.
– 'Political and Religious Propaganda at the Court of Charles V: A Newly-Identified Tract by Alfonso de Valdés.' *Historical Research* 70, no. 171 (February 1997): 23–33.
Sánchez-Barbudo, Angela. 'Algunos aspectos de la vida religiosa en la España del Siglo XVI: los alumbrados de Toledo.' PhD diss., University of Wisconsin, 1953.
Sánchez León, Pablo. *Absolutismo y comunidad: Los orígenes sociales de la guerra de los comuneros de Castilla*. Madrid: Siglo XXI de España Editores, S.A., 1998.
Santa María, Domingo de. *Juan de Valdés 1498(?)–1541: su pensamiento religioso y las corrientes espirituales de su tiempo*. Rome: Apud Uedes Universitatis Gregorianae, 1957.

Seaver, Henry Latimer. *The Great Revolt in Castile: A Study of the Comunero Movement of 1520–1521*. New York: Octagon Books, 1966.

Selke de Sánchez, A. 'Algunos datos nuevos sobre los primeros alumbrados; el edicto de 1525 y su relación con el proceso de Alcaraz.' *Bulletin Hispanique* 54 (1952): 125–52.

Serrano y Sanz, Manuel. 'Pedro Ruiz de Alcaraz, iluminado alcarreño del siglo XVI.' *Revista de archivos, bibliotecas y museos* 7 (1903): 1–139.

Smith, Paul Julian. *Writing in the Margin: Spanish Literature of the Golden Age*. Oxford University Press, 1988.

Stephens, John. 'Giovanbattista Cibo's Confession.' In *Essays Presented to Myron P. Gilmore*. 2 vols., ed. Sergio Bertelli and Gloria Ramakus, 1: 255–69. Florence: La Nuova Italia Editrice, 1978.

Stinger, Charles. 'The Place of Clement VII and Clementine Rome in Renaissance History.' In *The Pontificate of Clement VII: History, Politics and Culture*, eds. Kenneth Gouwens and Sheryl E. Reiss, 165–84. Aldershot: Ashgate, 2005.

Stockwell, B. Foster. 'Juan de Valdés.' In *Alfabeto Cristiano* by Juan de Valdés. Buenos Aires: Editorial 'La Aurora,' 1948.

Surles, Robert L. 'Juan de Valdés' El *Diálogo de la lengua*: The Erasmian Humanism of a Spanish Expatriate.' *College Language Association Journal* 2 (1991): 224–35.

Tellechea Idigoras, Ignacio. 'Juan de Valdés y Bartoloméo de Carranza : La apasionante historia de un papel.' *Revista española de teología*, 20 (1961): 289–324.

– 'Juan de Valdés y Bartoloméo de Carranza: Sus normas para leer la Sagrada Escritura.' *Revista Española de teleogía* 22 (1962): 373–400.

Thomas, Werner. 'La creciente represión del protestantismo en la España carolina.' In *Carlos V y la quiebra del humanismo político en Europa (1530–1558)*, vol. 4, ed. Jesús Bravo Lozano and Carlos J. de Carlos Morelos. Madrid: SDAD Estatal Felipe II, 2001: 281–307.

Torre y del Cerro, Antonio de la. 'La Universidad de Alcalá: Datos para su Historia.' *Revista de archivos, bibliotecas y museos* 20 (1909): 412–23; 21 (1909): 48–71, 261–85, 405–33.

– 'La Universidad de Alcalá, estudio de la enseñanza según las vistas de cátedras de 1524–1525 a 1527–1528.' In *Homenaje a Menendez y Pelayo*, 3: 361–78. Madrid: Librería y Casa Editorial Hernando S.A., 1925.

Torres Fontes, Juan. 'La conquista del Marquesado de Villena en el reinado de los Reyes Catolicos.' *Hispania: revista española de historia* 50 (1973): 37–151.

Urriza, Juan. *La preclara facultad de artes y filosofía de la Universidad de Alcalá de Henares en el siglo de Oro 1509–1621*. Madrid: Consejo Superior de Investigaciones Científicos, Instituto Jerónimo Zurita, 1941.

Vales Failde, Javier. *La emperatriz Isabel*. Madrid: Gráficas Ultra, S.A., 1944.
Venacio D. Carro, Paulino. *Los Dominicos y el concilio de Trento: Estudio histórico-teológico del concilio y de la aportación de la orden Dominicana*. Salamanca: Calatrava, 1948.
Wiffen, Benjamin. 'Julia Gonzaga.' Translated by Adam F. Sosa. In *Alfabeto Cristiano* by Juan de Valdés. Buenos Aires: Editorial 'La Aurora,' 1948.
– *Life and Writings of Juan de Valdés, Spanish Reformer in the Sixteenth Century*. London: Bernard Quartich, 1865.
Williams, George. *The Radical Reformation*. Philadelphia: Westminister Press, 1962.
Woodhouse, J.R. *Baldesar Castiglione: A Reassessment of The Courtier*. Edinburgh: Edinburg University Press, 1978.
Young, G.F. *The Medici*. New York: Random House, 1930.
Zimmermann, T.C. Price. *Paolo Giovio: The Historian and the Crisis of Sixteenth-Century Italy*. Princeton: Princeton University Press, 1995.

Index

Accolti, Benedetto, Cardinal of Ravenna 4, 48, 50, 55, 72–8, 82, 105, 120, 160, 215n25; case, 77–8; corruption, 75; court, 73; imprisonment, 75; lawyers, 76; prebends, 74, 78
Acuña, Luisa de, 43
Aesop, 33
Aguilar, Marquis of, 137–42, 167, 242n22
Alarcón, Gregorio de, 9
Alarcón, Marquis of, 97
Alba, Duke of, 98
Alba, Pedro de, Archbishop of Granada, 35–6, 38
Albornoz, Pedro Carillo de, 9
Alcalá, Cristóbal of, 18
Alcalá, University of, 10, 15–16, 20–2, 25, 27–32, 34–5, 39–42, 44–6, 52, 155, 167; assembly, 39–40; press, 29, 31, 44; curriculum, 31–2; *visita* of, 29, 33
Alcaraz, Pedro Ruiz de, 7, 92, 162, 166–7; doctrines, 23, 25, 37, 163; investigation, 25–6, 29, 32 195n8, 205n122; letters of defence, 23
Alcionio, Pietro, 52
Alcor, Archdeacon of, 34–5
Alderete, Diego Gracián de, 22

alumbrados, 19–20, 29, 162, 204n108, 205n120, 207n17; doctrines, 20, 21, 25; errors, 21, 45, 46; factions, 24; sexual excesses, 22
Amadis of Gaul, 21
Amalfi, Duke of, 94
Ancona, Cardinal of, 74
Andrea, Giovann, 83
Angleria, Pedro de, 15, 16, 30, 196n11, 200n59
Angoulême, Charles of Valois, Duke of, 86
Angulo, Diego Ortiz de, 46
Aquinas, Thomas, 23, 31, 44
Aragon, 14, 197n34; Chancellery, 58; Council of, 30
Aragon, Juana de, 94
Aragon, María de, 94
Archbishop of Toledo, 9, 19, 33, 40, 43, 167
Aretino, Pietro, 73, 101
Ariosto, 80; *Orlando Furioso*, 73, 80; Aristotle, 33, 52, 54; *De animalibus*, 52; *Politics*, 33
Augsburg, Diet of, 48, 50–1, 55, 214n18; *Augsburg Confession*, 49, 51, 226n104

Augustine, St, 23–4, 119
Avalos, Constanza d', 94, 166
Ayala, Martín Pérez de, 167–8
Azevedo, Francisco de, 25

Barbarossa, Kheireddin, 61, 64, 70–1, 80
Barcelona, 68; treaty of, 48–9, 57
Barrera, María de, 9
Bataillon, Marcel, 6, 29, 194n8, 200–1n67, 206n3, 207nn16, 17, 209n59
Bembo, Pietro, 92, 99, 102, 137, 142; *Gli Asolani*, 92; *Prose of the Common Language*, 99
Benavente, Bartolomé de, 115–16, 121–2, 125, 127, 129–30; audit of viceroyalty, 115, 237n54; reform, 122, 127
Bergamo, Bishop of, 96
Bijar, Antonio de, 141
Bitonto, Marquis of, 94
Bobadilla, Nicolás de, 95, 138, 167, 228n36
Boccaccio, 22, 99
Boehmer, Eduard, 108–10, 146, 148, 245n100
Bologna, 48, 57; League of, 48; treaties of, 4, 7, 48, 52, 56–7, 62, 74–5, 81, 136; University of, 28, 52
Bonaventure, St, 23
Bonfadio, Giacomo, 95–6, 100
Borgo Delle Vergine, 152
Boyden, James, 132
Brísegna, Isabella, 94, 166
Brucioli, Antonio, 106
Burgundy, 49; faction, 9, 11, 14; wool trade, 8

Calvin, John, 150, 154, 162–3
Calabria, Antonio, 123

Cambrai, Peace of, 48
Camerino: crisis, 62, 64, 68, 71; negotiations, 65–8, 242n22
Campeggio, Cardinal, 49
Candido, Juan Luis, 235n22
Capua, Pietro Antonio of, Archbishop of Otranto, 95, 162
Capuana, Palace of, 122
Caracciolo, Galeazzo de, 96
Carauz, Pedro de, 117
Cardenete, 15, 200n57
Cardona, Isabel Villamari y, 94
Cardona, María de, 94
Carillo, Luis, 12, 15
Carnessechi, Pietro, 55, 57, 95, 103, 151, 154, 217n60; execution, 162, 249n186; trial, 146
Carpi, Geronimo of, 84
Carranza, Bartolomé de, Archbishop of Toledo, 10–12, 31–2, 40, 44, 60, 155–8, 167, 212–13n134, 248n165
Cartagena, Bishop of, 60
Castiglione, Baldesar 35, 230n74; *Book of the Courtier*, 79, 99
Castile: Admiral of, 19; chancellery in Valladolid, 13, 16, 21, 36, 58; Council of, 43, 66, 116, 118, 167; Council of State, 30, 48, 59, 65, 68, 133; finance, 43
Castillo, Juan de, 45, 63
Castle Saint Angelo, 35, 77–8, 83–4
Catherine of Siena, St, 24
Cato, 32
Cazalla, Bishop Pedro de, 41
Cazalla, María de, 21, 37, 39, 41–2, 45, 166
Charles V, Emperor, 3–13, 15–19, 27–31, 34–6, 42–4, 47–72, 75–6, 79, 81–90, 96–8, 100, 102–4, 106, 111–24, 126–7, 129–33, 135–43, 150–9,

161–2, 164, 167–8, 214n18, 215n29, 219n97, 221nn156, 167, 240n112; Algerian campaign, 135, 152; administrative reorganization, 30; finances, 97, 114; household, 132; Italian alliance system, 7, 47–8, 50; marriage alliance, 138; propaganda efforts, 27–8, 30, 164; religious colloquies in Germany, 5, 106, 138, 143; Tunisian campaign, 4, 7, 61–5, 68, 70–1, 83, 85, 231n111
Cheronissa, Bishop of, 96
Chiaja, 97
Chinchilla, Gregorio, 16
Christ, 19, 31, 109–10, 138, 143, 145–6, 148–50, 154, 157–8, 161, 163–4
Cibo, Caterina, Duchess of Camerino, 62, 93–4, 166
Cibo, Giovanbattista, 82–3
Cicero, 102
Cifuentes, Count of, 58, 60–6, 68–72, 75–6, 78, 81–4, 87, 136–7, 153, 163, 221nn156, 167
Cisneros, Jiménez de, Cardinal and Archbishop of Toledo, 9, 19, 28, 32–3, 202n83
Clairvaux, Bernard of, 23
Clement VII, Pope, Giulio de Medici, 4, 12, 27–8, 34–5, 48–9, 50, 52, 55–7, 60–4, 68–9, 74–5, 79, 164, 217n67
Climacus, John, 23–4
Cobos, Francisco de los, 4–6, 43, 45–7, 49–50, 56–60, 63–4, 76, 85–6, 90–1, 96–8, 100, 103, 108, 111–12, 114, 116–18, 121, 123–9, 131–5, 139, 142–3, 151–2, 158–9, 164–8, 218n86, 219n97, 229n47, 243n33; adaptability, 132; entourage, 58; faction, 47, 58, 124; home town, 58; influence, 58, 97; *privanza*, 132–4

Cognac, League of, 27
College of Cardinals, 23–4, 49–50, 55, 65, 75, 82, 139, 150–1
Colocci, Angelo, 47, 73, 52, 99
Colonna: clan, 3, 80, 88; family jewels, 108, 141; imperial support, 90, 104; palace, 137
Colonna, Ascanio, Constable of Naples, 52, 64, 88–90, 94, 111, 130, 137, 140–2, 151, 153, 157, 160, 240n121
Colonna, Isabella, 80, 88, 91, 94, 103–4, 107, 134, 140, 158
Colonna, Vespasiano, Duke of Trajetto and Count of Fondi, 3, 79–80, 88, 103
Colonna, Vittoria, 93, 137, 142, 146, 152–4, 166
Comunero Revolt, 15, 16–20, 27, 34, 85, 161
Constantinople, 70–1, 135
Contarini, Gasparo Cardinal, 5, 27, 52, 106, 139, 143, 151; death, 153; Diet of Regensburg, 140–2; doctrine of double justification, 143–4, 148–50; nomination as legate, 138–40
Coronel, Doctor Luis Núñez, 31, 40–1
Cortese, Abbot Gregorio, 142, 154, 159
Croce, Benedetto, 6
Cruz, Isabel de la, 20, 22, 41, 166
Cruz, Luis de la, 156
Cuenca, 4, 9, 11–17, 19–20, 60, 120, 161, 168, 197n33, 199n47; archivists of, ix, 10–11; city council, 10–14, 17–18; jurisdiction, 13; liberty, 13, 165; loyalty, 17; militia, 9–10, 12, 16–18
Curione, Celio Secondo, 133, 163
Cusano, Benedetto 96

276   Index

Dalmatian coast, 138
Della Casa, Giovanni, 100
Demosthenes, 33, 102
Dilfo, Francisco, 44
Dominican order, 155
Doria, Andrea, 114, 121, 127, 237n59
Duns Scotus, 41

Eguía, Miguel, 29, 44
England, 49, 87
Enzinas, Francisco de, 46
Erasmus, 21, 27–9, 31–4, 36, 38, 41–2, 44, 47, 51–5, 163, 216n54; *Adages*, 29, 32, 101; *Colloquies*, 5, 34, 36; concern, for J. de Valdés, 42; *Enchiridion*, 29, 34, 36; New Testament, 28; Sepúlveda's relation with, 52–4; Spanish Erasmianism, 27–9, 34, 43, 206n3, 207n17

Farnese, Cardinal Alessandro, 61, 71, 140
Farnese, Pier Luigi, 81, 86–7, 138
Farnese, Ottavio, 72, 81, 137–8, 243n43
Ferdinand, King, 8–9, 11, 13–15, 43, 48, 50, 65, 68, 218n86
Feros, Antonio, 132
Ferrara, 48, 57, 66, 71, 78, 162; Duke of, 48, 50, 56, 62–4, 69, 71
Figueroa, Juan de, 89, 111, 124, 126–7, 238nn81, 87
Firenzuola, Agnolo, 93
Flaminio, Marcantonio, 95, 100, 143, 146, 150–1, 154–5, 157
Flanders, 11–12, 15, 123–4, 139
Florentine succession crisis of 1537, 136–7
Foligno, Angela of, 23
Fonseca, Alonso de, 40

Fonseca, Galeoto de, 89
France, 24, 27, 29, 48–9, 62, 64–5, 67, 69–70, 81, 87, 90, 97
Francis I, 27, 47, 56–7, 61, 64–5, 69, 71, 85–7; Turkish alliance, 7, 27, 51
Frankfurt, Colloquy of, 138
French war of 1536, 96
Fuente, Doctor Francisco de la, 39

Gaddi, Niccolò, 79, 81
Galeota, Mario, 96, 117
Gattinara, Mercurino, Grand Chancellor, 6, 27, 29–30, 113, 167
Gennaro, Juan Thommaso de, 115
Germany, 5, 20, 27, 31, 49, 51, 65, 68, 70, 73, 106, 126, 133, 135, 138–9, 141–2, 146, 151, 167
Gerson, Jean, 24
Giberti, Gian Matteo, 47
Gilly, Carlos, 7
Giovio, Paolo, 47, 57, 83
Gonzaga, Ercole, Cardinal of Mantua, 3, 6, 55, 64, 68–9, 73–4, 76, 84–5, 88–9, 96, 103–4, 150, 153, 166, 232n113
Gonzaga, Dorotea, 94
Gonzaga, Elisabetta, Duchess of Urbino, 64, 79, 85
Gonzaga, Ferrante, Viceroy of Sicily, 85–6, 94
Gonzaga, Giulia, 3, 6, 16, 74, 76, 79, 83–4, 88–93, 94, 96, 102–5, 107–12, 125, 137, 143–4, 146–7, 151–2, 154, 157, 160, 166, 168, 240n112; death, 159; depression, 103, 108, 110; fame, 3, 80, 102; lawsuit, 45, 88, 90, 107, 109, 112, 137, 158–9; letters, 111
Gonzaga, Isabella, 79
Gonzaga, Ludovico, 79, 107–8, 111, 137, 151, 158

Gonzaga, Luigi, 88
Gonzaga, Vespasiano, 88–9, 107–8, 111–12, 152, 155, 166, 168
Granvelle, Lord of, Nicholas Peronet, 48–9, 61, 86, 103, 124, 133, 231n111, 238n87
Gregory, St: College of, 155; *Morals on the Book of Job*, 24
Gumiel, Cristóbal 40

Habsburg: dynasty, 8, 14–16, 132; heartland, 27; Margaret of, 48, 75, 81, 136–8; Spanish succession, 13–15, 161
Headley, John, 27
Henry VIII, 27, 138
Hernández, Diego, 44–5
Hernández, Francisca, 21, 24, 39, 44, 166, 203n97
Hesse, Philip of, 61, 65
Holy League, 138
Homer, 101
Hugh of St Victor, 23
humanism, 27, 47, 51–2, 73, 97, 100–1, 106, 118
Hungary, 27, 56, 59, 75, 80, 135

Idiáquez, Alonso de, 57–9, 77, 118, 124
Indies, Council of, 43–4; administration of, 43
Isabel of Portugal, 18
Isabel, Queen, 8, 12–15, 22, 43; daughter Juana, 14, 198n43; death, 8
Italy, 3–7, 18, 27, 30, 40, 44, 46–9, 52–3, 56–8, 60, 61–2, 65–8, 79–80, 86, 90–1, 94, 97, 99, 101, 106, 117, 124, 130–3, 146, 151, 153–4, 161, 163, 165, 167; administration of, 30, 49–50, 57–8; alliances, 47, 50, 57, 137; courts, 90–2, 99; military weakness, 52; sack of Rome, 30, 45, 47–8, 51–2, 74, 100; vernacular movement, 5, 91–2, 99–100, 102

Jaen, Bishopric of, 71
Jerome, St, 23–4
Jewish history, 107
Jewish state, 161
judaizing: accusations of, 20, 25
Juvenal, 32

La Mancha, 3, 7–8, 22, 25, 27
Lallemand, Jean, 35, 43
Lannoy, Charles of, Prince of Sulmona and Viceroy of Naples, 89, 98, 104
Lannoy, Philippe of, Prince of Sulmona, 89
Latin, 14, 16, 29–32, 97, 99, 101; ciceronians, 28–9, 51; Vulgate, 28
Lázaro, Elena, 10
Lea, Henry Charles, 44
Lee, Edward, 207–8n26
Lerma, Duke of, 132
Lerma, Pedro de, 39
Limos, Bishop of, 69, 221n162
Llorente, Juan Antonio, 44, 212n134, 248n170
Loaysa, Cristóbal de, 39
Loaysa, García de, 43, 49–50, 214n18, 215nn25, 29
Lombard, Peter, 23
Longhurst, John, 42, 44
Lucena, Gaspar, 40
Ludolf of Saxony: *Life of Christ*, 24
Luther, Martin, 27–8, 31, 33–4, 161–3
Lutheran, 19, 45; doctrine of justification, 6, 37, 144; Lutheranism, 20, 44–5, 162; military aid, 27, 51, 135; seizure of Württemberg, 61–2, 138

278 Index

Machiavelli, 119, 131
Madrid, 8, 12
Madrigal, Alonso Fernández de, 23
Magno, Marcantonio, 100, 155
Mai, Ambassador Miguel, 50, 55–8, 85, 214n18
Manrique, Inquisitor General Alonso, 34, 39, 41, 43, 44–5, 202n76
Manrique, Diego, 13, 17, 202n76
Manrique, García, 94
Manrique, Isabella, 94
Manrique, Canon Juan del Pozo, 13
Manrique, Rodrigo, Alguacil of Cuenca and Comendador of Salamanca, 13, 17, 198n37
Mantua, 48, 56, 69, 79, 87–8, 151; Council of, 87, 226n104, 232n113; Duke of, Frederigo Gonzaga, 80, 85, 87–8
Marcial, Juan, 89
Martirano, Coriolano, 101
Matheson, Peter, 139
Medici: papacies, 47; restoration in Florence, 48, 57; rule, 48
Medici, Alessandro de', Duke of Tuscany, 48, 62, 74–5, 79, 81–3, 136–7, 139, 242n13
Medici, Catherine de', 56–7, 81
Medici, Cardinal Giulio de', 52
Medici, Cardinal Ippolito de', 3, 69, 72–5, 78–84, 224n53; death, 79–80, 84–5, 88; ecclesiastical offices, 81; sodality, 74, 79–80
Medina, Doctor Juan de, 39–40
Melanchthon, Philip, 49
Mendoza, Diego Hurtado de, Duke of Infantado, 9, 13–15, 17–20, 137, 157, 161, 199n49, 201n70
Michelangelo, 94
Mignoz, Sigismundo, 96

Milan, 27, 48, 56, 86–7, 103, 231nn111–12; governor of, 130, 137
Minadois, Germano, 96
Miranda, Sancho Carranza de, 39, 155
Modena, 48–50, 56–7, 62–3, 66, 71; Ferrara's seizure of, 48; imperial territory, 57
Monteserín, Miguel Jiménez, 9, 11
Montesinos, José, 6
Moretti, Giuseppe, 81
Monreal, Cardinal, 106
Morone, Giovanni, 138, 142, 146, 150–1, 153–4
Moya, Marquis of, Andres de Cabrera 9, 12, 15–17, 200n57

Naples, 3–5, 12, 48, 55, 57–8, 61, 69, 71–4, 76, 78–80, 84–5, 87–90, 94–101, 103, 106, 112–14, 120–3, 125–9, 131, 136–8, 140, 142–3, 151–3, 155–6, 165, 167; administration, 4, 89, 113–14, 122, 131, 133; archivist of, 57, 59; autonomy, 165; Chancellery, 49, 57–9, 236n46; Collateral Council, 51, 59, 108, 111, 113, 121, 127, 129, 136, 238n81; courts, 89, 115, 121–3, 126–7, 129; finance, 96, 115, 123, 127, 129–30; Franciscan convent, 104; taxation, 122–3; *visita* of, 114–15, 120–31, 133, 142, 158–9, 165
Navagiero, Bernardo, 238n87
Nebrija, Antonio de, 28–9, 32, 100, 206n8, 230n90; *Grammar*, 101; Spanish imperial language, 29, 101, 206n13
Neocastro, Cardinal, 139
Nice, Truce of, 97, 133
Nieto, José, ix, 6, 10, 162, 166, 195nn8, 9, 204n112, 208n32, 210n74, 211n116, 250n16, 251n29

Nürnberg, Peace of, 51, 56, 59, 61, 151, 215n33
Nursia, Benedict of, 23

Ocaña, Francisco de, 24
Ochino, Bernardino, 95, 102–3, 153
Olmillos, Juan de, 24
Orduña, Luis de, 9
Orleans, Duke of, Henry of Valois, 56–7, 81

Pacheco, Juan de, 197n34
Pacheco, Pedro de, Bishop of Mondonedo, Pamplona, Cardinal of Jaén, 90, 100–1, 115, 120–3, 126–8, 158, 161
Paliano: fortress of, 88, 90, 137
Pamplona, 10
papal: authority, 38, 49, 146–7, 149, 151, 167–8; Chamberlain, 11, 120; concession, 139; court, 4, 47, 54–5, 64, 66–7, 86, 92, 100, 103, 153, 164; curia, 73, 125, 143; forces, 65, 83, 88; independence, 57; indulgence, 48; Inquisition, 6, 10, 55, 138, 150, 153–5, 159, 162, 164; office, 146–7; Reform Commission, 5, 91, 106, 138; States, 48, 56, 61–2, 88, 90, 137, 139
Parma, 87
Paul, St, 25, 107, 146
Paul III, Pope, Alessandro Farnese, 4–5, 61–3, 70, 71, 72, 74–6, 81–5, 87, 90, 101, 137, 139–40, 151, 160, 168, 228n36; Florentine ambitions, 81, 84; marriage alliance, 137
Paul IV, Pope, Gian Pietro Carafa, 153, 164
Pavia, Battle of, 27, 29–30
Peasants War, 20

Peñalosa, Comendador, 117
Pérez, Gonzalo, 58, 143
Peru, 97
Perugia, 48, 62–3, 139, 140, 165
Petrarch, 22, 99, 149
Philip II, 131–2
Pio, Alberto, 52–3
Plato, 33, 101; doctrine of innate ideas, 150; Platonic desire, 93; *Symposium*, 91–2
Pliny, 54
Pole, Reginald, Cardinal of England, 96, 137, 142, 146, 151, 153–4, 157–8, 249n186
Protestant, 49, 51, 144, 151, 155, 162–3
Puente, Antonio de, 235n22
Puente, Doctor Diego de la, 39

Regensburg, Diet of, 5, 84, 106, 133, 135, 139, 146, 150, 154, 163
Ridolfi, Cardinal Niccolò, 79, 81, 153
Rome, 4, 6, 11, 24, 28, 30, 31, 35, 40, 42, 45, 47, 48–9, 51–8, 60–1, 66–70, 72–7, 78, 80–6, 88, 90–1, 94, 98–100, 103, 114, 120, 125, 136–7, 140–1, 143, 147–8, 150–1, 153, 155, 157, 164; humanism in, 47, 51, 54; courtesans, 229n50

Saavedra, Miguel Cervantes, 8; *Don Quixote*, 8
Sadoleto, Jacobo, 47, 142
Sabelo, Juan Batista, 22, 67
Salamanca, 12; University of, 20–1, 28
Salazar, Luis de, 9, 12
Salinas, Martín de, 58, 218n86
Salviati, Cardinal Giovanni, 82
San Clemente, Church of, 60, 96, 120,
San Eugenio, colleges of, 32

San Giovanni Maggiore, 102
San Jerónimo, College of, 32
San Isidoro, 32
San Lázaro, 11, 42, 44, 63
San Marco, Bishop of, 101
San Yuste, Church of, 39
Sánchez, Alonso, 114–15, 121, 123–4, 126, 128–9, 151–2, 158, 165, 237n54
Sanchez, Juan, 95, 109
Santa Chiara, Convent of, 94
Santa Junta, 17
Santa María de la Granada, Monastery of, 36
Santo Domingo, Convent of, 43
Santo Pietro ad Ara, Prior of, 96
Sarmiento, Don Juan, 117
Scaglione, Lucrezia, 98
Schmalkaldic League and War, 7, 49
Sepúlveda, Juan Ginés de, 47, 52–5, 216n54
Seven Mortal Sins, 36
Severino, Hieronimo, 122–3, 237n54, 239n105
Seville, 8, 39, 43, 155
Sforza, Francisco, 86
Sicily, 61, 79
Siena, 81, 87, 131
Silva, Cesare de, 115
Silva, Ruy Gómez de, 131–2
Socrates, 36; Socratic injunction of self-examination, 109; Socratic voice, 36
Soranzo, Vittore, 96, 153
Spain, 4, 7–8, 13, 15, 18, 27–8, 29–30, 34–5, 40, 42–6, 48–9, 51–3, 57–9, 66, 81, 91, 94, 97, 125, 131–2, 138, 152, 156, 161, 167; bishopric of Tarazona, 85; diplomatic corps, 50, 167; domain, 7, 30, 48, 125; global empire, 91; Inquisition, 4–6, 26, 41, 44–5, 59, 64, 162, 164; Inquisitor General, 19, 34, 39, 43, 45, 94, 106; language, 5, 22, 38, 99–102, 165; translation of *Enchiridion*, 29; troops, 48, 50, 59, 137, 139, 165
Stigliano, Princess of, 94
Strozzi, Filippo, 75, 81–3, 137, 242n13
Strozzi, Piero, 83
Suleiman, Sultan, 61, 96
Sulmona, Prince of, 89
Sulmona, Princess of, 94, 96, 104

Tajo River, 8
Tasso, Bernardo, 92–3, 166
Tavera, Cardinal Juan de, 43, 45, 167
Terenziano, Giulio, 96, 153
Thucydides, 33
Toledo, 8, 15, 17, 19, 24–5, 29, 31, 42, 93
Toledo, Eleanor de, 137
Toledo, Fadrique de, 133, 218n93
Toledo, García de, 97, 240n121
Toledo, Juan de, Cardinal of Burgos 135, 140, 152–3
Toledo, Pedro de, Viceroy of Naples, Marquis of Villafranca, 4, 7, 59–67, 85, 108, 111–14, 117–18, 121–31, 136–41, 151–3, 158, 220n120, 237n54, 240n112, 243nn33, 43; appointment as viceroy, 59; baronial enemies, 130–1; reforms, 113; Regensburg diplomacy, 139–41; reputation, 5, 238n81
Tovar, Bernardino 21, 42; case, 39–40; disciples, 44
Trent, Council of, 6–7, 97, 137, 146, 148, 154–7, 162, 164, 167–8
Tunis, 4, 61–5, 68, 71, 83, 85
Turkish war, 50, 58, 69, 87, 118, 135, 138–9

Urbino, Duke of, Francesco Maria della Rovere, 62, 65, 66–9, 72, 81, 87, 138
Utrecht, Adrian of, 17, 201n70

Valdés family, 9–11, 15–19, 161; *converso* heritage, 9, 12, 19–20, 24, 26, 33, 48, 161–2, 164
Valdés, Alfonso de (brother), 4–6, 9, 11–12, 15–16, 21, 29–32, 34–5, 42, 44–6, 48–51, 53–9, 120, 132–3, 143, 165, 168, 207–8n26, 214n18, 215n36, 216n54, 249n177; administrative appointments, 132; death, 56, 59, 94; *Dialogue on Events in Rome*, 31, 35, 42, 45; *Dialogue of Mercury and Charon*, 21, 31, 45, 157, 212–13n134
Valdés, Alonso de (uncle), 9–10, 16–17, 19, 200n61
Valdés, Andrés de (brother), 9, 11–12, 15–18, 26, 63, 152, 168, 200n61, 202n79
Valdés, Diego de (brother), 9, 11–12, 15, 45, 57, 60, 63, 120, 132, 196nn23, 25, 197n27
Valdés, Fernando de (father), 4, 9–18, 26, 42, 120, 196n15, 197n30, 199n47, 199n51, 200n61, 200–1n63, 209n48, 212n123
Valdés, Juan Alfonso de (nephew), 12
Valdés, Juan de, 3–7, 9–10, 14, 19, 22, 25–9, 31–4, 36–42, 44–7, 51–3, 55–7, 59–60, 63–74, 76–9, 81–91, 93–112, 114–20, 124–8, 132–3, 152–65, 167–8; *Advice Concerning Interpreters of Scripture*, 156, 248n170; anti-Farnese comments, 96, 160, 249n1; appointments, 55–6, 59, 63–4, 66, 73, 133, 219n97, 222n170; birth date, 10–11, 196n14; book of Spanish proverbs, 101–2; Camerino negotiations, 64–72, 85, 87, 138, 167; childhood, 9, 161; *Christian Alphabet*, 4, 99–100, 102–3, 109, 145, 147, 155, 163, 231n102, 232n128; *Commentary on First Corinthians*, 106, 144–5, 155, 163; *Commentary on Matthew*, 19, 95, 149; *Commentary on the Psalms*, 107, 119; *Commentary on Romans*, 106, 108, 143–4, 146, 148, 150, 155; death, 5, 151–4, 158; *Dialogue on Christian Doctrine*, 6–7, 15, 23, 28, 31, 33, 35, 37–9, 41–2, 44–5, 55, 58, 94, 102, 105, 145, 150, 155, 157, 163–5, 167, 250n8; *Dialogue on Language*, 15–16, 21, 23, 32, 98–102, 161, 166, 231n107; disciples, 93–6, 142–3, 151–3; doctrine of justification, 6, 37, 94, 143–7, 151, 154, 156, 162; doctrine of self-examination, 156; heresy, 7, 79, 137, 151, 154, 157–8, 162; house, 95, 97; ideal Church, views on, 149; intelligence reports, 65–71, 78, 82, 86–7, 221nn162, 163, 167; last wishes, 152; *One Hundred Ten Divine Considerations*, 6, 79, 95, 106, 109, 133, 146–7, 156, 244n71, 246nn119, 122, 248nn165, 170; sodality/circle, 5, 79, 91–6, 102, 106–7, 131, 137, 142, 151, 154, 161, 166; stature, 138, 154, 158, 167; women, views on, 93, 227n21
Valdés, Margarita de (sister), 9, 12
Valdés, María de (mother), 9, 12
Valdés, Teresa Gómez de (sister), 9
Valencia, Countess of, 43
Valeriano, Pierio, 52, 99

Varano, Giovanni Maria, Duke of Camerino, 62
Varano, Ercole, 62
Varchi, Benedetto, 81, 224n61
Vargas, Doctor Francisco de, 39
Vasto, Marquis of, Alfonso D'Avalos, Governor of Milan/Lombardy, 94, 108, 111, 130, 136–7, 142
Vázquez, Hernán, 33, 39
Vázquez, Juan, 58–9, 123, 129
Venice, 6, 27, 48, 52, 62, 66–8, 138, 146–7, 162
Verdura, Giovan Francesco, 96
Vergara, Francisco de, 33
Vergara, Juan de, 10–11, 21, 33, 39–41, 44, 46, 59, 101, 196n13
Vergerio, Pietro Paolo, 96
Vermigli, Pietro Martyr, 96, 143, 152–3
Vienna, 27, 108, 146
Villaescusa, Diego Ramírez, 13
Villalar, Battle of, 19
Villamarina, Marcantonio, 151
Villanueva, 9
Villena, Marquis of, Pedro de Pacheco, 13–14, 16, 19–20, 24–5, 101, 195n8

War of League of Cognac, 30
Worms, Diet of, 27, 30
Württemberg, 57, 61–2, 138

Zurich, 94

www.ingramcontent.com/pod-product-compliance
Lightning Source LLC
Chambersburg PA
CBHW030307080526
44584CB00012B/480